NEW ENGLAND AND THE BAVARIAN ILLUMINATI

BY

VERNON STAUFFER, A. M.

Dean and Professor of New Testament and Church History
Hiram College

SUBMITTED IN PARTIAL FULFILMENT OF THE REQUIREMENTS
FOR THE DEGREE OF DOCTOR OF PHILOSOPHY
IN THE FACULTY OF POLITICAL SCIENCE
COLUMBIA UNIVERSITY

ACKNOWLEDGMENT

The obligations incurred in the preparation of the following study are much too numerous and varied to admit of adequate notice. Special mention must, however, be made of my indebtedness to the staffs of the following libraries: The Boston Athenaeum, Congregational, Masonic (Boston), American Antiquarian Society, Connecticut Historical Society, New York Historical Society, Library of Congress, the public libraries of the cities of Boston and New York, the library of Hiram College, and the university libraries of Harvard, Yale, and Columbia. In addition to the many courtesies received from these sources, I have had valuable assistance from the following persons: Mr. Newton R. Parvin, grand secretary of the Grand Lodge of Iowa, A. F. & A. M., Cedar Rapids, Iowa, whose warm personal interest in my investigation has found expression in the loan of many valuable volumes; Mr. Worthington C. Ford, of the Massachusetts Historical Society, who besides opening freely to me the unpublished treasures of the Society, has given me the benefit of peculiarly stimulating suggestions; Mr. Walter C. Green, librarian of Meadville Theological School, who has most generously met all my drafts upon his patience and time; and Professor Guy Stanton Ford, of the University of Minnesota, who has made it possible for me to use his copy of Forestier's *Les Illuminés de Bavière et la Franc-Maçonnerie allemande*, without which in this war period, with its partial stoppage of the inflow of European literature, my chapter on "The European Order of the Illuminati" could scarcely have been written.

My greatest debt is to Professor William Walker Rockwell, of Union Theological Seminary, who from the day that he suggested the theme not only has followed the progress of the work with unwearied interest, but at many points has guided my efforts and helped me to avoid numerous pitfalls. Whatever excellencies the study contains are due to Professor Rockwell's stimulating criticism; the faults are altogether chargeable to me.

There remains to acknowledge my obligation and express my best thanks to my colleagues, Professors Ralph Hinsdale Goodale, Lee Edwin Cannon, and John Samuel Kenyon, and to Miss Bertha Peckham, Registrar of Hiram College, who have greatly assisted me by correcting copy, reading proof, and otherwise helping to see the work through the press. To my wife a special obligation is due because of the benefits derived from her critical insight and heartening sympathy throughout the performance of the task.

V. S

HIRAM, OHIO.

INTRODUCTION

Few if any periods in our national history have been marked by a greater variety of clashing interests than the closing decade of the eighteenth century. Owing in part to inexperience in grappling with the problems of government, in part to widely belligerent and irreconcilable elements among the people, in part to grave international complications and concerns, and in part, confessedly, to rumors and excitements for which, as events proved, no adequate grounds existed, the lives of the people of New England were tossed rudely about on rough currents and counter-currents of mingled hope and anguish. To a dispassionate observer (if anywhere on the green earth at the close of the eighteenth century such an individual might have been found) it must have seemed as though the citizens of New England were as so many bits of wood, bobbing up and down on waters excessively choppy but otherwise motionless. The agitation, however, was not merely superficial; issues and movements of the most profound significance were pouring their impetuous torrents through channels freshly cut and steadily deepened by new streams of human interest which the erection of the national government, in particular, had started on their tortuous ways.

The development of this thesis calls for an evaluation of the more significant elements and forces which gave to the period the characteristic temper of nervous excitability by which it was stamped. The profound spirit of apprehension, amounting to positive distress, with which for many a thoughtful religious patriot of New England the eighteenth century closed, constitutes a phenomenon as impressive as it is curious. To isolate that spirit, to analyze it, to explain its genesis and its development, to take account of its attachments and antipathies with respect to the special interest under consideration,—this must be regarded as no inconsiderable portion of the general task.

On the morning of May 9, 1798, in the pulpit of the New North Church in Boston, and on the afternoon of the same day in his own pulpit at Charlestown, the occasion being that of the national fast, the Reverend Jedediah Morse[1] made a sensational pronouncement. He first discussed with his hearers "the awful events" which the European Illuminati had precipitated upon an already distracted world, and then proceeded solemnly to affirm that the secret European association had extended its operations to this side of the Atlantic and was now actively engaged among the people of the United States, with a view to the overthrow of their civil and religious institutions. In the eyes of the distinguished clergyman, the matter was of such serious moment that he felt moved to remark:

I hold it a duty, my brethren, which I owe to God, to the cause of religion, to my country and to you, at this time, to declare to you, thus honestly and faithfully, these truths. My only aim is to awaken in you and myself a due attention, at this alarming period, to our dearest interests. As a faithful watchman I would give you warning of your present danger.[2]

Morse's warning by no means fell upon deaf ears. The "due attention" he claimed for the alarm which he that day sounded was promptly and generally accorded. Soon ministers were preaching, newspaper editors and contributors writing and clearheaded statesmen like Oliver Wolcott, Timothy Pickering, John Adams, and even the great Washington, inquiring, and voicing their serious concern over the secret presence in America of those conspirators whose greatest single achievement, a multitude had come to believe, was the enormities of the French Revolution.

It is true that before two years had passed men generally began to admit the baseless nature of the alarm that Morse had sounded. None the less one may not dismiss the incident with the light and easy judgment that it signified nothing more than the absurd fears of a New England clergyman who, under the strain of deep political and religious concern, and after a hasty reading of the latest volume of religious and political horrors that had just arrived from Europe,[3] rushed into his pulpit and gave utterance to preposterous statements which his imagination for the moment led him to believe were justified. The episode has considerably larger and more important bearings. No man could possibly have awakened such wide-spread concern as the minister of Charlestown succeeded in awakening if it had not been true that significant concurrent and related circumstances gave both setting and force to the alarm which with such stout conviction he sounded.

What previous influences and events had tended to predispose the public mind favorably to Morse's alarm? What was the peculiar combination and cast of events which gave the notion of a conspiracy against religion and government in Europe and in America a clear semblance of truth? In what ways, and to what extent, did the alarm affect the lives and the institutions of the people of New England? Finally, what were the grounds, real or imaginary, upon which the charge of an Illuminati conspiracy rested? To answering these questions the following pages are devoted.

CHAPTER I

THE UNDERMINING OF PURITAN STANDARDS AND INSTITUTIONS

1. RAPID DISINTEGRATION OF PURITANISM AFTER THE REVOLUTION

Back of the War of Independence was the less absorbing but scarcely less harrowing contest of the French and Indian War. Thus for a period of fully thirty years the people of New England had been subjected to the rough and unsettling experiences of military life. This consideration, taken in connection with the fact that a growing declension from the standards of the Puritan fathers had been the occasion of increasing comment and concern from the middle of the seventeenth century on,[4] will make explicable the fact that the average citizen of New England emerged from the Revolutionary struggle with the edge of his conscience dulled. The secularizing spirit of the post-Revolutionary period, when questions of national organization and unity, of the rehabilitation of commerce and industry, and of international relations and policies were foremost in the thought of the day, left marks upon the human spirit over which stern and rigorous adherents to the old order wept copiously and long. For one thing, the lives of the men and women of New England were never again to be as barren of diversified interests as they had been in the past. The successful issue of the struggle for political independence had so enlarged the mind of the common man that he of necessity entertained considerations of private desire and of public policy which he formerly would have rejected entirely. The avenue of retreat to the ancient simplicity and seclusion was forever closed.

The soundness of this estimate of the rapid disintegration of Puritanism will be apparent if the changing attitude of the people on the subject of theatrical entertainments is considered.[5] As early as the year 1750 the General Court of Massachusetts had found it necessary to enact legislation to prevent stage-plays and other theatrical entertainments.[6] That Puritan standards dominated the situation at the time is evidenced both by the reasons advanced by the framers of the law for its enactment and by the stringent penalties attached to it. The justification of the measure was found in the economic waste, the discouraging effect upon industry and frugality, and the deleterious effect upon morality and religion which stage-plays were believed to exercise. The penalties imposed called for a fine of twenty pounds upon any owner of property who permitted his property to be used for such purposes, while a fine of five pounds was to be assessed upon any actor or spectator found in attendance upon or participating in any such exercises where more than twenty persons were assembled together.[7] How meekly the craving for pleasurable excitement bowed its head in submission, there is no evidence to show; but it is very clear that as the century drew toward its close the people of Massachusetts began to manifest a decidedly intractable spirit with respect to legislative control of their amusements and pleasures.

The days of the Revolution supplied thrills of their own, and the colonists gave themselves in devotion to their great task-at-arms, with little desire for the amenities of life. Accordingly, when the Continental Congress, on October 16, 1778, passed a resolution deprecating every species of public entertainment which would be likely to divert the minds of the people from the considerations of public defence and the safeguarding of their liberties,[8] there was nothing singular about the episode, and we may believe readily that the people of New England, fortified by their grim spirit of determination and their long tradition of self-denial, in no sense fell short of the general standard. But by the year 1790 the people living in and about Boston had come to a very different state of mind. In that year by petition to the General Court they sought to have the prohibitory act of 1750 revoked.[9] The incident has importance because it registers a determined effort to feed desires whose hunger-pains had grown insistent.

The history of this particular effort to remove legislative restrictions in the way of harmless amusements is illuminating. The petition referred to received scant consideration at the hands of the legislators of Massachusetts. The following year certain gentlemen of Boston, to the number of thirty-nine, presented a memorial to the selectmen of that city, requesting that a vote of the citizens be taken on the questions of permitting the erection and use of a building for theatrical entertainments, and the issuing of instructions to Boston's representatives in the legislature calling for the repeal of the obnoxious law. Apparently the plebiscite was not taken; but the general question was debated in town meeting. A committee was appointed to prepare instructions. The committee reported favorably concerning the proposed instructions to Boston's representatives in the legislature, and these representatives later undertook the task of bringing a majority of the members of the General Court to the more liberal point of view; not, however, with immediate success. Meanwhile, to the scandal of Governor John Hancock, and doubtless many another advocate of decency and order, theatrical entertainments, "under the Stile & Appellation of Moral Lectures,"[10] flourished openly in Boston.[11]

It was during the progress of the debate in the legislature over the proposed repeal of the law against theatrical entertainments that John Gardiner, one of Boston's representatives in that body, delivered himself of sentiments touching what he styled "the illiberal, unmanly, and despotic act" of 1750. His speech gave evidence of how fresh and independent the judgments of some minds had come to be. Addressing the presiding officer, Gardiner said:

Sir! I really and truly venerate; I would rather say, I sincerely and almost enthusiastically admire the many great and splendid virtues of our renowned puritan ancestors ...; but still, Sir, they were only men; and, like all other men, were fallible; liable to frailties, to prejudices, and to error. Some errors, and some unjust prejudices, they undoubtedly had. Would to God a veil was drawn over all their absurd prejudices which, like spots in the sun, tend in some small degree to bedarken and obscure the otherwise truly-resplendent glories of their character. One of these prejudices, in my opinion, was their inveterate opposition and abhorrent aversion to the theatre.[12]

That Gardiner was the spokesman of a very considerable number of citizens is demonstrated by the fact that on March 28, 1793, a bill drawn to take the place of the older legislation against theatrical amusements and granting specifically to the people of Boston the right to erect a theatre and to have "stage plays performed under certain regulations and restrictions," was enacted by the legislature of Massachusetts.[13] It is very evident that public sentiment had veered round to a radically new and different view respecting the place and function of the theatre. So much so, indeed, that some who sought to shape the thought and determination of the times recommended the establishment of the theatre as the only possible way of drawing the desires and interests of the people away from grosser and more injurious excitements toward which, it was believed, an alarming growth of frivolity and lack of moral concern was rapidly sweeping the people of New England.[14]

This alleged declension of morals may be more vitally viewed from the standpoint of the subject of intemperance. Convivial habits were a fixed part of the New England character, and the sin of drunkenness was as old as the settlement of the country. The practice of brewing was numbered among the employments of the first settlers.[15] Rum was generally used by the people, and the commercial life of the colonies was inextricably woven with its importation and exportation.[16] Cider was the native New England beverage.[17] The importation of wine was large from the first.[18] A general tendency in the direction of increased habits of drinking was to be expected.[19]

The period of the Revolution made its own special contribution to the gravity of the case. The soldiers of the Continental armies received regular rations of liquor,[20]and at the expiration of the war carried back to their respective communities the habits of intemperance which in many cases their army life had strengthened. Rum was more and more coming to be regarded as one of the necessities of life;[21] and with the revival of industry and commerce after the war the business of distilling mounted rapidly to amazing proportions.[22]

A growing uneasiness over the social and economic consequences involved in the spread of alcoholism is apparent. Under the date of July 29, 1789, the Reverend Jeremy Belknap, minister of the church in Long Lane, Boston, is found writing thus to Dr. Benjamin Rush, Philadelphia's celebrated physician and early apostle of temperance reform:

With respect to spirituous liquors I believe some good has been done, but much more remains to be done. The distilleries here are so ready a source of gain, that, till the *auri sacra fames* shall cease to be a ruling passion, I fear there will no end be put to them. The demand from abroad I am told increases, particularly from the north of Europe, & while the stills are kept going there will be a large home consumption. In an excursion of about 80 miles into the country a few weeks since, I met many loads of pot & pearl ashes coming down, & on my return the teams which I met were loaded with dry fish, hogsheads of salt, & barrels of rum. The thirst for spirits in the back country is so ardent, that in the fall & winter they will sell their wheat for this sort of pay, & then in the spring and summer following go 40 or 50 miles after bread. However, we do what we can by way of precept & example, & we do not intend to be discouraged.[23]

The correspondence which the Reverend Bulkley Olcott, minister of the church in Charlestown, New Hampshire, had with Belknap is of like import.[24] He had tried to obtain accurate statistical information from the Excise Master as to the quantity of spirituous liquors consumed in his county, and had not succeeded. However, it is a matter of his personal knowledge that many good estates have been squandered through drinking, and much time, labor, and health, and many lives destroyed in the same way. He recognizes that many concurring circumstances come to the aid of spirituous liquors in working fatal results; still the general abuse of drink is declared to be one of the heaviest and most threatening evils under which the country groans.

The taverns of the day on all public occasions,[25] and frequently in the ordinary course of their business, were filled with gambling, carousing, drinking crowds. The extent to which the great occasions of state were seized upon as opportunities for open and shameless drinking had become a scandal. The custom of granting a certain allowance of rum per day to laborers was honored in at least some sections of the country.[26] Accidental deaths due to drunkenness, and cases of suicide and insanity traceable to the same cause, were frequently reported.[27] All classes of society, young and old, rich and poor, men and women, fell victims to the great scourge. The colleges were not immune. At Yale, wine and liquors were kept in the rooms of many of the students and intemperance was one of the commonest of student faults.[28]Clergymen, though generally restraining themselves from gross indulgence, were accustomed to feel that the spirit of conviviality and the discussion of the affairs of church and state went hand in hand;[29] and now and then the bounds of propriety were overstepped.

Other unfavorable aspects of the situation may be found in the habits of card-playing and gambling which everywhere prevailed, and in the frequent allusions to instances of social vice and illegitimacy with which the pages of the diary of such a careful observer as the Reverend William Bentley were laden.[30]

The opinion that the social life of the period was desperately unsound was accepted without question by many a so-called interpreter of the times. The observations which President Timothy Dwight, of Yale, made in his Century Sermon[31] expressed the views of many minds. Dating "the first considerable change in the religious character of the people of this country" with the beginning of the French and Indian War,[32] he continued:

The officers and soldiers of the British armies, then employed in this country, although probably as little corrupted as those of most armies, were yet loose patterns of opinion and conduct, and were unhappily copied by considerable numbers of our own countrymen, united with them in military life. These, on their return, spread the infection through those around them. Looser habits of thinking began then to be adopted, and were followed, as they always are, by looser conduct. The American war increased these evils. Peace had not, at the commencement of this war, restored the purity of life which existed before the preceding war. To the depravation still remaining was added a long train of immoral doctrines and practices, which spread into every corner of the country. The profanation of the Sabbath, before unusual, profaneness of language, drunkenness, gambling, and lewdness were exceedingly increased; and, what is less commonly remarked, but is perhaps not less mischievous than any of them, a light, vain method of thinking concerning sacred things and a cold, contemptuous indifference toward every moral and religious subject.[33]

But this sweeping judgment of Yale's president, together with the specific explanation of the situation which he offered, are to be checked up by other and less pessimistic considerations. That there was much pertaining to the customs and manners of the times to be deplored, is not to be denied. On the other hand, that society in New England, as the eighteenth century drew toward its close, was actually lapsing from soundness and virtue to the extent that its fundamental views and habits were being altered, is far from clear. Observers who spoke to the contrary listened chiefly to the murmurs of the shallows and were unresponsive to the deeps.

The fact is, new ideals and new forces were working upward in the common life of the age. The new sense of freedom which the War of Independence ushered in, the steadily growing prosperity of the people, the development of social intimacies as the population of the country increased, the intrusion and growing influence of foreign ideas and customs, the steadily diminishing domination of the clergy—these all tended to inaugurate a new order which clashed more or less violently with the old. The memories of the old Puritan régime were still sufficiently vivid to make every lapse from liberty into license appear ominous in the extreme.

A general relaxing of social customs expressed itself in manifold ways over all those areas where actual stagnation had not come to pass; but this loosening was by no means characterized by deep-seated coarseness or general immorality.[34] The people had begun to claim for themselves some relaxation, and hence to amuse and satisfy themselves in the light of their enlarged conceptions of the freedom and privileges of life. On the whole, their enjoyments and amusements were such as characterize a state of healthy-mindedness at a time of marked transition.

In the main, the condition of the people was deplorable for what they lacked in the way of incitements to pleasurable and helpful social and cultural employments rather than because of what they possessed.[35] When it is recalled how considerable was the dearth of material for mental occupation; how undeveloped, for example, were music and painting;[36] how the newspapers and magazines of the day supplied little or nothing of a constructive or inspiring character; how science was almost totally undeveloped,[37] libraries few in number and destitute of stimulating material, the colleges for the most part mooning the years away over insipid and useless abstractions and dogmatic formulations, the wonder is that the rebound against Puritanism, in this period of intense political excitement and the growing secularization of thought, was not tenfold more violent and subversive than it was.[38]

The impression communicated by this view is heightened when it is recalled that the struggle for political independence not only had affected profoundly the status of the people of New England with respect to both their internal and their external relations; it had also made substantial and significant modifications in the very constitution of society itself. When the reorganization of affairs after the Revolutionary struggle was over, it became increasingly apparent that the control of the forces and institutions of society in New England was in the hands of new leaders and arbiters. The aristocracy of unquestioned conservatism which had all society under its thumb before the Revolution, had been swept away generally in the flood of that epochal event. Up from the small towns and villages of the country to the great centers, to Boston particularly, came a small army, made up largely of squires and gentry,[39] to establish a new but less secure sovereignty, to assume control of the social and political forces of the day, and, more or less unaware of the precise significance of the turn of events, to measure its strength against those new forces of democracy which in New England, as no place else in the nation, were to find themselves compelled to fight a long and stubborn battle to secure their emancipation.

Assuming without question the direction of affairs, this new aristocracy, after the fashion of the old leaders who were gone, addressed itself to the task of social, political, and religious control.[40] Manifestly the situation was big with possibilities with respect to the effect to be produced upon the thought and habits of the people. There they dwelt in their spacious houses,[41] these modern aristocrats and autocrats of fashion and custom, by no means rolling in luxury and idleness, yet claiming and enjoying a degree of relaxation and social pleasure vastly more lavish than that accorded to their plebeian neighbors, occupying themselves with their parties, their weddings and dances,[42] their refinements of dress[43] and behavior, but with little or no disposition to abandon themselves to scandalous conduct.

The constant challenge of the political necessities of the times, it may be urged, was altogether too compelling to admit of any such looseness. Still, one cannot scan the newspapers of the period, or read the story of the social commerce of the times as it pieces itself together out of the private records and correspondence of the day, or listen even to the pulpit's copious flood of denunciations,[44] without a feeling of mingled admiration and astonishment that in an age everywhere characterized by upheaval and ferment there was really as little of shameless and wanton conduct in New England as the records of the period reveal. It cannot but be viewed as a notable tribute to the essential soundness and nobility of that type of moral and religious culture which Puritanism had supplied from the first that the New England character should be able to pass through a period of profound social readjustment, of the discarding of old value judgments and the adoption of new, such as came near the close of the eighteenth century, and this without serious loss of moral power and prestige. Manifestly, whatever hollowness and insincerity Puritanism may have developed in other lands and times, it did not so cramp and fetter the human spirit in New England as to render it incapable of self-guidance when the old restraints and limitations were no more.[45]

Now that its controlling spirit of gravity and provincialism was being replaced by a general temper of comparative light-heartedness and open-mindedness, of unaffected enjoyment of the good things of life, of the acceptance of standards far more natural than those of the earlier day, the transition was accomplished with a relative absence of accompanying instances of moral lapse and disaster nothing less than remarkable. A considerable amount of the boisterousness and heat of the day over which clerical Jeremiahs and others of like conservative leanings ceased not to pour out their complaints,[46] is explicable on the ground of the growing habit of the mass of the people to exercise the rights of citizenship through direct participation in the affairs of the day. For far more significant than any evidence of moral blindness and perversity on the part of the people in general is the fact that a great, crowding, hungry democracy was knocking at the gates of the old aristocratic régime and insistently urging the consideration of its rights.

The general impression of a revolt against morality and religion in New England near the close of the eighteenth century was deepened by the bitterness of spirit which marked the last stages of the long struggle waged by dissenters to cut the bond between church and state.[47] The Congregational Church was one of the fundamental institutions of New England, and from the first the sword of the magistrate had been invoked to enforce conformity to its worship and polity. Strange enough seem the terms "Establishment" and "Standing Order"[48] in the history of a people whose forefathers came to America in quest of religious freedom. The freedom sought, however, was to be construed as loyalty to a new order rather than as the embodiment of tolerance. Thus it happened that for two whole centuries the battle on behalf of the rights of dissent had to be waged in New England.[49] To have this struggle construed by the aggrieved representatives of the Establishment as the crowning expression of what they had come to regard as the deep-seated and widespread irreligion of the age, was not the least of the bitter taunts which dissenters had to bear.

(a) *Massachusetts*

In Massachusetts the eighteenth century dawned with some faint promise of a kindlier day. The Charter of 1691 granted full liberty of conscience to all Christians except Roman Catholics.[50] The practical effects of this apparently sweeping reform were largely nullified, however, when in the following year the General Court made it obligatory for each town to have a minister for whose support all its inhabitants should be taxed.[51] With the removal of all bonds upon conscience and of all religious restrictions upon the right of suffrage on the one hand, but with the principle of enforced support of the institutions of religion on the other, the hallowed union of church and state in Massachusetts obviously stood in no immediate danger. The slight modifications speedily made in the law of 1692 did not touch the principle of taxation in the interests of religious worship.[52]

A measure of relief came to the Episcopalians in 1727,[53] and to the Quakers and Baptists in 1728,[54] in the form of exemption laws. In the case of the Baptists the exemption granted was not absolute, but only for a limited period of years. With the expiration of this period the struggle for relief of necessity had to be renewed.[55]The rights of dissent had begun to receive some recognition, but the limitations embodied in the foregoing legislation bore convincing testimony of a grudging temper of mind which would yield no ground without strong pressure.

The spirit of excitement and controversy which characterized the revival of religion of the third and fourth decades of the eighteenth century (*i. e.*, the Great Awakening) led to new complications and difficulties. Stirred by the revival, itinerant preachers, some of them of little learning and of less tact, invaded parishes of their clerical brethren without their consent, and presumed to censure the ministers and congregations that had not yielded to the emotional impulses of the revival.[56] A clash of parties followed, producing new antipathies and cleavages. Many who were in sympathy with the revival withdrew from orthodox congregations to organize new churches, nominally Baptist, with a view to obtaining exemption from the obligation to support the state church. To meet this evasion in 1752 the General Court of Massachusetts passed an act which provided

That no person for the future shall be so esteemed an A(n)nabaptist as to have his poll or polls and estate exempted from paying a proportionable part of the taxes that shall be raised in the town or place where he or they belong, but such whose names shall be contained in the lists taken by the assessors, as in said act provided, or such as shall produce a certificate, under the hands of the minister and of two principal members of such church, setting forth that they conscientiously believe such person or persons to be of their perswasion, and that he or they usually and frequently attend the publick worship in such church on Lord's days.[57]

A further provision of the act denied to Baptist ministers and their parishioners the right of furnishing the required certificates unless three other Baptist churches previously should have certified that the persons granting the certificates were regarded as members of that body.[58] To make the situation more galling, if that were possible, certificates so obtained had to be lodged annually with the town clerk before the time to pay the rates arrived.

From every point of view this legislation was objectionable to the Baptists. Their protest was instant and vigorous.[59] It was decided to send one of their number as agent to England, to carry their case before the government of the mother country.[60] A sharp remonstrance, so plain in its language that its signers came very near being taken into custody, was drawn up and presented to the General Court at Boston.[61] But great as was the sense of injustice under which the Baptists smarted, the operations of the act appear to have been most severe in the case of those who had drawn off from the orthodox churches on account of the disturbances created by the Great Awakening. The position of these Separatists[62] was peculiarly vulnerable. Baptist leaders found themselves embarrassed when called upon to certify to the Baptist affiliations of the Separatists; such a distasteful judgment of the motives and scruples of others was to be avoided wherever possible.[63] On the other hand, if the Separatists sought to set up churches and establish ministers of their own, they were confronted by the fact that a second Congregational church could not be formed in a parish without legislative permission, and the orthodox party usually showed itself capable of forestalling all such sanction on the part of the state. It was left, therefore, to the Separatists either for conscience' sake to bear the double burden of taxation,[64] or to seek a permanent religious home in one of the recognized dissenting bodies.[65]

Five years later, when the exemption law of 1752 expired and with it the exemption laws that previously had been passed for the relief of the Quakers, a new law was enacted governing both sects.[66] Henceforth a Baptist who desired exemption must have his name upon a list to be presented annually to the assessor and signed by the minister and three principal members of the Baptist congregation to which the applicant belonged, with the accompanying certification that the applicant was recognized as a conscientious and faithful Baptist. Quakers were placed under the same regulations. For thirteen years this law was in operation, with manifold instances of distress resulting, particularly in the case of Baptists.[67] Through difficulty in obtaining the certificates, goods were seized, expensive and otherwise irritating court trials were held, and not a few victims, either because of poverty or on account of conscientious scruples, found their way to prison. In some instances, despite the fact that the certificates were duly obtained and presented, they were waved aside and the payment of the tax required or the process of distraint invoked.[68]It is little wonder that the feeling in the minds and hearts of New England Baptists that there was a spirit of iniquity back of the oppressive measures of the Standing Order, came to have all the significance of a settled conviction.[69]

Further modifications in the exemption laws, made in 1770, were so slight, leaving as they did the certificate principle practically untouched,[70] that Baptist opposition was aroused even more deeply and the determination struck deeper root to push the battle for religious freedom to a decision. The times also were propitious. The near approach of the Revolutionary struggle focused attention upon the subject of tyranny and caused acts of oppression, whether civil or ecclesiastical in character, to stand out in a new relief before the eye of the public. That dissenters were quick to see the bearing of political events will appear from the following pithy comments in the address which the Committee of Grievances[71] drew up late in 1774 and presented to the Provincial Congress of Massachusetts:

It seems that the two main rights which all America are contending for at this time, are,—Not to be taxed where they are not represented, and—To have their causes tried by unbiased judges. And the Baptist churches in this province as heartily unite with their countrymen in this cause, as any denomination in the land; and are as ready to exert all their abilities to defend it. Yet only because they have thought it to be their duty to claim an equal title to these rights with their neighbors, they have repeatedly been accused of evil attempts against the general welfare of the colony; therefore, we have thought it expedient to lay a brief statement of the case before this assembly…. Great complaints have been made about a tax which the British parliament laid upon paper; but you require a paper tax of us annually. That which has made the greatest noise, is the tax of three pence a pound upon tea; but your law of last June laid a tax of the same sum every year upon the Baptists in each parish, as they would expect to defend themselves against a greater one…. All America is alarmed at the tea tax; though, if they please, they can avoid it by not buying tea; but we have no such liberty. We must either pay the little tax, or else your people appear even in this time of extremity determined to lay the great one upon us. But these lines are to let you know, that we are determined not to pay either of them; not only upon your principle of not being taxed where we are not represented, but also because we dare not render homage to any earthly power, which I and many of my brethren are fully convinced belongs only to God. We can not give the certificates you require, without implicitly allowing to men that authority which we believe in our conscience belongs only to God. Here, therefore, we claim charter rights, liberty of conscience.[72]

As the event proved, the Revolutionary period brought little legislative relief to dissenters in Massachusetts. Wherever the distractions of the war did not interrupt the ordinary course of ecclesiastical affairs, the state church continued to assert its time-honored prerogatives. The new constitution of the commonwealth which was adopted in 1780 gave conclusive proof that the Standing Order still had the situation well in hand. That instrument contained a bill of rights which reaffirmed the authority of the legislature to authorize and require the various towns and parishes "to make suitable provision, at their own expense, for the institution of the public worship of God";[73] affirmed also that the legislature had authority to enjoin attendance upon public worship; that towns and parishes were to have the right to elect their ministers and make contracts with them for their support; and that moneys, in the form of rates paid by the people in the support of public worship, were to be applied according to the preference of the rate-payer, "provided, there be any [minister] on whose instructions he attends"; otherwise the minister selected by the town or parish was to receive the benefit of the tax.[74] There is no difficulty in discerning here the outlines of the old ideal of a state church. The day of deliverance for dissent was not yet.[75]

What did take place during the Revolutionary period to promote the cause of religious freedom and to hasten the day of its triumph was the publication of various pamphlets and treatises devoted to the cause of toleration or championing the closely allied cause of democracy in church and state.[76] Several of these[77] were from the pen of the indomitable Isaac Backus, whose unwearied advocacy of the rights of the individual conscience was exceeded by none. The likeness of the struggle which dissenters were making for freedom of conscience to that which the colonists were making for civil liberty was a favorite notion of this doughty penman; and such an argument presented when the imaginations of his countrymen were stirred by the political situation, could not fail of its appeal. Three years before the war broke out, in his *Appeal to the Public for Religious Liberty*, Backus had drawn for the benefit of the public a sharp distinction between the spheres of ecclesiastical and civil governments. The former was armed only with *light* and *truth*, and was commissioned to "pull down the strongholds of iniquity," to gather into Christ's church those who were willing to be governed by His teachings, and to exclude those who would not be so governed;

while the latter "is armed with *the sword to guard the peace and to punish those who violate the same.*"[78] In his *Government and Liberty Described, and Ecclesiastical Tyranny Exposed*, published in 1778, he attacked the notion of men "assuming a power to govern religion, instead of being governed by it," and asserted that the essence of true religion is a voluntary obedience to God.[79] Here was strong meat for a people for whom the word freedom was rapidly coming to have an enlarged signification.

The most convincing exposition of the democratic tendencies of the age came from another quarter, and in a sense belonged to the past. Spurred by the fact that at the beginning of the century a resolute effort had been made, both in Massachusetts and Connecticut, to obtain more compact and rigid ecclesiastical control,[80] the Reverend John Wise, of Ipswich, Massachusetts, in 1710 had issued a satirical tract entitled, *The Churches' Quarrel Espoused*, and later, in 1717, a more serious production entitled, *A Vindication of the Government of the New England Churches*. In 1772 a new edition of these tracts, published by subscription, came from the Boston press.[81] The enduring quality of the task Wise had performed is shown by the fact that, while these two slight volumes had been conceived as a protest against the encroachments of ecclesiastical tyranny in the first two decades of the century, they now, a half-century later, served equally well to voice the deep passions and impulses of a people who for the moment were engrossed in the concerns of civil government.[82] Wise rejected the ideals of monarchy and aristocracy for the church, and took his stand upon the proposition that democracy alone stands the test of reason and revelation.[83] Of all systems, democracy alone cherishes the precious interests of man's original liberty and equality. It alone serves effectually to restrain the disposition to prey and embezzle, and to keep the administration of government firmly fixed upon the main point, "the peculiar good and benefit of the whole." "It is as plain as daylight, there are no species of government like a democracy to attain this end."[84]

Such literary assaults upon the usurpations of government, upon the violation of individual rights, and upon obstructions erected in the path of democracy, were frontal. As has been said, they were also happily timed. The oppressed would have to content themselves a little longer with a type of toleration which seemed but the shadow of genuine freedom; but the broad dissemination of such principles as those proclaimed by Backus and Wise had had the effect of altering appreciably the spirit of the times.

The close of the struggle for political freedom gave early proof that the cause of religious toleration had passed into a new stage. Dissent had grown in numbers and influence.[85] Distant voices, too, were being heard. Virginia's noble example in adopting the *Act Establishing Religious Freedom* had given a practical demonstration of the complete severance of church and state. The impression created by this determination of the issue of religious freedom on the broadest possible basis had been profound throughout the country. When the Constitution of the United States was before the people of Massachusetts for ratification, in the fall and winter of 1787–88, they found in it a single provision concerning religion. Article VI provided: "No religious test shall ever be required as a qualification to any office or public trust in the United States." So far had the eyes of dissenters in Massachusetts been opened to dangers lurking in legislative measures that a large proportion of the Baptist delegates in the state constitutional convention voted against the adoption of the instrument.[86] Besides, their hearts were set on some broad and yet specific guarantee of religious freedom under which their liberties would be safe. The First Amendment to the Constitution, which Congress proposed in 1789, seemed to fulfil their desire. It provided that "Congress shall make no law respecting an establishment of religion, or prohibiting the free exercise thereof." With the adoption of this law by the majority of the states, the principle of full liberty of mind, conscience, and worship, had been written finally into the law of the land.

Yet this pronouncement of the national government could not bring to a full end the long struggle which had been waged. Only the sphere of the federal government was involved, and individual states were still free to deal with the institutions of religion and the rights of individuals as they might feel disposed, as long as the national welfare was not involved.[87] What actually happened in Massachusetts is well expressed by Isaac Backus: "The amendment about liberty of conscience is kept out of sight."[88] The goods of Baptists continued to be levied upon to meet the ministerial tax.[89] Dissensions continued to arise in parishes over the settlement and support of ministers, dissenting minorities usually contesting the right of the majority to saddle upon them clergymen for whose ministrations they had no desire.[90] The annoyances and disabilities that dissenters and disaffected members of the Establishment suffered were clearly not so numerous nor so severe as they had been in the past;[91] none the less they were able to keep alive the impression that nothing but a spirit of bigotry and obdurate tyranny could explain the prolonged attitude and policy of the Standing Order.[92]

(b) *Connecticut*

Before directing attention to the effect which this weakening of the forces of ecclesiastical domination had upon the minds of the leaders of the Establishment, it will be necessary to review briefly the course which affairs took in Connecticut.[93]

Despite the fact that the founding of Connecticut had directly resulted from the ecclesiasticism of Massachusetts, the forces of ecclesiastical tyranny proved to be more strongly entrenched in Connecticut than in the parent state.[94] This was due in part to the homogeneity of the population,[95] but more largely to the degree of oversight of the religious life of the people, unusual even for Puritan New England, which the General Court of Connecticut exercised from the first.[96] In this connection it is to be observed that the impulses that lay back of the oppression of dissenters in Connecticut were not the same as those that shaped the situation in Massachusetts. The founders of Connecticut were out of sympathy with the theocratic ideal that prevailed in the mother colony; they frowned upon the harsh measures of repression which the authorities of Massachusetts adopted.[97] They held before them the ideal of a state wherein the maintenance of religion and the exercise of individual freedom should not be incompatible.

Yet as the event proved, the hand of religious tyranny fell heavily upon their posterity.[98] This happened, not because they were disposed to exercise harsher repressive measures than their fathers in curbing dissent, but because, in their extraordinary devotion to the churches of their own order, in their extreme care and watchfulness to strengthen them and to safeguard the whole range of their interests, they came into open conflict with the interests of dissenting bodies.[99] As early as 1669 the Congregational church was formally adopted as the state church.[100] From that day forward an intimate and intense paternalism characterized the attitude of the civil government toward the Establishment. Its most serious and permanent, as well as its lighter and occasional concerns, all were provided for with equal constancy. Contingencies of every description were either prudently anticipated or, arising suddenly, received the immediate and painstaking attention of the magistrates.[101]

The following list, though far from complete, will serve to illustrate this point. Without the consent of the General Court, churches could not be organized,[102] nor bonds be severed between pastors and their flocks.[103] The formation of new parishes and the fixing of their limits,[104] the calling of new ministers,[105] the determination of the time at which arrearages in ministers' salaries must be paid fully,[106] the fixing of the location of new houses of worship,[107] the disposition of cases of discipline appealed from the decisions of local church courts,[108] the settlement of the question as to who were to be permitted to receive the Lord's Supper,[109]the proffer of counsel concerning the behavior offended members were expected to manifest toward pastors for whom they entertained no affection nor respect[110]—these all were regarded as part of the proper business of the General Court.

The dangers inherent in such a system are not difficult to divine. The churches themselves upon which such paternal legislative care was imposed generally found their affairs taken out of their hands. Civil authority disciplined them and their members, and made independent ecclesiastical rule little more than a fiction. Again, the committal of the political government to a particular type of religious polity and worship aroused antagonisms in the minds of men who hated the palest shadow of the principle that the religion of a prince or government must be the religion of the people. However tolerant toward non-conformity such a state may show itself to be—and none will deny that Connecticut rose to comparatively high levels of justice in this regard[111]—the favoritism of government puts dissent at a disadvantage; and when narrow and intolerant men are at the helm of state, disadvantage passes rapidly into positive deprivation and injury. Once more, so close an alliance between politics and religion as the Standing Order in Connecticut represented, invites similar combinations on the part of men, some of whom have political and some religious objects to serve, and who, therefore, in the presence of a common foe gladly make common cause. All of which we shall see illustrated later.

Another general aspect of the situation in Connecticut concerns the development of synodical government within the Congregational church. At the beginning of the eighteenth century, out of a sense of the decay of religion in New England, as evidenced by the loosening of discipline and the weakening of ministerial influence,[112]the clergy of Massachusetts attempted to buttress church government and ministerial authority through the "Proposals of 1705." These provided for the grouping of ministers in Associations which were to function in the following ways: pastors were to adopt their advice in all difficult cases; ministerial candidates were to be examined and licensed by them; pastorless, or "bereaved" churches were to be urged to apply to them for candidates; they were also to exercise a general oversight of religion, and to inquire into charges made against the character, conduct, or faith of any of their members. The "Proposals" also made provision for Standing Councils to be made up of delegates from these Ministerial Associations and lay members of the churches. These Standing Councils were "to consult, advise, and determine all affairs that shall be proper matter for the consideration of an ecclesiastical council within their respective limits." Their judgments were to be accepted as final and obedience was to be enforced on penalty of forfeiting church-fellowship.[113] This bold step in the direction of bringing the churches of Massachusetts under more rigorous ecclesiastical control was not destined to succeed. Liberalizing elements stirred up powerful opposition, the legislature failed to give to the "Proposals" its support, and the movement fell through.[114]

A very different situation developed in Connecticut. The yearning for the strengthening of church government in the interests of a general improvement of religion was if anything stronger in that commonwealth; and a propitious hour for the inauguration of such a movement came when, in 1707, the most influential minister of the colony, Gurdon Saltonstall, of New London, was raised to the governor's chair. The following May the General Court issued the call for the famous Saybrook Synod.[115] Ministers and messengers of the churches were to assemble in their respective county towns, "on the last Monday in June next ... to consider and agree upon those methods and rules for the management of ecclesiastical discipline which by them shall be judged agreeable and conformable to the word of God."[116] By these county councils ministers and delegates were to be chosen to meet at Saybrook, at the commencement of the "infant college" (i. e., Yale), there "to compare the results of the ministers of the several counties, and out of them and from them to draw a form of ecclesiastical discipline which by two or more persons delegated by them shall be offered to this Court ... to be considered of and confirmed by them."[117]

The directions of the General Court were complied with. The doctrinal results of the Saybrook Synod are no part of our concern; but this is not so with regard to its ecclesiastical formulations. The principles contained in the "Proposals of

1705" were accepted and worked out in more complete detail. Churches were to be grouped in Consociations, one or more in each county as the churches might determine. Cases of discipline too difficult of management in local congregations were to be heard and determined by these Consociations. Refusal to answer to the summons of a Consociation, or to submit to its decision, incurred excommunication, whether a church or a pastor might be the guilty party. All matters relating to the installation, ordination, and dismissal of ministers were to be submitted by the churches to these Consociations. In like manner the ministers of the various counties were to be grouped together in Associations to consult concerning the affairs of the church, provide ministerial licensure, examine complaints, and make recommendations to the legislature concerning the settlement of pastors with "bereaved" churches.[118]

The result of the deliberations of the Saybrook Synod was laid duly before the sessions of the General Court, in October, 1708, and formally adopted by that body in the following terms:

This Assembly do declare their great approbation of such a happy agreement, and do ordain that all the churches within this government that are or shall be thus united in doctrine, worship, and discipline, be, and for the future shall be owned and acknowledged established by law. Provided always, that nothing herein shall be intended and construed to hinder or prevent any society or church that is or shall be allowed by the laws of this government, who soberly differ or dissent from the united churches hereby established, from exercising worship and discipline in their own way, according to their consciences.[119]

This reëstablishment of the Congregational church in Connecticut determined the course of events, as far as the religious interests of the commonwealth were concerned, for a hundred years to come. By this it is not meant that the ecclesiastical system which was thus worked out and imposed upon the churches of the colony continued to operate in full force for that period; the Saybrook Platform was abrogated in 1784. But the Congregational church in Connecticut, by the act of 1708, "attained the height of its security and power,"[120] and, as one of the chief consequences of the act, ministerial domination was accorded a recognition and support, the tradition of which outlived by at least a quarter of a century the system by which it had been so firmly established.

Thus to the paternalism of the state the authority and sense of importance of the clergy had been added. These principles established, it was to be expected that the religious history of Connecticut during the eighteenth century would reveal the following characteristics and tendencies: a disposition on the part of the state to treat the clergy of the Establishment as the pillars of conservative thought and custom; and a disposition on the part of the clergy to exercise a controlling hand over all the religious activities of the people, as well as to react violently against all radical impulses and movements which appeared to endanger centralization of government, whether ecclesiastical or political. Certainly these were the tendencies, expressed in the attitude of mind and the activities of the Standing Order, with which the forces of non-conformity and democracy had to contend throughout the whole of the century.

We may now turn to take a brief survey of the more important events in the course of this conflict. The concluding statement of the act whereby the Connecticut General Court adopted the recommendations of the Saybrook Synod,[121] gave evidence of a tender regard for the consciences and rights of dissenters which subsequent occurrences far from justified. The fact is, the act of reëstablishment did not stand alone. Earlier in the same year (1708) the General Court had written into the law of the colony another statute whose provisions were in no way affected by the later act. For the worthy object of granting liberty of worship to sober dissenters, a liberty which they were to be permitted to enjoy "without let, or hindrance or molestation," it was provided that dissenting congregations were to qualify (*i. e.*, obtain license) under the law.[122] It was likewise provided that this permission to qualify should in no way operate to the prejudice of the rights and privileges of the churches of the Establishment, or "to the excusing any person from paying any such minister or town dues, as are now, or shall hereafter be due from them."[123] This double burden of obtaining license and supporting the state church was not to be borne easily. An agitation to obtain relief promptly began.[124]

After two decades of effort the Episcopalians were the first to meet with any measure of success. Henceforth their rate money was to be spent in the support of their own ministers and they were no longer to be required to help build meeting-houses for the state church.[125] Two years later, relief was granted to Baptists and Quakers. The exemption laws passed in their behalf, however, made necessary the presentation of certificates vouching for the claims of the holders that they were conscientious supporters of the principles and faithful attendants upon the worship of one or the other of these bodies.[126]

The introduction of the custom of requiring certificates encountered the same sense of injustice and bitter resentment that dissenters in Massachusetts manifested. Besides, the exemption laws just referred to failed to operate in a uniform and equitable manner. Episcopalians and Baptists, particularly, found frequent occasion to complain of the miscarriage of this legislation and to groan under the double burden of taxation from which they had obtained no actual relief.[127]

But as in Massachusetts, so in Connecticut, the greatest hardships befell the Separatists who went out from the fold of the orthodox church. Unable to achieve within the Establishment that reformation of doctrine, polity, and spiritual life which they deemed requisite, they associated themselves together in churches committed to their own convictions. Opposition confronted them at every turn. Obstructions were thrown in the way of their efforts to obtain legal permission to constitute their churches; the civil power persisted in treating them as law-breakers and incorrigibles; their ministers were drastically dealt with by Consociations which regarded them as wicked men filled with the spirit of insubordination.[128] A group of laws as severe and intolerant as any the statute books of Connecticut ever contained were enacted in 1742–43 to curb and if possible to eradicate the Separatist defection.[129] Ordained ministers were forbidden to preach outside the bounds of their parishes unless expressly invited so to do.[130] Ministerial Associations were restrained from licensing candidates to preach outside the territorial jurisdiction of the Association granting licensure.[131] Ministers of the Establishment were empowered to lodge certificates with society clerks, attesting that men had entered their parishes and preached therein without first having received permission. No provision for ascertaining the facts in such cases was contemplated by the law. Justices of the peace were forbidden to sign a warrant authorizing the collection of a minister's rates until they were assured that no such certificate had been lodged against the clergyman involved.[132]Heavy bonds were to be imposed upon ministers from outside the colony who might venture to preach within its limits without invitation, with the added provision that such men were to be treated as vagrants and bundled out of the colony as speedily as possible.[133] Ministers who had not been graduated from Yale or Harvard, or some other Protestant college or university, were debarred from all benefits of ministerial support as provided by law.[134]

The climax of the high-handed measures of the supporters of the Establishment was doubtless reached in this legislation. A retrograde movement in the cause of religious toleration set in,[135] the direct effects of which were not quickly overcome. Henceforth dissenters were to be annoyed and hampered as they had not been before. The necessity of appearing in person before the General Court when seeking exemption from ecclesiastical burdens,[136] the embarrassments and hardships that dissenting ministers suffered in their efforts to supply religious counsel to their people,[137] the growing aversion of the General Court to granting permission to unorthodox and dissenting groups to organize,[138] all serve to indicate the strength of the reaction that had set in.

The impressions produced by this excess were even more significant than the direct results, deplorable as the latter were.[139] In the middle of the eighteenth century the Standing Order in Connecticut had gained for themselves an unenviable record for bigotry and persecution from which the events of the latter half of the century by no means cleared them.

For a quarter of a century following the enactment of the legislative measures just considered, no advance step, general in its nature, was taken. Here and there a little larger measure of freedom was doled out to this or that aggrieved dissenting minister or church; but the situation as a whole was not materially changed. "Restriction was the rule, freedom the exception, and government the absolute and irresponsible dispenser of both."[140] Finally, in 1778 some evidence that a change in sentiment was under way appeared in the fact that Separatists were exempted from taxes to support the state church. Six years later, in 1784, more satisfactory proof was forthcoming. That year, by the passing of an act entitled, "An Act for Securing the Rights of Conscience in Matters of Religion, to Christians of Every Denomination in this State,"[141] the General Court tacitly abrogated the Saybrook Platform and set the institutions of religion in Connecticut upon a new base. The act declared

That no Persons in this State, professing the Christian Religion, who soberly and conscientiously dissent from the Worship and Ministry by Law established in the Society wherein they dwell, and attend public Worship by themselves shall incur any Penalty for not attending the Worship and Ministry so established, on the Lord's Day, or on account of their meeting together by themselves on said Day, for public Worship in a Way agreeable to their consciences.

It was further declared that Christians of every Protestant denomination, "whether Episcopal Church, of those Congregationalists called Separates, or of the people called Baptists, or Quakers, or any other Denomination who shall have formed themselves in distinct Churches or Congregations," and who helped to maintain their worship, were to be exempted from the support of any other church than their own. Further, all such dissenting congregations were to enjoy the same power and privileges in the support of their ministry, and in the building and repairing of their houses of worship, as those churches which were established by law. Such persons as did not belong to any of these dissenting bodies were to be taxed for the support of the state church.[142]

The spirit of toleration had traveled far; but that the struggle for complete religious freedom was yet by no means won will immediately appear from the following restrictions: (1) Protestants only were contemplated as beneficiaries under the act; (2) the principle of taxation for the support of the state church was retained; (3) the obligation to support some form of Christian worship was required; (4) the benefits of that provision of the act which guaranteed to dissenters exemption from ecclesiastical taxation were to be available only on the condition that a certificate, signed by an officer of a dissenting congregation, should be deposited with the clerk of the state church near which the dissenter lived.

A formidable number of the objectionable features of the older legislation were thus retained. The state church was still in existence. Taxation for the support of religion was still the law of the commonwealth. Dissenters were still compelled to put themselves to the trouble and humiliation of obtaining the detested certificates. Besides, the ghost of religious persecution was not yet laid. Goods and chattels of the religiously indifferent, or of conscientious dissenters, continued to be seized and sold by officers of the law, to discharge unsatisfied levies made for the support of the Establishment.[143]

The principle of requiring certificates proved to be the chief bone of contention between the Standing Order and dissenters as the century drew to its close. The rapid growth of dissenting bodies in the period following the Revolution, aided as they were by a zeal for proselyting on the part of their leaders and by a set of the public mind decidedly favorable to their propaganda because of their democratic leanings, was met by corresponding anxiety and sternness on the part of the supporters of the Establishment. Confusing, as they habitually did, the interests of the state church with the cause of religion, the representatives of the Standing Order led themselves to believe that a contagion of irreligion was spreading alarmingly, and therefore restrictive religious legislation was in order.[144] In line with this conviction, in May, 1791, the legislature enacted a law requiring dissenters to have their certificates signed by at least one, and preferably two, civil officers, instead of as provided in the act of 1784. This law proved peculiarly distasteful to dissenters.[145] A powerful opposition developed; and the authorities, made aware of the fact that they had over-reached themselves, six months later withdrew the obnoxious act, substituting for it another which permitted each dissenter to write and sign his own certificate, but requiring him, as before, to file it with the clerk of the state church near which he lived.[146] The momentary wrath of dissenters was thus mollified; however, the retention of the certificate principle continued to gall and to excite them. A disagreeable discussion dragged itself along, marked by acrimony, pettiness, and personal attacks on both sides; by a consolidation of the forces and interests of dissenters and Republicans on the one hand, and a growing sense of injured innocence and of concern for the fate of religion on the part of the Standing Order.[147]

(c) *Summary*

By way of summary, a few general comments, based upon the situation in Massachusetts and Connecticut jointly considered, are now in order. Looking back upon the activities of the Standing Order after the lapse of something more than a century, we see that they were zealously contending for an ideal which had won their whole allegiance—a body politic safeguarded and made secure by a state church. To prevent deterioration of the state and its people the bulwark of a religion established by law seemed imperative.[148] The interests involved were far too serious to put them at the mercy of a voluntary support of the institutions of religion.[149] Moreover, an established church seemed to this group of men no necessary enemy of non-conformity. The degree of toleration possible under an establishment of religion was deemed sufficient actually to favor the growth of sects, and at the same time to make the sway of orthodoxy secure.[150]

How, then, were men of such opinions to interpret the ever-growing agitation for a larger measure of toleration, accompanied as it was by an ever-growing resentment toward the political influence and activities of the Standing Order, as anything other than a covert attack upon religion itself? These bitter complainings over the religious measures adopted by government, these flauntings of authority through stubborn refusal or passive resistance to the payment of ecclesiastical rates, these unrelenting efforts to dispossess the clergy of the Establishment of their traditional honors and emoluments—what were they all but so many proofs of the impiety of the age and an abominable conspiracy to drive pure religion from the land? As the representatives of the Standing Order saw the situation, the church was obviously in grave danger and to steady the tottering ark of the Lord was the most imperative duty of the hour.

On the other hand, in the light of the growing liberality of the times, it was impossible for the forces of dissent to be patient with such men. They were men of the past, callously unresponsive to the spirit of the new age. They were an embittered minority, exerting themselves to keep a struggling and confident majority a little longer under their thumb. They were mischievous meddlers in the affairs of others, using religion as a cloak to hide their social and political self-seeking. As for the cry, "The church is in danger!", that was to be regarded as the most signal proof of the hypocrisy of those who raised it.[151]

3. ALARMS DUE TO THE SPREAD OF RELIGIOUS RADICALISM AND SCEPTICISM

During the eighteenth century the progress of religious thought in New England in the direction of liberal positions was marked. Near the beginning of the century, in his *Ratio Disciplinae*, Cotton Mather was able to speak confidently of the solid and compact character of religious opinion in his generation, and felt free to dispose of the subject with a few general statements regarding the universal adherence of the churches of New England to the orthodox standards of the mother country. He made the added comment: "I can not learn, That among all the Pastors of Two Hundred Churches, there is one Arminian: much less Arian, or a Gentilist."[152] At the end of the century, it is very certain that no such all-inclusive generalization, by the widest stretch of the imagination, would have been possible. Indeed, when a noted Philadelphia minister of the day, the Reverend Ashbel Green, visited New England in 1791, he found an aptitude for polemical discussion on the part of the clergy which impressed him as most extraordinary. Through his contact with the Boston Ministerial Association he encountered "Calvinists, Universalists, Arminians, Arians," and at least one "Socinian," all participating in pleasant social intercourse, despite their radical differences of religious opinion. To the mind of the visiting Philadelphia clergyman the situation was explicable only on the basis of an extreme laxness in the matter of religious sentiments and doctrines, a judgment which obviously requires some modification in view of the predilection for doctrinal controversy which he himself remarked.[153]

From the days of the Great Awakening, the lines of doctrinal cleavage had grown increasingly distinct in the religious thought of New England. Apart from those effects of the revival which already have been noted,[154] it may be said that the one really permanent result of that notable wave of religious enthusiasm was the polemical controversy which it precipitated.[155] The question concerning the "means of grace," around which the controversy in its initial stage raged,[156] became larger and more complicated by virtue of the massive system of theology which Jonathan Edwards developed upon the fundamental notion of the utter worthlessness of man, due to his depravity and consequent helplessness.

Into the metaphysical subtleties of the Edwardean system we are not called to go; it is sufficient to observe that the reaction against such a conception of human nature was bound to be marked in the midst of an age generally responsive to enthusiasms born of fresh conceptions of the essential dignity and worth of man. The virtue of humility was destined to divest itself of much of that abject quality with which the whole Calvinistic theology had clothed it, and to accommodate itself to candid and unblushing convictions of human endowments, abilities, excellencies, and prospects, because of which it would be impossible to retain the traditional contempt for human nature.[157]

The reaction against the Edwardean theology was fruitful in the encouragement of liberal notions along other closely related lines. The bold necessitarianism of that system could not but produce an effect generally favorable to the promotion of man's confidence in himself, in the midst of an age characterized by prodigious political initiative and love of liberty, and by conceptions of the Deity which stressed the very vastness of those reaches of space stretching between God and the world. The heavy emphasis which the new theological system laid upon the notion of the divine sovereignty, true as it was in spirit to the traditional Puritan interest in the cause of theocracy, was doomed to find itself belated within an age beginning to glow with humanitarian passion and with enthusiasm for the ideal of democracy; and, positively considered, to give impulse in the general direction just noted. The very heat and intensity of the controversy which, from the middle of the century on, filled New England with its din and confusion, in itself bore witness to the degree of pressure which the more secularized notions of human worth and destiny had begun to exert. That a system so staggering in its assumptions, so all but invulnerable in its logical self-consistency, and withal so inexorable in its demands upon the human spirit for the abandonment of all thought of independent ability and worth, having been brought to close quarters with more or less vague and undefined, but none the less vital human interests and passions, should tend to give rise to a variety of radical opinions and judgments, was to be expected. And thus it operated,[158] not, to be sure, without the assistance of significant concurrent causes.

The wash of the wave of the great deistic controversy on the other side of the Atlantic was not without its effect upon the religious thought of New England. The direct evidence of this is, however, much more elusive than one might at first suppose.[159] That the reading public was acquainted with the writings of the great English deists, Herbert, Chubb, Shaftesbury, Tindal, Wollaston, Toland, Hume, is clear from references to their works which appear with considerable frequency in the private and public records of the day; but invariably these references are made in a more or less casual manner, and, for the most part, in connection with sweeping generalizations made by the clergy respecting the prevailing scepticism of the age. Apart from such allusions and the appearance of titles in the lists of booksellers who were advertising their stocks in the newspapers, it would be difficult to cite specific evidence, Thomas Paine's *Age of Reason* alone excepted, to the effect that the impact of English deism upon the thought of New England was anything like direct.

The amount of independent literary expression which the doctrines of deism obtained in New England was practically negligible.[160] The quality was even less noteworthy. Ethan Allen's *Reason the Only Oracle of Man*,[161] published in 1784, was perhaps the only production of native orig into which anything like general attention was accorded; and the evident inability of this work to root itself deeply in the thought of the people, despite the prestige due to the author's Revolutionary record, was demonstrated the moment Paine's more serious work began to circulate in this country. The crudeness of Allen's style, coupled with the ferocity of his onslaught on the advocates and absurdly credulous devotees of supernaturalism, as Allen regarded the orthodox party of his day, went far toward determining the attitude of contempt and high-minded scorn with which his work was generally treated, when leaders of conservative thought deigned to notice it at all.[162]

But Thomas Paine's attack upon the foundations of supernaturalism was by no means taken lightly. From the time of its arrival in this country, the *Age of Reason* produced an amount of excited comment which gave to its appearance and circulation all the elements of a sensation.[163] The natural interest of the public in the appearance of the production was admittedly great; but at least a partial explanation of the attention which the book received is to be found in the fact that its author was able to effect plans to have the work published cheaply abroad and extensively circulated in this country.[164] In any event, whatever may have been the precise influences which promoted the distribution and perusal of the book, the *Age of Reason* aroused an immediate public interest, chiefly antagonistic, the like of which probably had been accorded to no other volume circulated in America before its day. The bumptious and militant nature of its deism, as well as its raw and unceremonious ridicule of much that passed in the thought of the times for essential orthodoxy, drew popular attention from the worthier and more exalted passages in the volume,[165] and irritated the opposition beyond control. A vociferous chorus of hostile criticism arose.[166] Clergymen poured out the vials of their wrath and execration, despite their evident desire to appear undisturbed; newspaper editors and contributors gave voluminous expression to their sense of chagrin and pained disappointment that so scandalous and impious a publication should be in circulation;[167] observers of and participants in the college life of the day felt called upon to lament the extent to which unsettling opinions of the nature of those expressed by Paine had laid hold of the imaginations and altered the convictions of youthful minds.[168] The impression that Paine had aided and abetted the cause of impiety and irreligion was general.[169]

It was not the doctrinal controversies of the period, however, nor yet the intrusion of the principles of natural religion, by which the unsettling tendencies of the times were believed to be promoted most directly and powerfully. In the judgment of practically every leader of conservative thought in New

England, and of all America for that matter, that unholy preëminence belonged to the effect produced upon the public mind in this country by the French Revolution, and more especially the impious principles of infidelity and atheism by which, they concluded, that colossal overturning of institutions was stimulated and guided. No single phenomenon of our national history stands out in sharper relief than the impression which the great European convulsion made, first upon the imaginations and later upon the political and religious ideals of the citizens of this young republic in the West, who followed the earlier fortunes of the French Revolutionary cause with breathless interest and concern. The memory of the recent struggle of the American colonists for independence, for the happy issue of which France had made such timely and substantial contributions, in itself supplied a pledge of profound sympathy for that country. That the spark of revolution had been communicated originally by America to France was, moreover, one of the favorite conceits of the day. Gratitude, the bonds of political friendship and alliance, the supposed similarity of popular enthusiasms and passions—all the essential factors requisite for the development of a spirit of tender and affectionate regard were clearly present.

Thus it happened that from the hour when the first rumblings of the impending European revolution were heard on this side of the Atlantic, the citizens of these states evinced an earnest and sympathetic concern;[170] and as the revolutionary drama unfolded through its earlier scenes the enthusiasm and lively sympathy of the people grew apace. The atmosphere was electric. Anticipations of citizens ran high. Liberty was again in travail.[171] The institutions of freedom were about to descend upon another nation. The shackles of political and ecclesiastical tyranny were being torn from the limbs of twenty-five millions of slaves.[172] Having revolutionized France, America's ideals might be expected to leaven the whole of Europe.[173] The millennium could not be far away. Admiration for the French cause and devotion to it swept all before them. So much so that when, in the autumn and winter of 1792–93, the thrilling news of the successes achieved by the French armies in repelling the invaders of the new republic began to arrive in America, a wave of irresistible and uncontrolled enthusiasm swept over the land.[174] The "French Frenzy," with its maudlin outbursts of professed attachment for the great watchwords of the Revolution—Liberty, Equality, Fraternity—with its pageants and civic feasts, its cockades and liberty caps, its ribald singing of republican songs and dramatic intertwinings of the standards of the two sister republics, deserves a place altogether by itself as an extraordinary expression of the public mind.

To this wild riot of tumultuous and spectacular enthusiasm an effectual check was soon to be given. With the execution of Louis XVI, in January, 1793, the admiration of the more thoughtful observers of the Revolution, who had accustomed themselves to pass soberly but apologetically over the earlier excesses of the revolutionists as unavoidable concomitants of a struggle necessarily desperate in its character,[175] received a rude shock.[176] The brutal death of a monarch whose personal services on behalf of their own cause during the days of deep necessity had been considerable, brought home to American citizens their first clear conviction respecting the excessively bloody and relentless spirit of the forces in control of the Revolution. The day of disillusionment had dawned. Leaders of thought made no effort to conceal their sense of mingled horror and regret. The amount of popular sympathy for the cause of the Revolution was still too great to allow anything approaching a general condemnation; but none the less a decided chill was felt.[177]

The murder of the king soon enough appeared to Americans a mere incident in a wild orgy of unbridled violence and blood-letting. A stream of information concerning the swift march of events in France, mostly having to do with enormities and excesses which gave all too patent proof of the fury of the currents of passion upon which the participants in the Revolution were being tossed, began to pour its waters through the channels of public utterance and discussion in America. The atrocities of the Reign of Terror brought fully home to the

American public, to the conservative-minded particularly, the conviction that the Revolution had become diverted from its original principles and aims, and had descended to the plane of brutal despotism, reprehensible both in principle and practice above anything the eyes of men had ever beheld.[178] The leaders of the Revolution clearly were not the high-minded patriots and emancipators their admirers on this side of the ocean had adjudged them to be. The terms "assassin," "savage," "monster," "regicide," began to be employed as the only fit terms whereby to characterize the leading figures in an awful spectacle of butchery and rapine.[179]

But not until the religious aspects of the French Revolution are considered, is the deep revulsion of feeling which took place in New England completely laid bare. This feature of the situation had been regarded with deep solicitude from the beginning;[180] and as time went on through the cloud of confusion raised by the dust and smoke of the political developments of the Revolution, it became increasingly clear to the conservative class in New England that an alliance between the forces of anarchy and impiety had been effected. What else could explain the rapid development of a fierce reforming spirit, which in turn, within the space of not more than two or three years at the most, stood forth as a spirit of overt persecution in the handling of all ecclesiastical affairs? The vociferous affirmation of deistical and atheistical principles on the part of Revolutionary leaders in the councils of clubs and in sessions of the National Assembly, the reiteration and growing boldness of the demand for the elimination of the ancient system of religious faith, the successive efforts to supplant that system, first with the cult of Reason and later with the cult of the Supreme Being,—how were these to be construed other than as the expressions and performances of men who were bent upon the utter abolition of the Christian faith? There was wanting in New England, of course, intimate knowledge of the true state of French religious affairs and of the reactionary spirit displayed by the higher clergy and their devotion to the cause of monarchy. Little was known of the growing sense of resentment felt by a people who had begun to contemplate frankly the burdens which had been imposed upon them under the ancient régime, the multiplication of religious offices and establishments, the absorption of the land into vast ecclesiastical estates, and the indifference of the spiritual guides of the nation to private and public distress. It was hardly to be expected that spectators as far removed from the scene as the shores of New England would be able to interpret correctly the essential spirit of a people who had grown weary of the abuses of a religious system in whose principles and purer forms they still believed, despite the momentary violence of their leaders.[181]

By the year 1794 the belief that the revolutionists in France had added atheism to their program of anarchy was well established in New England. The difficulty of weighing this opinion exactly is greatly enhanced on account of the political handling which the situation received. Over the question of foreign alliances the Federalists and Republicans had split violently in 1793. The war which had broken out between England and France, regarded from any point of view, was of vast consequence in the eyes of the citizens of this young nation, just beginning to cope with the problems of diplomacy and international relations. The outbreak of hostilities between the two European nations with which the United States had had and must continue to have its most intimate and important intercourse forced an alignment among its citizens so sharp and decisive as to constitute the outstanding political feature of the country for years to come.[182] For reasons which we shall not now pause to consider, Federalists championed the cause of England in the European conflict, and Republicans the cause of France. Seizing upon the issue of "French infidelity," Federalist editors were disposed to see in it the gravest peril by which the American people were threatened. The anti-religious spirit of the French Revolutionary leaders represented a danger-point of infection against which every citizen must needs be warned. On the other hand, Republican editors felt it incumbent upon them to do their utmost to minimize the genuineness and importance of all such damaging views of the case.[183]

But considerations of party advantage fall far short of furnishing a full explanation of the general sense of alarm the people of New England experienced on account of the open hostility to religion which they saw manifest in France. Out of France came a series of reports which taken together were calculated to raise their fears to the highest pitch. The confiscation of the property of the church, the abolition of religious vows, the promulgation of the "Civil Constitution of the Clergy,"[184] the banishment of non-juror priests, the infamy of the Goddess of Reason, the abolition of the Christian Sabbath, the secularization of festivals[185]—here were evidences of impiety as shameless as they were shocking.[186] Such principles and measures appeared as so many deadly thrusts at the Christian faith. It was difficult, if not impossible, for the most sympathetic admirers of France to find a way to explain this ominous cast of events.[187]

How thoroughly the fear of "French infidelity" had gripped the imaginations of men in New England will appear more clearly if the following considerations are weighed. The presumption that the intimate relations which Americans had been having with the people of France had produced a serious blight of morals and religion among the former, seemed to find its justification in the currents of skepticism and irreverence which, by common consent, had set in among the youth of the land. This phase of the situation as reflected in conditions within the colleges was held to be particularly deplorable. It was the settled conviction of President Dwight of Yale that "the infidelity of Voltaire and his coadjutors" had a special attractiveness for youth, for reasons which do not impress one as being highly charitable, to say the least:

Youths particularly, who had been liberally educated, and who with strong passions, and feeble principles, were votaries of sensuality and ambition, delighted with the prospect of unrestrained gratification, and panting to be enrolled with men of fashion and splendour, became enamored of these new doctrines. The tenour of opinion, and even of conversation, was to a considerable extent changed at once. Striplings, scarcely fledged, suddenly found that the world had been involved in a general darkness, through the long succession of the preceding ages; and that the light of wisdom had just begun to dawn upon the human race. All the science, all the information, which had been acquired before the commencement of the last thirty or forty years, stood in their view for nothing.... Religion they discovered on the one hand to be a vision of dotards and nurses, and on the other a system of fraud and trick, imposed by priestcraft for base purposes upon the ignorant multitude. Revelation they found was without authority, or evidence; and moral obligation a cobweb, which might indeed entangle flies, but by which creatures of a stronger wing nobly disdained to be confined.[188]

This somewhat theoretical view of the case was not unsupported by tangible evidence. The students of Yale were sceptical.[189] In the religious discussions of the lecture-rooms the cause of infidelity stood high in student favor.[190] Of seventy-six members of the class that graduated in 1802 only one was a professed Christian at the time of matriculation.[191] At the time President Dwight entered upon the leadership of the college, the college church was practically extinct.[192] Altogether the situation was highly alarming to the friends of Christianity.[193]

The condition of affairs at Harvard showed little if any improvement. When William Ellery Channing matriculated in that institution in 1794 he found the thought and principles of the students on a lower level than they ever before had reached.[194] The French Revolution, which generally throughout the country had shown itself to be contaminating, already had left its marks deep upon the life of the college. The old loyalties were shaken; conversation had become bold and daring in tone; the foundations upon which morals and religion had been built in the past were now believed to be seriously undermined.[195]

On the part of men who held themselves responsible for the education of youth, everywhere the feeling prevailed that a popular mood of skepticism had developed for which the precepts and example of the French were chiefly responsible.

With the clergy—and in their state of mind we are interested especially—this feeling was hardly less than an obsession. The special conservators of the moral and religious health of the people, they had long been concerned over the possible effects of radical French political and religious notions; and when they seemed to see the triumph of those notions in the excesses of the French Revolution, their sense of alarm was intense. It was, of course, the exhibition of violent hostility to organized Christianity in France which the Revolutionists were making, over which their hands were flung high in horror.

The clergy of New England, like the majority of their fellow-countrymen, in the beginning had not adopted an attitude of hostility toward the French upheaval. There was that in the earlier struggles of the French people to tear the yoke of despotism from their necks which appealed mightily to the sympathies of the clerical heart. It was not without some travail of spirit that clergymen arrived at the conclusion that their sympathy and enthusiasm for the French Revolution had been misplaced.[196]Two factors contributed to this result. In the first place, the changed complexion of the Revolution; in the second place, the new party alignments at home which brought the orthodox clergy, almost to a man, into the Federalist camp.

Which of these two factors was the more decisive in its power of control over the clerical mind, it would be difficult to say. As a matter of fact, the two influences were interrelated to an extraordinary degree. Political alignments, as we have seen, were interwoven closely with the question of foreign alliances. Conversely, the status of foreign affairs was bound to react strongly upon the judgments of clergymen with whom patriotic concerns were second in importance only to the interests of religion. Be that as it may, the years 1793 and 1794 saw the Federalist clergy in New England rapidly veering round to the fixed position of vehement antagonism to French principles. The following is a brief account of the course they pursued.

On the occasion of the annual fast in Massachusetts, April 11, 1793, the Reverend David Tappan, professor of divinity in Harvard College, preached a sermon that indicated the trend of a clerical mind.[197] In language not unmarked by vagueness, he called upon his hearers to bear witness to the present corrupted state of religion, due to the bold advance and rapid diffusion of "sceptical, deistical, and other loose and pernicious sentiments." Waxing more confident, he continued: "May I not add that a species of atheistical philosophy, which has of late triumphantly reared its head in Europe, and which affects to be the offspring and the nurse of sound reason, science, and liberty, seems in danger of infecting some of the more sprightly and free-thinking geniuses of America."[198]

Something more than a year later, a pulpit deliverance was made at Medford, Massachusetts, on the occasion of the annual state Thanksgiving, which supplied ample evidence that clerical fears were rapidly gathering force. Medford's minister, the Reverend David Osgood,[199] was heard in a vigorous discussion of the leading political and religious concerns of the day.[200] First taking occasion to eulogize the Federal government by way of atonement for the failure of Governor Samuel Adams to make reference to the same in his Thanksgiving proclamation, the reverend gentleman thereupon launched into a vehement denunciation of the Democratic Societies,[201] because of their subservience to foreign emissaries, and because of the outrageous activities of Minister Genet. Not content with this, he proceeded to lay heavy emphasis upon the ferocious zeal and desperate fury which the French were manifesting in their attacks upon the institutions of religion, the far-reaching import of which, he declared, was already apparent in the fact that, under the power of their blind devotion to the French cause, not a few American citizens were casting off their allegiance to the Christian religion.[202]

The notes of warning sounded by Osgood in this sermon were both clear and loud. They fell on numerous sympathetic and responsive ears. Committed promptly to type, the sermon passed rapidly through six editions, a sufficient proof of the extent of the sensation which it produced. Its author's reputation was established; but beyond this, and what is more to the point, the shibboleths of future clerical pronouncements had been uttered. Henceforth the public utterances of the Federal clergy were to be characterized by a violent antagonism to the French Revolution and the spread of French influence in America.[203]

The chorus of clerical complaint on account of the dangers that threatened the cause of religion, either because of the progress of the Revolution abroad or the overt and secret diffusion of infidel principles at home, grew steadily in volume. One or two added instances of this type of pulpit utterance will suffice.

Tappan was again heard from, in February, 1795, on the day set for the observance of the national thanksgiving.[204] He dealt with the political situation at length, and emphasized particularly the destructive effects of French influence. Before his sermon was committed to the hands of the printer, Tappan was made acquainted with the fact that the minister of Rowley, the Reverend Ebenezer Bradford, had made certain apologetic comments, on the occasion of the national thanksgiving, respecting the importance of French success to the peace and tranquility of America, and the propriety of seeking the reason for the recent insurrection in western Pennsylvania in "impolitic laws" rather than in French influence exerted through Democratic Clubs,[205] as Federalists had made bold to claim.[206] To these observations Tappan made the following sharp retort:

The destructive effects of them [*i. e.*, secret political clubs] in France have been noticed in the preceding discourse. Their unhappy influence in this country is sufficiently exemplified in that spirit of falsehood, of party and faction, which some of them, at least, assiduously and too successfully promote, and especially in the late dangerous and expensive western insurrection, which may be evidently traced, in a great degree, to the inflammatory representations and proceedings of these clubs, their abettors and friends.[207]

Medford's minister acquitted himself with something more than his customary fiery earnestness on the occasion of this same national festival. Mounting his pulpit, he pictured to his hearers "the reign of a ferocious and atheistical anarchy in France," whose authors had "formed the design of bringing other nations to fraternize with them in their infernal principles and conduct."[208] Their emissaries, Osgood argued, have spread themselves abroad and entered into every country open to them. In Geneva these abandoned creatures have been "horribly successful in overthrowing a free government but lately established, and in bringing on, in imitation of what had happened in their own country, one revolution after another." The same identical agents have found their way into the United States and have begun here their poisonous fraternizing system.[209] The sermon as a whole could scarcely have been more violent in tone. It is very clear that Osgood had resolved to do what he could to rouse the country.

As a direct result of this kind of pulpit utterance—a result that doubtless had much to do with persuading the clergy that an alarming decline of religion was under way in New England—the charge of "political preaching" rapidly developed into one of the standing accusations of the day. The bitterness of party strife grew apace. Opposition to Federalist measures of government, such as Jay's Treaty and the handling of diplomatic relations with France, mounted steadily higher. In consequence, the Federal clergy found themselves drawn farther and farther into the maelstrom of political discussion. Out of this developed the sentiments entertained by the opposition that the clergy were the tools of the Federalists, and that public occasions were eagerly pounced upon by them and used to promote the cause of party advantage.

This shaft struck home; and yet not so much in the nature of a personal affront as an added proof that a state of deep impiety had settled down upon the land. Well might the clergy lament, not that they had been so foully slandered, but that they were called upon to reckon with a people who had drifted out so far upon the sea of irreverence and disrespect. To illustrate: The Reverend Jeremy Belknap was before the convention of the clergy of Massachusetts, in May, 1796, to preach the convention sermon. His mind turned to this new burden which had lately fallen on the already heavily-laden shoulders of the ministry. Thus he sought to mollify the wounded feelings of his brethren:

Another of the afflictions to which we are exposed, is the resentment of pretended patriots, when we oppose their views in endeavoring to serve our country. There is a monopolizing spirit in some politicians, which would exclude clergymen from all attention to matters of state and government; which would prohibit us from bringing political subjects into the pulpit, and even threaten us with the loss of our livings if we move at all in the political Sphere. But, my brethren, I consider politics as intimately connected with morality, and both with religion. … How liberal are some tongues, some pens, and some presses, with their abuse, when we appear warm and zealous in the cause of our country! When we speak or write in support of its liberties, its constitution, its peace and its honor, we are stigmatized as busy-bodies, as tools of a party, as meddling with what does not belong to us, and usurping authority over our brethren.[210]

A couple of years later another staunch clerical supporter of Federalist policies, the Reverend John Thornton Kirkland, minister of the New South Church in Boston, came somewhat closer to the main point. The spirit of the times, he urged, had greatly changed, and that for the worse. Clergymen now were being severely censured for what only a few years earlier they had been warmly commended for as constituting a peculiar merit. The leaders of the American Revolution, for example, had praised the clergy for throwing the weight of their influence into the political scale, recognizing that there exists a moral and religious as well as a civil obligation on the part of ministers to warn the people of the dangers which threaten their liberty and happiness. But now, however, at a time when the dearest interests of religion and patriotism, of church and state, are fiercely assailed and imperiled, the clergy are met with calumny and insult when they venture to speak out. Only the debasement of morals and piety could explain so lamentable a transformation.[211]

A growing sensitiveness to the objections of Republican partisans that they were stepping aside from the legitimate responsibilities of their calling and prostituting the functions of their sacred office to unworthy ends, is apparent on the part of the clergy;[212] but when the very slander and abuse which they suffered supplied added evidence, if that were needed, that the institutions of religion and of government were being rapidly undermined, there could be no damping of their spirit nor turning back from the performance of a service, however unappreciated, to which by tradition and by present necessity they believed themselves bound.

Thus matters stood with the clergy of the Standing Order in New England at the close of the eighteenth century. Whether they were mistaken or not, a state of general irreligion seemed to them to have been ushered in. On all sides the positions of traditional orthodoxy were being called in question. The cause of revealed religion had found new enemies, and the cause of natural religion new agencies for its promotion. The French Revolution had given a terrifying exhibition of what might be expected to happen to a nation in which radical and sceptical opinions were allowed to have complete expression. As for the progress of impiety at home, the youth of the land were contaminated, the state of public morals was unsound, opposition to measures of government was increasing in power and virulence, the institutions of religion were commanding less and less respect, the clergy were treated with a coldness and criticalness of spirit they had never faced before. Seeking for the causes of this baneful condition of affairs, the clergy believed they were to be found mainly in the dissemination of revolutionary opinions issuing from France, but in part also in native tendencies to exalt reason and throw off the restraints of government in church and state.

Before taking leave of the subject, a few final illustrations may be considered by way of fixing upon the mind the strength of this general impression which the New England clergy entertained.

On the occasion of the general fast, May 4, 1797, at West Springfield, Massachusetts, the Reverend Joseph Lathrop preached a sermon to which he gave the expressive title, *God's Challenge to Infidels to Defend Their Cause*.[213] The inspiration of the discourse was drawn from the conviction that "this is a day when infidelity appears with unusual boldness, and advances with threatening progress, to the hazard of our national freedom and happiness, as well as to the danger of our future salvation."[214] According to this interpreter of the signs of the times, the dissemination of infidelity was to be regarded as the outstanding fact in the life of America, as well as in the life of the world.

An unusually lugubrious view of the situation was that taken by the Reverend Nathan Strong, in the sermon which he preached, April 6, 1798, on the occasion of the Connecticut state fast. In the eyes of this modern Jeremiah, the situation was desperate almost beyond remedy:

There are dark and ominous appearances. I do not mean the wrath and threatening of any foreign nations whatever, for if we please God and procure him on our side, we may bless his providence, and hear human threatenings without emotion. But the dark omens are to be found at home. In our hearts, in our homes, in our practice, and in a licentious spirit disposed to break down civil and religious order. In affecting to depend on reason in the things of religion, more than the word of God; so as to reject all evangelical holiness, faith in Jesus Christ, the Son of God, and the ministrations of the spirit in the heart. In substituting anarchy and licentiousness, in the room of rational and just liberty. In supposing that freedom consists in men's doing what is right in their own eyes; even though their eyes look through the mist of wicked ambition and lust. Here is our real danger, and these are the omens that augur ill to us.[215]

Far less subjective in its analysis was the sermon which the now celebrated minister of Medford, the Reverend David Osgood, preached not many days later, on the occasion of the national fast.[216] Once more the eyes of his hearers were invited to contemplate the horrible spectacle abroad. It had now become certain that the legislators of France had abolished the Christian religion. Preposterous indeed was the idea of those who supposed that they were engaged in anything so beneficent as "stripping the whore of Babylon, pulling down the man of sin, destroying popery,"[217] and making way for the introduction of the millennium. That which they had set their hearts upon was to bring it to pass that Christ and His religion should no longer be remembered upon the earth. The French republicans were so many infernals who had broken loose from the pit below.[218] Their profession of principles of liberty and philanthropy were deceptive in the highest degree. They sought to fraternize with other nations merely to seduce them. Their emissaries employed the arts of intrigue and corruption, they were charged to stir up factions, seditions, rebellions, so as to disorganize established governments and make them more readily the prey of thc infamous French government.[219]

That these were not the pulpit utterances of men of peculiarly morbid dispositions, who stood apart from the main currents of thought and life in their day, would seem to be proved by the following instances of formal declarations issued by associations of churches.

On the 17th of May, 1798, the General Assembly of the Presbyterian Church in the United States, then in session in the city of Philadelphia, issued an address to the members of its various congregations scattered throughout the country, urging attention to the extraordinarily gloomy aspect of affairs. The situation was interpreted as follows:

The aspect of divine providence, and the extraordinary situation of the world, at the present time, indicate that a solemn admonition, by the ministers of religion and other church officers in General Assembly convened, has become our indispensable duty. When formidable innovations and convulsions in Europe threaten destruction to morals and religion; when scenes of devastation and bloodshed, unexampled in the history of modern nations, have convulsed the world; and when our own country is threatened with similar calamities, insensibility in us would be stupidity; silence would be criminal. The watchmen on Zion's walls are bound by their commission to sound a general alarm, at the approach of danger. We therefore desire to direct your awakened attention, towards that bursting stream, which threatens to sweep before it the religious principles, institutions, and morals of our people. We are filled with a deep concern and an awful dread, whilst we announce it as our real conviction, that the eternal God has a controversy with our nation, and is about to visit us in his sore displeasure. A solemn crisis has arrived, in which we are called to the most serious contemplation of the moral causes which have produced it, and the measures which it becomes us to pursue.[220]

As to the "moral causes" referred to, the address proceeds to define them as "a general defection from God and corruption of the public principles and morals," the evidences whereof are such as a general dereliction of religious principle and practice, a departure from the faith and simple purity of manners for which the fathers were remarkable, a visible and prevailing impiety, contempt for the laws and institutions of religion, and "an abounding infidelity."[221]

The same year, on May 31, the Congregational clergy of Massachusetts, assembled in annual convention, "without a dissenting vote" adopted an address to their churches, wherein they expressed their deep sorrow and concern on account of "those atheistical, licentious and disorganizing principles which have been avowed and zealously propagated by the philosophers and politicians of France; which have produced the greatest crimes and miseries in that unhappy country, and like a mortal pestilence are diffusing their baneful influence even to distant nations."[222] A year later the same body of clergy, again assembled in their annual convention, formulated and later published an address similar in tone, but strongly emphasizing the American aspects of the case. The growing disbelief and contempt of the Gospel are loudly lamented; the lack of exemplary piety and morality even among the members of churches, and the dissipation, irreligion, and licentiousness prevalent among the youth of the day, are accounted to be of so much weight as to constitute a national apostasy. "The voice of God to us in these events," continues the address, "is emphatically this: Come out of the infidel, antichristian world, my people; that ye be not partakers of her sins, and that ye receive not of her plagues."[223]

To a very considerable number of earnest lovers of religion in New England and elsewhere throughout the nation, the century's sun seemed to be setting amid black and sullen clouds of the most ominous character.

CHAPTER II

POLITICAL ENTANGLEMENTS AND HYSTERIA

1. THE SITUATION PRIOR TO 1798

Party history in New England, as elsewhere throughout the Union, began with the inauguration of the new government in 1789.[224] Such differences of opinion concerning matters of public policy as had previously existed were confined to unorganized groups whose leaders depended chiefly on the devotion of their personal following to mould popular opinion. But the setting up of the Federal government and the fixing of national standards brought to light issues which challenged fundamental conceptions and interests, and a definite rift in public sentiment was not long in appearing. By 1793 the main line of political cleavage was plainly visible. The Federalists, who stood for the importance of a strong central government, found themselves confronted with an organized opposition to which in time the terms Anti-Federalists, Republicans, and Democrats were applied.[225]

In 1793 the war between England and France came into American politics, providing issues for party controversy for years to come. The sympathies of the Federalists, who numbered in their ranks the conservative and aristocratic elements in the population, inclined strongly toward England; whereas the sympathies of Republicans, who attracted to their standard the radicals of the country concerned in the democratization of government, were disposed with equal warmth toward France.

The promulgation of the Neutrality Proclamation[226] of President Washington, April 22, 1793, seemed to settle the question of foreign alliances before the matter had become acute. On the whole, the response which New England gave to the President's proclamation was gratifying. Messages of cordial approval came pouring in from many quarters.[227] The majority of the people rejoiced in the course of prudence and foresight which the national government had been led to pursue.

Still New England was not wholly satisfied. The sentiments of all her people had not been served. An opposition of respectable proportions developed. The columns of the public press carried numerous articles[228] voicing various degrees of hostility to the President's cause of neutrality and affording ample evidence that instead of solidifying the sentiments of the people on the subject of foreign alliances, the proclamation had the effect of widening the breach between the political forces of the country.

This aspect of the case was much aggravated by two important circumstances, one of which developed simultaneously with the publication of the proclamation of neutrality, and the other came to light soon after. These two circumstances were the coming of Genet and the rise of the Democratic Societies.

In no part of the country was the news of the arrival of the French minister received with less suspicion than in New England.[229] Republican newspapers were, of course, loud in their exclamations of satisfaction over the word that came out of the south concerning the arrival and subsequent activities of the amazing French diplomat, so young, so ardent, so eloquent, and so absurd. Editors of Federalist journals, while in no mood to be swept off their feet by the latest excitement of the hour, yet showed no disposition to cavil or express distrust.

Such, however, were the exceptional performances of this altogether exceptional diplomat, who insisted on comporting himself more like a ruler of the people of this nation than an accredited representative to their government, that the day of revulsion and deep resentment could not long be postponed.[230]

The stir created by the activities of Genet, great as it was, soon was swallowed up in the excitement produced by the sudden emergence of a new factor in American politics; *viz.*, indigenous political organizations that were secret. Coincident with the arrival of Genet, and with a view to capitalizing the state of public feeling that his arrival and reception brought to a head, there sprang up in various parts of the country a group of organizations devoted to the propagation of ultra-democratic ideals. These Democratic Societies, or Clubs, were destined to exert a degree of baneful influence upon political feeling out of all proportion to their actual number and weight.[231] Needless to say, the excited state of public feeling, together with the total unfamiliarity of American citizens with political agencies of a secret character, were responsible for this result. The embarrassments under which the French cause in America momentarily suffered on account of reports concerning the multiplied atrocities of the Reign of Terror and the swelling tide of popular resentment because of the indiscretions of Minister Genet, might induce the judgment that the times were unpropitious for the development of organizations whose sympathy for the principles of the French Revolution was notorious.[232] But there was another side to the situation. The heated public discussions provoked by Madison's Commercial Resolutions, Clark's Non-Intercourse Resolution, and the appointment of John Jay as Minister Extraordinary to Great Britain, set free such a torrent of anti-British feeling that the spirit of republicanism lifted its head with renewed vigor and stimulated a public sentiment decidedly favorable to the rapid formation and spread of the new organizations. From the day that the first of these sinister Societies was established, and its statement of principles blazoned forth in a multitude of newspapers throughout the country,[233] the public mind found itself wrought upon by a new species of excitement, by suggestions of tricks and plots, by appeals to passion and unreasoning fear, all conspiring to inject into the national spirit an element of haunting suspicion from which it was not soon to be cleared.

The fact that at least five of these Democratic Societies were located in New England strongly suggests the immediate concern which the people of that section were bound to have because of these unexpected and ominous secret political associations.[234] The creation of the Boston Society became at once the occasion of virulent opposition and infuriated comment. Organized in the late fall of 1793[235] under the innocent title, the Constitutional Club, the principles and alliances of the organization became quickly known, with the result that the already agitated waters of local party feeling were disturbed beyond all previous experience. Citizens whose sympathies were fully with the conduct of affairs under the Federalist régime were quick to believe that henceforth they might expect to be threatened, brow-beaten, and checkmated in a ruthless and scandalous fashion because of the activities of this pernicious Club.[236] They anticipated an amount of secret and dastardly political interference on the part of the Club, because of which the lives of their public officials would be filled with distraction and the minds of decent men aspiring to public office would be thrown into a state of disinclination and repugnance.

Nor in this did they prove to be false prophets. Newspaper innuendoes, sharp and poisonous as deadly arrows, were let fly with abandon; town meetings were disturbed and the opponents of democracy and French republicanism put to rout; the public mind was so altered that Democrats who sought to deprive Federalists of their hold upon the "Boston Seat" in the legislature were completely successful in their efforts. In these and similar ways the citizens of Boston were given tangible proofs of how effective an instrument of political action such an organization as the Constitutional Club could be.[237]

The address which President Washington delivered before both houses of Congress, November 19, 1794, wherein he traced a causal connection between the Democratic Societies and the Whiskey Rebellion, characterizing the former as "self-created societies" which had "assumed a tone of condemnation" of measures adopted by the government, being actuated by "a belief that, by a more formal concert" they would be able to defeat those measures,[238] proved to be a mortal blow to these secret organizations, and in New England, as elsewhere throughout the country, had consequences beyond the disappearance of the Clubs. Eagerly and with unconcealed joy, Federalist editors and orators seized upon the President's denunciation and turned it to immediate political account.[239] A flood of condemnation and answering vituperation was instantly released. The champions of Federalism were at pains to secure publication of the discussions which took place in the national congress respecting the precise character of the response to be made to the President's address, with special reference to his condemnation of the Democratic Clubs.[240]They were at equal pains, also, to lay hold of the President's pregnant phrase, "self-created societies," and turn it to account: that phrase should be regarded as a designation equally applicable to the odious Jacobin Clubs of France.[241] Henceforth the whole democratic faction might reasonably be expected to work under cover "to unhinge the whole order of government, and introduce confusion, so that union, the constitution, the laws, public order and private right would be all the sport of violence or chance."[242]

Mortified and discomfited Republican editors made such response as they could. The members of the Clubs were declared to be independent citizens who were acting within their rights in so banding together. They were "proceeding in the paths of patriotic virtue with a composure and dignity which become men engaged in such important and timely services";[243] whereas their opponents were men who hungered for the loaves and fishes of the government and who shared the secret fear that they would be discovered or have their plans deranged.[244]

The continual harping of the Federalist press on the phrase "self-created societies" particularly touched the raw. Was not the Society of the Cincinnati self-created? And are not many of the members of that organization war-worn soldiers of the American Republic? In a state of society in which we see such veterans toiling for their daily sustenance, while other men, enjoying the hard-earned property of the former, riot in all the luxuries of life, how can one but exclaim, *O Tempora! O Mores!* [245]The national congress, moreover, might well be expected to be engaged in much more serious and timely business than to be burdening its sessions with discussions respecting the affairs of private societies.[246]

The hostile attitude that the Federalist clergy took toward the Democratic Societies gave special irritation to the editors of the *Independent Chronicle*. Because he ventured in his thanksgiving sermon of November 20 (1794) to denounce all Constitutional Societies, the rector of the Episcopal congregation in Boston was held up to ridicule in the columns of the *Chronicle* as a "*ci-devant* lawyer" and "a certain Episcopalian 'thumper of the pulpit drum,'" whose pastoral care many of his substantial members had already renounced because of his injection of political discussion into the sacred sphere of the pulpit; while others had given evidence of their disposition to follow the example of the more courageous members of the flock, "if virulence is to take the place of religion."[247] But the Reverend David Osgood, Medford's "monk," on account of his more extended and violent treatment of the Democratic Societies in his thanksgiving day sermon,[248] gave much deeper offence. That he should have represented these organizations as controlled by the same principles as the incendiary French Jacobin Clubs, and as set to watch the Federal government and plot its overthrow through the support of pernicious and inveterate faction, was more than ardent democratic patriots could endure. "A Friend to the Clergy and an Enemy to Ecclesiastical Presumption," together with "A Friend of Decency and Free Inquiry," sought entrance to the willing columns of the *Chronicle* in order to express their contempt for "a Rev. gentleman" who could lend himself to the peddling of such illiberal sentiments and could show himself capable of acting in a manner unbecoming the character of a Christian and a gentleman, and also in order to draw conclusions derogatory to his reputation as a scholar.[249] The castigations of "Stentor" were not less caustic. The red-hot anathemas of the Reverend Parson Osgood, whining preacher of politics that he was, had no other effect than to singe and sear the reputation of their author. "On the Constitutional Society their influence has been as small as though they had been issued in the form of a BULL from the Chancery of the Pope."[250]

Thus were protracted for a time the frantic efforts of Democratic editors and scribblers to repair the damage which "the clownish Bishop of Medford"[251] and his clerical confederates were supposed to have effected.[252] But the main injury had by no means come from that quarter. Such was the veneration for the name and person of the great Washington throughout New England that few men had the hardihood to launch their resentment and abuse against him; yet it was his hand, and none other, that wrote the word *Ichabod* across the brow of these secret political associations. From the day that his address reproaching them was made, their doom was sealed. That doom might tarry for a season, but it could not long be averted. The apologists and defenders of these organizations which the presidential censure had made odious, might fiercely exert themselves to show how innocent they were of the offences charged and how unimpaired in usefulness they remained after the thrust had been made. This was but whistling to keep up their courage. The prestige of the Societies had been effectually destroyed by the President's denunciation; in a surprisingly short time these ambitious and troublemaking organizations sank into desuetude and were lost to view.

The deep impression they had made upon the public mind was, however, much less readily effaced. That impression resolved itself into a memory most unpleasant and disturbing. For us the significance of these organizations is found chiefly in the fact that, appearing at a time when the two great opposing political parties were developing, and having vehemently espoused the cause of France in a rabidly democratic spirit, they consequently added enormously to the passion and the suspicion of the day. To the Federalists they were dangerous intruders, groups of unprincipled demagogues organized for unpatriotic purposes, working in the dark, ashamed to stoop at nothing in the way of duplicity and subterfuge, of deception and intrigue, if by any means the vicious designs of their hearts could be furthered. Thus they not only helped to make the strife of parties vituperative and bitter; in addition they made familiar to the thought of a great body of citizens in America the idea that the intrigues of secret organizations must needs be reckoned with as one of the constant perils of the times. Henceforth it would be easier to fill the public mind with uneasiness and gloomy forebodings on account of the supposed presence of hidden hostile forces working beneath the surface of the nation's life. Should inexperienced and unsuspecting souls profess their incredulity, the appeal to the example of the Democratic Societies might be expected to go far toward dissolving all indifference and trusting unconcern.[253]

To trace in detail the increasingly bitter party strife in New England would not only call for the canvassing of material already well known, but would lead us far afield from the special object of this investigation. Only the main features of the case need to be noted.

The temporary check the Democrats suffered on account of the suppression of the secret political clubs was soon removed by the wave of anti-British sentiment that swept the country upon the publication of the treaty which John Jay negotiated between Great Britain and the United States, late in the autumn of 1794.[254]

The truth is, nothing less than a howl of rage went up from the throats of the people of the United States, and the voices of the men of New England were by no means lost in the chorus.[255] Nothing that could have been said to inflame the blind and passionate anger of the people was omitted. The United States, it was asserted, had been resolved back into the colonies of Great Britain.[256] The Senate had bargained away the blood-bought privileges of the people for less than the proverbial mess of pottage. It had signed the death-warrant of the country's trade and entailed beggary on its inhabitants and their posterity forever.[257] The people's cause had been most perfidiously betrayed. The trading class, whose pecuniary interests would be jeopardized if England were to be left free to prey upon our commerce, especially if the way should remain open for the two countries to drift into actual war, might show itself disposed to make a choice of the lesser of two evils and accept the treaty; but the great mass of the people were indignantly hostile, it must be added, to the point of unreason.[258]

The promulgation of the treaty by Washington, February 29, 1796, as the law of the land, had the effect of bringing to a close a period of agitation which deeply affected the national life.[259] For one thing, the violence of party spirit had been so augmented that henceforth there were to be no limits to which men would not go in the expression of their antipathies and prejudices. Even the great Washington had not been able to escape the venom of the tongue of the partisan in the controversy which had raged over the treaty.[260] A condition of the public mind which not only permitted but supported the burning in effigy of its public servants; which consented to brutal campaigns of newspaper calumniation, so unrestrained and indecent that the reader looks back upon them with shame; to the circulation of incendiary handbills and scurrilous pamphlets; to participation in lawless gatherings in which riotous utterances of the most violent character were freely made and disgraceful actions taken[261]—this could not possibly make for a wholesome discipline of the passions of the people.[262]

For another thing, the spirit of devotion to the cause of France had been greatly refreshed and quickened by the agitation over the treaty. From the moment that information concerning the nature of the treaty began to circulate, the cry of "British faction" was taken up by the Democrats and used with telling effect. That the treaty was an infamous instrument arranged for no other purpose than to injure the French cause was generally believed.[263] From beginning to end, Democrats could find nothing in the treaty which had not been directly inspired by hostility to France. Apart from the damage that would ensue to American commerce, the treaty would work for the elevation of monarchical and the undoing of republican principles.[264] Once again George the Third had become the master of the citizens of America, and thus the great accomplishments of the American Revolution had been made to count for nought. British gold had succeeded in effecting the betrayal of the republican cause in this country, and thus had worked itself into a strategic position where it could more easily strangle the life out of the spirit of republicanism in Europe, now so sorely beset in France.[265]

One other by-product of the agitation that arose over the treaty has been dwelt upon at length in another connection, but it should be adverted to briefly here. It was inevitable that a discussion so vital, so heated, and so protracted as that of which we have just been taking account, should draw into it those guardians of morals and mentors of public spirit in New England, the Federalist clergy.[266] The disturbance of the public mind over the treaty had been marked by two features full of grave import in the clerical view: vicious attacks upon the officers and measures of the existing government, and a reinvigorated crying-up of French political and religious notions.

The offices of government were all, or nearly all, in the hands of Federalists. This being the case, their occupants were doomed to be the chief targets of resentment and villification by men who found such a measure of government as Jay's Treaty obnoxious in the extreme. But if officers of government were to be pilloried in the stocks of public slander and abuse, how then was the government itself to command the respect and obedience of its citizens? The Federalist clergy of New England saw the pathway of duty shining clear: they must hold up the hands of government at any hazard. Hence it happened that the outcry against "political preaching" grew rapidly in volume from 1795 on.[267]

As for the renewed zeal of the Democrats in the interests of French revolutionary ideals, that found a special point of interest and concern for the Federalist clergy in the prominence which the rapid growth of republicanism secured for Thomas Jefferson. An ardent friend of the French Revolution, a lover of French philosophy, the enemy of religious intolerance, in personal faith a deist—were not these sufficient to damn the man as an unbeliever and an atheist in the eyes of New England clergymen, to whom the faintest breath of rationalism was abhorrent and the very notion of toleration suspect? Accordingly the New England clergy launched a fierce attack upon him as the arch-apostle of the cause of irreligion and free-thought.[268] In language carefully guarded, his name usually being omitted, Jefferson was pointed out as the leader of the hosts of infidelity whose object was the extermination of the institutions of religion and the inauguration of an era wherein every man should think and do that which was right in his own eyes.[269]

2. THE SITUATION FROM 1798 TO 1800

Very few of the events in our national affairs which link together the history of the last decade of the eighteenth century are significant for our purpose. Having sought to discover the chief occasions for the apprehension and distress which weighed upon the minds of the citizens of New England, we may now proceed to focus attention exclusively upon the last three years of the century, within which developed that special disturbance of the public mind with which we are primarily concerned.

And first let it be said, we are approaching a period of as intense strain and nervous excitability as this nation in all its history has known. When Thomas Jefferson, in November, 1796, wrote Edward Rutledge of his deep personal satisfaction that he had escaped the presidency, he may have been influenced by unworthy but certainly not by imaginary constraints. "The newspapers," so his letter runs, "will permit me to plant my corn, peas, &c., in hills or drills as I please … while our Eastern friend will be struggling with the storm which is gathering over us; perhaps be shipwrecked in it. This is certainly not a moment to covet the helm."[270] Never has a defeated candidate for the presidency had more solid grounds for the justification of his fears, or shall we say, his hopes? The severe strain of domestic strife was about to be enormously augmented by a series of untoward and alarming events in the field of foreign relations, certain of which must receive our particular attention.

The complete change in the character of the relations between the United States and France is for us a matter of the first importance. The publication of the treaty negotiated between the United States and Great Britain by Jay produced definitive results as respects the attitude of France. With some reason that instrument was interpreted as inimical to the interests of the latter country, and the government and people of this nation were not long left in doubt of the fact.[271] By the employment toward her former ally of a policy of coercion, of which two chief instruments were the destruction of American commerce upon the high seas and the overbearing and insolent conduct of diplomatic negotiations, France speedily addressed herself to the task of attempting to gain by pressure what she conceived she had lost in the way of prestige and material advantage. The result was, to the discomfiture and disgrace of the Democrats in particular and to the alarm of the country in general, that the United States was made aware of the fact that its government was being driven into a corner from which, as far as a human mind could foresee, the only avenue of honorable escape would be recourse to arms.

The damage which American commerce sustained at the hands of French privateers is rendered appreciable when the following circumstances are taken into account. Within the year following the publication of the extraordinary decrees against the commerce of neutral nations, which the French Directory promulgated, beginning with June, 1796, something over three hundred American vessels had been captured. The crippling blow to American commerce was by no means the sole consideration in the case. In numerous instances the crews of captured vessels were treated in such an outrageous and brutal manner as to inflame and gall the American spirit beyond endurance. On account of abuses which American shipping and commerce had suffered previously, by virtue of methods adopted by England and France to gain control of the seas, the strain imposed upon the nation had been severe; but now that a sweeping and utterly ruthless policy of commerce-destruction had been inaugurated by the French, forbearance was no longer possible. In his maiden speech in the national congress, Harrison Gray Otis, Massachusetts' gifted young representative, put the case with dramatic eloquence:

If any man doubted of the pernicious measures of the French nation, and of the actual state of our commerce, let him inquire of the ruined and unfortunate merchant, harassed with prosecutions on account of revenue, which he so long and patiently toiled to support. If any doubted of its effects upon agriculture, let him inquire of the farmer whose produce is falling and will be exposed to perish in his barns. Where ... are your sailors? Listen to the passing gale of the ocean, and you will hear their groans issuing from French prison-ships.[272]

It was not to be expected that a deeply injured people, to whose just sense of wrong and indignation the youthful Federalist orator had given such exact expression, could long be restrained from acts of reprisal and war.

To the sense of injustice was added the burden of fear. The idea began to take possession of the minds of leaders of thought in America that France had darker and more terrible purposes in her councils than the blighting of American commerce in retaliation for the treaty-alliance which had recently been concluded with Great Britain; she sought *war*, war which would supply to her the opportunity to visit upon this nation the same overwhelming disasters which her armies had heaped upon the nations of Europe. The French, it was believed, were busy with schemes for employing the world in their favor and were drunk with the vision of universal dominion.[273] The true explanation of French violence and arrogance was to be sought in her aims at universal empire.[274] Her ravenous appetite could not be satisfied; she had resolved to make of the United States another mouthful.[275] What reason had the citizens of this country to claim exemption from the general deluge? Having fastened the chains of slavery upon nation after nation in

Europe, the generals of France were now planning fresh triumphs; with our armies of the Mississippi and Ohio, of the Chesapeake and Delaware, her forces would contest the field on American soil.[276] Had not her geographers already partitioned the country according to the new system of government which would here be imposed?[277] Did not her agents and spies fill the land, constantly exerting themselves to thwart the purposes of the American government and to render fruitless its policies of administration?[278]

Such fears may not be brushed aside as silly and chimerical, in view of the steady stream of information which came across the Atlantic, announcing the downfall of one nation after another as the result of French intrigue and the prowess of French arms.[279] Besides, there was probably not a solitary Federalist leader in the United States who did not believe that French ministers and agents were in secret league with influential representatives of the Democratic party.

The bullying treatment which the French Directory accorded the ministers and envoys of this nation added much to the heat as well as to the dark suspicions which characterized public feeling in America. A government which boldly assumed to treat with impudent indifference and coldness one accredited minister of the United States, while at the same time it lavished the most extravagant expressions of friendship upon another whose disappointed executive had reluctantly summoned him home,[280] was obviously pursuing a course so high-handed and insolent as to stir the last dormant impulse of national honor. But the hot flame of public indignation which burst forth in this country when it became known that its Minister Plenipotentiary, Charles Cotesworth Pinckney, after months of painful embarrassment and hazard, marked by neglect, evasions, and threats of arrest, was returning home, defeated in purpose, was as nothing to the lava-like stream of infuriated anger which swept through the land when it became known how treacherously the three envoys of the national government, Pinckney, Marshall, and Gerry, had been used.

By common consent the publication of the X.Y.Z. despatches, early in April, 1798, put the top sheaf upon a long series of intolerable actions which this nation had suffered at the hands of the government of France. Like a flash it was made clear that not mere whimsicality and offended hauteur were at the bottom of the unsatisfactory dealings which our ministers had had with the French: we had sent our ambassadors to negotiate with men who knew how to add bribery to threats. Though the government of France might seek to save its face on the pretext that the mysterious French emissaries had acted without proper warrant, yet back of the negotiators was Talleyrand, and back of Talleyrand the Directory. The revulsion of feeling in the United States was complete. All innocent delusions were shattered; all veils torn away. What the French government desired in its negotiations was not political sympathy, not commercial cooperation, not a fraternal alliance between two sister republics in order that the flame of liberty might not perish from the earth; what it desired was *money*—money for the pockets of the Directory and its tools, "for the purpose of making the customary distribution in diplomatic affairs," money for the public treasury that the Directory might find itself in a position to give a "softening turn" to certain irritating statements of which President Adams had delivered himself in his message to the Fifth Congress.[281]

The passion for war with France became the one passion of the hour. Only abandoned men, men whose desire for "disorganization" was the one yearning of their hearts, were unresponsive to the spirit of militant patriotism which swayed the people's will:[282] such at least was the confident and boastful view of Federalist leaders, and for once they were able to gauge accurately the depth and power of the currents of popular sympathy. That hour had passed when men could say, as Jefferson had but a brief day before President Adams turned over to Congress the astounding despatches, "The scales of peace & war are very nearly in equilibrio."[283] The heavy weight of the despatches had sent the bowl of war to the bottom with a resounding thud.

So it seemed at the moment; and yet, though there has seldom been an hour in our national history when all purely factional counsels were more effectually hushed and when the war fever mounted higher, an amazing period of uncertainty and of conflicting impulses and passions immediately set in.

Addresses and memorials to the President came pouring in, pledging to the government the full confidence of its citizens and unswerving loyalty and support. Volunteer military companies sprang into existence in every quarter over night. War vessels were purchased, or their construction provided for, by public subscription and presented to the government. The white cockade, new emblem of an aroused public spirit, generally appeared. The fierce slogan, "Millions for defence, but not one cent for tribute!" and the tuneful strains of "Hail Columbia" and "Adams and Liberty" went ringing through the land. Within a brief period of little more than three months, Congress passed no less than twenty acts for the strengthening of the national defence.[284]

This was one side of the matter; there was another, as events soon made clear. The President, it appeared, was not at one with the more ardent leaders in his own political camp, whose resolution for war was unbounded; he exhibited an attitude of indifference to the whole notion of open war with France that became increasingly manifest as the weeks went by. The President would temporize; he would try to avoid the crisis by sending new commissioners to France to reestablish friendly relations. Against such a policy many of his advisers protested furiously. Besides, the problem of supplying the army with leaders who should serve with Washington had resulted in an unseemly struggle as to whether this or that patriot should stand next to the great hero of Mount Vernon. The President's policy of conciliation took on the appearance of shameless procrastination;[285] the imbroglios of the Federalist leaders aroused public suspicion, and invited to the garnished hearth the spirits of confusion and clamor.

Those evil spirits, however, which most effectively coöperated to make the last state worse than the first came as the result of the extraordinarily stupid and blundering measures which the Federalists adopted to curb the activities of resident aliens and the abuse of free speech. Beginning with the Naturalization Act of June 18, 1798, there followed in quick succession three other repressive measures, the Act Concerning Aliens of June 25, the Act Respecting Alien Enemies of July 6, and the Act for the Punishment of Certain Crimes against the United States (the Sedition Act) of July 14.[286] The purpose of these famous acts has already been indicated; the impulse out of which they grew is not so easily determined. Was it that the heads of the national government really anticipated danger on account of the presence of a multitude of foreigners and the unlicensed freedom of action and public utterance which thus far had been allowed?[287] Was it that the memory of more than four years of biting satire and vicious calumny which the opposition had visited upon the heads of Federalist leaders had filled the latter with longings for revenge? Or was it that, conscious of their undisputed control of national affairs and carried away by the sense of their power, the Federalist leaders proposed to show how strong and effective a centralized government could become? No single alternative, doubtless, suggests the full truth. No matter; the effect which these measures produced is, with us, the main point, and to that we turn.

No milder word than *maddening* will adequately describe the effect of these measures. All the old wounds were opened, all the old antipathies aggravated. Editors and pamphleteers, statesmen and demagogues, tore at each others' throats as they had never done before and have never done since. A veritable "reign of terror" filled the land.[288] Insult and violence were everywhere. Mobs tore down liberty-poles which Federalist hands had erected and put in their place other poles bearing symbols of defiance to "British faction" and tyrannous Federal government; or the action was reversed, with Federalist mobs tearing down the standards of the opposition. White cockades were snatched from the hats of men who supported the government, and once more the black cockade blossomed forth.

Toasts were drunk over tavern bars and on public occasions to the confusion of the British Eagle or the Gallic Cock; to the health and prosperity of the Federal government or to the downfall of tyrants; to the alien and sedition laws, with the fervent wish that "like the sword of Eden [they] may point everywhere to guard our country against intrigue from without and faction from within";[289] or to "freedom of speech, trial by jury, and liberty of the press,"[290] according as the adherents of one faction or the other were assembled for patriotic or convivial purposes. Raucous and ribald outbreaks of party feeling burst out in the theaters to the interruption of performances, the confusion of performers, and the breaking of not a few heads. Such was the lighter and more ludicrous aspect of affairs.

But beneath this effervescence honest and whole-hearted antagonism to the odious legislation surged in countless breasts. In the power of an anger which scorned all frivolous and tawdry action, men declared their deep and irrevocable opposition to such measures of government. That respectable and well-meaning aliens, from lack either of inclination or opportunity to become citizens, should be expelled from the country, or remaining here should become the targets of suspicion and the victims of political oppression; that opposition to government must henceforth wear a muzzle, with a heavy bludgeon meanwhile held menacingly over its head; that the damage done by favored partisan scribblers was not to be repaired by answering opponents; and all this under the guise of laws which, whatever their intention, operated to the enormous disadvantage of one of the two great political bodies of the day—these were things not to be endured by men to whom liberty was the very breath of life.

The actual amount of personal injury inflicted by the operation of the alien and sedition laws was not enormous, though certainly not negligible. A considerable body of aliens fled the country, either during the period when the alien laws were pending or immediately after they went into effect.[291] Probably something more than a score of individuals were arrested under the sedition law, less than half of whom were compelled to stand trial.[292] But once again popular judgment was based upon qualitative rather than quantitative grounds. The popular sense of personal liberty had been outraged by these acts.[293] The Federalist leaders by their precipitate and inconsiderate action had very much overshot the mark and were about to bring their house tumbling down about their heads. As for the opposition, those of its leaders whose highest political interest was party advantage lived to bless the day when, blinded by hysteria or lust of power, the Federalist party made the alien and sedition acts the law of the land. Six months after these unsavory measures were passed, discerning Democrats were able to rejoice that this body of legislation was operating as a powerful sedative to quiet the inflammation which that "God-send" to the Federalists, the X.Y.Z. despatches, had incited.[294] By their own blunder in party strategy the Federalists had alienated the sympathies of the people and given to the ground-swell of republican principles a tremendous impetus which carried them to a speedy triumph.

Once again our special interest must be allowed to center upon a secondary element in the situation, *i. e.*, the over-wrought tension of nerves because of which the most fantastic and unlikely of happenings seemed wholly within the circle of reason and probability. The circumstances which have just been considered were, in the main, upon the surface. As such they were capable of being evaluated and weighed. But who was to say that they were not attended by subterranean influences and designs? Affairs everywhere, be it remembered, were moving with incredible swiftness. In every quarter the beleaguered forces of conservatism found themselves surrounded and hemmed in by radical elements which manifested a spirit of militancy and a resolute will to conquer. With the European situation to lend strong emphasis to the suggestion of sinister tendencies and secret combinations, it cannot be thought extraordinary that here in America, where traditional opinions and institutions were as certainly being undermined, the conviction should take root that beneath all this commotion over foreign and domestic policies secret forces must be at work, perfecting organizations, promoting conspiracies, and ready at any hour to leap forth into the light to throttle government and order.

There is, of course, no desire to make it appear that apprehensions concerning hidden designs and movements were generally shared by the citizens of the United States. There was then, as there has always been, a very large body of citizens whose faith in the stability and high destiny of the nation made them immune to such fears; calm and philosophic souls who were equally unmoved by the rant of the demagogue or the distracted mood of the self-deceived alarmist. Their sympathy for and their faith in the democratic tendencies of the age inhibited every impulse to despair. But there were also other men, as has been the case in every deeply agitated generation, who were fully persuaded that they were able to catch deeper tones than their neighbors, to whom the gift had been given to read the signs of the times more accurately than their fellows. For them the conclusion was inescapable that no postulate which did not leave room for secret combinations was adequate to explain the peculiar cast of events in the United States at the end of the eighteenth century. To dismiss the case of such men with the casual judgment that they were temperamentally susceptible to such impressions, is to rule out of account the extraordinary character of the age to which they belonged. Apropos of this observation, the two following items are deserving of notice.

Some time previous to the celebration of the national fast of 1798, three anonymous letters were flung into President Adams' house, announcing a plot to burn the city of Philadelphia on the day of the approaching fast. Convinced that the matter was of moment, the President made the contents of the letters publicly known. As a result, many people of the city packed their most valuable belongings and prepared to make a quick departure in the event that the threats made should come to fulfilment.[295] Was this a mere "artifice to agitate the popular mind," the work of "war men" who were restless and impatient for an immediate declaration of hostilities against France? Quite possibly. Such, at least, was the private opinion of Thomas Jefferson.[296] But who was to *know*? The true lay of the land was not easily to be discovered in the midst of an age when, in the language of a contemporary, "all the passions of the human heart are in a ferment, and every rational being from the throne to the cottage is agitated by the picturesque circumstances of the day."[297]

Alexander Hamilton left among his manuscripts certain comments which he had made upon the character and import of the French Revolution. Before we turn to consider the European Illuminati and the outcry against its alleged presence in the United States, we may, by perusing this document, throw a little added light upon the gnawings of anxiety and fear which were felt at the time by very rational gentlemen in America.

Facts, numerous and unequivocal, demonstrate that the present AERA is among the most extraordinary which have occurred in the history of human affairs. Opinions, for a long time, have been gradually gaining ground, which threaten the foundations of religion, morality and society. An attack was first made upon the Christian revelation, for which natural religion was offered as a substitute. The Gospel was to be discarded as a gross imposture, but the being and attributes of God, the obligations of piety, even the doctrine of a future state of rewards and punishments, were to be retained and cherished.

In proportion as success has appeared to attend the plan, a bolder project has been unfolded. The very existence of a Deity has been questioned and in some instances denied. The duty of piety has been ridiculed, the perishable nature of man asserted, and his hopes bounded to the short span of his earthly state. DEATH has been proclaimed an ETERNAL SLEEP; "the dogma of the *immortality* of the soul a *cheat*, invented to torment the living for the benefit of the dead." Irreligion, no longer confined to the closets of conceited sophists, nor to the haunts of wealthy riot, has more or less displayed its hideous front among all classes….

A league has at length been cemented between the apostles and disciples of irreligion and anarchy. Religion and government have both been stigmatized as abuses; as unwarrantable restraints upon the freedom of man; as causes of the corruption of his nature, intrinsically good; as sources of an artificial and false morality which tyrannically robs him of the enjoyments for which his passions fit him, and as clogs upon his progress to the perfection for which he is destined....

The practical development of this pernicious system has been seen in France. It has served as an engine to subvert all her ancient institutions, civil and religious, with all the checks that served to mitigate the rigor of authority; it has hurried her headlong through a rapid succession of dreadful revolutions, which have laid waste property, made havoc among the arts, overthrown cities, desolated provinces, unpeopled regions, crimsoned her soil with blood, and deluged it in crime, poverty, and wretchedness; and all this as yet for no better purpose than to erect on the ruins of former things a despotism unlimited and uncontrolled; leaving to a deluded, an abused, a plundered, a scourged, and an oppressed people, not even the shadow of liberty to console them for a long train of substantial misfortunes, or bitter suffering.

This horrid system seemed awhile to threaten the subversion of civilized society and the introduction of general disorder among mankind. And though the frightful evils which have been its first and only fruits have given a check to its progress, it is to be feared that the poison has spread too widely and penetrated too deeply to be as yet eradicated. Its activity has indeed been suspended, but the elements remain, concocting for new eruptions as occasion shall permit. It is greatly to be apprehended that mankind is not near the end of the misfortunes which it is calculated to produce, and that it still portends a long train of convulsion, revolution, carnage, devastation, and misery.

Symptoms of the too great prevalence of this system in the United States are alarmingly visible. It was by its influence that efforts were made to embark this country in a common cause with France in the early period of the present war; to induce our government to sanction and promote her odious principles and views with the blood and treasure of our citizens. It is by its influence that every succeeding revolution has been approved or excused; all the horrors that have been committed justified or extenuated; that even the last usurpation, which contradicts all the ostensible principles of the Revolution, has been regarded with complacency, and the despotic constitution engendered by it slyly held up as a model not unworthy of our imitation.

In the progress of this system, impiety and infidelity have advanced with gigantic strides. Prodigious crimes heretofore unknown among us are seen....[298]

CHAPTER III

THE EUROPEAN ORDER OF THE ILLUMINATI

1. THE RISE AND THE DISAPPEARANCE OF THE ORDER

That great European movement in the direction of the secularization of thought to which the expressive term, the *Aufklärung* or Enlightenment, has been applied, and which reached its apogee in the latter half of the eighteenth century, encountered a stubborn opposition in southern Germany in the electorate of Bavaria. The pivot of Bavarian politics, particularly from the beginning of the sixteenth century, had been the alliance which had been effected between the clerical party and the civil power. The counter reformation which followed in the wake of the Lutheran movement was able to claim the field in Bavaria without the necessity of a combat.

In the third quarter of the eighteenth century Bavaria was a land where sacerdotalism reigned supreme. Religious houses flourished in abundance; the number of priests and nuns was incredibly large.[299] So easy were the ways of life in that fertile country that a lack of seriousness and intensity of feeling among the masses flung open the door for superstitious practices which made the popular religion little better than gross fetichism. So-called "miraculous" images were commonly paraded through the streets; innumerable statues and sacred relics were exposed to the gaze of crowds of the faithful; the patronage of the saints was assiduously solicited. Among the educated there was a widespread conviction that the piety of the people was ignorant and that their trustful attitude made them the prey of many impostors.

The degree of power to which the representatives of the Society of Jesus had been able to attain in Bavaria was all but absolute.[300] Members of the order were the confessors and preceptors of the electors; hence they had a direct influence upon the policies of government. The censorship of religion had fallen into their eager hands, to the extent that some of the parishes even were compelled to recognize their authority and power. To exterminate all Protestant influence and to render the Catholic establishment complete, they had taken possession of the instruments of public education. It was by Jesuits that the majority of the Bavarian colleges were founded, and by them they were controlled. By them also the secondary schools of the country were conducted.[301]

The prevailing type of education in Bavaria had little more to commend it than the popular type of religion.[302] The pedagogical aim of the Jesuits was the development of the memory with scant regard for other faculties of the mind. To learn the catechism, or in the case of advanced pupils to receive unquestioningly the dogmatic instruction offered by clerical pedagogues, was the ideal honored throughout the Bavarian schools. Books which bore the slightest taint of Protestant influence, or which in any other way gave evidence of a liberalizing spirit, were ruthlessly banned.[303]

Such were the conditions of life under which the great mass of the people lived. There was, however, a relatively small group of cultivated people in Bavaria who, despite the clerical oppression and bigotry from which they suffered, had contrived to share in the liberalizing spirit of the larger world. The censorship exerted by the Jesuits had found no adequate means to guard against the broadening influences of travel or of contact with travelers from other lands, or even to prevent the introduction of all contraband journals and books. The effect of the former had been to create a humiliating and galling sense of inferiority on the part of liberal-minded Bavarians,[304] while the latter had served to stimulate a thirst for the new knowledge which the rationalism of the age made available. To this small group of discontented and ambitious spirits the ancient faith had ceased to be satisfactory, and the burden of clericalism had become insufferable.

The University of Ingolstadt, established in 1472, was destined to become a rallying point for these radical tendencies. In the middle of the sixteenth century the Jesuits had gained control of its faculties of philosophy and theology, and for two centuries thereafter the university had been counted upon as the chief fortress of clericalism in Bavaria.[305] By the middle of the eighteenth century the deadening effect of the rigorous censorship exerted by the Jesuits had produced its full fruitage at Ingolstadt. The university had fallen into a state of profound decadence.[306]

With the accession of Maximilian Joseph[307] as elector, in 1745, the breath of a new life soon stirred within its walls. For the position of curator of the university the elector named a well-known and resolute radical of the day, Baron Johann Adam Ickstatt, and charged him with the responsibility of reorganizing the institution upon a more liberal basis.[308] Measures were adopted promptly by the latter looking to the restoration of the prestige of the university through the modernization of its life. The ban was lifted from books whose admission to the library had long been prohibited, chairs of public law and political economy were established, and recruits to the faculty were sought in other universities.[309]

It was, of course, not to be expected that the clerical party, whose power in the university, as has been intimated, was particularly well entrenched in the faculties of philosophy and theology, would retire from the field without a struggle.[310] A sharp contest arose over the introduction of non-Catholic books, into which the elector himself was drawn, and which in addition to the substantial victory that Ickstatt won, had the further effect of aligning the two parties in the university squarely against each other.[311] It was only a few years after this episode, when the Jesuits were still chafing under the sharp setback which their policies had suffered, that the name of Adam Weishaupt first appeared (in 1772) on the roll of the faculty of the university as professor extraordinary of law.

Weishaupt (born February 6, 1748; died November 18, 1830) entered upon his professional career at Ingolstadt after an educational experience which had made him a passionate enemy of clericalism. His father having died when the son was only seven, his godfather, none other than Baron Ickstatt, compelled doubtless by the necessities of the case, had turned the early training of the boy over to the Jesuits. The cramming process through which he thus passed was destined to prove unusually baneful in his case[312] on account of certain influences which penetrated his life from another quarter. Accorded free range in the private library of his godfather, the boy's questioning spirit was deeply impressed by the brilliant though pretentious works of the French "philosophers" with which the shelves were plentifully stocked.[313] Here was food for the fires of imagination just beginning to flame up in this unsophisticated and pedantic youth. Here, also, were ready solvents for the doubts with which his experience with Jesuit teachers had filled his mind. The enthusiasm of the most susceptible of neophytes seized him: he would make proselytes, he would deliver others from their bondage to outworn beliefs, he would make it his duty to rescue men from the errors into which the race had long been plunged.[314] His object in life thus early determined, he threw himself with great zeal into the study of law, economics, politics, history, and philosophy. He devoured every book which chanced to fall into his hands.[315]

After graduating from the University of Ingolstadt in 1768, he served for four years in the capacity of tutor and catechist until his elevation to the rank of assistant instructor took place. The favor he was permitted to enjoy as the protégé of Ickstatt[316] brought him more rapid advancement than that to which his native abilities entitled him. In 1773 he was called to the chair of canon law, which for a period of ninety years had been held by representatives of the Jesuits.[317] Two years later, when he was but twenty-seven years of age, he was made dean of the faculty of law. Such a rapid improvement in his professional standing proved far from salutary. The young man's vanity was immensely flattered and his reforming resolution unduly encouraged. His sense of personal worth as the leader of the liberal cause in the university quite outran his merit.[318]

Meantime the Jesuits, observing with deep resentment Weishaupt's meteoric rise,[319] together with a growing disposition on his part to voice unrestrained criticism of ecclesiastical intolerance and bigotry, entered into intrigues to checkmate his influence and undermine his position.[320] The payment of his salary was protested and the notion that he was a dangerous free-thinker industriously disseminated.[321] On his part, Weishaupt did not scruple to furnish Ickstatt's successor, Lori, with secret reports calculated to put the Jesuit professors in the university in an unfavorable light.[322] A disagreeable squabble resulted, marked on the one hand by clerical jealousy and pettiness and on the other by Weishaupt's imprudence of speech[323] and indifference to considerations of professional honor.

The effect of this unseemly strife upon Weishaupt was to establish firmly in his mind the conviction that as the university's most influential leader against the cause of ecclesiastical obscurantism he was being made a martyr for free speech.[324] In no way disposed to be sacrificed to the animosity of enemies whose power he greatly over-estimated, he arrived at the conclusion that a general offensive against the clerical party ought immediately to be undertaken. A secret association was needed which, growing more and more powerful through the increase of its members and their progress in enlightenment, should be able to outwit the manœuvres of the enemies of reason not only in Ingolstadt but throughout the world. Only by a secret coalition of the friends of liberal thought and progress could the forces of superstition and error be overwhelmed. Over the scheme of such an association consecrated to the cause of truth and reason, the self-esteem of Weishaupt kindled anew as he contemplated none other than himself at its head.[325]

His imagination having taken heat from his reflections upon the attractive power of the Eleusinian mysteries and the influence exerted by the secret cult of the Pythagoreans, it was first in Weishaupt's thought to seek in the Masonic institutions of the day the opportunity he coveted for the propagation of his views. From this original intention, however, he was soon diverted, in part because of the difficulty he experienced in commanding sufficient funds to gain admission to a lodge of Masons, in part because his study of such Masonic books as came into his hands persuaded him that the "mysteries" of Freemasonry were too puerile and too readily accessible to the general public to make them worth while.[326] He deemed it necessary, therefore, to launch out on independent lines. He would form a model secret organization, comprising "schools of wisdom," concealed from the gaze of the world behind walls of seclusion and mystery, wherein those truths which the folly and egotism of the priests banned from the public chairs of education might be taught with perfect freedom to susceptible youths.[327] By the constitution of an order whose chief function should be that of teaching, an instrument would be at hand for attaining the goal of human progress, the perfection of morals and the felicity of the race.[328]

On May 1, 1776, the new organization was founded, under the name of the Order of the Illuminati,[329] with a membership of five all told. The extremely modest beginning of the order in respect to its original membership was more than matched by the confusion which existed in Weishaupt's mind as to the precise form which the organization had best take. Only three elementary grades, or ranks, had been worked out by him, and these only in a crude and bungling fashion, when the enterprise was launched. A feverish regard for action had full possession of the founder of the order; the working-out of his hazy ideas of organization might wait for quieter days.[330]

Out of the voluminous and rambling expositions which Weishaupt at various times made of the three primary grades, *viz.*, Novice, Minerval, and Illuminated Minerval, the following brief descriptions are extracted.

To the grade of Novice youths of promise were to be admitted, particularly those who were rich, eager to learn, virtuous, and docile, though firm and persevering.[331] Such were to be enrolled only after their imaginations and desires had been artfully aroused by suggestions concerning the advantages to be derived from secret associations among like-minded men, the superiority of the social state over that of nature, the dependence of all governments upon the consent of the governed, and the delight of knowing and directing men.[332] Once enrolled, the instruction of each Novice was to be in the hands of his enroller, who kept well hidden from his pupil the identity of the rest of his superiors. Such statutes of the order as he was permitted to read impressed upon the mind of the Novice that the particular ends sought in his novitiate were to ameliorate and perfect his moral character, expand his principles of humanity and sociability, and solicit his interest in the laudable objects of thwarting the schemes of evil men, assisting oppressed virtue, and helping men of merit to find suitable places in the world.[333] Having had impressed upon him the necessity of maintaining inviolable secrecy respecting the affairs of the order, the further duties of subordinating his egoistic views and interests and of according respectful and complete obedience to his superiors were next enjoined. An important part of the responsibility of the Novice consisted in the drawing-up of a detailed report (for the archives of the order), containing complete information concerning his family and his personal career, covering such remote items as the titles of the books he possessed, the names of his personal enemies and the occasion of their enmity, his own strong and weak points of character, the dominant passions of his parents, the names of their parents and intimates, *etc.* [334] Monthly reports were also required, covering the benefits the recruit had received from and the services he had rendered to the order.[335] For the building-up of the order the Novice must undertake his share in the work of recruitment, his personal advancement to the higher grades being conditioned upon the success of such efforts.[336] To those whom he enrolled he became in turn a superior; and thus after a novitiate presumably two years in length,[337] the way was open for his promotion to the next higher grade.

The ceremony of initiation through which the Novice passed into the grade Minerval was expected to disabuse the mind of the candidate of any lingering suspicion that the order had as its supreme object the subjugation of the rich and powerful, or the overthrow of civil and ecclesiastical government.[338] It also pledged the candidate to be useful to humanity; to maintain a silence eternal, a fidelity inviolable, and an obedience implicit with respect to all the superiors and rules of the order; and to sacrifice all personal interests to those of the society.[339] Admitted to the rank of Minerval, the candidate received into his hands the printed statutes of the order, wherein he learned that in addition to the duties he had performed as novice, his obligations had been extended with special reference to his studies.[340] These were to be more highly specialized, and the fruits of his researches from time to time turned over to the superiors. In the prosecution of difficult labors of this character, he was to be free to call to his assistance other Minervals in his district.[341] He might also count upon the assistance of his superiors in the form of letters of recommendation in case he undertook travels in the pursuit of his studies; and should he form the resolve to publish his material, the order pledged itself to protect him against the rapacity of booksellers who might show themselves disposed to overcharge him for the works he wished to consult, as well as to render assistance in attracting the attention of the public to his work.[342]

In the assemblies of this grade the Minerval for the first time came into contact with the members of the order. In other words, his life within the society actually began.[343] The thirst for the sense of secret association with men of like interests and aims, which the members long novitiate had developed, began to find its satisfaction.[344] Ordinary Minervals and "illuminated" Minervals mingled together in these assemblies[345] and mutually devoted their deliberations to the affairs of the order.

To the grade Illuminated Minerval were admitted those Minervals who in the judgment of their superiors were worthy of advancement. Elaborate initiatory ceremonies fixed in the candidates mind the notions that the progressive purification of his life was to be expected as he worked his way upward in the order,[346] and that the mastery of the art of directing men was to be his special pursuit as long as he remained in the new grade. To accomplish the latter, *i. e.*, to become an expert psychologist and director of men's consciences, he must observe and study constantly the actions, purposes, desires, faults, and virtues of the little group of Minervals who were placed under his personal direction and care.[347] For his guidance in this difficult task a complicated mass of instructions was furnished him.[348]

In addition to their continued presence in the assemblies of the Minervals, the members of this grade came together once a month by themselves, to hear reports concerning their disciples, to discuss methods of accomplishing the best results in their work of direction and to solicit each other's counsel in difficult and embarrassing cases.[349] In these meetings the records of the assemblies of the Minervals were reviewed and rectified and afterwards transmitted to the superior officers of the order.

Such, in brief, was the system of the Illuminati as it came from the brain of Weishaupt, its founder. By means of such an organization he proposed to effect nothing less than the redemption of the world. In its assemblies the truths of human equality and fraternity were to be taught and practised.[350] Its members were to be trained to labor for the welfare of the race; to strive for a civilization, not like that of the present, which left men savage and ferocious under its thin veneer, but one which would so radically change their moral dispositions as to put all their desires under the control of reason—the supreme end of life, which neither civil nor religious institutions had been able to secure.[351] The study of man was to be made at once so minute, so comprehensive, and so complete[352] that two immense advantages would result: first, the acquisition of the art of influencing favorably the wills of one's fellows, thus making social reformation possible; and second, self-knowledge.[353] That is to say, the thorough scrutiny of the instincts, passions, thoughts, and prejudices of others, which the order imposed upon him, would react in turn upon the member's judgment of his own personal life. As a result his conscience would be subjected to frequent examination, and the faults of his life might be expected to yield to correction. From both of these advantages, working together, a moral transformation of the whole of society would result, thus securing the state of universal well-being.[354]

But this conception of the order as essentially an instrument of social education requires to be balanced by another, *viz.*, its anticlericalism. Its founder professed that at the time when the idea of the order was taking shape in his mind he was profoundly influenced by the persecutions which honest men of unorthodox sentiments had been compelled to suffer on account of their views.[355] Considerations growing out of his own personal embarrassments and imagined peril on account of his clashings with the Jesuits were also admittedly weighty in his thought.[356] It is therefore to be regarded as a substantial element in his purpose to forge a weapon against the Jesuits, and in a larger sense to create a league defensive and offensive against all the enemies of free thought.[357]

Accordingly, the expression of utterances hostile to Christian dogmas was early heard within the assemblies of the order,[358] and only the difficulty experienced in working out the supreme grade of the order inhibited Weishaupt's intention of converting it into a council of war to circumvent and overwhelm the advocates of supernaturalism and the enemies of reason.[359] The pure religion of Christ, which, doctrinally conceived, had degenerated into asceticism and, from the institutional standpoint,[360] had become a school of fanaticism and intolerance, was pronounced a doctrine of reason, converted into a religion for no other purpose than to make it more efficacious.[361] To love God and one's neighbor was to follow in the way of redemption which Jesus of Nazareth, the grand master of the Illuminati, marked out as constituting the sole road which leads to liberty.[362]

The objects of the order were such as to appeal to the discontented elements in a country suffering from intellectual stagnation due to ecclesiastical domination.[363]Despite this fact, its growth during the first four years of its existence was anything but rapid. By that time four centers of activity, in addition to Ingolstadt, had been established, and a total of possibly sixty members recruited.[364] While its visionary founder considered that a solid basis for encouragement had been laid,[365] as a matter of fact at the termination of the period just indicated the organization was seriously threatened with failure. Fundamental weaknesses had developed from within. Chief among these was the tension which existed almost from the first between Weishaupt and the men whom he associated with him in the supreme direction of the affairs of the order.[366] The thirst for domination, which was native to the soul of Weishaupt, converted the order into a despotism against which men who had been taught by their leader that they shared with him the innermost secrets of the organization, rebelled. The result was the constant breaking-out of a spirit of insubordination and a series of quarrels between the founder and his associates which rendered the future progress of the order very precarious.[367] The extreme poverty of the organization constituted another serious obstacle to its rapid growth. With a view to demonstrating the genuine disinterestedness of the society, an effort had been made from the beginning to emphasize the financial interests of the order as little as possible.[368] The rules of the organization were far from burdensome in this regard, and it is by no means surprising that many of the proposed measures of the leaders in the interests of a more extensive and effective propaganda proved abortive for the very practical reason that funds were not available to carry them into effect.[369]

A decidedly new turn in the wheel of fortune came some time within the compass of the year 1780,[370] with the enrollment of Baron Adolf Franz Friederich Knigge[371] as a member.

In the recruiting of this prominent North German diplomat Weishaupt and his associates found the resourceful and influential ally for which the organization had waited, a man endowed with a genius for organization and so widely and favorably connected that the order was able to reap an immense advantage from the prestige which his membership bestowed upon it. Two weighty consequences promptly followed as the result of Knigge's advent into the order. The long-sought higher grades were worked out, and an alliance between the Illuminati and Freemasonry was effected.[372]

Such was the confidence which Knigge's presence immediately inspired in Weishaupt and his associates that they hailed with enthusiasm his admission to the order, and gladly abandoned to him the task of perfecting the system, their own impotence for which they had been forced to admit.[373] Manifesting a zeal and competency which fully justified the high regard of his brethren, Knigge threw himself into the task of elaborating and rendering compact and coherent the childish ideas of organization which Weishaupt had evolved.

The general plan of the order was so shaped as to throw the various grades or ranks into three principal classes.[374] To the first class were to belong the grades Minerval and Illuminatus Minor; to the second,[375] (1) the usual three first grades of Masonry, Apprentice, Fellow, and Master, (2) Illuminatus Major, and (3) Illuminatus Dirigens, or Scottish Knight; and to the third class were reserved the Higher Mysteries, including (a) the Lesser Mysteries, made up of the ranks of Priest and Prince, and (b) the Greater Mysteries, comprising the ranks of Magus and King.[376]

A detailed description of the various grades of Knigge's system would far outrun the reader's interest and patience.[377] The present writer therefore will content himself with making such comments as seem best suited to supply a general idea of the revised system.

The grade Novice (a part of the system only in a preparatory sense) was left unchanged by Knigge, save for the addition of a printed communication to be put into the hands of all new recruits, advising them that the Order of the Illuminati stands over against all other forms of contemporary Freemasonry as the one type not degenerate, and as such alone able to restore the craft to its ancient splendor.[378] The grade Minerval was reproduced as respects its statutes but greatly elaborated in its ceremonies under the influence of Masonic usages with which Knigge was familiar.[379] The grade Illuminatus Minor was likewise left identical with Weishaupt's redaction, save in unimportant particulars as to special duties and in the working-out and explanation of its symbolism.[380]

The three symbolic grades of the second class seem to have been devised solely for the purpose of supplying an avenue whereby members of the various branches of the great Masonic family could pass to the higher grades of the new order.[381] Membership in these grades was regarded as a mere formality, the peculiar objects and secrets of the order having, of course, to be apprehended later.

A candidate for admission to the grade of Illuminatus Major was first to be subjected to a rigorous examination as respects his connections with other secret organizations and his objects in seeking advancement. His superiors being satisfied upon these points, it was provided that he should be admitted to the grade by means of a ceremonial highly Masonic in its coloring. His special duties were four in number: (1) to prepare a detailed analysis of his character, according to specific instructions furnished him; (2) to assist in the training of those members of the order who were charged with the responsibility of recruiting new members; (3) to put his talents and his social position under tribute for the benefit of the order, either by himself stepping into places of honor which were open or by nominating for such places other members who were fitted to fill them; and (4) to coöperate with other members of his rank in the direction of the assemblies of the Minervals.[382]

Advanced to the grade of Illuminatus Dirigens, or Scottish Knight, the member bound himself with a written oath to withhold his support from every other system of Masonry, or from any other secret society, and to put all his talents and powers at the disposition of the order.[383] His obligations in this rank were purely administrative in their character. The inferior grades of the order were territorially grouped together into prefectures, and upon these the authority of the Illuminatus Dirigens was imposed. Each Illuminatus Dirigens had a certain number of Minerval assemblies and lodges assigned to him, and for the welfare of these he was responsible to the superiors of the order. The members of this grade constituted the "Sacred Secret Chapter of the Scottish Knights," from which issued the patents of constitution for the organization of new lodges.[384]

To the first grade of the third class, that of Priest,[385] were admitted only such members as, in the grade Minerval, had given proof of their zeal and advancement in the particular sciences which they had chosen.[386] The initiatory ceremonies of the grade emphasized the wholly unsatisfactory character of existing political and religious systems and sounded the candidate's readiness to serve the order in its efforts to lead the race away from the vain inventions of civil constitutions and religious dogmas from which it suffered.[387] Relieved entirely of administrative responsibilities, the members of this grade devoted themselves exclusively to the instruction of their subordinates in the following branches of science: physics, medicine, mathematics, natural history, political science, the arts and crafts, and the occult sciences. In brief, the final supervision of the teaching function of the order was in their hands, subject only to the ultimate authority of their supreme heads.[388]

Knigge's statutes provided that only a very small number of members were to be admitted to the grade of Prince.[389] From this group the highest functionaries of the order were to be drawn: National Inspectors, Provincials,[390] Prefects, and Deans of the Priests. Over them, in turn, at the apex of the system and as sovereign heads of the order, ruled the Areopagites.[391]

So much for the external structure of the system which Knigge reshaped. With respect to the aims and principles of the order the modifications introduced by him were considerable, although scarcely as comprehensive as in the former case.[392] In certain instances the ideas of Weishaupt were retained and developed;[393] in others significant alterations were made or new ideas introduced. Of the new ideas the two following were unquestionably of greatest weight:[394] the notion of restricting the field of recruiting solely to the young was abandoned, and this phase of the propaganda was widened so as to include men of experience whose wisdom and influence might be counted upon to assist in attaining the objects of the order;[395] the policy was adopted that henceforth the order should not occupy itself with campaigns against particular political and religious systems, but that its energies should be exerted against superstition, despotism, and tyranny.[396] In other words, the battle for tolerance and enlightenment should be waged along universal and not local lines. Accordingly, the esoteric teaching of the order, under Knigge's revision, was reserved to the higher grades.

The progress of the order from 1780 on[397] was so rapid as to raise greatly the spirits of its leaders. The new method of spreading Illuminism by means of its affiliation with Masonic lodges promptly demonstrated its worth. Largely because of the fine strategy of seeking its recruits among the officers and other influential personages in the lodges of Freemasonry, one after another of the latter in quick succession went over to the new system.[398] New prefectures were established, new provinces organized, and Provincials began to report a steady and copious stream of new recruits.[399] From Bavaria into the upper and lower Rhenish provinces the order spread into Suabia, Franconia, Westphalia, Upper and Lower Saxony, and outside of Germany into Austria[400] and Switzerland. Within a few months after Knigge rescued the order from the moribund condition in which he found it, the leaders were able to rejoice in the accession of three hundred members, many of whom by their membership immensely enhanced the prestige of the order. Students, merchants, doctors, pharmacists, lawyers, judges, professors in *gymnasia* and universities, preceptors, civil officers, pastors, priests—all were generously represented among the new recruits.[401] Distinguished names soon appeared upon the rosters of the lodges of the new system. Duke Ferdinand of Brunswick, Duke Ernst of Gotha, Duke Karl August of Saxe-Weimar, Prince August of Saxe-Gotha, Prince Carl of Hesse, Baron Dalberg,[402] the philosopher Herder, the poet Goethe,[403] the educationist Pestalozzi,[404] were among the number enrolled. By the end of 1784 the leaders boasted of a total enrollment of between two and three thousand members,[405] and the establishment of the order upon a solid foundation seemed to be fully assured.[406]

But just at the moment when the prospects were brightest, the knell of doom suddenly sounded.[407] Dangers from within and from without, with bewildering celerity and concurrence, like a besom of destruction swept from the earth the order which Adam Weishaupt, with such exaggerated anticipations, had constituted out of a little group of obscure students at Ingolstadt, on May Day, 1776.

The internal difficulties were of the nature of dissensions among the chiefs. The old jealousies that existed between Weishaupt and the Areopagites[408] before Knigge reconstructed the order were not eradicated by the introduction of the new system, and in course of time they flamed forth anew.[409] But ugly in temper and subversive of discipline and order as these petty contentions were, they were of little importance as compared with the fatal discord which arose between Weishaupt and Knigge. The spirit of humility that the former manifested in 1780, when in desperation he turned to Knigge for assistance, did not long continue. Aroused by the danger of seeing his personal control of the order set aside and himself treated as a negligible factor, Weishaupt sought opportunities of asserting his prerogatives, and the ambition of Knigge being scarcely less selfish than that of Weishaupt, the two men quarreled repeatedly and long.[410] So bitter and implacable the spirit of the two became that in the end, exercising a discretion dictated by despair rather than generosity, Knigge withdrew from the field, leaving Weishaupt in undisputed possession of the coveted headship of the order.

But the fruits of his victory the latter had little chance to enjoy.[411] On June 22, 1784, Carl Theodore[412] launched the first of his edicts against all communities, societies, and brotherhoods in his lands which had been established without due authorization of law and the confirmation of the sovereign.[413] The edict, to be sure, was general in its character, and the Bavarian Illuminati were glad to believe that their system was not specially involved: by lying low for a season the squall would speedily blow over and the activities of the order might safely be resumed.[414] These anticipations, however, were doomed to disappointment. Having surrendered himself completely to the spirit of reaction, and spurred by reports of the covert disobedience of the order which his *entourage* spread before him,[415] the Bavarian monarch, on March 2 of the following year, issued another edict that specifically designated the Illuminati as one of the branches of Freemasonry, all of which were severely upbraided for their failure to yield implicit obedience to the will of the sovereign as expressed in the previous edict, and a new ban, more definite and sweeping in its terms than the former, was thereby proclaimed.[416]

A fixed resolution on the part of the government to give full force to the provisions of the interdict left no room for evasion.[417] In response to the call of its enemies, former members of the order who, either because of scruples of conscience or for less honorable reasons, had withdrawn from its fellowship, came forward to make formal declarations respecting their knowledge of its affairs.[418] In this direct manner the weapons needed for the waging of an effective campaign against the society were put into the government's hands.[419] Judicial inquiries were inaugurated, beginning at Ingolstadt.[420] Measures of government, all aimed at nothing short of the complete suppression and annihilation of the order, followed one another in rapid succession. Officers and soldiers in the army were required to come forward and confess their relations with the Illuminati, under promise of immunity if ready and hearty in their response, but under pain of disgrace, cassation, or other punishment if refractory.[421] Members and officers of consular boards were subjected to similar regulations.[422] Officers of state and holders of ecclesiastical benefices who were found to have connections with the order were summarily dismissed from their posts.[423] Professors in universities and teachers in the public schools suffered a like fate.[424] Students who were recognized as adepts were dismissed, and in some cases were banished from the country.[425]

As a system the order was shattered, but its supporters were not wholly silenced. Weishaupt particularly, from his place of security in a neighboring country, lifted his voice against the men who had betrayed the order and the government which had ruined it. Taking recourse to his pen, with incredible rapidity he struck off one pamphlet and volume after another,[426] in a feverish effort, offensive and defensive, to avert if possible total disaster to the cause which, despite all his frailties, he truly loved. The one clear result of his polemical efforts was to draw the fire of those who defended the denunciators of the afflicted order and who supported the clerical party and the government. A war of pamphlets developed, the noise and vehemence of which were destined to add, if possible, to the embarrassment and pain of those members of the order who still remained in Bavaria. Once more the suspicions of the government were aroused; a search was made by the police for further evidence, and in the month of October, 1786, at Landshut, in the house of Xavier Zwack,[427] one of the order's most prominent leaders, decisive results were achieved. A considerable number of books and papers were discovered,[428] the latter containing more than two hundred letters that had passed between Weishaupt and the Areopagites, dealing with the most intimate affairs of the order, together with tables containing the secret symbols, calendar, and geographical terms belonging to the system, imprints of its insignia, a partial roster of its membership, the statutes, instruction for recruiters, the primary ceremony of initiation, *etc.* [429]

Here was the complete range of evidence the authorities had long waited for. Out of the mouths of its friends, the accusations which its enemies made against the order were to be substantiated. By the admissions of its leaders, the system of the Illuminati had the appearance of an organization devoted to the overthrow of religion and the state, a band of poisoners and forgers, an association of men of disgusting morals and depraved tastes. The publication of these documents amounted to nothing less than a sensation.[430] New measures were forthwith adopted by the government. Leading representatives of the order, whose names appeared in the telltale documents, were placed under arrest and formally interrogated. Some of these, like the treasurer, Hertel, met the situation with courage and dignity, and escaped with no further punishment than a warning to have nothing to do with the organization in the future under fear of graver consequences.[431] Others, like the poltroon Mändl,[432]adopted the course of making monstrous "revelations" concerning the objects and practices of the order. Still others, like Massenhausen, against whom the charge of poison-mixing was specifically lodged,[433] sought safety in flight.

As a final blow against the devastated order, on August 16, 1787, the duke of Bavaria launched his third and last edict against the system.[434] The presentments of the former interdicts were reëmphasized, and in addition, to give maximum force to the sovereign's will, criminal process, without distinction of person, dignity, state, or quality, was ordered against any Illuminatus who should be discovered continuing the work of recruiting. Any so charged and found guilty were to be deprived of their lives by the sword; while those thus recruited were to have their goods confiscated and themselves to be condemned to perpetual banishment from the territories of the duke.[435] Under the same penalties of confiscation and banishment, the members of the order, no matter under what name or circumstances, regular or irregular, they should gather, were forbidden to assemble as lodges.[436]

The end of the order was at hand. So far as the situation within Bavaria was concerned, the sun of the Illuminati had already set.[437] It remained for the government to stretch forth its hand as far as possible, to deal with those fugitives who, enjoying the protection of other governments, might plot and contrive to rebuild the ruined system. Accordingly, Zwack, who had sought asylum first in the court of Zweibrücken and had later obtained official position in the principality of Salm-Kyburg, was summoned by the duke of Bavaria to return to that country. The summons was not accepted,[438] but the activities of Zwack as a member of the Illuminati, as the event proved, were over. Count (Baron) Montgelas, whose services on behalf of the order do not appear to have been significant, but who, upon the publication of the correspondence seized in the residence of Zwack, had likewise sought the protection of the duke of Zweibrücken, found the favor of that sovereign sufficient to save him from the power of the Bavarian monarch.[439] As for Weishaupt, whose originary relation to the order the Bavarian government had discovered in the secret correspondence just referred to, his presence in Gotha, outside Bavarian territory but in close proximity to the Bavarian possessions, added greatly to the concern of Carl Theodore.[440] Efforts were made by the latter to counteract any possible influence he might exert to rehabilitate the Illuminati system.[441] They were as futile as they were unnecessary. Broken in spirit, making no effort to regain the kingdom which his vanity insisted he had lost, contenting himself with the publication of various apologetic writings,[442] permitted for a considerable period to enjoy the bounty of his generous patron, Duke Ernst of Gotha, he sank slowly into obscurity.[443]

As for the fortunes of the order outside of Bavaria, the measures adopted by the government of that country proved decisive. Here and there, especially in the case of Bode,[444] a Saxon Illuminatus, efforts were made to galvanize the expiring spirit of the order, but wholly without result.

BIBLIOGRAPHICAL NOTE: The amount of literature, chiefly polemical in character, which has sprung up about the subject of the European Illuminati is astonishingly large. Wolfstieg, *Bibliographie der Freimaurerischen Literatur*, vol. ii, pp. 971–979, lists ninety-six separate titles of principal works, not counting translations, new editions, *etc.* In the same volume (pp. 979–982) he lists the titles of one hundred and fourteen "kleinere Schriften". In addition, he also lists (*ibid.*, p. 982) three titles of books occupied with the statutes of the order, and the titles of five principal works devoted to the order's ritual (*ibid.*, p. 983), together with the titles of nine smaller works likewise occupied (*ibid.*). No student penetrates far into the study of the general topic without being made aware that not only were contemporary apologists and hostile critics stirred to a fierce heat of literary expression, but that a swarm of historians, mostly of inferior talents, have been attracted to the subject.

In view of the thoroughgoing work which bibliographers like Wolfstieg have performed, no necessity arises to repeat the task. For the benefit of the student who may wish to acquaint himself at first hand with the principal sources of information respecting the order, the following abbreviated list has been compiled. For convenience the titles are grouped in three principal divisions.

I. Apologetic writings.

Weishaupt, *Apologie der Illuminaten*, Frankfort and Leipzig, 1786.

" *Vollständige Geschichte der Verfolgung der Illuminaten in Bayern, I*, Frankfort and Leipzig, 1786.

" *Das verbesserte System der Illuminaten mit allen seinen Graden und Einrichtungen*, Frankfort and Leipzig, 1787.

" *Kurze Rechtfertigung meiner Absichten*, Frankfort and Leipzig, 1787

" *Nachtrag zur Rechtfertigung meiner Absichten*, Frankfort and Leipzig, 1787.

Bassus, *Vorstellung denen hohen Standeshäuptern der Erlauchten Republik Graubünden*, Nuremberg, 1788.

Knigge, *Philo's endliche Erklärung and Antwort auf verschiedene Anforderungen und Fragen*, Hanover, 1788.

II. Documents of the order, published by the Bavarian government or otherwise, and hostile polemics.

Einige Originalschriften des Illuminaten Ordens, Munich, 1787.

Nachtrag von weiteren Originalschriften, Munich, 1787.

Der ächte Illuminat, oder die wahren, unverbesserten Rituale der Illuminaten, Edessa (Frankfort-on-the-Main), 1788.

Cosandey, Renner, and Grünberger, *Drei merkwürdige Aussagen die innere Einrichtung des Illuminatenordens*, Munich, 1786.

Same (with Utzschneider), *Grosse Absichten des Ordens der Illuminaten mit Nachtrag, I, II, III*, Munich, 1786.

Der neuesten Arbeiten des Spartacus and Philo, Munich, 1793.

Illuminatus Dirigens, oder Schottischer Ritter, Ein Pendant, etc., Munich, 1794.

III. Historical treatments of the precise character and significance of the order.

Mounier, *De l'influence attribuée aux philosophes, aux franc-maçons et aux illuminés, sur la révolution de France*, Tübingen, 1801.

Mounier, J. J., *On the Influence attributed to Philosophers, Freemasons, and to the Illuminati, on the Revolution of France.... Translated from the Manuscript, and corrected under the inspection of the author, by J. Walker*, London, 1801.

Engel, *Geschichte des Illuminaten-Ordens*, Berlin, 1906.

Forestier, *Les Illuminés de Bavière et la Franc-Maçonnerie allemande*, Paris, 1915.

2. THE LEGEND OF THE ORDER AND ITS LITERARY COMMUNICATION TO NEW ENGLAND

Although the Order of the Illuminati was dead, the world had yet to reckon with its specter. So intense and widespread was the fear which the order engendered, so clearly did the traditionalists of the age see in its clientele the welding together into a secret machine of war of the most mischievous and dangerous of those elements which were discontented with the prevailing establishments of religion and civil government, that it was impossible that its shadow should pass immediately.[445]

The emergence of the order had attracted public attention so abruptly and sharply, and its downfall had been so violent and so swift, that public opinion lacked time to adjust itself to the facts in the case. In Bavaria, particularly, the enemies of the order were unable to persuade themselves that the machinations of the Illuminati could safely be regarded as wholly of the past.[446] The documents of the order were appealed to, to supply proof that its leaders had made deliberate calculations against the day of possible opposition and temporary disaster and with satanic cunning had made their preparations to wring victory out of apparent defeat.[447] Besides, the depth of the governments suspicions and hostility was such that additional, though needless measures of state[448] kept very much alive in that country the haunting fear of the continued existence of the order.

Outside of Bavaria numerous factors contributed to create the same general impression in the public mind. Among these were the efforts of the Rosicrucians to play upon the fears that the Illuminati had awakened, the mistaken connections which, in the Protestant world, were commonly made between the members of the Order of the Illuminati and the representatives and promoters of the *Aufklärung*, and the emergence of the German Union. To each of these in turn a word must be devoted.

Following the suppression of the Jesuits in 1773, members of that order in considerable numbers, attracted by the rapid growth and the pretentious occultism of the Rosicrucians,[449] had united with the latter system.[450] The result was the infusion of a definite strain of clericalism into the order of the Rosicrucians and, in consequence, a renewal of the attack upon the Illuminati. In Prussia, where the Rosicrucians had firmly established themselves in Berlin, King Frederick William II was under the influence of Wöllner, one of his ministers and a leading figure in the Rosicrucian system.[451] Through the latter's relations with Frank, who at the time stood at the head of the Rosicrucian order in Bavaria, the Prussian monarch was easily persuaded that the operations of the Illuminati had not only been extended to his own territories, but throughout all Germany.[452] Encouraged by Wöllner, Frederick William took it upon himself to warn neighboring monarchs respecting the peril which he believed threatened, a course which bore at least one definite result in the measures taken by the elector of Saxony to investigate the situation at Leipzig where, according to the king of Prussia, a meeting of the chiefs of the Illuminati had been effected.[453] Thus the notion that the order of the Illuminati was still in existence was accorded the sanction of influential monarchs.

The disposition of orthodox Protestants to confuse the advocates of rationalism with the membership of the Illuminati finds its suggestion of plausibility at a glance and stands in little need of specific historical proof. The general effect of the undermining of traditional faiths, for which the dominating influences of the period of the *Aufklärung* were responsible, was to create the impression among the more simple-minded and credulous elements in the Protestant world that a vast combination of forces was at work, all hostile to the Christian religion and all striving to supplant faith by reason. So vast and significant a movement of thought naturally enough tended to engender various suspicions, and among these is to be numbered the naïve conviction that the order which the Bavarian government had felt compelled to stamp out, on account of its alleged impiety and its immoral and anarchical principles, was but a local expression of the prevailing opposition to the established systems and orthodox doctrines of the age.[454]

The excitement occasioned by the appearance of the German Union (*Die Deutsche Union*), on account of its definite connections with one of the former leaders[455]of Weishaupt's system and the unsavory private character and avowed unscrupulous designs of its originator, gave still more specific force to the Illuminati legend. Charles Frederick Bahrdt,[456] a disreputable doctor of theology, in 1787, at Halle, proposed to reap advantage from the ruin of Weishaupt's system and to recruit among its former members the supporters of a new league, organized to accomplish the enlightenment of the people principally by means of forming in every city secret associations of men[457] who were to keep in correspondence with similar groups of their brethren and who, by the employment of reading-rooms, were to familiarize the people with those writings which were specially calculated to remove popular prejudices and superstitions, and to break the force of appeals to tradition. Further, these associations were to supply financial assistance to writers who enlisted in the Union's campaign, and to fill the palms of booksellers who for the sake of a bribe showed themselves willing to prevent the sale of the works of authors who withheld their coöperation.[458]

As an organization the German Union scarcely emerged from the stage of inception; but the absurd policy of publicity pursued by its founder gave to the project a wide airing and provoked hostile writings[459] that added immensely to the importance of the matter. The new system was boldly denounced as continuing the operations of the odious order dissolved in Bavaria, with a shrewd change of tactics which substituted "innocent" reading-rooms for the novitiate of Weishaupt's organization, and thus, it was urged, the way was opened for the exertion of a really powerful influence upon the thought of the German people.[460]

By such means, and in such widely diverse and irrational ways, the popular belief in the survival of the defunct Order of the Illuminati was kept alive and supplied with definite points of attachment; but it remained for the French Revolution, in all the rapidity and vastness of its developments and in the terrifying effects which its more frightful aspects exercised upon its observers, to offer the most exciting suggestions and to stimulate to the freest play the imaginations of those who were already persuaded that the secret associations that plagued Bavaria still lived to trouble the earth.[461]

The supposed points of connection between the Order of the Illuminati and the French Revolution were partly tangible, though decidedly elusive,[462] but much more largely of the nature of theories framed to meet the necessities of a case which in the judgment of dilettante historians positively *required* the hypothesis of a diabolical conspiracy against thrones and altars (*i. e.*, the civil power and the church), though the labors of Hercules might have to be exceeded in putting the same to paper.

Of the exiguous resources of interpreters of the Revolution who made serious efforts to trace its impious and anarchical principles and its savage enormities to their lair in the lodges of the Illuminati, the following are perhaps the only ones worthy of note.

The public discussion of the affairs and principles of Weishaupt's organization, to which attention has already been called in various connections, continued with unabated zeal even beyond the close of the eighteenth century. At the very hour when the Revolution was shocking the world by its lapse from its original self-control into its horrible massacres, execution of monarchs, guillotine-lust, and ferocious struggles between parties, new pamphlets and reviews bearing on the demolished order's constitution and objects found their way into the channels of public communication. Conspicuous among these were the following: *Die neuesten Arbeiten des Spartacus und Philo in dem Illuminaten Orden, jetzt zum ersten Mal gedruckt und zur Beherzigung bei gegenwärtigen Zeitläuften herausgegeben*,[463] and *Illuminatus Dirigens oder Schottischer Ritter*,[464] announced as a continuation of the former. These works, published at the instigation of the authorities at Munich, attracted public attention anew to the most extreme religious and social doctrines[465] of the order. Thus the revolutionary character of Illuminism received heavy emphasis[466]synchronously with contemporary events of the utmost significance to the imperilled cause of political and religious conservatism.

In Austria an independent literary assault upon Illuminism developed. At Vienna, Leopold Hoffman,[467] editor of the *Wiener Zeitschrift*, fully convinced that the Order of the Illuminati had exercised a baneful effect upon Freemasonry, to which he was devoted, abandoned his chair of language and German literature at the University of Vienna to dedicate his talents and his journal to the overthrow of Illuminated Freemasonry.[468] Finding a zealous collaborator in a certain Dr. Zimmerman, a physician of Hannover, a radical turned an extreme conservative by the developments of the French Revolution, the two labored energetically to stigmatize the Illuminati as the secret cause of the political explosion in France.

The discontinuance of the *Wiener Zeitschrift* in 1793 by no means marked the end of the campaign. A deluge of pamphlets[469] had been precipitated, all based upon the assumption that the order Weishaupt had founded had subsided only in appearance. Declamation did not wait upon evidence. It was alleged that the lower grades of the Illuminati had been dissolved, but the superior grades were still practised. Under cover of correspondence, recruits of the system were now being sought. Freemasonry was being subjugated by Illuminism only that it might be forced to serve the ends of its conqueror. Journalists partial to the interests of the *Aufklärung* had been enlisted for the same purpose. The German Union was thus only one of the enterprises fostered by the Illuminati to further their designs. The dogmas of the order had been spread secretly in France by means of the clubs of that country, and the effectiveness of the propaganda was being vividly demonstrated in the horrors of the Revolution. Unless German princes should promptly adopt rigorous measures against the various agents and enterprises of the order in their territories, they might confidently expect similar results to follow.[470]

Much more of like character was foisted upon the reading public. As for contemporary historians who searched for specific evidence of an alliance between the Illuminati of Germany and the Revolutionists in France, their energies were chiefly employed in the development of a clue which had as its kernel the supposed introduction of Illuminism into France at the hands of the French revolutionary leader, Mirabeau, and the German savant, Bode.[471] Unfolded, this view of the case may be stated briefly as follows: Mirabeau, during his residence at Berlin, in the years 1786 and 1787, came into touch with the Illuminati of that city and was received as an adept into the order. Upon his return to Paris he made the attempt to introduce Illuminism into that particular branch of Masonry of which he was also a member, the *Philalèthes* or *Amis Réunis*.[472] To give force to his purpose, he called upon the Illuminati in Berlin to send to his assistance two talented and influential representatives of the order. The men chosen by the Illuminati-circle in Berlin, Bode and von dem Busche,[473] arrived in Paris in the early summer of 1787. To conceal their purpose from prying eyes, they spread the report that they had come from Germany to investigate the subjects of magnetism and the extent of the influence exerted by the Jesuits upon the secret societies of the age. Meantime, the lodges of the *Philalèthes*, and through them the French Masonic lodges in general, were inoculated with the principles of Illuminism. French Freemasonry thus became committed to the project of forcing the overthrow of thrones and altars. So transformed, these lodges created secret committees who busied themselves with plans for the precipitation of a great revolutionary movement. To these committees belonged the subsequent leaders and heroes of the French Revolution—de Rochefoucauld, Condorcet, Pétion, the Duke of Orléans (Grand Master of French Masonry), Camille-Desmoulins, Danton, Lafayette, de Leutre, Fauchet, *et al.* Through these and their associates the connection between the lodges of Illuminated French Freemasonry and the powerful political clubs of the country was effected. Thus Illuminism was able to inspire Jacobinism. Finally, on the 14 of July, 1789, the revolutionary mine was sprung, and the great secret of the Illuminati became the possession of the world.[474]

At every point this fantastic exposition suffered the fatal defect of a lack of historical proof. Even the specific assertions of its inventors which were most necessary to their hypothesis were disproved by the facts brought to light by more cautious and unbiased investigators who followed. *E. g.*, the idea of Mirabeau's intimate connection with the program of the Order of the Illuminati and his profound faith in it as the best of all instruments for the work of social amelioration is rendered untenable the moment the rash and unrepublican temper of his spirit is called seriously to mind.[475] Again, the real object of Bode's visit to Paris, a matter of vital importance in the Illuminati-French Revolution hypothesis, was not to communicate Illuminism to French Freemasons, but to attend an assembly of representatives of the *Philalèthes*, called to consider the results of an inquiry previously undertaken, respecting the occult interests and tendencies of that order. Convinced that that branch of French Masonry was yielding to an inordinate passion for the occult sciences, Bode had been prevailed upon by German Masons, von dem Busche[476] among the number, to make a journey to Paris to warn his French brethren of their mistake. A subsidiary personal interest in the newly-discovered "science" of animal magnetism[477] helped to form his decision to make the trip.[478]

The much more important contention that the Illuminati were instrumental in starting the French Revolution, shows a lack of historical perspective that either leaves out of account or obscures the importance of the economic, social, political, and religious causes, tangible and overt, though complex, that rendered the Revolution inevitable.

Yet the legend of Illuminism as the responsible author of the French Revolution found numerous vindicators and interpreters,[479] to the efforts of two of which, because of their intimate relation to the interests of the investigation in hand, our attention in the remainder of this chapter is to be confined.

In the year 1797 there appeared at Edinburgh, Scotland, a volume bearing the following title: *Proofs of a Conspiracy against All the Religions and Governments of Europe, carried on in the Secret Meetings of the Free Masons, Illuminati, and Reading Societies.*[480] Its author, John Robison,[481] an English savant and Freemason, whose position in the academic world entitled his statements to respect, had had his curiosity regarding the character and effects of continental Freemasonry greatly stimulated by a stray volume of the German periodical, *Religions Begebenheiten,*[482] which came under his notice in 1795, and in which he found expositions of Masonic systems and schisms so numerous and so seriously maintained by their advocates as to create deep wonderment in his mind.[483] Bent upon discovering both the occasion and the significance of this tangled mass, Robison obtained possession of other volumes of the periodical mentioned[484] and set himself the task of elucidating the problem presented by Masonry's luxuriant growth and its power of popular appeal.

The conclusions Robison came to are best stated in his own words:

I have found that the covert of a Mason Lodge had been employed in every country for venting and propagating sentiments in religion and politics, that could not have circulated in public without exposing the author to great danger. I found, that this impunity had gradually encouraged men of licentious principles to become more bold, and to teach doctrines subversive of all our notions of morality—of all our confidence in the moral government of the universe—of all our hopes of improvement in a future state of existence—and of all satisfaction and contentment with our present life, so long as we live in a state of civil subordination. I have been able to trace these attempts, made, through a course of fifty years, under the specious pretext of enlightening the world by the torch of philosophy, and of dispelling the clouds of civil and religious superstition which keep the nations of Europe in darkness and slavery. I have observed these doctrines gradually diffusing and mixing with all the different systems of Free Masonry; till, at last, AN ASSOCIATION HAS BEEN FORMED for the express purpose of ROOTING OUT ALL THE RELIGIOUS ESTABLISHMENTS, AND

OVERTURNING ALL THE EXISTING GOVERNMENTS OF EUROPE. I have seen this Association exerting itself zealously and systematically, till it has become almost irresistible: And I have seen that the most active leaders in the French Revolution were members of this Association, and conducted their first movements according to its principles, and by means of its instructions and assistance, *formally requested and obtained*: And, lastly, I have seen that this Association still exists, still works in secret, and that not only several appearances among ourselves show that its emissaries are endeavouring to propagate their detestable doctrines, but that the Association has Lodges in Britain corresponding with the mother Lodge at Munich ever since 1784 …. The Association of which I have been speaking is the order of ILLUMINATI, founded, in 1775 [*sic*], by Dr. Adam Weishaupt, professor of Canon-law in the University of Ingolstadt, and abolished in 1786 by the Elector of Bavaria, but revived immediately after, under another name, and in a different form, all over Germany. It was again detected, and seemingly broken up; but it had by this time taken so deep root that it still subsists without being detected, and has spread into all the countries of Europe.[485]

The "proofs" to which Robison appealed to support these conclusions betrayed the same lack of critical mind[486] with which all the advocates of the Illuminati-French Revolution hypothesis are to be charged. Only the more significant elements are here brought under survey.[487]

That inclination for a multiplication of the degrees and an elaboration of the ceremonies of simple English Freemasonry which Robison found operative among French Freemasons from the beginning of the eighteenth century on,[488] had resulted in making the lodges attractive to those elements in France whose discontent over civil and ecclesiastical oppressions had grown great.[489] Under the pressure imposed upon private and public discussion by the state and by the church, men of letters, *avocats au parlement*, unbeneficed abbés, impecunious youths, and self-styled philosophers thronged the halls of the lodges, eager to take advantage of the opportunity their secret assemblies afforded to discuss the most intimate concerns of politics and religion.[490] Despite the wide contrariety of minor views thus represented, one general idea and language, that of "cosmopolitanism," was made familiar to a multitude of minds. Worse still, the popular interest of the period in mysticism, theosophy, cabala, and genuine science was appealed to, in order to provide a more numerous clientele among whom might be disseminated the doctrines of atheism, materialism, and discontent with civil subordination.[491] Thus the Masonic lodges in France were made the "hot-beds, where the seeds were sown, and tenderly reared, of all the pernicious doctrines which soon after choaked every moral or religious cultivation, and have made ... Society worse than a waste …."[492]

The introduction of French Freemasonry into Germany, according to Robison, was followed by similar results.[493] Thither, as to France, simple English Freemasonry had first gone, and because of its exclusive emphasis upon the principle of brotherly love the Germans had welcomed it and treated it with deep seriousness;[494] but the sense of mystery and the taste for ritualistic embellishments which the advent of French Masonry promoted, speedily changed the temper of the German brethren.[495] A reckless tendency to innovation set in. The love of stars and ribbons,[496] and the desire to learn of ghost-raising, exorcism, and alchemy,[497]became the order of the day. Rosicrucianism flourished,[498] rival systems appeared, and questions of precedency split German Freemasonry into numerous fiercely hostile camps.[499]

Meantime, on account of the propaganda carried on by the Enlighteners,[500] a revolution of the public mind took place in Germany, marked by a great increase of scepticism, infidelity, and irreligion, not only among the wealthy and luxurious but among the profligate elements in the lower classes as well.[501] Rationalistic theologians, aided and abetted by booksellers and publishers and by educational theorists,[502] coöperated to make the ideas of orthodox Christianity distasteful to the general public.[503] To give effect to this campaign of seduction, the lodges of Freemasonry were invaded and their secret assemblies employed to spread free-thinking and cosmopolitical ideas.[504] Thus German Freemasonry became impregnated with the impious and revolutionary tendencies of French Freemasonry.[505]

At such an hour, according to Robison, Weishaupt founded his Order of the Illuminati.[506] Employing the opportunities afforded him by his connections with the Masons,[507] he exerted himself to make disciples and to lay the foundations of an "Association … which, in time, should govern the world,"[508] the express aim of which "was to abolish Christianity and overturn all civil government."[509]

To accomplish this end a most insinuating pedagogy was adopted,[510] the members were trained to spy upon one another,[511] and hypocrisy which did not stop short of positive villainy was practised.[512] As a fitting climax to a program that involved the complete subversion of existing moral standards, women were to be admitted to the lodges.[513]

Following an analysis of the grades of the order,[514] lifted little if any above the general plane of ineptitude upon which the author moved, Robison incorporated into his history of the Bavarian Illuminati a table of the lodges that had been established prior to 1786.[515] Drawing professedly upon the private papers of the order as published by the Bavarian government, he worked out a list which included five lodges in Strassburg; four in Bonn; fourteen in Austria; "many" in each of the following states, Livonia, Courland, Alsace, Hesse, Poland, Switzerland, and Holland; eight in England; two in Scotland; and "several" in America.[516]

The suppression of the Illuminati by the Bavarian government was regarded by Robison as merely "formal" in its nature:[517] the evil genius of the banned order speedily reappeared in the guise of the German Union.[518] Into the discussion of the German Union Robison read the "proofs" of an enterprise truly gigantic both as to its proportions and its baneful influence. The *illuminated* lodges of Freemasonry were declared to have given way to *reading societies* wherein the initiated, *i. e.*, the members of the Union, actively employed themselves, apparently to accomplish the noble ends of enlightening mankind and securing the dethronement of superstition and fanaticism,[519] but actually to secure the destruction of every sentiment of religion, morality and loyalty.[520] The higher mysteries of Bahrdt's silly and abortive project were declared to be identical with those of Weishaupt's order: natural religion and atheism were to be substituted for Christianity, and political principles equally anarchical with those of the Illuminati were fostered.[521]

Although Robison confessed himself driven to pronounce Bahrdt's enterprise "coarse, and palpably mean,"[522] and although the archives and officers of the Union were held to be "contemptible,"[523] none the less an elaborate though most disjointed tale was unfolded by him. This involved the organization of the German literati and the control of the book trade, with a view to forming taste and directing public opinion;[524] and the establishment of reading societies to the number of eight hundred or more,[525] among whose members were to be circulated such books as were calculated to fortify the mind against all disposition to be startled on account of the appearance of "doctrines and maxims which are singular, or perhaps opposite to those which are current in ordinary societies."[526] Thus it would be possible "to work in silence upon all courts, families, and individuals in every quarter, and acquire an influence in the appointment of court-officers, stewards, secretaries, parish-priests, public teachers, or private tutors."[527]

Robison was unable to present anything beyond the most tenuous "proofs" that a direct relation existed between Weishaupt's system and Bahrdt's enterprise;[528] still he did not hesitate to affirm that, on account of the emergence of the latter, it had been made clear that the suppression of the Illuminati had been futile.[529] "Weishaupt and his agents were still busy and successful."[530]

Arriving finally at the subject of the French Revolution, Robison devoted something more than sixty pages to an effort to connect the system of Weishaupt with the great European debacle. Approaching the matter with unconcealed dubiety,[531] he found his confidence and boldness growing as he proceeded. Relying chiefly upon such uncritical and promiscuous sources as the *Religions Begebenheiten*, the *Wiener Zeitschrift*, and the *Magazin des Literatur et Kunst* (*sic*), and a work entitled *Mémoires Posthumes de Custine*, he sought a point of direct contact between the Illuminati and the French revolutionary movement by stressing the enlistment of Mirabeau,[532] the mission of Bode and von Busche,[533] and the instructions which, he alleged, were given by the latter to the *Amis Réunis* and the *Philalèthes* through their chief lodges at Paris.[534]

The mission of Bode and von Busche, according to Robison, had been undertaken at the request of Mirabeau and the Abbé Perigord[535] (Talleyrand). When Weishaupt's plan was thus communicated to the two French lodges mentioned, "they saw at once its importance, in all its branches, such as the use of the Masonic Lodges, to fish for Minervals—the rituals and ranks to entice the young, and to lead them by degrees to opinions and measures which, at first sight, would have shocked them."[536] By the beginning of 1789 the lodges of the *Grand Orient* [537] had received the secrets of the Illuminati.[538] The Duke of Orléans, who had been "illuminated" by Mirabeau,[539] and whose personal political ambitions were strongly stressed by Robison,[540] gave hearty support to the enterprise; and thus in a very short time the Masonic lodges of France were converted into a set of secret affiliated societies, all corresponding with the mother lodges of Paris, and ready to rise instantly and overturn the government as soon as the signal should be given.[541] The political committees organized in each of these "illuminated" lodges familiarized not only their brethren but, through them, the country in general, with the secret revolutionary program.[542] Thus it happened that the "stupid Bavarians" became the instructors of the French "in the art of overturning the world";[543] and thus, also, it happened that "the whole nation changed, and changed again, and again, as if by beat of drum."[544]

Such in its main outlines and in its "principal links" of evidence is the *Proofs of a Conspiracy against all the Religions and Governments of Europe.* Yet to obtain a just appraisal of the book it must not be overlooked that its author wrote an additional one hundred and fifty pages, not of "proofs" but of argument, partly to defend errors of judgment he may have committed in his treatment of the subject, but chiefly to persuade his fellow countrymen that the principles of Illuminism were false and to urge them to turn a deaf ear to these doctrines.

We turn now to consider another and much more elaborate exposition of the Illuminati-French Revolution legend. Almost at the moment of the appearance of Robison's book, there appeared in French, at London and Hamburg, a far more finished production, devoted to the same thesis and bearing the title, *Mémoires pour servir à l'histoire du Jacobinisme.*[545] Its author, the Abbé Barruel,[546] who had been trained as a Jesuit, enjoying literary talents much superior to those of Robison and relying upon documentary evidence more copious if not more convincing, defined his purpose in the following manner:

We shall show that with which it is incumbent on all nations and their chiefs to be acquainted: we shall demonstrate that, even to the most horrid deeds perpetrated during the French Revolution, everything was foreseen and resolved on, was combined and premeditated: that they were the offspring of deep-thought villainy, since they had been prepared and were produced by men, who alone held the clue of those plots and conspiracies, lurking in the secret meetings where they had been conceived, and only watching the favorable moment of bursting forth. Though the events of each day may not appear to have been combined, there nevertheless existed a secret agent and a secret cause, giving rise to each event, and turning each circumstance to the long-sought-for end. Though circumstances may often have afforded the pretense of the occasion, yet the grand cause of the revolution, its leading features, its atrocious crimes, will still remain one continued chain of deep-laid and premeditated villainy.[547]

The amazing breadth of Barruel's canvass, as well as the naiveté of the artist, are immediately disclosed in his foreword respecting the "triple conspiracy" which he proposes to lay bare.[548] To present this "triple conspiracy" in his own words will do more than define the abbé's conception of his task: its transparent incoordination will make it apparent that much of the work of examination that might otherwise seem to be called for is futile.

1st. Many years before the French Revolution, men who styled themselves Philosophers conspired against the God of the Gospel, against Christianity, without distinction of worship, whether Protestant or Catholic, Anglican or Presbyterian. The grand object of this conspiracy was to overturn every altar where Christ was adored. It was the conspiracy of the *Sophisters[549] of Impiety*, or the ANTICHRISTIAN CONSPIRACY.

2dly. This school of impiety soon formed the *Sophisters of Rebellion*: these latter, combining their conspiracy against kings with that of the Sophisters of Impiety, coalesce with that ancient sect whose tenets constituted the whole secret of the *Occult-Lodges* of Free-Masonry, which long since, imposing on the credulity of its most distinguished adepts, only initiated the chosen of the elect into the secret of their unrelenting hatred for Christ and kings.

3dly. From the Sophisters of Impiety and Rebellion arose *Sophisters of Impiety and Anarchy*. These latter conspire not only against Christ and his altars, but against every religion natural or revealed: not only against kings, but against every government, against all civil society, even against all property whatsoever.

This third sect, known by the name of Illumines, coalesced with the Sophisters conspiring against Christ, coalesced with the Sophisters who, with the Occult Masons, conspired against both Christ and kings. It was the coalition of the adepts of *impiety*, of the adepts of *rebellion*, and the adepts of *anarchy*, which formed the *CLUB of the JACOBINS*.... Such was the origin, such the progress of that sect, since become so dreadfully famous under the name JACOBIN. In the present Memoirs each of these three conspiracies shall be treated separately; their authors unmasked, the object, means, coalition and progress of the adepts shall be laid open.[550]

The sole proposition which Barruel proposed to maintain is thus made clear enough. *All* the developments of the French Revolution were to be explained on the basis of the following postulate: The Encyclopedists, Freemasons, and Bavarian Illuminati, working together, not unconsciously but with well-planned coördination, produced the Jacobins, and the Jacobins in turn produced the Revolution. Over all, embracing all, the word "conspiracy" must needs be written large.

The first volume of the Memoirs was devoted to the conspiracy of the philosophers. Voltaire, D'Alembert, Frederick II, and Diderot—"Voltaire the chief, D'Alembert the most subtle agent, Frederick the protector and often the adviser, Diderot the forlorn hope"[551]—these were the men who originally leagued themselves together "in the most inveterate hatred of Christianity."[552] Bringing out into bold relief the most malignant and brutal of the anticlerical and anti-Christian utterances of Voltaire and his friends,[553] as well as all available evidence of a crafty strategy on the part of the conspirators to avoid detection of their plan,[554] Barruel was emboldened to affirm a desperate plan to overturn every altar where Christ was adored, whether in London, Geneva, Stockholm, Petersburg, Paris, Madrid, Vienna, or Rome, whether Protestant or Catholic.[555]

The first definite step in this campaign of the philosophers is declared to have been the publication of L'*Encyclopédie*;[556] the second, the suppression of the Jesuits and the widespread elimination of religious houses;[557] and the third, the capture of the French Academy by the philosophers and the diversion of its honors to impious writers.[558]

The foregoing were measures which primarily concerned "the chiefs," or "better sort."[559] Efforts to extend the conspiracy to the hovel and the cottage were also made. Accordingly, appeals to toleration, reason, and humanity became the order of the day.[560] These were intended to impress the populace and, by a show of sympathy with those who complained of their condition, prepare the way for the days of rebellion, violence, and murder which were yet to come.[561] Free schools were established, directed by men who, privy to the great conspiracy, became zealous corrupters of youth.[562] All was carefully calculated and planned to render possible the full fruitage of the designs of the conspirators when the harvest day should come.

Having thus dealt with the conspiracy against altars, Barruel turned in his second volume to consider the plot against thrones. The great inspirers of this covert attack upon monarchy were Voltaire, Montesquieu, and Rousseau. Voltaire, though by nature a friend of kings, whose favor and caresses were his delight, yet, since he found them standing in the way of his efforts to extirpate Christianity, was led to oppose them, and to substitute the doctrines of equality of rights and liberty of reason for his earlier emphasis upon loyalty to sovereigns.[563] Unwittingly, through his *Spirit of Laws*, Montesquieu had helped on the anti-monarchical resolution by his heavy emphasis upon the essential differences between monarchies and democracies, thus for the first time suggesting to the French people that they lived under a despotic government and helping to alienate them from their king.[564] As for Rousseau, in his *Social Contract* he had widened the path which Montesquieu had opened.[565] His doctrines had the effect of placing monarchy in an abhorrent light. They filled the minds of the people with a passion for Liberty and Equality.

The systems of Montesquieu and Rousseau, particularly, induced the Sophisters of Impiety to combine the task of overthrowing monarchy with the task of overthrowing religion.[566] A sweeping attempt to popularize the leveling principles embodied in those two systems immediately developed. A flood of antimonarchical writings appeared,[567] governments were sharply criticized, despotism was roundly denounced, the minds of the people were agitated and inflamed, and the notion of revolution was rendered familiar both by precept and example.[568]

Some powerful secret agency was needed, however, to promote this vast conspiracy. The lodges of Freemasonry suggested a tempting possibility. The members of the craft gave ample evidence that they were susceptible.[569] The occult lodges,[570] moreover, already had traveled far toward the goal of revolution. All their protests to the contrary, their *one* secret was: "Equality and Liberty; all men are equals and brothers; all men are free."[571] Surely it would not be difficult for the enemies of thrones and altars to reach the ears of men who cherished such a secret, and to convert their lodges into council-chambers and forums for the propagation of the doctrines of impiety and rebellion.

An alliance was speedily consummated,[572] and a fresh torrent of declamation and calumnies, all directed against the altar and the throne, began to pour through these newly discovered subterranean channels.[573] The *Grand Orient* constituted a central committee which as early as 1776 instructed the deputies of the lodges throughout France to prepare the brethren for insurrection.[574] Condorcet and Sieyès placed themselves at the head of another lodge, to which the Propaganda was to be traced.[575] In addition, a secret association bearing the title *Amis des Noirs* created a *regulating committee*, composed of such men as Condorcet, the elder Mirabeau, Sieyès, Brissot, Carra, the Duc de la Rochefoucauld, Clavière, Lepelletier de Saint-Fargeau, Valade, La Fayette, and Bergasse.[576] This *regulating committee* was also in intimate correspondence with the French lodges of Freemasonry. Thus a powerful secret organization was at hand, composed of not less than six hundred thousand members all told, at least five hundred thousand of whom could be fully counted upon to do the bidding of the conspirators, "all zealous for the Revolution, all ready to rise at the first signal and to impart the shock to all other classes of the people."[577]

However, all these machinations might have come to naught had it not been for the encouragement and direction supplied by the Illuminati. In the latter Barruel saw the apotheosis of infamy and corruption.[578] With diabolical ingenuity the chiefs of the Illuminati succeeded in evolving an organization which put into the hands of the conspirators, *i. e.*, the philosophers and Freemasons, the very instrument they needed to give full effect to their plans. The superiority of that organization was to be seen in its principles of general subordination and the gradation of superiors, in the minute instructions given to adepts and officers covering every conceivable responsibility and suggesting infinite opportunities to promote the order's welfare, and in the absolute power of its *general*.[579] Thus was built up a hierarchy of savants, an association held under a most rigid discipline, a formidable machine capable of employing its maximum power as its governing hand might direct.[580] With the close of the third volume Barruel considers that he has been able to present a "complete academy of Conspirators."[581]

Barruel's last volume, the most formidable of all, was devoted by its author to the forging of the final link in his chain: the coalescence of the conspiring philosophers, Freemasons, and Illuminati into the Jacobins. To establish a connection between the "illuminated" Masons and the immediate "authors and abettors of the French Revolution,"[582] *i. e.*, the Jacobins, Barruel had recourse to the familiar inventions of the reappearance of the Bavarian Illuminati after its suppression,[583] the rise and corrupting influence of the German Union,[584] that treacherous "modification of Weishaupt's *Minerval* schools,"[585] and, particularly, the pretended mission of Bode and von Busche to Paris.[586]

With respect to this last invention, no more worthy of our comment than the others except for the fact that it was supposed to supply the direct point of contact between the conspirators and the French Revolution, Barruel was obliged to admit that he was unable to place before his readers evidence of the precise character of the negotiations that took place between the deputation from Berlin and the French lodges:[587] "facts" would have to be permitted to speak for themselves.[588] These "facts" were such as the following: the lodges of Paris were rapidly converted into clubs, with *regulating committees* and *political committees*;[589] the resolutions of the *regulating committees* were communicated through the committee of correspondence of the *Grand Orient* to the heads of the Masonic lodges scattered throughout France;[590] the day of general insurrection was thus fixed for July 14, 1789;[591] on the fatal day the lodges were dissolved, and the Jacobins, suddenly throwing off their garments of secrecy and hypocrisy, stood forth in the clear light of day.[592]

His last two hundred pages were devoted by Barruel to arguments shaped chiefly to show that the principles of the Revolutionary leaders were identical with the principles of the illuminated lodges;[593] that the successes of the Revolutionary armies, of Custine beyond the Rhine,[594] of Dumouriez in Belgium,[595] of Pichegru in Holland,[596] and of Bonaparte in Italy, in Malta, and in Egypt,[597] were explicable only on the ground of treacherous intrigues carried on by the agents of Illuminism; and that no country, moreover, need flatter itself it would escape the seductions and plots of the conspirators. The dragon's teeth of revolution were already sown in Switzerland, in Sweden, in Russia, in Poland, in Austria, in Prussia, *and in America*.[598] With Barruel's comment upon America,[599] our discussion of the *Memoirs of Jacobinism* may well come to a close.

As the plague flies on the wings of the wind, so do their triumphant legions infect America. Their apostles have infused their principles into the submissive and laborious negroes; and St. Domingo and Guadaloupe have been converted into vast charnel houses for their inhabitants. So numerous were the brethren in North America, that Philadelphia and Boston trembled, lest *their rising constitution should be obliged to make way for that of the great club*; and if for a time the brotherhood has been obliged to shrink back into their hiding places, they are still sufficiently numerous to raise collections and transmit them to the insurgents of Ireland;[600] thus contributing toward that species of revolution which is the object of their ardent wishes in America.[601]God grant that the

United States may not learn to their cost, that Republics are equally menaced with Monarchies; and that the immensity of the ocean is but a feeble barrier against the universal conspiracy of the Sect!

NOTE: The literary relationship between the works of Robison and Barruel is of sufficient interest and significance to warrant some comment. Robison's volume was published before its author saw Barruel's composition in its French text.[602] Later, Robison was moved to rejoice that Barruel had confirmed his main positions and contentions. A few things in the *Memoirs of Jacobinism*, however, impress him as startling. He confesses that he had never before heard the claim seriously made that "irreligion and unqualified Liberty and Equality are the genuine and original Secrets of Free Masonry, and the ultimatum of a regular progress through all its degrees."[603] He is driven to assert that *this* is not the secret of Masonry as he has learned it from other sources. Robison also recognizes differences in the two works respecting the exposition of certain Masonic degrees. For his part he is not willing to admit that his sources are unreliable.[604]

Barruel, on the other hand, did not get sight of Robison's volume until just as his third volume was going to press.[605] He comments in part as follows: "Without knowing it, we have fought for the same cause with the same arms, and pursued the same course; but the Public are on the eve of seeing our respective quotations, and will observe a remarkable difference between them."[606] That difference Barruel attempts to explain on the ground that Robison had adopted the method of combining and condensing his quotations from his sources. Besides, he thinks his zealous confederate "in some passages … has even adopted as truth certain assertions which the correspondence of the Illuminées evidently demonstrate to have been invented by them against their adversaries, and which," he continues, "in my Historical Volume I shall be obliged to treat in an opposite sense."[607] Barruel also differs with Robison respecting the time of the origin of Masonry.[608] But all such matters are of slight consequence; all suggestions of opposition and disagreement between Robison and Barruel are brushed aside by him in the following summary fashion: " ... It will be perceived that we are not to be put in competition with each other; Mr. Robison taking a general view while I have attempted to descend into particulars: as to the substance we agree."[609]

It was one of the most confident boasts of the supporters of the idea of a "conspiracy against thrones and altars" that these two writers, Robison and Barruel, had worked at the same problem without the knowledge of each other's effort, and thus following independent lines of investigation, had reached the same conclusion. The merit of the claim may safely be left to the reader's judgment.

CHAPTER IV

THE ILLUMINATI AGITATION IN NEW ENGLAND

1. MORSE PRECIPITATES THE CONTROVERSY

The fast day proclamation of President John Adams, issued March 23, 1798, expressed unusual solemnity and concern. Therein the United States was represented as "at present placed in a hazardous and afflictive position."[610] The necessity of sounding a loud call to repentance and reformation was declared to be imperative, and the people were fervently urged to implore Heaven's mercy and benediction on the imperiled nation.

On the day appointed, the 9th of May, among the multitude of pastors who appeared before their assembled flocks and addressed them on topics of national and personal self-examination, was the Reverend Jedediah Morse. The deliverance which he made to his people[611] was destined to have far more than a passing interest and effect. He took for his text fragments of the language that King Hezekiah addressed to the prophet Isaiah, as found in II Kings 19: 3, 4: "This is a day of trouble, and of rebuke (or reviling), and blasphemy.... Wherefore lift up thy prayer for the remnant that is left." Then the well-known minister of Charlestown proceeded to suggest a parallel between the desperate state of affairs within the little kingdom of Judah when the Assyrians, fresh from their triumph over the armies of Egypt, renewed their insolent and terrifying campaign against the city of Jerusalem, and the unhappy and perilous condition of affairs within the United States.[612]

From this general observation Morse proceeded to take specific account of the circumstances that made the period through which the nation was passing "*a day of trouble*, of *reviling and blasphemy*." The main source from which the *day of trouble* had arisen, as the President's fast day proclamation had indicated, was the very serious aspect of our relations with

France, owing to the unfriendly disposition and conduct of that nation. Here, and not elsewhere, was to be found the occasion of the unhappy divisions that existed among the citizens of the United States, disturbing their peace, and threatening the overthrow of the government itself.[613] The settled policy of the French government, that of attempting the subjugation of other countries by injecting discord and division among their citizens before having recourse to arms, had been faithfully adhered to with respect to America.

Their too great influence among us has been exerted vigorously, and in conformity to a deep-laid plan, in cherishing party spirit, in vilifying the men we have, by our free suffrages, elected to administer our Constitution; and have thus endeavoured to destroy the confidence of the people in the constituted authorities, and divide them from the government.[614] They have abused our honest friendship for their nation, our gratitude for their assistance in our revolution and our confidence in the uprightness and sincerity of their professions of regard for us; and, by their artifices and intrigues, have made these amiable dispositions in the unsuspecting American people, the vehicles of their poison.[615]

Emboldened by its knowledge of the power which the French party in America has acquired, Morse continued, the government of France has shown itself disposed to adopt an increasingly insolent tone toward the government of this nation. The insurrections which the government of France has fomented here, its efforts to plunge the United States into a ruinous war, its spoliation of our commerce upon the high seas, its insufferable treatment of our ministers and commissioners as shown in the lately published state papers[616]—these all tend to show how resolute and confident in its determination to triumph over us the French government has become.[617]

If, said Morse, a contributory cause for the present "hazardous and afflictive position" of the country is sought, it will readily be found in "the astonishing increase of irreligion."[618] The evidence of this, in turn, is to be found, not only in the prevailing atheism and materialism of the day, and all the vicious fruits which such impious sentiments have borne, but as well in the slanders with which newspapers are filled and the personal invective and abuse with which private discussion is laden, all directed against the representatives of government, against men, many of whom have grown gray in their country's service and whose integrity has been proved incorruptible. It is likewise to be discovered in the reviling and abuse which, coming from the same quarter, has been directed against the clergy, who, according to their influence and ability, have done what they could to support and vindicate the government. Nothing that the clergy has done has been of such a character as to provoke this treatment. And how "can *they* be your friends who are continually declaiming against the Clergy, and endeavouring by all means—by falsehood and misrepresentation, to asperse their characters, and to bring them and their profession into disrepute?"[619]

When the question is raised respecting the design and tendency of these things, their inherent and appalling impiety is immediately disclosed. They give "reason to suspect that there is some secret plan in operation, hostile to true liberty and religion, which requires to be aided by these vile slanders."[620] They cannot be regarded as mere excrescences of the life of the times; they are not detached happenings; they go straight down to the roots of things; they are deadly attacks upon the civil and religious institutions whose foundations were laid by our venerable forefathers. They mean that all those principles and habits which were formed under those institutions are to be brought into contempt and eventually swept aside, in order to give a clear field "for the spread of those disorganizing opinions, and that atheistical philosophy, which are deluging the Old World in misery and blood."[621]

That this preparatory work has begun, that progress in the direction of its fatal completion has been made, that what is now going on in America is part of the same deep-laid and extensive plan which has been in operation in Europe for many years—these, Morse continued, are reasonable and just fears in the light of the disclosures made "in a work written by a gentleman of literary eminence in Scotland, within the last year, and just reprinted in this country, entitled, 'Proofs of a Conspiracy against all the Religions and Governments of Europe'."[622] The following facts are brought to the light of day in this volume: For more than twenty years past a society called THE ILLUMINATED has been in existence in Germany; its express aim is "to root out and abolish Christianity, and overthrow all civil government";[623] it approves of such atrocious principles as the right to commit self-murder and the promiscuous intercourse of the sexes, while it condemns the principles of patriotism and the right to accumulate private property;[624] in the prosecution of its infamous propaganda it aims to enlist the discontented, to get control of all such cultural agencies as the schools, literary societies, newspapers, writers, booksellers, and postmasters;[625] it is bent upon insinuating its members into all positions of distinction and influence, whether literary, civil, or religious.[626]

Practically all of the civil and ecclesiastical establishments of Europe have already been shaken to their foundations by this terrible organization; the French Revolution itself is doubtless to be traced to its machinations; the successes of the French armies are to be explained on the same ground.[627] The Jacobins are nothing more nor less than the open manifestation of the hidden system of the Illuminati.[628] The order has its branches established and its emissaries at work in America.[629]Doubtless the "Age of Reason" and the other works of that unprincipled author are to be regarded as part of the general plan to accomplish universal demoralization: the fact that Paine's infamous works have been so industriously and extensively circulated in this country would seem to justify fully this conclusion.[630] The affiliated Jacobin Societies in America have doubtless had as the object of their establishment the propagation of "the principles of the illuminated mother club in France."[631]

Before making room for the admonitions which Morse based upon this exposition of the underlying significance of "this ... day of trouble, ... rebuke ... and blasphemy," his treatment of the Masonic bearings of the subject should be noticed. As delivered by Morse, the fast day sermon of May 9, 1798, contained no reference to the relations alleged to exist between the Order of the Illuminati and the lodges of Freemasonry. The Charlestown pastor's silence upon this important phase of the matter is best explained in the light of the pains which he took, when the sermon was committed to type, to handle this delicate and embarrassing aspect of the case.[632]

Extended foot notes dealing with the omitted topic and expressive of great reserve and caution comprise a substantial part of the printed sermon. In these Morse repeated the charge which Robison had made before him that the Order of the Illuminati had had its origin among the Freemasons, but hastened to add that this was because of corruptions which had crept into Freemasonry, so that Illuminism must be viewed as "a vile and pestiferous *scion* grafted on the stock of simple Masonry."[633] As if further to ward off the blows of incensed and resentful members of the craft, Morse proceeded to dilate upon the artifice which men of wicked purpose commonly resort to in attempting "to pervert and bend into a subserviency to their designs ancient and respectable institutions."[634] The Illuminati, it is suggested, may thus have taken advantage of the schisms and corruptions with which European Masonry has been cursed, and have employed many members of the lodges to serve as "secret conductors of their poisonous principles": the high estimation in which the order of Masonry is generally held may be construed as making such a presumption probable.[635] And in this country, if one may base his judgment upon the considerations that the immortal Washington stands at the head of the Masonic fraternity in America and that the Masons of New England "have ever shown themselves firm and decided supporters of civil and religious order," then it may safely be assumed that the leaven of Illuminism has not found its way into the American lodges, at least not into the lodges of the Eastern States.[636] If it *should* be found true that some of the branches of Masonry have been corrupted and perverted from their original design, need *that* circumstance occasion more serious humiliation and embarrassment than Christians face as they contemplate the apostasies of which certain churches in Christendom have been guilty?[637] Finally, the readers are urged to keep in mind that Robison's book has been commended, not because of its animadversions upon Freemasonry, but for the reason that "it unveils the dark conspiracies of the *Illuminati* against civil government and Christianity, ... and because it is well calculated to excite in this country a just alarm for the safety and welfare of our civil and religious privileges, by discovering to us the machinations which are deployed to subvert them."[638]

Thus having canvassed the situation abroad and at home, the sermon drew toward its close in the following manner:

By these awful events—this tremendous shaking among the nations of the earth, God is doubtless accomplishing his promises, and fulfilling the prophecies. This wrath and violence of men against all government and religion, shall be made ultimately, in some way or other, to praise God. All corruptions, in religion and government, as dross must, sooner or later, be burnt up. The dreadful fire of *Illuminatism* may be permitted to rage and spread for this purpose.... But while we contemplate these awful events in this point of view, let us beware, in our expressions of approbation, of blending the *end* with the *means*. Because atheism and licentiousness are employed as *instruments*, by divine providence, to subvert and overthrow popery and despotism, it does not follow that atheism and licentiousness are in themselves good things, and worthy of our approbation. While the storm rages, with dreadful havoc in Europe, let us be comforted in the thought, that God directeth it, and that he will, by his power and wisdom, so manage it, as to make it accomplish his own gracious designs. While we behold these scenes acting abroad and at a distance from us, let us be concerned for our own welfare.... We have reason to tremble for the safety of our political, as well as our religious ark. Attempts are making, and are openly, as well as secretly, conducted, to undermine the foundations of both. In this situation of things, our duty is plain, and lies within a short compass.[639]

With one heart, as citizens to cleave to the national government and as Christians to be alert to the open and secret dangers which threaten the church, these, according to the last word of the preacher, were the paramount concerns of the hour.

Such was Jedediah Morse's fast day sermon of May 9, 1798. Such at least it was when it came from the press; surely not even by the widest stretch of the imagination an epoch-making sermon; not even notable, except when viewed from a single angle. Nothing could be clearer than that the sermon moved, for the most part, well within the circle of conventional ideas to which on state occasions the minds of the clergy of New England generally made response. But for the introduction of one element it is safe to say the deliverance of Charlestown's minister would have passed for one of the ordinary "political sermons" of the day, and so have accomplished nothing perhaps beyond helping to swell the chorus of protests from disgusted Democrats against "political preaching." That element, needless to say, was *Illuminism.*

The public sanction which Morse gave to the charge that the Illuminati were responsible for the afflictions of both the Old World and the New was a new note on this side of the Atlantic. Sounded in New England at a time when Europe was in convulsion and when the shift from traditional social, political, and religious positions in America was extremely rapid in its movement, this new alarm could not fail to arrest attention. We have seen that the air of New England was already surcharged with notions of implacable hostility to the forces in control of church and state,[640] and with gloomy forebodings born of surmises of intrigue and conspiracy.[641] The hour was electric. The hard-pressed forces of religious and political conservatism were bound to receive the new Shibboleth with unquestioning and eager joy. Henceforth their arsenal would be enlarged to include a new weapon. They would be able to point to the villainies, impieties, and blood-lettings in Europe, to the flauntings, contumelies, and crafty counter-manœuverings which the clergy and the heads of government had to suffer in America, and assert that back of all these and binding all together into a single vicious whole was a conspiracy whose object was nothing less than the complete overthrow of civil government and orthodox Christianity. To be able to brand political and religious radicalism with a word as detestable as this new word "Illuminism" which had just come across the Atlantic, should indeed prove sufficient to damn that cause.

The immediate effect produced by the sermon fell considerably short of a sensation. For one thing the subject of the Illuminati was new and unfamiliar in New England. Much more significant, however, is the fact that at the time the sermon came to public attention, the long-expected X. Y. Z. despatches were passing through the newspaper presses of the country and inflaming the national spirit to an incredible degree. In view of the fact that innumerable public assemblies were being held and innumerable patriotic addresses drawn up and presented to the President, all inspired by the prospect of and the demand for an immediate rupture with France, it is not surprising that the minister of Charlestown did not succeed in creating a more instant and widespread alarm than he did.

However, he had no reason to be disappointed. The spark which he had communicated to the tinder might seem to smoulder for a season,[642] but in due course it was bound to burst into flame. That Morse was himself well content with the degree of interest which the public manifested in his disclosure of the "conspiracy" is evident from the following letter that he addressed to Oliver Wolcott, within a fortnight of the date of the national fast:

Charlestown, May 21, 1798.

Dear Sir,

I enclose for your acceptance my Fast Sermon, & one on the death of my worthy friend Judge Russell, both whh. together with one other occasional discourse, besides two common sermons, I was obliged to compose after my return from Phila., and under the disadvantage of general fatigue.—I owe you and myself this apology.—The fast discourse was received with very unexpected approbation—& with no opposition even in Charlestown, whose citizens many of them have been the most violently opposed to the measures of Govt. & the most enthusiastic in favor of France.—This same discourse delivered two months ago would have excited such a flame, as would in all probability have rendered my situation extremely unpleasant, if not unsafe.—I hope it has done some good, & that it may have a chance of doing more, however small, I have permitted its publication…. The fast was celebrated in this quarter with unexpected solemnity & unanimity. Its effects, I hope & believe will be great both as respects our civil & religious interests….

Your friend,
JED^H MORSE.[643]

TO HONORABLE OLIVER WOLCOTT,
Comptroller of the Treasury

Here and there Morse's sermon promptly became the occasion of public comment. To illustrate: The Reverend John Thayer, beloved and trusted shepherd of the Catholic flock in Boston, following the patriotic example of the Protestant clergy, preached a sermon on the occasion of the national fast appropriate to the solemnity of the day.[644] In the published text of this sermon Thayer took occasion to commend Morse "for his interesting abridgement of the infernal society of the Illuminati."[645]For the most part, however, the comment of the clergy was reserved for subsequent occasions when the clerical mind should have had opportunity to inform itself more fully concerning the matter.

As for the newspapers, they began to pay their respects to Morse's sensational utterance soon after the latter's fast day sermon came from the press. Thus "An American" contributed an article of generous length and of somewhat hostile tone to the *Independent Chronicle* of May 24 (1798), calling upon Morse to substantiate more fully the charge he had made. This pseudonymous contributor professed to have experienced great astonishment upon reading Morse's sermon and finding that Robison's *Proofs* alone had been relied upon as a source of information and authority. So serious a matter seemed to demand fuller evidence. Thinking that perhaps Dr. Morse had been imposed upon and that the work in question was possibly apocryphal, the writer had been constrained to search through foreign literary journals with a view to discovering how the "performance" attributed to Robison was regarded abroad. Thus employed he had come across an article in *The Critical Review, or Annals of Literature*, London, 1797, wherein he found severe strictures upon Robison's volume. In view of this, "since the *Doctors* of Europe and America differ so widely in their estimation of its importance," but a single course of honor and obligation would seem to be open to Dr. Morse. Having stood sponsor for the authenticity of such an extraordinary publication, he should now submit to the public decided proofs of the authority and correctness of the book in question.[646]

To this sharp challenge of "An American," Morse was not indifferent. Replying to his critic in a subsequent issue of the *Chronicle*,[647] he expressed the hope that the public would not form its judgment respecting Robison's volume before reading the same, or at least not until it shall have heard further from its "humble servant, Jedidiah Morse." Meantime, if his readers shall be pleased to peruse the observations clipped from the *New York Spectator* by which his (Morse's) letter to the *Chronicle* is accompanied they will learn that "there is at least *one* other person in the United States who has *read this* work, [and] whose opinion of it accords with" his own.[648]

A few days later, through the columns of the same paper,[649] Morse replied at greater length to the criticisms which "An American" had brought to public attention. That he had not "too hastily recommended Professor Robison's late work" Morse regards as sufficiently demonstrated by the fact that he had had a copy of the book in his possession since the middle of the previous April. This he had examined with care, and he had satisfied himself that it was entitled to the recommendation he had given it in his fast day sermon. So far as the hostile criticism of the authors of *The Critical Review* is concerned, he has no doubt that their *caricature* of Robison's book is to be construed as expressive of their determination to destroy its reputation and thus prevent its circulation, since it probably exposed and thwarted their favorite schemes. Besides, over against the contemptuous estimate that the authors of *The Critical Review* had seen fit to place upon Robison's volume, Morse was able to oppose a very different judgment. *The London Review* of January, 1798, extracts from which he was glad to be permitted to offer in evidence,[650] placed an estimate upon Robison's book which was both accurate and just. From this "An American" will be able to gather that "'the Doctors in Europe and America'" do not "differ so widely in their estimation" of the importance of Robison's volume as had been asserted. The observations that Morse is now offering to the public, it is his expectation, will serve to effect his personal justification; but if doubts still remain in the minds of any, he can only recommend as the best and perhaps the only sure means of dissolving them that such persons read *Proofs of a Conspiracy* for themselves.[651]

With respect to the inception of the Illuminati agitation in New England, the utterances of two other clergymen require attention. One of these, the Reverend David Tappan, professor of divinity at Harvard, in a discourse[652] delivered before the senior class of that institution on the 19th of June, 1798, cautioned the young people before him who were about to quit the life of the college to guard against the dangers of speculative principles, the pleasures of idleness and vicious indulgence, the degrading tendency of selfish sentiments, *and* "a more recent system, which … has for its ostensible object THE REGENERATION OF AN OPPRESSED WORLD TO THE BLISSFUL ENJOYMENT OF EQUAL LIBERTY." This "more recent system," Tappan explained, was the philosophy of the Order of the Illuminati.[653]

Drawing, as he professed, upon Morse's fast day discourse and upon President Dwight's sermons on *infidel philosophy*,[654] Tappan essayed a sketch of the objects and operations of the Illuminati, from the time of the founding of the order by Weishaupt to its supposed connections with the French Revolution, and the successes which it had enabled the

French armies to accomplish through its intrigues "in various and distant parts of the world." The conspiracy, it is true, might not be as extensive in its scope as had been claimed; but even so, the *undoubted* aspects of the situation were sufficient to afford ground for most grave apprehension. "If these and similar facts," the clergyman continued, "do not evince so early and broad a system of wickedness as this writer[655] supposes (the truth of which in *all* its extent the speaker is not prepared to support), yet they indicate a real and most alarming plan of hostility against the dearest interests of man."[656]

The question of the general credibility of the claims which Robison had made, as well as the implication of the Masons in the "conspiracy," came in for special consideration by Tappan when his sermon was prepared for publication.[657] Concerning the former, the observation is made that the ridicule and incredulity which have opposed themselves to the report of a scheme so novel, extravagant, and diabolical, were to have been expected. At any rate, much of the opposition has come from men whose wishes and opinions have been offended, or from those who have shown themselves to be ardent friends of political and religious innovation. And with regard to the Masons, it is urged that the displeasure which certain worthy members of that fraternity have expressed against Robison ought not to be permitted to become so violent as to render impossible a candid and thorough examination of the proofs he has submitted. Robison's *opinion* respecting the universal frivolity or mischievous tendency of the assemblies of the European Masons may be incorrect and injurious, and at the same time the leading facts upon which he founds that opinion may be true. To manifest a willingness to investigate with candor the proofs that have been presented, while continuing to hold in esteem "the approved characters of the principal Masons in this country, especially in the Eastern States," this, Tappan advises, represents the middle course that his readers should attempt to steer.[658]

Thus it will appear that Tappan became an echo of Morse. As for Timothy Dwight, the contribution he made to the awakening of public interest in the subject of Illuminism requires somewhat stronger statement. In the person of the president of Yale this new idea of a definite and deep-laid conspiracy against religion and civil government encountered a highly sensitized mind. Upon the subjects of infidelity and the general irreligious tendencies of the times, Dwight had been speaking frequently and for years from his lecture-desk in the classroom and from his pulpit in the church. It is safe to say that among all the men of New England no man's spirit was more persistently haunted by the fear that the forces of irreligion were in league to work general ruin to the institutions of society than his. When, therefore, on the occasion of the Fourth of July, 1798, the people of New Haven assembled to do honor to the day in listening to a sermon by the honored president of their college, it was to be expected that if the latter had any new information to impart or any new pronouncement to make respecting malign efforts that were making to plunge the world into irremediable scepticism and anarchy, he would seize the occasion that the day offered to arouse in his hearers a sense of the new perils which threatened. And President Dwight *had* new information and a new pronouncement to offer.

The subject which he chose to discuss on that Independence Day, and the text upon the elucidation of which he relied for the illumination of the subject, were in themselves calculated to excite concern. These were respectively, THE DUTY OF AMERICANS AT THE PRESENT CRISIS, and "Behold I come as a thief: Blessed is he that watcheth, and keepeth his garments, lest he walk naked, and they see his shame." (Revelation xvi: 16.)[659] Having first explained the setting of the text, President Dwight then proceeded to define the thesis of his sermon in the following manner: "From this explanation it is manifest that the prediction consists of two great and distinct parts: *the preparation for the overthrow of the Antichristian empire; and the embarkation of men in a professed and unusual opposition to God, and to his kingdom, accomplished by means of false doctrines, and impious teachers.*"[660]

The first of these predictions, it was asserted, had been fulfilled in the repressive and secularizing measures that during the century had operated to weaken greatly the Catholic hierarchy and its chief political supports among the states of Europe.[661] The second was experiencing a fulfilment not less remarkable in the open and professed war against God and his kingdom, in which Voltaire, Frederick II, the Encyclopedists, and the Societies of the Illuminati had confederated.[662]

This systematical design to destroy Christianity, which Voltaire and his accomplices formed, found its first expressions in the compilation of the *Encyclopédie*, the formation of a new sect of philosophers to engineer the assaults upon the church, the prostitution of the French Academy to the purposes of this sect, and the dissemination of infidel books and other publications, all of which were so prepared "as to catch the feelings, and steal upon the approbation, of every class of men."[663] Eventually the labors of this group of men and their disciples were widened so as to include not only religion but morality and civil government as well, with the object in view of unhinging "gradually the minds of men, and destroying their reverence for everything heretofore esteemed sacred."[664]

Simultaneously the Masonic Societies of France and Germany had been drawn away from the pursuit of the objects of friendly and convivial intercourse for which they were originally instituted, to the employment of their secret assemblies in the discussion of "every novel, licentious, and alarming opinion"[665] that innovators and other restless spirits might choose to advance. Thus,

Minds already tinged with philosophism were here speedily blackened with a deep and deadly die; and those which came fresh and innocent to the scene of contamination became early and irremediably corrupted…. In these hot beds were sown the seeds of that astonishing Revolution, and all its dreadful appendages, which now spreads dismay and horror throughout half the globe.[666]

The Society of the Illuminati, springing up at this time and professing itself to be a higher order of Freemasonry, availed itself of the secrecy, solemnity, and mysticism of Masonry, of its system of correspondence, to teach and propagate doctrines calculated to undermine and destroy all human happiness and virtue. Thus God's being was derided, while government was pronounced a curse, civil society an apostasy of the race, the possession of private property a robbery, chastity and natural affection groundless prejudices, and adultery, assassination, poisoning and other infernal crimes not only lawful but even virtuous.[667] To crown all, the principle that the end justifies the means was made to define the sphere of action for the members of the order.

The triumphs of this system of falsehood and horror, Dwight continued, have already been momentous. In Germany "the public faith and morals have been unhinged; and the political and religious affairs of that empire have assumed an aspect which forebodes its total ruin."[668] In France the affairs of the people have been controlled by the representatives of this hellish society. Not only this, but by means of the establishment of the order in those countries which France has opposed, the French government has been able to triumph in its military campaigns and to overthrow religion and governments in the countries which have been attacked. Neither England nor Scotland have escaped the foul contagion; and private papers of the order, seized in Germany, testify to the fact that several such societies had been erected in America prior to the year 1786.[669]

When the preacher passed to the head of *improvement*, it was therefore natural that he should prescribe as one of the "duties" that especially needed to be observed, the breaking off all connection with such enemies as had been mentioned. The language in which this particular duty was enforced certainly did not lack boldness and vigor.

The sins of these enemies of Christ, and Christians, are of numbers and degrees which mock account and description. All that the malice and atheism of the Dragon, the cruelty and rapacity of the Beast, and the fraud and deceit of the false Prophet, can generate or accomplish, swell the list. No personal or national interest of man has been uninvaded; no impious sentiment, or action, against God has been spared; no malignant hostility against Christ, and his religion, has been unattempted. Justice, truth, kindness, piety, and moral obligation universally have been, not merely trodden under foot, ... but ridiculed, spurned, and insulted, as the childish bugbears of drivelling idiocy. Chastity and decency have been alike turned out of doors; and shame and pollution called out of their dens to the hall of distinction and the chair of state.... For what end shall we be connected with men of whom this is the character and conduct? Is it that we may assume the same character, and pursue the same conduct? Is it that our churches may become temples of reason, our Sabbath a decade, and our psalms of praise Marsellois [*sic*] hymns? ... Is it that we may see the Bible cast into a bonfire, the vessels of the sacramental supper borne by an ass in public procession, and our children, either wheedled or terrified, uniting in the mob, chanting mockeries against God, and hailing in the sounds of *Ca ira* the ruin of their religion, and the loss of their souls? ... Shall we, my brethren, become partakers of these sins? Shall we introduce them into our government, our schools, our families? Shall our sons become the disciples of Voltaire, and the dragoons of Marat; or our daughters the concubines of the Illuminati?[670]

With equally fiery speech, all doubting Thomases are urged to

... look for conviction to Belgium; sunk into the dust of insignificance and meanness, plundered, insulted, forgotten, never to rise more. See Batavia wallowing in the same dust; the butt of fraud, rapacity, and derision, struggling in the last stages of life, and searching anxiously to find a quiet grave. See Venice sold in the shambles, and made the small change of a political bargain. Turn your eyes to Switzerland, and behold its happiness and its hopes, cut off at a single stroke, happiness erected with the labour and the wisdom of three centuries; hopes that not long since hailed the blessings of centuries yet to come. What have they spread but crimes and miseries; where have they trodden but to waste, to pollute, and to destroy?[671]

From these excerpts and this extended survey of President Dwight's sermon it will readily appear that his espousal of the notion that the Illuminati were immediately responsible for the riotous overturnings and bitter woes of the age was as unequivocal as it was vigorous. To this view of things he boldly committed himself, and that on a great national anniversary occasion when public interest was bound to be peculiarly alert. Moreover, the crisis through which his country was passing had seemed to him to require that his countrymen should especially be put on their guard respecting this new peril which threatened. Though he had been silent respecting personal observations and evidence of his own bearing on the operations of this infamous organization in the United States, nevertheless he had given his hearers to understand that he accepted at its face value Robison's statement regarding the existence of the Order of the Illuminati in this country. Here, then, was a man high in the councils of the church,[672] of education, and the state, lending the full weight of his personality and his office to this fresh and startling explanation of the true cause of the agitations and disorders of the day.[673] The undoubted effect was to give more solid standing to the sensational charge that Jedediah Morse had made.

But preachers were not the only public characters who early caught up and echoed the new alarm. Orators, too, lent the aid of their voices in an effort to persuade the people that their liberties and institutions were in danger of a deadly thrust from this new quarter. A number of these, on the Fourth of July just referred to, delivered themselves of sentiments similar to those which President Dwight expressed. Thus at Sharon, Connecticut, the orator of the day, a certain John C. Smith, supplied a new thrill to his patriotic address by informing his hearers that the French Revolution was the result

chiefly of *a combination long since founded in Europe, by Infidels and Atheists, to root out and effectually destroy Religion and Civil Government,*—not this or that creed of religion,—not this or that form of government,—in this or that particular country,—but all religion,—all government,—and that through the world.[674]

At Hartford, Theodore Dwight, brother to Yale's president, publicly averred it was a fact well ascertained that the French Revolution "was planned by a set of men whose avowed object was the overthrow of Altars and Thrones, that is, the destruction of all Religion and Government."[675] At the midnight orgies of the "modern Illuminati" the plan had been conceived and nourished. For six years past, the orator declared, the government of France has been directed by men who have been schooled in that society of demons.[676] In the same city, and on the same occasion, another voice was raised to declaim against the reckless impiety of French partisans in the United States.[677] These conspiring men, so this orator somewhat vaguely declared, are said to have substituted the wild dogmas of infidel philosophy for the benevolent principles of Christianity. They have adopted "a philosophy originating in wickedness, founded in error, and subversive of the peace and happiness of society."[678]

From this early handling of the subject by clergymen and orators, we are now called away to consider a significant exposition of the matter in the columns of a Boston newspaper. To the issue of the *Massachusetts Mercury* of July 27, 1798, "Censor" contributed an article that was destined to have important bearings on the course of public discussion. Professing a spirit of reasonable moderation, "Censor" offered the practical suggestion that the time had come to inquire what evidence Professor Robison possessed respecting the authenticity of his sources. "At this distance," he urged, "it is impossible to decide on the truth of his assertions, or the respectability of his testimonies." Yet the writer had had his attention drawn to certain evidences of prejudice, misrepresentation, and unrestrained imagination on the part of Robison which tended to destroy confidence in his judgment. Dr. Morse, too, he continued, on the unsupported assertion of an individual three thousand miles distant, to the effect that several lodges of the Illuminati had been established in America prior to '86, in his fast sermon had seen fit to declare that the Illuminati were here, that they had made considerable progress among us, and that to them were to be traced the torrent of irreligion and the abuse of everything good and praiseworthy which threatens to overwhelm the world. For all these assertions, "Censor" inquired, where were the evidences?[679]

The tone of "Censor's" article was decidedly hostile. The spirit of cynicism and distrust had lifted its head, not apologetically but boldly. The evidence in the case was called for. To Jedediah Morse, original and chief sponsor for the outcry against the Illuminati, it must have seemed clear that the obligation of meeting the issue thus joined rested squarely upon his own shoulders. Nor was he minded to evade responsibility. And thus it happened that the columns of the *Massachusetts Mercury*, for some weeks to come,[680] carried a succession of articles over Morse's signature, all laboring to prove that the judgment their author had passed upon Robison's volume had not been hasty, but was well grounded in reason. To these articles, rambling and inconclusive as they were, we must now devote attention.

Expressing first his gratitude that Professor Robison's *Proofs of a Conspiracy* had attracted the attention of so large and respectable a portion of the community, Morse thereupon professed surprise that his own commendation of that work in his late fast day sermon should have exposed him to the necessity of vindicating both the author of the *Proofs* and his own composition.[681] He had assumed that every reader of Robison's production would be impressed as he had been with the evidence of the author's talents, views, candor, and integrity. The sensitiveness and irritation which members of the Masonic fraternity had shown had also astonished him. His hope had been that the notes by which his published fast day sermon had been accompanied would forestall censure from that quarter. However the necessity to vindicate Professor Robison and his book had been imposed upon him, and that he would proceed to do. He would first introduce extracts from his fast day sermon to show that he had recommended Robison's book, not because of any observations unfavorable to the Masons which it contained, but for the sole reason that it exposed the dark conspiracies of the Illuminati against civil government and Christianity.[682]

The vindication of Professor Robison's character and reputation as a man and writer was next undertaken. These points Morse considered to be fully established by the positions that Robison occupied as Secretary of the Royal Society of Edinburgh and Professor of Natural Philosophy in one of the best universities of the world. If further proof should be required, the contributions that Robison had made to the *Encyclopædia Britannica* certainly vouched for his respectability and prominence. Beyond this Morse could go no further than to add that private advices which had come to him from one of his foreign correspondents, the Reverend Dr. Erskine, of Edinburgh, fully confirmed the reputation of the Scotch professor.[683]

But since it was likely to be remarked in this instance that "great men are not always wise," Morse proposed to deal next with the marks of the book's credibility. As to *external* marks, the approbation and support of the book by very respectable men in England and Scotland, and its approval and recommendation by clergymen and laymen of discernment and ability in America, he argued, were to be weighed as impressive considerations.[684] If by way of rejoinder it should be urged that the English reviewers were not of one mind respecting the merits of the book, then his reply would be that having read on both sides of the controversy that had been waged in the English journals, he had been forced to the conclusion that "the balance of *candor* and *truth* are [*sic*] clearly on the side of those who are in favor of Professor Robison, and give credit to his work."[685]

Respecting the favorable reception which the book had been accorded in America, he was glad to be privileged to point to the sentiments of Professor Tappan,[686]President Dwight,[687] and Theodore Dwight, Esq.[688] It is true that in America the book had excited warm, even virulent opposition; but certainly it had received respectable support, "such as ought to exempt any person from the charge of *weakness* or *credulity* who believes it authentic."[689]

An effort to marshal the *internal* evidence of the book's credibility is next promised by Morse.[690] This anticipation remained a promise, however, for the disingenuous reason that Morse offered that a book which has met such a flattering reception as Robison's *Proofs* absolves its friends and supporters of the necessity of defending its contents as well as the authenticity of the documents from which it has been drawn. The burden of proof rests upon those who have nothing to offer against the work in question but bold assertions, contemptuous sneers, and vilifying epithets.[691] Professor Robison's critics have failed to take sufficient account of the fact that he was engaged in a delicate and arduous undertaking. He was attempting to unveil a deep and dark conspiracy.[692] It is not pretended that all the links in the chain of evidence have been discovered; nor is it claimed that there has been an entire absence of confusion, disconnection, and imperfection in the work of ferreting out the conspiracy. But certainly enough has been accomplished to merit confidence in the effort, and to justify serious alarm on the part of the friends of the civil and religious interests of the country.[693]

This, it need scarcely be said, did not amount to a satisfactory handling of the case. In truth, from the standpoint of the main issue involved, *viz.*, the reliability of Robison's "proofs," it was little more than so much dust thrown into the air. Evidence had been asked for. In its place arguments, and it must be confessed very inconclusive arguments at that, were submitted. The vital questions in the case had scarcely been touched. Were the Illuminati still in existence? If so, did they actually aim at the universal overthrow of religion and civil government? Was the French Revolution the result of their machinations? More momentous still to the interests of Americans, had the net of conspiracy been thrown over this country, with the result that nefarious secret organizations were at work among her people, corrupting them and plotting the downfall of their institutions? No definite, independent word had yet been spoken in America in answer to these questions. Thus far the issue was joined over the merits or demerits of a *book*,[694]—a book that had recently come across the Atlantic and whose readers in America, according as they were credulous or incredulous, boldly asserted or as vehemently denied that the questions which have just been propounded should be answered in the affirmative.

Thus matters stood in the early fall of 1798. The newspapers generally had begun to take hold of the subject, and the volume of public discussion steadily increased. But as to progress in the clarifying of the fundamental questions at issue, no advance was made. No additional facts were forthcoming; no new light was shed. The alarm that Morse and his allies had raised may be said to have been something like a ship which has been able to make its way out as far as the harbor mouth, but lingers there becalmed, waiting for a favoring gale to speed it on its way. Or was it that the winds were ample, but wholly unfavorable? In the late summer and the fall of 1798 practically every other public interest in New England was eclipsed by two surpassingly important concerns: the bitter agitation over the Alien and Sedition Acts, and the distress and terror of the people over the ravages of an epidemic of yellow fever which was sweeping the towns and cities of the Atlantic seaboard, extending well up along the New England coast.

2. INCONCLUSIVE DEVELOPMENTS OF MORSE'S SECOND FORMAL DELIVERANCE

With the approach of the anniversary thanksgiving in Massachusetts, late in November, 1798, public discussion of the Illuminati broke out afresh. Once more the columns of the *Massachusetts Mercury* became the chief medium of communication. Stirred, it appears, by the announcement from abroad that the first three volumes of the Abbé Barruel's

Memoirs of Jacobinism had been translated into English, a contributor to the *Mercury* took occasion to comment at length on the marvelous corroboratory evidence which that work was about to supply to the English reading public with respect to the great and terrible conspiracy which Professor Robison had laid bare.[695]

This advance commendation of Barruel's composition was not destined to be received with unanimous approval. "A Friend to Truth" was unable to restrain the impulse to exclaim:

The paper signed "A Customer" could find but one man contemptible enough to write it. It has his ignominy and his guilt…. No excuse can be made for the late publication. If Barruel's work be not yet in America, why not wait till it comes? … The public are cautioned against all anonymous defamers, from whom our Country has suffered its greatest evils.[696]

Time and space were claimed by this writer to call attention also to alleged discrepancies of a serious nature between Robison's account of the rise of the Illuminati and its early relations with Freemasonry and the account of the same matters by Barruel, as reflected in English reviews of the latter's work. Quite incidentally "A Friend to Truth" threw out the suggestion that Robison was not always in command of his reason.[697]

Such an indecisive passage at arms obviously called for further hostilities. The aspersion upon Robison's sanity must immediately be branded as infamous, and the charge that Barruel had contradicted Robison boldly pronounced a lie.[698] "Trepidus" felt drawn to enter the combat at this juncture, with satire as his principal weapon. He knew of nothing so amazing and so wonderful as the discoveries which Mr. Robison and his commentators had made respecting the achievements of the Illuminati in America.[699] Surely there was nothing half so dreadful about the Catalinarian conspiracy, the Sicilian Vespers, the massacre of St. Bartholomew, or the Gunpowder Plot. But he, too, had a mysterious cabal to expose. The people who were vulgarly called "Quakers," but who had assumed the suspicious name of "Friends," were they not conspirators?

The Illuminati esteem all ecclesiastical establishments profane, irreligious, and tyrannical; so do the Quakers. They hold also the obligations of brotherly love and universal benevolence. The Quakers not only profess these Atheistical principles, but actually reduce them to practice. The Illuminati hold the enormous doctrine of the Equality of mankind. So do these Quakers. They, like the Illuminati, have a general correspondence through all their meetings, delegates constantly moving, and one day, at every quarterly meeting, set apart for *private business*; and I engage to prove at the bar of any tribunal in the United States, that these Friends, these men so horribly distinguished for benevolence and philanthropy, (Ah! philanthropy!) have held, and do still hold a constant correspondence with their nefarious accomplices in Europe.... *Awake, arise, or be forever fallen!* [700]

These, however, were the sentiments of mere scribblers. Such were able to handle the subject seriously or lightly according as their sympathies or their prejudices were most appealed to. It was evident that in either case such men charged themselves with no personal responsibility to get at the precise facts. What was needed was the testimony and counsel of one who, recognizing the gravity of the interests involved and having accumulated and weighed the evidence, should be able to speak the language of enlightened conviction, backed by the force of a position among his fellow citizens which would entitle his words to respect. An attempt to meet that need was about to be made, how successfully we shall soon be in a position to judge.

On the day of the anniversary thanksgiving referred to in the beginning of this chapter, the Reverend Jedediah Morse was again before his people in his Charlestown pulpit, to speak to them under the inspiration of another high occasion in the commonwealth's life. Of what would he speak? The day had, of course, its own definite suggestions. Governor Increase Sumner, in appointing it, apparently had felt that Massachusetts' measure of providential mercies had been well filled.[701] The earth had yielded a sufficient supply for the wants of the people, and the efforts of industrious husbandmen had been well rewarded. The state's fisheries had been prospered, and its commerce, although much interrupted by the violence and rapacity of unreasonable men, had been generally attended with success. Order and tranquillity had continued to reign in the commonwealth, and although a mortal contagious disease had been permitted for a time to afflict the city of Boston, yet Providence had been pleased to set bounds to the progress of the plague, and once more the voice of health and plenty was generally heard. The constitutions of civil government were still enjoyed; the life and usefulness of the nation's chief magistrate had been spared and continued; and despite the past impenitence of the people, they were still indulged with the Christian religion.[702]

Would these considerations engage the thought of the minister of Charlestown and inspire his tongue to speak the language of thanksgiving and praise? Only in part.[703] Morse's mind was occupied, not so much with the thought of mercies bestowed as with that of perils to be faced. Passing lightly over the more favorable and reassuring aspects of the state of public affairs, he seized upon various items in the governor's proclamation to point out those untoward elements in the situation which seemed to him to supply ample warrant for alarm.

The proclamation of the governor had referred to the uninterrupted order and tranquillity of the state. True; this was a mercy with which, under the favor of Providence, the people of Massachusetts had been blessed. Yet, unhappily, serious differences in political and religious opinions had been permitted to exist. Men might call these differences a mere war of words; but words are often calculated to bring on a more serious conflict. Such party zeal and animosities as had been raging would now somewhat abate, let it be hoped, and thus the heat of battle would be found to be past. But undeniably the crisis had been grave.[704]

The "Constitutions of Civil Government" were still enjoyed; but they had been, and still were seriously threatened. The main sources from which such dangers issue deserved to be pointed out. The vices and demoralizing principles of the people generally, their selfish spirit as conspicuously expressed in their insatiable ardor to become rich, the spread of infidel and atheistical principles in all parts of the country, the increase of luxury, extravagance, and dissipation, the spirit of insubordination to civil authority,—these constituted the perils against which the most powerful precautions must be taken.[705] The people of the United States were not sufficiently aroused to a sense of the high importance of the experiment of free government which they were making before the eyes of the world. Unless prompt reformation took place, they must make their choice between a voluntary increase in the power of government on the one hand, and revolution, anarchy, and military despotism on the other.[706]

The real nub of the matter, however, was yet to be considered. "The blessings of good government have been most imminently and immediately endangered by *foreign intrigue*."[707] Enlarging upon this proposition, Morse argued that for twenty years and more foreign intrigue had been the bane of the country's independence, peace, and prosperity. By it, insidious efforts had been made to diminish the nation's limits, its importance, and its resources. By it, national prejudices had been kept alive. By it, efforts had been made to render efficient government impossible.[708] This spirit, which in other nations had brought about their downfall and left them, like the republics of Europe, prostrate at the feet of France,[709] had thus far been thwarted here only by means of the administration of government, wise, firm, dignified, and "supported by the enlightened and ardent patriotism of the people, seasonably manifested, with great unanimity, from all quarters of the Union, in patriotic addresses, in a voluntary tender of military services, and liberal means of naval defence."[710]

As to the country's continued indulgence with the Christian religion,[711] it should be said that this blessing was regularly recognized in the governor's proclamation, and always called for loudest praise. However, at that particular hour there were extraordinary reasons why the praise of citizens should be unusually fervent; for were not those times

... when secret and systematic means have been adopted and pursued, with zeal and activity, by wicked and artful men, in foreign countries, to undermine the foundations of this Religion, and to overthrow its Altars, and thus to deprive the world of its benign influence on society, and believers of their solid consolations and animating hopes; when we know that these impious conspirators and philanthropists have completely effected their purposes in a large portion of Europe, and boast of their means of accomplishing their plan in all parts of Christendom, glory in the certainty of their success, and set opposition at defiance; when we can mark the progress of these enemies of human happiness among ourselves, in the corruption of the principles and morals of our youth; the contempt thrown on Religion, its ordinances and ministers; in the increase and boldness of infidelity, and even of Atheism?[712]

The foregoing abstract takes account of all the important points in the text of Morse's anniversary thanksgiving sermon. The reader will not need instruction as to the commonplace character of Morse's pulpit performance. The distinguishing character of the production, however, is not to be sought in the sermon proper, but in the astonishing array of supplementary material by which it was accompanied when it appeared in its printed form. This material consisted of numerous foot notes and a bulky appendix of some fifty pages. The foot notes frequently commented upon passages in the works of Robison and Barruel. Since they throw no light upon the fundamental questions at issue, we may pass them by. One, however, was unique; and because of its suggestiveness for the future trend of public discussion respecting the Illuminati, it must be cited in full.

The probable existence of Illuminism in this country was asserted in my Fast Discourse of May last. The following fact, related by a very respectable divine, while it confirms what is above asserted, shews that my apprehensions were not without foundation. "In the northern parts of this state [Massachusetts] as I am well informed, there has lately appeared, and still exists under a licentious leader, a company of beings who discard the principles of religion, and the obligations of morality, trample on the bonds of matrimony, the separate rights of property, and the laws of civil society, spend the sabbath in labour and divertion, as fancy dictates; and the nights in riotous excess and promiscuous concubinage, as lust impels. Their number consists of about forty, some of whom are persons of reputable abilities, and once, of decent characters. That a society of this description, which would disgrace the natives of Caffraria, should be formed in this land of civilization and Gospel light, is an evidence that the devil is at this time gone forth, having great influence, as well as great wrath." *Cf.* a Sermon on "the Dangers of the times, especially from a lately discovered Conspiracy against Religion and Government. By Rev. Joseph Lathrop, D. D., of West Springfield."[713]

This foot note speaks for itself. The Appendix, or supplement of Morse's sermon, was made up of a curious mixture of heterogeneous documents, such as an original survey of the history of the United States from the time that the Federal government was established, extracts from the confidential correspondence which passed between French agents in this country and the French government,[714] and extracts from the correspondence of various public characters in the United States, all tending to enforce the point that from the beginning of the relations between our government and that of France, the controlling aim and spirit of the latter had been to work despicable and ruinous intrigue.[715]

All of this, it may be said, was fairly typical of the pabulum which Federalist leaders were regularly serving up to the people in 1798, and signified little or nothing concerning the existence of French conspirators wearing the Illuminati brand who may, or may not, have been at work in America at the time.

One section of the Appendix, however, supplied some evidence of a definite effort to leave generalities and deal intimately with the point at issue. In this section[716]Morse sought to connect the Illuminati with "the Jacobin Clubs instituted by Genet."[717] Like their sister organizations in France they had been constituted after the manner and with the principles of the European Illuminati. The fact that the members of these American organizations have been the leading disseminators of the *principles* of Illuminism in this country, as well as the circulators of all those publications, like Paine's *Age of Reason*, whose object is to discredit and throw contempt upon the Christian religion, clearly fixes their status as "the apostles of Illuminism."[718] Frowned upon by the Federal government, these American organizations have ceased to act openly; "but, like their parent society in Bavaria which, when suppressed under one form, was soon revived again under the name of the German Union,"[719] so their offspring in the United States now hypocritically mask themselves under the name of The American Society of United Irishmen.[720]

Taken by itself, it would be impossible to state how favorably this presentation of the case against Illuminism impressed the public mind.[721] But as a matter of fact, on the occasion of the Massachusetts anniversary thanksgiving referred to, Morse was by no means compelled to bear his testimony alone. By the time that occasion came round, the subject of Illuminism had solicited the attention and concern of the Federalist clergy generally; on which account it happened that a considerable amount of clerical artillery was unlimbered and trained upon the new foe.

At Haverhill, the Reverend Abiel Abbott, in language emphatic, if somewhat high-flown, voiced his alarm:

Upon the authority of a respectable writer in Europe and of corroboratory testimonies, it is now generally believed that the present day is unfolding a design the most extensive, flagitious, and diabolical, that human art and malice have ever invented. Its object is the total destruction of all religion and civil order. If accomplished, the earth can be nothing better than a sink of impurities, a theatre of violence and murder, and a hell of miseries. Its origination was in Germany; its hot-bed now is Paris. Its nursing fathers are the French Government; its apostles are their generals and armies. Its fruits have been seen in France; Christianity expelled; its priesthood seized and murdered, or hunted down in neutral countries and demanded of their hospitable protectors at the peril of war and ruin.—And now, were our first magistrate an Illuminatus, a conspirator in league with the horde in Europe, the grand master of the demoralizers in America, how soon might the American republic have been degraded to the deplorable state of the French?[722]

At Deerfield, the Reverend John Taylor dwelt upon "the good effect ... produced upon the public mind by the fortunate discovery of a secret conspiracy in Europe, against all the religions and governments on earth."[723] One of the evidences of this salutary impression, he said, was to be found in the fact that even the confirmed infidels in America had been shocked.[724] At Andover, the Reverend Jonathan French did not consider his full duty discharged when he had uttered a general warning against men of treachery, slander, and falsehood in the nation, men who have spared no pains in fomenting difficulties and divisions.[725] He believed it to be incumbent upon him to strike out at that "envenomed serpent in the grass," France, whose tools, said he, were here, according to two writers of eminence and credit, Professor Robison and the Abbé Barruel.[726] The works of these two authors, French's hearers were informed, "ought to rouse the attention, awaken the vigilance, and excite the endeavors of every friend to religion, to develop the dark designs, and to guard against the baneful influence of all such dangerous secret machinations."[727] Through the pulpit ministrations of the Reverend Joseph Eckley, auditors at the Old South Church in Boston had their attention drawn to the same topic, although the language employed by this clergyman was somewhat less specific than that which has just been noted.[728]

Other pastors, while refraining from definite reference to the Illuminati, took occasion to exploit the subject of French intrigue, with a view to awakening in their hearers a keen sense of instant alarm. Of such, the efforts of the Reverend Nathan Strong, pastor of the North Presbyterian Church in Hartford,[729] and the Reverend Henry Cumings, pastor of the church in Billerica, deserve mention. Strong contended that foreign influence, if not promptly checked, would work here the same havoc it had wrought in France, *i. e.*, the demoralizing principles of infidelity and political engagements and alliances would chain the people of the United States to "a burning pile";[730] and Cumings developed the idea that the war impending between this country and France possibly amounted to an act of intervention on the part of God to rescue the United States as a brand from the burning.[731] By the breaking out of war a providential check would be put

… to that alarming inundation of impiety and infidelity, which, having overwhelmed a great part of Europe, has lately rolled its swelling waves across the Atlantic … threatening our happy country with an universal devastation of every religious sentiment, moral principle, and rational enjoyment, together with the consequent introduction of that wretched unhallowed philosophy which degrades a man to a level with the beasts that perish,"[732] *etc.*

On the whole, the idea of secret and systematic plottings against the liberties and institutions of the people of the United States was extensively promoted by clerical agency during the autumn and winter of 1798–99. For it is not to be lost sight of that such pulpit utterances as have just been noticed were considerably more than *mere* pulpit pronouncements. Issued from the presses of New England, these sermons were scattered widely through the country[733] and, no doubt, were widely read. Some representatives of the clergy, as we have seen, spoke out with distinctness regarding the Illuminati, asserting that this organization would have to be reckoned with by their fellow citizens. Others committed themselves no farther than to emphasize foreign intrigue of the French stripe, and to characterize it as a vital thrust at the country's peace and prosperity. The total effect was to invite a general airing of the issue which Jedediah Morse had raised in his fast day sermon of May 9, 1798, and to render imperative a sifting of evidence.

The part played by the newspapers is less easily interpreted, since it calls for the survey of a much less solid body of opinion. Some journals adopted an attitude of discreet silence, apparently waiting for the mists which enveloped the subject to clear. Others opened their columns impartially to champions and antagonists, willing to be used to let light in upon a dark and perplexing matter. The policy (the word seems strangely out of place in connection with the average New England newspaper of the period) of several of these journals can best be stated in terms of their own behavior.

The course pursued by the *Columbian Centinel* [734] left nothing to be desired as respects impartiality. As early as August 11, 1798, there appeared in this paper the following sarcastic "epistles":

Epistle from Professor Robison, in Scotland, to Professor Morse, in America:

"*Dear Brother*,
Will you scratch my back?
Yours affectionately,
J. ROBISON."

Another Epistle, from Professor Morse, in America, to Professor Robison, in Scotland:

"*Dear Brother*,
I'll scratch your back, if you will scratch
my elbow.
Yours affectionately,
JED. MORSE."

A few weeks later there appeared in the same paper an article whose author professed that having read "The Cannibals' Progress, the Freemason's illuminati, and some other documents of the French nation," he had been brought round to the conclusion that the depravity of the human race was astounding. He could no longer doubt that the conspiracy against religions and governments was not only deeply laid, but was likewise spreading far and wide. He was convinced that the proofs of its existence in America were to be observed generally throughout the country, "in every society where there is the least prospect of success, in misleading and dividing our citizens."[735] To this another contributor was given opportunity to respond with an expression of sentiments intended to sweep the views of the former aside as inordinately nonsensical and silly.[736]

After the autumn crop of thanksgiving sermons had revived interest in the subject of the Illuminati, the *Centinel* published one article which really shed a modicum of light upon the subject. This consisted of a letter which had originally been received in England from Germany, together with certain observations from the pen of the anonymous contributor who offered it in evidence.[737] The letter bore the signature of one Augustus Böttiger, who identified himself as "Counsellor of the Upper Consistory, and Provost of the College of Weimar."[738] It concerned itself with the amused astonishment with which, according to its author, Professor Robison's *Proofs of a Conspiracy* had been received in Germany, in view of the fact that from 1790 on every interest in the Illuminati had ceased in that country. The Freemasons of Germany, Böttiger asserted, had had absolutely nothing to do with Illuminism from the date mentioned. In the observations which accompanied this letter the information was advanced that in England all public interest in Illuminism had likewise died out, owing to the contemptuous estimate which the people of that country had come to place upon the works of Robison and Barruel.[739]

In the heat which had arisen over the subject of Illuminism it was impossible that this bit of evidence should pass without being sharply challenged. A rough and scurrilous rejoinder to these productions appeared in the *Centinel* of January 19, 1799. Questions were boldly raised concerning the identity of the addressee of the Böttiger letter; how the letter had chanced to find its way to America; where it had been translated; what were the religious and political sentiments of the author; who was the person that penned the remarks by which it had been accompanied in the *Centinel*; how the latter had come into possession of his pretentious stock of information respecting the state of public opinion in England, *et cetera, et cetera*. Neither the writer nor his friends were favorably impressed. "The naked declaration of an unknown paragraphist, probably enough an emigrant illuminatist, will not be sufficient with enlightened Americans to convict Professor Robison or Abbé Barruel of criminality or even of error in their publications."[740]

Another newspaper that sought to hold to a noncommittal course was the *Massachusetts Mercury*, as might have been anticipated in view of circumstances already related. After the generous hearing which this journal, in the summer and fall of 1798, accorded to both sides in the controversy, a marked diminution of its interest for a season is noticeable. A search through its files for the winter of 1798–99 discloses nothing more than an occasional article bearing on the subject. One of these came to light in the issue of December 7.[741] "Anti-Illuminism" solicited the public ear that he might testify to the change that had taken place in his personal convictions. An examination of Robison's volume and reflection upon the amount of abuse which that author had been compelled to suffer had persuaded him that there was positive truth in the charge of conspiracy that had been made. He was now certain that the Masons were not the harmless persons he had formerly believed them to be. The vociferous attempt which had been made to vindicate American Freemasonry impressed him as decidedly premature. It was clear to him that *all* secret societies were dangerous.

It might have been expected that a Democratic sheet as violent and aggressive as the *Independent Chronicle* would range itself squarely against the alarmists, and seek, if not by argument at least by unlicensed vituperation, to distract the public interest. But as a matter of fact, the *Chronicle* elected to adopt a very different attitude.[742] Morse and his associates in the special cause which he and they were pleading should be treated with contemptuous indifference. The *bête noire* of the editors of the *Chronicle* was "political preaching." This new agitation over Illuminism, for which the clergy were chiefly responsible, was but one other proof of their incorrigible impertinence in turning aside from their legitimate functions. In displaying "his over-heated zeal ... in silly tales about the 'illuminati',"[743] Morse was but holding true to type.[744]

At Hartford, next to Boston the main center of the Illuminati agitation in New England, two papers, the *American Mercury* and the *Connecticut Courant*, assisted materially in giving publicity to the controversy. The former at first gave some evidence of a disposition to treat Morse's presentation of the case with respect. Extracts from the latter's fast day sermon of May 9, 1798, were given to this journal's readers;[745] and the annual poem which at the beginning of the new year (1799) it furnished to its patrons, testified to the widespread interest that the general public in Connecticut had come to have in the subject of the Illuminati.[746] It was not long after this, however, that Elisha Babcock, editor of the *Mercury*, found reason to become rabidly hostile to Morse and his agitation.[747]

As for the *Connecticut Courant*, its behavior was precisely what one should expect from a journal breathing always a spirit of arrogant and unreasoning Federalism. Quick to take advantage of any new issue which gave promise of offering discomfiture to the Democrats, and all too often impatient to the point of exasperation over so slight a question as the essential soundness of the facts involved, from the first day that it was made aware of the agitation against the Illuminati, the *Courant* gave every encouragement to the men who were trying to awaken the people of the country to a sense of the gravity of the peril that threatened. The books, pamphlets, sermons, orations, and leading newspaper contributions that appeared upon the subject, these the *Courant* urged upon the attention of its readers, and gave such assistance as it was able in the exposition of their respective merits.[748]

The political possibilities in the situation supplied the chief, if not the only animus for this playing-up of the case by the *Courant*. On this point little room for doubt is left. One contributor who heard Theodore Dwight's Fourth of July oration asserted that not till then had his eyes been opened to see in Mr. Jefferson "anything more than the foe of certain men, who were in possession of places to which he might think himself entitled;" but Dwight convinced him that Jefferson "is the *real Jacobin*, the very child of *modern illumination*, the foe of man, and the enemy of his country."[749] Another argued that the zeal of the Democrats for office was to be treated as a part of the scheme of Illuminatism in America "to worm its votaries into all offices of trust, and importance, that the weapon of government, upon signal given, may be turned against itself."[750] Still another contended that the one concern of the Democrats of Connecticut was to dispense "to the people of this state the *precious doctrines* of the Illuminati."[751]

The contributions to the agitation made by two newspapers that were published outside of New England but which were extensively circulated and much quoted in that region, are entitled to consideration at this point. These were *Porcupine's Gazette* and the *Aurora General Advertiser*, both Philadelphia publications and, it may be remarked in passing, both tremendously influential throughout the entire country.

William Cobbett, the editor of the former, participated in the publication of the first American edition of Robison's *Proofs of a Conspiracy*. As soon as the book was ready for distribution he announced the fact in his paper, accompanying the advertisement with flattering testimonials gleaned from the *London Review*.[752] Later, he gave to his readers his personal estimate of the merits of Robison's production.[753] In his judgment the *Proofs* was of such great value that it deserved to be read by every living man. For one thing, "it unravels everything that appears mysterious in the progress of the French Revolution."[754]

In the issue of *Porcupine's Gazette* for August 9, 1798, Cobbett expressed his deep interest in the reports which had come to him respecting Morse's fast day sermon and the "Vindication" with which, he understood, Morse had followed his sermon. He would be grateful to any gentleman who would send him a copy of the "Vindication," since there could be no doubt as to its great public utility. Very promptly his desire was gratified, and Morse's articles in vindication of Robison, which in the summer of that year he contributed to the *Massachusetts Mercury*, began to be spread before the readers of *Porcupine's Gazette*.[755]

Following their publication, other matters appear to have held the restless attention of Cobbett for a time and no further reference of an extended character to the affairs of the Illuminati appeared in this paper until February of the following year.

Upon the receipt of a copy of Morse's thanksgiving sermon, Cobbett communicated to his readers the joy he experienced in being able to put them in possession of extracts from it.[756] Morse's sermon, in his judgment, was an extraordinary performance. Of its Appendix he wrote:

"This Appendix is one of the most valuable political tracts that ever appeared in Amcrica, whether we view it as a collection of facts, or as an address to the reason and feelings of the people."[757] Of the sermon as a whole he wrote:

It has gone through two editions, and a third is about to be commenced. Doctor Morse has long been regarded as a benefactor to his country; but notwithstanding his former labours have been of great utility, this last work, I have no hesitation to say, surpasses them all in this respect; and it must, if there be any such thing as *national gratitude* in America, render the author the object of universal esteem. He has brought to light facts which people in general never before dreamed of, and however deaf the middle and southern states may be to his warning voice, New-England will listen to it.[758]

This was very strong language, providing the personality of William Cobbett is left out of account! How soothingly it fell upon the ears of a certain clergyman in New England, which ears, it may be remarked, were growing accustomed to much less kindly comment, we may leave to conjecture.

As for Benjamin Franklin Bache, the editor of the *Aurora* [759] and as militant an advocate of Democratic principles as this country contained, all such views of the case were so much puerile *fol de rol*. Robison's *Proofs* was a blending of "a most absurd collection of stories respecting the mystical societies in Germany with some fragments of histories of French Free Masonry, ... [an] inconsistent Farrago."[760] Weak indeed must be the cause of despotism "when its Satellites can imagine a dissemination of such contemptible mummery would calumniate the friends of Liberty or paralize their efforts to explore the *divinity of kings*, or the *dogma of priests*."[761] The explanation of Morse's faith in Robison's book is to be sought in the fact that the minister of Charlestown received his doctor's degree from the University of Glasgow; and therefore on the principle, "Tickle me and I'll scratch you," the Glasgow professor's production was entitled to credit.[762]

3. MORSE SUBMITS HIS INEPT DOCUMENTARY EVIDENCE

The national skies had by no means cleared of threatening clouds when, in the early spring of 1799, the time arrived for President Adams to issue his annual fast day proclamation. In the view of the nations chief executive the questions of the hour were still of great urgency and it was a season of imminent danger.[763] Accordingly, in appointing Thursday, April 25, as the day for the people of the nation to perform acts of solemn humiliation, fasting and prayer, he justified in part the issuance of the proclamation on the following grounds:

The most precious interests of the people of the United States are still held in jeopardy by the hostile designs and insidious acts of a foreign nation, as well as by the dissemination among them of those principles, subversive of the foundations of all religious, moral, and social obligations, that have produced incalculable mischief and misery in other countries.[764]

Seldom, if ever, has a presidential proclamation breathed deeper concern for the moral and religious interests of the people.[765] Its challenge to citizens who were already of fearful heart was unmistakable.

To the observance of this fast day the Reverend Jedediah Morse must have turned in no ordinary frame of mind. A spirit of exultation possessed him. It is impossible to read the sermon which on that occasion he delivered before his people in the Charlestown meeting house and avoid the impression that to Morse personally the day had been anticipated as one of triumph rather than of humiliation.[766] Not that in any sense he was out of sympathy with the objects for which the day had been set apart, or with the President's extremely solemn language in proclaiming the fast; but it was given him, as he believed, to make before his people a pronouncement of such a startling and convincing character as would perform for the country at large that great and needed service which for months he had been eager to accomplish. Incidentally, the scoffers who had sought to cry down the alarm which a year before he had sounded should be put to rout. Timid apologists for the outcry against the Illuminati were about to see their case tremendously strengthened. Honest doubters, by the overwhelming weight of the evidence which was about to be spread before them, would be forced to acknowledge the folly of their distrust.

The text that Morse employed for the occasion directly echoed a sentiment in the President's proclamation, and besides was well suited to the purpose in view. From the Hebrew Psalms he selected the following passage: "If the foundations be destroyed, what can the righteous do?"—Psalm xi:3. With this text he proposed to make an effective appeal. The Psalm from which it was taken was composed by David while he was in great peril and distress from the persecuting hand of Saul; while, too, he was hard pressed to find a way of escape out of the destructive snares set by his enemies, whose *secret* machinations involved both his character and his life, and not only this, but the *foundations* of his country.[767] What word would better fit the circumstances of the present hour? Have not the enemies of David, of Christ his Antitype, and of the Church ... ever possessed similar *dispositions*, ... had in view similar *designs*, and in like circumstances, ... adopted and pursued the same means of gratifying the *former*, and of accomplishing the *latter*?"[768] Might it not be said that "the present situation is uncommonly critical and perilous?" Do not all persons of reflection agree upon that judgment, even though their opinions regarding the sources and degrees of the dangers may vary greatly?[769]

The "foundations" alluded to in the text were, of course, the foundations of religion and government.[770] This exegesis paved the way for the following statement:

With all the frankness and plainness becoming an honest and faithful watchman, I intend, my brethren, to lay before you what I humbly conceive to be our real and most alarming dangers; those which have a malign aspect, both on our religious and our political welfare. Believing, as I firmly do, that the foundations of all our *most precious interests* are formidably assailed, and that the subtil and secret assailants are increasing in number, and are multiplying, varying, and arranging their means of attack, it would be criminal in me to be silent. I am compelled to sound the alarm, and I will do it, so far as God shall enable me, with fidelity.[771]

Having thus prepared the minds of his auditors for the portentous revelation, Morse quickly descended to particulars.

It may as well be said plainly, he continued, that the passage in the President's fast day proclamation respecting the hostile designs, insidious arts, and demoralizing principles of a certain foreign nation, referred to France.[772] Did any one ask for proofs that the President's statement was true? The proofs were so abundant and so evident that the difficulty was to know where to begin. The war upon the defenceless commerce of the United States; the inhuman and savage treatment of those citizens of this country who have been so unfortunate as to fall into the hands of France's minions by whom they have been so grossly insulted, beaten, wounded and thrust into loathsome prisons and dungeons, even murdered; the recent plot of the

French Directory to invade the southern states from St. Domingo, using an army of blacks to effect an invasion, and by these attempting to excite to insurrection the blacks of this country;[773] here, surely, were ample proofs of the hostile and detestable designs of the French government against our own.[774]

But there was another matter. The disclosure that had recently been made regarding the secret machinations of the French on the Island of St. Domingo, focused attention upon a matter of the most serious moment. The most vigorous, active, and united measures must immediately be adopted to arouse from their slumber the citizens of this country, that they may give due attention to a particular aspect of the insidious and seductive activities of the French in the United States, of which, Morse averred, he stood prepared to speak with the utmost definiteness.[775] Continuing:

It has long been suspected that secret societies, under the influence and direction of France, holding principles subversive of our religion and government, existed somewhere in this country. This suspicion was cautiously suggested from this desk, on the day of the late National Fast, with the view to excite a just alarm, and to put you on your guard against their secret artifices. Evidence that this suspicion was well founded has since been accumulating, and I have now in my possession complete and indubitable proof that such societies do exist, and have for many years existed, in the United States. I have, my brethren, an official, authenticated list of the names, ages, places of nativity, professions, &c. of the officers and members of a Society of *Illuminati* (or as they are now more generally and properly styled *Illuminees*) consisting of *one hundred* members, instituted in Virginia, by the *Grand Orient* of FRANCE. This society has a deputy, whose name is on the list, who resides at the Mother Society in France, to communicate from thence all needful information and instruction. The date of their institution is 1786, before which period, it appears from the private papers of the European Societies already published, (according to Professor Robison), that several societies had been established in America. The seal and motto of this society correspond with their detestable principles and designs. The members are chiefly Emigrants from France and St. Domingo, with the addition of a few Americans, and some from almost all the nations of Europe. A letter which enclosed this list, an authentic copy of which I also possess, contains evidence of a society of like nature, and probably of more ancient date, at *New-York*, out of which have sprung *fourteen* others, scattered we know not where over the United States. Two societies of the same kind, but of an inferior order, have been instituted by the society first mentioned, one in Virginia, the other at St. Domingo. How many of equal rank they have established among us I am not informed.

You will perceive, my brethren, from this concise statement of facts, that we have in truth secret enemies, not a few scattered through our country; how many and, except in three or four instances, in what places we know not; enemies whose professed design is to subvert and overturn our holy religion and our free and excellent government. And the pernicious fruits of their insidious and secret efforts, must be visible to every eye not obstinately closed or blinded by prejudice. Among these fruits may be reckoned our unhappy and threatening political divisions; the increasing abuse of our wise and faithful rulers; the virulent opposition to some of the laws of our country, and the measures of the Supreme Executive; the Pennsylvania insurrection; the industrious circulation of baneful and corrupting books, and the consequent wonderful spread of infidelity, impiety, and immorality; the arts made use of to revive ancient prejudices, and cherish party spirit, by concealing or disguising the truth, and propagating falsehoods; and lastly, the apparent systematic endeavours made to destroy, not only the influence and support, but the official existence of the Clergy.[776]

The remainder of the sermon is void of originality and interest. Its utterances pale into insignificance alongside of the sensational and emphatic statements just recorded.[777]

When the sermon came from the printer's hands it contained the "complete and indubitable proof" that Morse had proudly told his hearers was in his possession. This "proof" was in the form of documents, conspicuous among which was the following letter:

A L'Ot∴ de Portsmouth, En Virginie le 17. du 5e. m. en L'an de la V∴ L∴ 5798∕:

La R∴ L∴ Pte∴ Fse∴ réguliérement constitué sous le titre distinctif de la Sagesse No. 2660, par le G∴

La T∴ R∴ L∴ L'union-française No. 14. constituée par le G∴ Ot∴ de New-York.

S∴ F∴ V∴

TT∴ CC∴ & RR∴ FF∴

La Planche dont vous nous avez favorisés en date du 16e. du 2e. mois de la présénte année Mque∴, ne nous est parvenuë que depuis peu de jours; Elle a été mise sous les yeux de notre R∴ L∴ en sa séance extraordinaire du 14e. du présent.

Nous vous félicitons TT∴ CC∴ FF∴ des nouvelles Constitutions que vous avez obténuës du G∴ Ot∴ de New-York. Nous avons ferons en conséquénce un plaisir & un devoir d'entretenir avec votre R∴ L∴ la correspondence la plus fraternelle, comme avec toutes les LL∴ réguliére qui voudront bien vous favoriser de la leur.

C'est a ce titre que nous croyons devoir vous donner Connoissance de l'éstablissement de deux nouveaux attellieres maçoniques réguliérement constitués et installés au rite français par notre R∴ L∴ provincialle, L'un depuis plus d'un an sous le titre de *L'amitiê* à L'Ot∴ de Petersburg, en Virginie; l'autre, plus récent, sous le titre de la *Parfaite-Egalité* à L'Ot∴ du Port de Paix isle St. Domingue.

Nous vous remettons cy-joint quelques exemplaires de notre Tableau de cette année que notre L∴ vous prie d'agréer en retour de ceux qu'elle a reçu de la votre avec reconnoissance.

Puisse la G∴ A∴ de l'U∴ bénir vos travaux et les couronner de toutes sortes de succés! C'est dans ces sentiments que nous avons la faveur d'être,

P∴ L∴ N∴ M∴ Q∴ V∴ S∴ C∴
TT∴ CC∴ et TT∴ RR∴ FF∴
Votre très affectionés F∴
Par Mandement de la T∴
R∴ L∴ Pte∴ de la Sagesse.

Guieu,
Sécrétaire.[778]

Following this letter and its translation appeared a list of the officers and members, resident and non-resident, of Wisdom Lodge, Portsmouth, Virginia, with explanatory data in each instance, covering such points as age, place of birth, profession, *etc.*, the whole concluding with a representation of the seal of Wisdom Lodge and the following motto: *Amplius Homines oculis quam auribus credunt. Iter longum est per precepta, breve et efficax per exempla.* [779]

Upon these documents Morse saw fit to make and publish certain "Explanatory Remarks,"[780] of which the following is the gist.

The Lodge Wisdom in Portsmouth, Virginia, is seen to be a branch of the *Grand Orient* of France. Its members consist chiefly of foreigners, that is to say, Frenchmen,—Frenchmen who come either from France or from the West India possessions of that country. From the seal it appears that Wisdom Lodge was established as early as 1786. It is also, as its number shows, "the TWO THOUSAND SIX HUNDRED AND SIXTIETH branch from the original stock."[781] It further appears that there is a sister lodge in the city of New York, styled the *Grand Orient* of New York. The latter, from the name and number of the lodges it has instituted, is quite likely the first and principal branch that the Mother Club in France has established in America. This New York lodge has established the French lodge, Union, to which the letter from the lodge Wisdom was addressed. As to the other thirteen branches from the parent stock, for the present there could be nothing more than conjecture as to their location.[782]

The documents also show that an intimate correspondence is maintained between the lodges in America and those in St. Domingo; also between the American lodges and the *Grand Orient* in France. It further appears that Wisdom Lodge has a regular deputy in the membership of the *Grand Orient* of France. Lists of names are exchanged between the two societies, so that their members may be fully known to each other.[783]

Masons to whom these documents issuing from Wisdom Lodge have been shown declare that the organization is not truly Masonic. The titles of its officers, its seal and motto, they affirm, are not regular. Thus the lodge in Portsmouth has been pronounced spurious by well-informed Masons.[784]

Wisdom Lodge, it appears, has one hundred members. Counting all the others referred to in the documents, there are seventeen lodges in all. Assuming that these have an equal number of members, it may be said that there are at least seventeen hundred Illuminati in the United States, all bound together by oath and intimate correspondence.[785] Beyond these there are to be considered, of course, the many thousands of Frenchmen scattered through the United States, all perhaps "combined and organized (with other foreigners and some disaffected and unprincipled Americans) in these societies, ... regularly instructed and directed by their masters in France, and ... systematically conducting the plan of revolutionizing this country."[786]

The principles and objects of this organization may be partly deduced from the motto and seal of Wisdom Lodge. The literal rendering of the former is not so significant as its spirit, which is best expressed in the following liberal translation: "Men more readily believe what they *see* than what they *hear*. They are taught slowly by *precept*, but the effect of *example* is sudden and powerful."[787] From this it may be inferred that the organization was formed, "not for *speculation*, but for activity." Precepts are scorned; actions are accepted as the only quick method of teaching mankind and of producing a change in their opinions. The change in opinions which the organization contemplates must have to do with government and religion. It cannot have to do with the minds of its members, for the society is *secret* and designs to work secretly. "The changes which they can produce by *secret influence and intrigue*, the novel arts which they can thus exhibit before the eyes of men, are doubtless to be the *efficaceous* means of teaching men the new system of philosophy, which sets at defiance, and contemns all old and settled opinions, by which the government of nations and the conduct of individuals have heretofore been directed."[788]

As to the organization's seal, no description can do it justice.[789] A view of its square and compass, pillars, and *skull and cross-bones* best indicates its horrid nature.[790]

Fortified by these documents, and flanked by the testimonies of Robison and Barruel,[791] Morse concluded his presentment in the following energetic manner:

That there are branches and considerably numerous too, of this infernal association in this country we have now full proof. That they hold and propagate similar doctrines and maxims of conduct is abundantly evident from what is passing continually before our eyes. They even boast that their plans are deeply and extensively laid, and cannot be defeated, that success is certain. If then, Americans, we do not speedily take for our motto, *Vigilance, Union and Activity*, and act accordingly, we must expect soon to fall victims to the *arts and the arms* of that nation, "on the title page of whose laws, as well as on its standards, is written the emphatic and descriptive motto
HAVOC AND SPOIL AND RUIN ARE OUR GAIN."[792]

Here, at last, was something reasonably concrete. After a full year, devoted mostly to the reiteration of vague suspicions and generalities, of reckless affirmations and denials, here was something which had the value of a definite point at which a rational investigation of the subject could begin, should any course so practical as this be thought of. The hour for the introduction of something tangible in the way of evidence had fully come, in any event. This was evidenced by the fact that in connection with the celebration of the national fast other clergymen, for the most part, had held back, apparently unwilling to commit themselves further on the subject of the Illuminati until clearer proof should be at hand.[793] This did not signify that public interest in the subject had abated; it was rather in suspense.[794]

With the appearance of Morse's third and last sermon dealing with the Illuminati,[795] the public discussion of the subject became immediately possessed of a new energy. In a letter to Wolcott, bearing date of June 5, 1799, Morse observed to his friend, "I expect that I have disturbed a hornet's nest."[796] There can be no doubt that, diction conceded, this was an apt estimate of the situation. In view of the experiences which were ahead of him, it was well that Morse found his serenity of mind such as to enable him to complete the remark just recorded, by adding, "Happily, I am fearless of their stings."[797]

The breaking-out of a heated newspaper discussion supplied the principal evidence that Morse's fast day sermon of 1799 inaugurated a new stage in the Illuminati agitation.

The *Independent Chronicle*, aware of the fact that something tangible was now before the public, something which might perhaps seriously influence the popular judgment, promptly abandoned its contemptuous and indiscriminative policy[798] and violently assailed Morse for his latest performance. The author of the fast sermon was sharply taken to task for handling the Illuminati matter as he did. If, in his judgment, there was substantial justification for the charges he had made, why then did he not submit the evidence to President Adams, or lay it before some other proper official of the government, instead of retailing "the alarming narrative in a nine-penny sermon?"[799] If it was true that there was a society plotting the overthrow of our government and Morse could throw any light whatever on the persons involved, what sense was there in treating the subject "in so loose a manner as to render it only subservient to a second or third edition of a political fulmination?"[800] Morse could have only political ends in view. His "plot" was another Federalist scheme. He wished to excite jealousies against a certain class of citizens,[801] *i. e.*, the Democrats. Or, was it to be inferred from the way he handled "the trifling story of the Illuminati," that he desired to incense and greatly anger the people of this country against France?[802] This suspicion would seem to be justified by the fact that Morse had preached and published a number of sermons, in all of which he had anathematized the French nation as the authors of the diabolical system of Illuminatism.[803] But whatever were the motives which animated him, his statements were not to be trusted. He had forfeited the right to be taken seriously.[804]

During the two or three months that followed the celebration of the national fast, a copious flood of contributed articles poured through the columns of the *Chronicle*.[805] "A Friend to a Real Clergyman, and an Enemy to Bigotry," "Bunker Hill," "Credulity," "Daniel," *et al.*, all made their offerings to the airing of what the opposition unanimously agreed should be styled "the preposterous documents of Morse." If a friend and supporter of the Charlestown pastor ventured to express his respect for the arguments of that gentleman, he had little to hope for in the face of the withering fire of sarcasm, ridicule, denial, and defiance that the opposition steadily maintained. Thus, for example, when "Senex," an old contributor to the *Chronicle*, made public profession of the fact that Morse's evidence had seriously shaken his earlier distrust of the "Illuminati conspiracy,"[806] "Credulity" hastened to "pooh-pooh" such anxious fears, and to insist that they were unworthy of a sensible man. Morse's declarations on the subject of Illuminism deserved only to be laughed at. They were certainly utterly out of reason.[807]

The *American Mercury* was another newspaper that rallied to the effort to break down any favorable impressions which Morse's latest deliverance upon the subject of Illuminism may have made upon the public mind. The respectfully attentive and receptive attitude of this journal during the earlier stages of the agitation has already been noted.[808] The appearance of the fast day sermon converted this into a spirit of violent antagonism. Morse's latest sermon was pronounced absurd. "His history of the *Lodge of Wisdom* is equally fabulous with his story of the ship Ocean,"[809] was the judgment of Editor Babcock.[810] A few weeks later the *Mercury* gave to its readers an article that had first seen the light in the *Farmer's Weekly Museum*,[811] a New Hampshire publication. How roughly Morse and the documentary proofs which he had recently laid before the public were handled in this article, the following excerpts will suggest:

Every person who had an opportunity of perusing the sermons which have been published by Dr. Morse, within the space of two years past, must be sensible how great have been his efforts and exertions, to sound an alarm amongst the people, and to create in the public mind the highest degree of astonishment.... From the assurance with which the Dr. speaks of his discovery and the great utility which must result from it to mankind, one would imagine that his name would be enrolled among the *worthies* of his day, as the greatest ornament of our country, and the glory of human nature.... He will undoubtedly do more honour to himself and his profession, to return again to his old business, "of writing geography," and not thus attempt to agitate the public mind, with such alarming discoveries of Illuminatism.

For trifles, light as air, are to the suspicious,
Strong as proofs of holy writ.[812]

Meanwhile the supporters of Morse were not idle, although it must be admitted that as far as the press was concerned the amount of sympathy and support that Morse received from that quarter was by no means commensurate to the weight of criticism with which his opponents sought to crush him. Extracts from his recent fast sermon appeared in such papers as the *Massachusetts Mercury* [813] and the *Salem Gazette*;[814] and with characteristic loyalty to every interest which in any way might be able to serve the cause of Federalism, the *Connecticut*

Courant proclaimed its complete satisfaction with Morse's production in the following reckless fashion:

This sermon is worthy the attention of every inhabitant in the United States on every account, as it contains an authentic letter from the Grand Lodge of Illuminated Free Masons in France, to the Grand Lodge of the Illuminated Free Masons in the United States, together with a list of about one hundred members—their names—birthplace—age—places of residence, and occupation. Every person who does not wish to be blind to his own destruction, will undoubtedly furnish himself with this document; since it establishes beyond a doubt the existence of that infernal club in the very heart of our country.[815]

A larger measure of support of Morse and his cause came from the public declaimers, who, on the occasion of the Fourth of July following, regaled their audiences with discursive observations on the state of national affairs. All over New England citizens were solemnly urged to take serious account of the conspiracy that recently had been partially dragged into the light.

At Ridgefield, Connecticut, the declaration was made that America had been caught in the meshes of the net which the Illuminati had attempted to cast over all the nations.[816] At New Haven it was asserted that the societies of Illuminism, having wrought fearful havoc and ruin in Europe, were now known to be extensively engaged in communicating infection and death to the citizens and institutions of this nation.[817] At Hartford the society of the Illuminati and the occult lodges of Freemasonry were represented as having "exhausted the powers of the human mind, in inventing and combining a series of dread mysteries, unhallowed machinations, and disastrous plots," with the dissemination of the principles of Voltaire and his school as the main objective in view.[818] At Boston direct connections were made between the secret affiliated societies which the virtuous frown of Washington drove into their lurking-places and the newly discovered organizations which had just been found to be "busily engaged in sapping the foundations of society, and may ere long spring a mine, which shall blow up our Constitution and Liberties."[819] At Portland, Maine, the unwilling prostitution of the Masonic lodges in Europe to the purposes of the Illuminati was pointed out as amounting to a threat against the institutions of America.[820] At Byfield[821] and Roxbury,[822] Massachusetts, similar warnings were heard.

To a certain extent, the general employment of this anniversary of national independence to arouse the country against the machinations of the Illuminati was due to an event, long anticipated, that had occurred shortly before. Less than a month prior to July 4, 1799, Barruel's *Memoirs of Jacobinism* made its first appearance in New England.[823] The hopes of the supporters of the agitation were immediately raised.

Before the publication of the documents which Morse gave to the world in his fast sermon of 1799, Robison's *Proofs of a Conspiracy* constituted the chief if not the sole resource of the friends of the agitation. Barruel had been appealed to, but only in the form of such scanty excerpts from his writings as percolated to America through the fingers of his English reviewers and, as we have seen, in settings which provided ammunition for both sides in the controversy. Now the hour had come when the supporters of the Illuminati alarm in New England were to be privileged to make a full and free appeal to their second great ally from abroad.[824]

The facts regarding the nature of the reception accorded Barruel's composition in New England are meagre in the extreme. In this very circumstance, one may suppose, is found the best of all evidences that the book failed to fulfil the hopes of its friends. It is true that within seven weeks after the public announcement of the fact that the *Memoirs of Jacobinism* were ready for distribution at Hartford, one of Morse's correspondents at that place was able to assure him that "the facts … in Du Pan, Robison, and Barruel have got into every farm house" in that section of the country.[825] It is also true that in order to insure a wide reading of what were supposed to be the more significant portions of Barruel's voluminous work, an abridgment of it was undertaken and published in the columns of such leading papers as the *Connecticut Courant* [826] and the *Massachusetts Mercury*.[827] Nevertheless, the inference is unavoidable that at the most the cause of the agitators received only a momentary quickening from this quarter. If anything, the very flatness of the reception accorded Barruel's work served to quiet the public mind in New England on the subject of Illuminism. The precious conceit which the supporters of the charge of an American conspiracy of the Illuminati had imported from abroad, *viz.*, that the two "great" European writers on the subject of Illuminism, Robison and Barruel, while working independently had unearthed the same set of facts and arrived at the same conclusion as to their import, fell quickly enough to the ground. Whatever the facts might be regarding the situation in Europe, it speedily became clear that Barruel had no clear and steady light to throw upon the situation in America, and even those who hoped most from the publication of the *Memoirs of Jacobinism* were soon forced to admit that the American reading public had little taste for the prolix romancings of the French abbé.[828]

Early in the fall of 1799 a new twist was given to the controversy. This developed out of an episode that for the time at least seriously embarrassed the personal integrity of Morse, and enveloped the issue generally in such a cloud of pettiness and disagreeable suspicions that the entire subject of Illuminism assumed an unsavory aspect, with the result that the public was all the more easily persuaded to turn to other and more fruitful topics. Compressed as much as the interests of clarity will allow, the facts were as follows.

The *American Mercury* of September 26, 1799, published an article asserting that in his efforts to substantiate his charges against the Illuminati, Morse had addressed a letter of inquiry to Professor Ebeling[829] of Hamburg, Germany, to which the latter made response that Robison's *Proofs of a Conspiracy* had no standing in Europe; that it was regarded there as a farrago of falsehoods, written by its author to obtain bread rather than in the hope that it would be believed.[830] It was further asserted that Ebeling's letter to Morse gave Robison an unsavory character; he was said to have lived too fast for his income, to be in trouble with the civil authorities in his native country, and to have been expelled from a Masonic lodge in Edinburgh on account of unworthy conduct.[831] This being the true state of affairs, why, it was urged, ought not "the terrible subject of illumination" to be dismissed forthwith as a wretched mass of absurdities? Let Morse publish the letter that he had received from Ebeling and the public would express itself quickly enough as to the silliness of the Illuminati conspiracy.[832]

Morse's rejoinder was spirited. He demanded the name of the author of the article in the *Mercury* and vigorously protested that the Ebeling letter referred to was a fabrication.[833] Denied the comfort of immediate attention and satisfaction,[834] he addressed the editor again and with even greater vehemence, insisting that the editor publicly brand the article referred to as "without foundation and a tissue of the most vile and calumnious falsehoods." But for the one consideration that the letter which he had actually received from Professor Ebeling was private, he averred that he stood ready to spread it before the public gaze.[835] As a guarantee of its character, however, he stood prepared to furnish the affidavits of Professors David Tappan and Eliphalet Pearson of Harvard, to whom he had submitted the letter of Ebeling for their inspection, and who were ready to depose that it was in no sense like the letter whose contents had been given to the public by the *American Mercury*.[836]

By the time these noisy verbal hostilities had taken place, the leading newspaper partisans on both sides of the controversy had accepted the responsibility of advising the public regarding the new issue. The *Connecticut Courant* roundly denounced the unprincipled editor of the *American Mercury* for having printed such a monstrous fabrication as its account of the Ebeling-Morse letter,[837] and later, on Morse's behalf, undertook to say that while the communication which Morse had received from Ebeling contained denials of the authenticity of many of the facts alleged in the *Proofs of a Conspiracy*, at the same time it was destitute of even the most distant suggestion of moral or other delinquencies on the part of Robison.[838] The *Columbian Centinel* regarded itself in duty bound to spread before its readers the indignant communication that Morse had sent to the editor of the *American Mercury*, for the reason that it believed Morse had been most shamefully treated in the matter.[839] As for the *Massachusetts Mercury*, one of its contributors felt moved to observe that the account of the Ebeling-Morse letter which the *American Mercury* had published was nothing less than a consummate piece of pure villainy, intended to ruin Mr. Robison's character; certainly no candid American would pay the slightest attention to it until the person who was responsible for the publication came forward and gave the public his name.[840]

On the other side, such rampant Democratic journals as the *Bee* and the *Aurora* came ardently to the support of the *American Mercury* and directed a searching cross-fire against Morse and his friends. Since the days of Salem witchcraft, the former observed, no subject had so much affected the minds of a certain class of people in New England as this pretended Illuminati conspiracy.[841] Because of the way in which preachers, orators, essayists, and newsmongers generally had declaimed upon the subject, a mist had overspread the public mind. Ebeling's letter to Morse, however, had given a fatal blow to the strife. It was now to be expected that the impressions made upon the minds of numerous over-credulous citizens by an insidious and designing set of men would be fully eradicated.[842] To give full force to these observations, the *Bee* published the text of the letter which, it averred, Morse had received from Ebeling.[843] This characterized Robison's *Proofs of a Conspiracy* as ridiculous and filled with statements many of which were faulty and others totally erroneous. Its author had composed the book in the interests of party and with a special animus against all men who asserted the use of reason in the sphere of theology. The authorities to which Robison appealed were declared to be questionable, and Robison's own standing as a historian was pronounced to be such that it was impossible to take his work seriously.[844]

The *Aurora* steered a similar course. Drawing upon the *Bee*, the text of the alleged Ebeling-Morse letter was printed[845] and the accompanying comment made that this effectually disposed of the Illuminati.[846] It was now fully apparent that Morse had seized upon the idea of a conspiracy against religion and the state in order to further selfish and partisan ends. He and Dr. Dwight, who were at the head of the clerical systems in Massachusetts and Connecticut respectively, were exhausting all the means in their power to exalt Federalism and to obtain a religious establishment which would deliver the consciences and purses of the nation into the hands of their party.[847] The rancor that these two men had recently stirred up against the respectable fraternity of Freemasons was due solely to their bigotry.[848]

Meantime a certain shrewd and none too scrupulous Democratic clergyman in Massachusetts was deriving such satisfaction as he could out of Morse's discomfiture and bitter resentment. The letter that the *Bee* and the *Aurora* published as a letter from Ebeling to Morse was in fact a letter from Ebeling to William Bentley,[849]inveterate hater of Morse.[850]

Ebeling, it appears, had written the letters to Bentley and to Morse at about the same time.[851] A little after the receipt of his letter, Bentley had learned from Ebeling that Doctors Pearson, Tappan, and Morse all were inquiring of Ebeling concerning Robison's standing as a historian, and that the Hamburg professor had addressed Morse at length upon the subject.[852] Further, he received clear hints from Ebeling as to the precise nature of the communications to Morse.[853] Bentley, therefore, had substantial reasons for believing that he was in full possession of the information that Ebeling had furnished Morse regarding the subsidence of the Illuminati craze in Europe and the unfavorable opinions of Robison that were entertained on the other side of the Atlantic. It certainly was not to his credit, however, that he should permit a letter which he himself had received from Ebeling to be published as a communication from Ebeling to Morse.[854]

Under the circumstances, Morse was placed in a position of embarrassment and humiliation from which he found it impossible wholly to extricate himself.[855] What is more to the point, the cause which in his misguided zeal he had been promoting was thus made to suffer an irreparable blow. With his personal integrity under grave suspicion and his main European ally held up to public ridicule and scorn, even Morse's obdurate spirit must have foreseen that the collapse of the agitation which he had fostered could not long be deferred. Even without this tumble into the slough of suspicion and contempt, time must soon have brushed aside as groundless the alarm that Morse had sounded. It is not difficult to imagine, however, that time might have found ways less vindictive and scurvy to dispose of the excited clamor of Morse.

Driven to undertake some further effort at self-justification,[856] the belated idea came to Morse to investigate the lodge Wisdom at Portsmouth, Virginia. Accordingly he addressed a letter to Josiah Parker, member of Congress for Virginia, soliciting information from Parker respecting the Portsmouth lodge. Parker responded to the effect that he had lived in Portsmouth until he went to Congress in 1789; that the lodge Wisdom was regarded in that city as a reputable Masonic society, made up of a few worthy people, mostly French; that some of its members were personally known to the writer to be men warmly attached to the cause of the government; that a good many Frenchmen had been admitted to the lodge about the time of the insurrection on the island of St. Domingo, but that the most of these were not now in America; that some of the Frenchmen whose names Morse had incorporated in his fast sermon of April 25, 1799, as members of Wisdom Lodge, were known to Parker to be honest and industrious men; in a word, that he, Parker, considered the lodge in question as entirely harmless as far as fomenting hostility to the institutions of the country was concerned.[857]

The receipt of Parker's letter left Morse without further resource. Promptly he wrote his friend and adviser, Oliver Wolcott, soliciting his counsel as to whether it would be better for him to remain silent and let matters take their course or whether he would better offer to the public such explanations and observations as he could.[858] The nature of Wolcott's counsel is unknown; but Morse, in any event, came to the conclusion that there was no further action he could take in the case, and his advocacy of the idea of an Illuminati conspiracy against religion and the government ceased. Henceforth, the reverberations of the controversy, with a single exception, were to be of the nature of jibes and flings on the part of irritated and disgusted Democrats who adopted the position that the controversy over the Illuminati had been introduced into American politics to serve purely partisan ends.

In 1802, the Reverend Seth Payson,[859] minister of the Congregational church at Rindge, New Hampshire, made an effort to revive the agitation. In a volume[860]characterized by dismal mediocrity Payson fulminated against the public stupor that, he admitted, had taken the place of the sense of alarm that the discovery of the Illuminati conspiracy had originally caused.[861] Payson's book was nothing more than a revamping of the earlier literature, European and American, on the subject. There is no evidence that it made the slightest impression on the country.

4. FREEMASONRY'S EMBARRASSMENT AND PROTEST

Freemasonry in New England, as throughout the United States in general, was very far from being in a favorable condition when the Illuminati controversy broke out. Like every other institution in the country, it had suffered greatly on account of the American Revolution. The membership of its lodges was depleted, and its affairs generally left in a chaotic condition. In the period of reconstruction which followed the Revolution, Masonry experienced the same difficulty in rebuilding its organizations and investing them with a fair degree of importance in the public eye as other social institutions of the times. To no little extent, this was due to internal dissensions and disintegrating tendencies generally. In the main these dissensions developed out of efforts which were made to create grand lodges of native origin, endowed with powers of sovereignty, to take the place in the system of American Masonry that formerly had been accorded to the grand lodges of England and Scotland. The spirit of independence communicated by the revolutionary struggle had to be reckoned with by Masonic leaders in their efforts to give unity and solidity to the system.[862]

But other concerns than those of organization engaged the attention of those who sought the rehabilitation of the institution. In the literature of the times appears more than one stinging reference to the reproach under which Freemasonry rested on account of the low standards of conduct by which the private lives of its members and its assemblies were marked. Coarseness, profligacy, boisterousness, and conviviality, which in the latter case did not stop short of drunken revels, were common indictments brought against the lodges by friend and foe alike.[863] It cannot be doubted that a considerable amount of the kind of rude and unlicensed behavior that displayed itself about many a New England tavern of the period was likewise to be observed in connection with the private and public performances of the craft.

To this must be added another and, from our special point of view, more serious criticism. The spirit of democracy, it should not be forgotten, was working itself out in the common life of the times in manifold ways. The idea of human equality had become the very touchstone of life. New applications of this conception were constantly being made. In such a day it was inevitable that the secret and exclusive character of the assemblies and practices of Freemasonry should make that institution widely suspected. Members of the fraternity were freely accused of supporting an institution that failed to respond to the spirit of the times.[864] As a result of the stir occasioned by Washington's bold denunciation of "self-created societies," in 1794, this charge of dangerous and unjustifiable secrecy became a more powerful weapon in the hands of

Freemasonry's enemies, whose blows were by no means easy to avoid.

That a retrograde movement was on in the ranks of American Masonry at the time the Illuminati controversy broke out is, however, by no means to be inferred. In most particulars, the faults and weaknesses which have been noted represented common faults and weaknesses of the times. On the whole, as the eighteenth century drew to its close, Freemasonry in this country appeared to be slowly working its way up out of the state of disorganization and weakness by which its progress had been retarded during the two decades that followed the Revolutionary War. It was in a day characterized by earnest and worthy striving, though not without its tokens of popular suspicion, that the accusation of an alliance with the odious Illuminati fell as a black shadow across its path.

The response which Massachusetts Masonry made to the aspersions of Robison and his supporters[865] on this side of the ocean was promptly forthcoming. On June 11, 1798, the Grand Lodge of that state drew up an address to President Adams, from which the following generous extract is taken:

Sir:—

Flattery, and a discussion of political opinions, are inconsistent with the principles of this ancient Fraternity; but while we are bound to cultivate benevolence, and extend the arm of charity to our brethren of every clime, we feel the strongest obligations to support the civil authority which protects us. And when the illiberal attacks of a foreign enthusiast, aided by the unfounded prejudices of his followers, are tending to embarrass the public mind with respect to the real views of our society, we think it our duty to join in full concert with our fellow-citizens, in expressing gratitude to the Supreme Architect of the Universe, for endowing you with the wisdom, patriotic firmness and integrity, which has characterized your public conduct.

While the Independence of our country and the operation of just and equal laws have contributed to enlarge the sphere of social happiness, we rejoice that our Masonic brethren, throughout the United States, have discovered by their conduct a zeal to promote the public welfare, and that many of them have been conspicuous for their talents and unwearied exertions. Among these your venerable successor is the most illustrious example; and the memory of our beloved Warren,[866] who from the chair of this Grand Lodge, has often urged the members to the exercise of patriotism and philanthropy, and who sealed his principles with his blood; shall ever animate us to a laudable imitation of his virtues.[867]

In addition to this formal action taken by the Grand Lodge, prominent Massachusetts Masons began at once to employ such public occasions as the calendar and special events of the order supplied, to refute the charge that Masonry was in league with Illuminism. Preëminent among these apologists were the Reverend William Bentley and the Reverend Thaddeus Mason Harris.[868]

On the occasion of the Masonic festival of St. John the Baptist, June 25, 1798, Bentley delivered a charge before Morning Star Lodge, at Worcester, Massachusetts.[869] The clergy, he maintained,—not all the clergy, to be sure, but particularly those representatives of the clergy "who ply the shuttle-cock of faith, with the dexterity of expert gamesters, and have the art of making the multitude fly with its feathers,"—are responsible for this new out-cry against the order.[870] It is the state of affairs in Europe that has caused general attention to be drawn to the order. During the century Masonry has flourished there in a remarkable way. In the midst of an age full of apprehension respecting everything that suggests political association, this rapid progress of Freemasonry, the character of its members, the coincidence of its designs, and its secrecy, have quite naturally conspired to give some appearance of danger. Yet no discoveries have been made which can fairly impeach the fraternity.[871] As for the principles and work of Weishaupt, these ought not to be condemned outright, solely on the testimony of Robison.[872] "We must leave Robison to an inquisitive public," Bentley concluded, and "forgive a worthy divine who has noticed the book, and has made our order ridiculous."[873]

Somewhat later in the year Harris delivered a number of addresses, in connection with the consecration of various lodges, in which he paid sufficient attention to the new issue that had been raised to make it clear that Masonic circles were greatly disturbed.[874] To Harris, this last assault upon the good name of Masonry was a most unreasonable performance; yet all he felt prepared to do was to enter a general denial, couched in a bombastic, windy style of utterance, of which the following is typical:

How much ... are we surprised to find opposers to an association whose law is peace, and whose whole disposition is love; which is known to discourage by an express prohibition the introduction and discussion of political or religious topics in its assemblies; and which forbids in the most positive and solemn manner all plots, conspiracies, and rebellions. But, notwithstanding the ignorant mistake, and the prejudiced censure the society, we are persuaded that its *real* character is too well known, and its credit is too well supported, to be injured by their misrepresentations, or destroyed by their invectives. When they charge us with demoralizing principles, we will tell them that some of the most orthodox and respectable *Clergymen* are of our order; and when they impute to us disorganizing attempts, we will remind them that Washington is our patron and friend.[875]

Much more of like character issued from this source.[876] We shall see, however, that the keen invective and unrestrained sarcasm of Bentley, rather than the platitudes of the amiable Harris, were needed to put Masonry's case before the public in an effective manner.

On the same occasion that the "Author of the Worcester Charge"[877] made his first formal answer to Robison and Morse, at least two other addresses were delivered, each of which require a word. One of these, *mirabile dictu!* was by Jedediah Morse.[878] Morse's "sermon" was dull and insipid enough. There was much talk about the cultivation and diffusion of the love of country, the duty of essaying the rôle of the peacemaker, and the wickedness of spreading base slanders and exciting unreasonable prejudices among one's fellows; but no discussion of the subject of Illuminism was attempted. All that was said was in entire good spirit, and but one consideration entitles Morse's performance to mention: the fact that its setting as well as its substance gave evidence of its author's earnest desire not to see the gulf widen between him and his Masonic neighbors.

The other address was different. Masonic Brother Charles Jackson, addressing the members and friends of St. Peter's Lodge, Newburyport, Massachusetts, showed no disposition to mince words with respect to the detractors of Freemasonry.[879] Robison was reprobated by him for launching "illiberal sarcasms" against the fraternity,[880] and particularly for making out the Masonic lodges to be "hot-beds of sedition and impiety," which the orator indignantly averred they were not.[881] It was granted that certain profligate and abandoned characters, as Robison claimed, had assumed the cloak of Masonry, with a view of shrouding their infernal plans under pretences of philanthropy and benevolence; but these men soon threw off this cloak, and there was no reason why Masonry should be sacrificed on their account.[882] The charges of atheism and unpatriotic spirit among the members of the fraternity were repelled with equal warmth by Jackson. As with Harris, these calumnies were countered, the charge of atheism by the fact that many of the clergy were members of the order, and the charge of unpatriotic spirit by the fact that Washington was the "illustrious brother" of American Masons.[883]

To a very limited extent the press was resorted to, in order that New England Masonry might have a chance to square itself before the public. The call for specific evidence that was made upon Morse, as voiced in the *Massachusetts Mercury* of July 27, 1798, and Morse's prolix but ineffective effort to meet the situation this created, have already been noticed.[884] In the course of the newspaper discussion referred to, the name of another prominent Mason of Massachusetts, the Reverend

Josiah Bartlett, was drawn into the controversy.[885] To Morse's somewhat unmanly plaint that "by necessary implication" he had been accused by the Massachusetts Masons before the President as being under the influence of unfounded prejudices, Bartlett made the conciliatory, though artful, response that the address of the Grand Lodge, to which Morse referred, was designed merely as a manly avowal of the true principles of Freemasonry. It was not necessary to believe, he continued, that they were influenced by irritation or resentment in making the *Address*, nor that Dr. Morse had hostile designs in the delivery and publication of his fast sermon.[886]

Such language, however, was much too mild and unduly exonerative for the "Author of the Worcester Charge." His aroused spirit required that censure should be imposed. Morse had been guilty of a base injustice; it was right that this fact should frankly be published to the world. Accordingly, the *Massachusetts Mercury* of August 10, 1798, contained a vigorous statement of the case of Masonry against Morse, from Bentley's pen. The following will suffice to indicate the author's spirit:

The notice taken of the American Geographer in the late Charge,[887] was on account of his zeal, in his public character, to give authority to a wicked and mischievous Book. That he did not understand the Charge he has proved in his attempt to apply it, and that he should not understand it, is easy to be conceived from the Strictures already published upon his Compilations, and from opinions of him, both at home and abroad. On a proper occasion, these opinions may be collected and published.[888]

Still refusing to depart from the pathway of amiability and clerical courtesy, Bartlett returned to the discussion of the subject of Illuminism in its relation to American Freemasonry, in the *Mercury* of September 7, 1798. In cumbrous sentences the appearance of Robison's book in this country was reviewed; the best of motives were imputed to its author and his supporters in America; but stress, very *gentle* stress, to be sure, was laid upon the question whether the Illuminati, in any form or other, had branches in this country. "If," Bartlett urged, "there is any citizen in the United States who can prove this, it is a duty which he really owes to God and his country, to come forward, 'as a faithful watchman,' with his documents." As for himself, he was fully persuaded that if the Masonic institution could be implicated fairly in the conspiracy, then the doors of every lodge ought to be flung wide open, and Masonry henceforth held in just derision and contempt.[889]

This seemed to open the way for such a polite and harmless handling of the subject as Morse coveted. In like spirit he replied to the foregoing.[890] He rejoiced in the candid utterances of his worthy friend. Bartlett's acceptance of the existence of the Illuminati persuaded him to hope that opposition to Robison would now soon cease. Had the latter's work not been opposed in the first place, he entertained no doubt that Freemasonry in the United States would not have been injured. While disclaiming all intention of pursuing a controversial course, he would, however, undertake an investigation to determine whether or not there were societies of the Illuminati in this country.[891]

A belated promise, to say the least, and one that found a certain belated fulfilment in Morse's fast sermon of the following spring.[892] Before turning to consider the effect of that sermon on Masonic thought, one other Masonic disclaimer of 1798 requires attention.

On October 23, the Grand Lodge of Vermont drew up an address to the President somewhat similar to the one which earlier in the year their Massachusetts brethren had presented.[893] Beginning with the familiar observation that Masonic principles forbade the introduction of political subjects into the discussions of the order, but that the serious cast of national affairs was such as to justify the present action, the address proceeded to notice the "slanders" that were in circulation respecting the order and to profess the ardent attachment of Vermont Masons to the cause of the government. The idea that Masons were capable of faction was repudiated with energy. An individual Mason here and there might possibly sell his birthright for a mess of pottage, or betray his country for paltry pelf; but as a body the Masonic fraternity stood committed to support the government. *All* should be risked in its maintenance and defence.[894]

The language of the address could hardly have been warmer. On the other hand, the President's response was cold, or, if not that, at least puzzling.[895] Asserting first that he had ever esteemed the societies of Freemasons in this country as not only innocent of base designs but actually useful, he seemed to dispel all the comfort which the reading of that assurance was calculated to impart by adding the following:

The principle, not to introduce politics in your private assemblies, and the other principle, to be willing subjects to the government, would, if observed, preserve such societies from suspicion. But it seems to be agreed, that the society of Masons have discovered a science of government, or art of ruling society, peculiar to themselves, and unknown to all the other legislators and philosophers of the world; I mean not only the skill to know each other by marks or signs that no other persons can divine, but the wonderful power of enabling and compelling all men, and I suppose all women, at all hours, to keep a secret. If this art can be applied, to set aside the ordinary maxims of society, and introduce politics and disobedience to government, and still keep the secret, it must be obvious that such science and such societies may be perverted to all the ill purposes which have been suspected. The characters which compose the lodges in America are such as forbid every apprehension from them, and they will best know whether any dangers are possible in other countries as well as in this.... I say cordially with you—let not the tongue of slander say, that Masons in America are capable of faction. I am very confident it can not be said by any one with truth of the Masons of Vermont.[896]

Was the President ironical or frank? He had intimated that the Masons were *capable* of corruption: did he, or did he not think they were guiltless of the charge of conspiracy that had recently been lodged against them? One could not be absolutely sure from what he had written. What the Masons of Vermont may have felt when the ambiguous response of the President was before them, we have no means of knowing; but there was one Mason in Massachusetts who read the response of the President to the address of the Vermont Masons, and who was displeased. In the view of William Bentley, the President had done anything but assist the cause of Masonry in the hour of its embarrassment. He has left us the record of his impressions in the following form:

The address to General Washington,[897] as brother, must have the best effect, because he gives his own testimony, that he is a stranger to any ill designs of our institution.[898] But the replies of President Adams, such as he was indeed obliged to offer, have only left us where he found us, if in so happy a condition. His answers are candid, but he could know nothing. His answer to Massachusetts Grand Lodge insinuates his hopes. To Maryland, he seems to express even his fears.[899] To Vermont, he says, he believes the institution has been useful But while he expressed a confidence in the American lodges, he consents to hold our lodges capable of corruption. His words are, "Masons will best know whether any dangers are possible in other countries, as well as in this."[900]

We have seen that the most appreciable and positive of all the evidence that the champions of the charge of Illuminism brought against the Masons was that which Morse embodied in his fast sermon in the spring of 1799. For once the tiresome reiterations of the theorist and the reporter of other men's suspicions were laid aside. For once a straight thrust was made at a definite point in the armor of American Masonry. The effect which Morse's sermon produced on the minds of New England Masons naturally stimulates inquiry.

Contrary to what might very properly be supposed, the literature of contemporary New England Freemasonry fails to yield full and convincing evidence as to the precise character of this reaction. A few formal public statements were made on the part of representatives of the craft, or in one or two instances by men who were sufficiently close to the institution to be used on occasions when Masonry threw wide its doors of seclusion that the profane might draw near. Some of these must be noticed.

Far removed from the chief centers of the agitation, at Portland, Maine, Masonic Brother Amos Stoddard addressed the craft, on the occasion of the festival of St. John the Baptist, June 24, 1799.[901] Stoddard did not balk at the admission that the fraternity "have, unfortunately, tolerated the Illuminati."[902] But there was this to be said by way of exculpation: the Illuminati were not legitimate Masons.[903] "To propagate their revolutionary poison, and to protract the period of detection" (*sic*), they attached themselves to Freemasonry and called themselves by its name. In this way the world had been deceived. But the main citadel of Masonry had not capitulated; only a section of the fraternity had been taken by treachery.[904] A temporary wound, undeniably, had been inflicted; but no lasting hurt would come to the craft.[905]

At Reading, Massachusetts, on the same occasion, Caleb Prentiss, a non-Mason, told the members and friends of Mt. Moriah Lodge that the lodges were under suspicion as they had never been before.[906] The eyes of the *world* were now turned upon Masonry. The suspicion that nefarious conspiracies had been formed or countenanced within the lodges was well fixed in the public mind. Masons would need to walk with more than ordinary circumspection. They must sedulously keep themselves spotless from the imputation of such designs, that the craft be not blamed. By striving to show themselves to be lovers of God and mankind, friends of religion, friends of their country, and firm and study supporters of the latter's civil constitution, government, and laws, they would be able to vindicate the principles, professions, and constitutions of true ancient Masonry.[907]

At Ashby, New Hampshire, on the same festival day, an assembly of Masons and their friends listened to a discourse which by way of concessions to the opponents of Masonry outstripped anything that went before or followed after.[908] The Reverend Seth Payson, that fatuous aspirant to literary fame who elected to be a tardy echo of the speculations of Robison,

Barruel, and Morse,[909] informed his auditors that while Masonry in its essential principles and constitution had shown itself to be useful to society, unhappily its name, veil of secrecy, symbols, and associative principles had been seized by a body of men in Europe, in order to mask their hellish purposes of eradicating from the human mind "all belief of a God, of a governing providence, of the immortality of the soul, and a future state,—to extinguish every principle of natural and revealed religion and moral sentiments, and to demolish every government but its own."[910] In all its horrid appendages, the French Revolution was the result of this conspiracy. This "vine of Sodom" was transplanted to the United States: witness the opposition which in this country developed against those "eminent benefactors to mankind in general," Drs. Robison, Morse, *et al.* [911] Without the faithful researches of Morse, in particular, a very much more serious infection of the Masonic body assuredly would have occurred.[912]

Such isolated and generally indefinite utterances, it may be urged, are scarcely to be trusted as offering an accurate reflection of the state of the Masonic mind. They do not, however, stand altogether alone. From various and perhaps more solid sources, the evidence is forthcoming that the year 1799 was a year of deep anxiety and concern on the part of the Masons of New England.

The diary of William Bentley supplies some evidence to this effect.[913] His disgust was great that the clergy continued to agitate concerning the pernicious principles and influence of Weishaupt, and that with equal pertinacity the press kept the affairs of that individual and his minions before the public.[914] The equally candid acknowledgments of other Masons are even more to the point. One spokesman for Rhode Island Masonry made public admission that the fraternity was suffering keenly from "a temporary odium."[915] Another in Massachusetts uttered the complaint that the industrious zeal of the unprincipled defamer had involved the craft in most serious embarrassment.[916] Some were driven to take refuge in the consolation that the lodges of the Illuminati were bastard organizations, and therefore Freemasonry could not justly be anathematized on their account.[917]

When the skies had cleared, as we have seen they soon did, and Masons began to take stock of the experience through which their institution had passed, their admissions of what the agitation had cost the order were even more significant. One confessed that Masonry had started back affrighted at the hideous spectre of Illuminism, and that the joy that filled the lodges because they were no longer suspected as "hot-beds of sedition" and "nurseries of infidelity" was very great.[918]Another likewise rejoiced in spirit that the dark period of suspicion and calumny through which the order has been passing was now over, and that political agitation against the institution was at an end.[919] Another admitted that after the lapse of a half dozen years it was difficult to plant a new lodge in one of the most cultured of New England's communities, on account of the influence exerted by the works of Robison and Barruel.[920] Still another confessed that the Illuminati controversy had cost the fraternity dearly in the matter of membership; a serious defection had resulted, representing many desertions.[921]

The various causes that contributed to bring about a collapse of the agitation over Illuminism have elsewhere received attention and for the most part require no special comment in this connection. One of these, however, was of such a nature that it has been reserved for brief exposition at this point.

The death of Washington, while confessedly an event of national significance, and, as such, shared as the common bereavement of all the citizens of the country, nevertheless assumed a very special importance in the eyes of Masons and exerted an immediate and weighty influence upon the fortunes of the order.

One who turns the pages of the black-bordered newspapers of the day, all sharing in the universal lamentation and doing their utmost to set before their readers the last detail regarding the closing hours in the great man's life and the arrangement and disposition of affairs in connection with his obsequies, is likely to find himself amazed because the Masons found it possible to figure in the circumstances as conspicuously and largely as they did. The Masons were in evidence, in very conspicuous evidence, it must be said, in all that pertained to the funeral rites of the nation's first chief. Not only was this true of the funeral ceremonies proper; in innumerable places where mourning assemblies gathered to pay respect to the memory of Washington, Masons claimed and were accorded the places of honor in the processions and concourses that marked these outpourings of popular sorrow.

It cannot be doubted that American Freemasons, while sincere in their expressions of sorrow on account of Washington's death, none the less found a peculiar comfort of soul in being able *at such a time* to point to the fallen hero as *their* "brother." At an hour when the tongue of scandal and the finger of suspicion were still active they esteemed it an opportunity not to be despised to be able to stand before the country and proudly say, "Washington was of us."

That this is not idle fancy the following utterances will help to make clear. At Middletown, Connecticut, a few days after Washington's death, a Masonic oration was pronounced in connection with the observance of the festival of St. John the Evangelist.[922] The orator, who recognized the season as one of unremitting calumny of Freemasonry,[923] sought refuge from the strife of tongues for himself and his brethren by urging the following sentiment:

If what Barruel has suggested of our institution is true; if it is among US that Jesus Christ is daily sacrificed, and all religion scoffed at; if our principles and doctrines, either in theory or practice, have a tendency to destroy the bonds of nature and of government; how could Washington, that *Perfect Man*, when his feet were stumbling upon the dark mountains of death, say, "I am ready to die," until he had warned the world to beware of the Masonic institution and its consequences? He was a thorough investigator, and a faithful follower of our doctrines.[924]

To this must be added the somewhat different apologetic of a prominent Massachusetts Mason. Speaking at Dorchester, at a Masonic service in Washington's memory, the Reverend Thaddeus Mason Harris acknowledged the value of Washington's connection with American Freemasonry in these words:

The honor thus conferred upon us has been peculiarly serviceable at the present day, when the most unfounded prejudices have been harbored against Freemasonary, and the most calumnious impeachments brought forward to destroy it. But our opposers blushed for the censures when we reminded them that Washington loved and patronized the institution.[925]

Washington's Masonic career, Masonry's uncontested claim to the right to be first among those who mourned at his burial,—these constituted a part, and a very substantial part of the demurrer which Freemasonry offered at the bar of public judgment in answer to its accusers. It is very certain that after the reinstatement in public favor which American Masonry was accorded when Washington was buried, the voice of censure was less and less disposed to be heard.[926]

NOTE.—The fiction of an alliance between American Freemasonry and the Illuminati had a curious revival in connection with the antimasonic excitement which swept the United States from 1826 to about 1832. The mysterious abduction of William Morgan had the effect of arousing the country to the peril of secret societies, the Masons particularly. The Antimasonic party for this and other reasons sprang into existence, and an elaborate political propaganda and program were attempted. See McCarthy, Charles, *The Antimasonic Party: a Study of Political Antimasonry in the United States, 1827–1840*. In Annual Report of the American Historical Association, 1902, vol. i, pp. 365–574. In connection with the Antimasonic conventions that were held in various states, efforts were made to establish a connection between American Masonry and Illuminism. Thus, in the state convention held in Massachusetts in 1828–1829, a committee was appointed "to inquire how far Freemasonry and French Illuminism are connected." This committee brought in a report establishing to the satisfaction of the convention that there was a direct connection between the two systems, and resulting in the passing of the following resolution: "Resolved, on the report of the Committee appointed to inquire how far Free Masonry and French Illuminism are connected, That *there is evidence* of an intimate connexion between the higher orders of Free Masonry and French Illuminism." *Cf. An Abstract of the Proceedings of the Anti-Masonic State Convention of Massachusetts, held in Faneuil Hall, Boston, Dec. 30 and 31, 1829, and Jan. 1, 1830.* Boston, 1830, p. 5. On the ground that the length of the committee's report made it inadvisable, the publishing committee deemed it inexpedient to print the "evidence."

The Vermont Antimasonic state convention of 1830 wrestled with the same question. Its committee brought in a report so naively suggestive as to merit notice. Citing the agitation that arose on account of the literary efforts of "Robison and Barruel in Europe, and Morse, Payson, and others in America," the committee expressed its judgment that those works "called Masonry in question in a manner which if assumed on any other topic, would have called forth disquisition and remark on the subject matter of these writings from every editor in the union; yet the spirit of inquiry, which these able performances were calculated to raise, was soon and unaccountably quelled—the press was mute as the voice of the strangled sentinel and the mass of the people kept in ignorance that an alarm on the subject of Masonry had ever been sounded, or even that these works had ever existed." See *Proceedings of the Anti-Masonic State Convention, holden at Montpelier, June 23, 24, & 25, 1830. Reports and Addresses.* Middlebury, 1830.

An exploration of the literature of the Antimasonic party yields nothing more significant. This literature as listed by

McCarthy may be found on pp. 560–574 of the *Report of the American Historical Association for 1902*, vol. i.

5. ATTEMPTS OF DEMOCRATS TO FIX THE COUNTERCHARGE OF ILLUMINISM UPON THE FEDERALISTS

By 1798 and 1799 the alignment of political parties in New England had arrived at such a stage that the suspicion of political jockeying to obtain party advantage was well grounded in the minds of leaders in both camps. This self-conscious and determined party spirit had been greatly promoted by the employment of electioneering methods.[927] The general public had not yet become accustomed to the precise significance of the broadside, the political pamphlet, and the newspaper canard; and these all, in a copious stream, had begun to flow from the country's presses. Party leaders, however, who knew the purposes of their own minds if not those of the opposition, were quick to scent anything that savored of political buncombe.

Coincident with the breaking out of the controversy over the Illuminati, a number of tales of plots or conspiracies were foisted upon the public.[928] One of these concerned a band of conspirators who were alleged to be agents of the French Directory, and who, with their secret documents concealed in the false bottom of two tubs, had taken ship from Hamburg to work sedition in this country.[929] Another concerned the operations of a tailor in the city of Philadelphia, of whom the report spread that he was engaged in making immense quantities of uniforms for French soldiers; and if for French soldiers, for whom could they be intended but for some French army which must be planning an invasion of the United States? A third tale had to do with the massacre which, rumor had it, had taken place on the good American ship Ocean, involving the brutal butchery of her entire crew by the French.[930]

All these preposterous "plots" were promptly exploded, and in due course all were traced to Federalist sources. The general effect upon the opposition scarcely needs to be stated. Such silly tales, said one Democrat, discredit everything that the Federalists affirm to be true.[931] They all had been artfully concocted and employed, said another, "to excite an indignation which might be played off for the purposes of party."[932] They were so many alarm-bells, a third said,[933] rung, we may add, to frighten the people into running to prop up the bowing walls and tottering pillars of the doomed temple of Federalism.

This mood of scepticism, imbedded as it was in a more serious mood of indignation arising from the rebuffs and discomfitures that citizens of democratic tastes and principles had long suffered at the hands of Federalist bigotry and intolerance, rendered it inevitable that the charge of Illuminism should be suspect from the first. One has but to recall that the year in which the controversy over the Illuminati broke out has still its characterization in political annals as "the reign of terror," to appreciate fully the statement that has just been made.

Beginning with 1799 a small group of pamphlets appeared, dedicated by their authors to an effort to convert the charge of Illuminism into a political boomerang, to be employed as a weapon against the Federalists. Conspicuous among these, and perhaps first in point of time, was *A View of the New England Illuminati*,[934] an anonymous composition, but one whose authorship was soon traced to the Reverend John Cosens Ogden,[935] an Episcopal clergyman.

Ogden wielded the pen of a ready and discursive writer, the latter more especially. To follow him step by step as he ranged from Barruel and Robison to meetings of New England ministers, from meetings of New England ministers to ecclesiastical usurpations, from ecclesiastical usurpations to the French Revolution, from the French Revolution to high-handed measures taken by New England college presidents, and so on *ad infinitum*, and the while to take equal account of all he touched upon, would be a formidable and, we may believe, largely unprofitable exercise. And yet, through a good deal of

Ogden's pamphlet the spirit of ecclesiastical and political dissent finds a certain earnest and even vivid expression.

It is true, said Ogden at the outset, that New England had its Illuminati. They were not, however, such as Robison and Barruel would represent them to be. The New England societies of the Illuminati were the monthly meetings of the clergy.[936] The work they did and the influence they exerted were so like the work and influence of the societies of which Robison and Barruel wrote that they deserved to be styled the New England Illuminati: readers could judge for themselves as to the appositeness of the title thus bestowed.[937] Their confederacy had been so successful that certain opulent and leading laymen, who supremely desired to perpetuate the union of church and state in New England, had lent to these clerical organizations their fostering care and support.[938] At these monthly clubs, the political issues of the times were discussed and prayers and orations filled with invectives against those who had not adopted the creeds and politics of the members were delivered.[939]

That which first gave offence to these clubs was the establishment of universal religious toleration in Canada and the petition of the Episcopalians inhabiting the colonies—now the United States—to their brethren in England, that a Protestant bishop might be granted them who would live in their midst.[940] To defeat these measures, the New England Illuminati were indefatigably busy; and when they discovered that they were foiled in their efforts, they languished for a season,[941] until the French Revolution stirred them to new life.

When the Revolution began in France, these New England Illuminated Clubs redoubled their energies. They prayed, they exhorted, they wrote and printed numerous dissertations and prophecies, all emphasizing the import of the Revolution as signalizing the overthrow of the Church of Rome, which was Antichrist, and of the Pope, who was the Beast of the Apocalypse, preparatory to the fulfilment of the eternal decree respecting the Millennium.[942] Everything that the clergy did at this time smacked loudly of their excessive interest in French affairs. In order more fully to influence public opinion they took the colleges into their confederacy, and soon teachers and pupils were busy disseminating throughout the land principles and prejudices favorable to the Revolution in France.[943] Nothing was omitted that might have been done to cement an attachment to the cause of the Revolution.

The fluctuating events of the European wars and the uncertain issue of French affairs soon cooled the ardor of these clerico-political societies.[944] For these men were not sincere in their devotion to France. They were not genuine supporters of the rights of man. They repudiated their former interest in French politics and turned fiercely upon those who maintained their interest in the principles of the Revolution. These men had but one interest. What they desired was *power*, a millennium in which the money and liberties of all men should be laid at the feet of the colleges and of the Illuminati Clubs.[945]

Such was the general indictment that Ogden drew. This attended to, he proceeded to file a bill of particulars.

The clergy, who constituted the predominating element in these New England Illuminati Clubs, from the first had occupied a position of commanding influence in New England. But the clergy *from the first* had steadily kept the people at a distance.[946] They courted the rich and schemed to obtain political influence. They united to themselves a formidable body from among the laity, who looked to them for votes and preferments. They freely wielded the weapons of ecclesiastical censure and discipline in efforts to coerce those who would not sell their consciences for gold or political honors.[947] In the army and the navy *their* sons and favorites received promotion; and in the distribution of college diplomas, because of the same influence, men were honored who could not construe the Latin parchments they received.[948]

Nominations to magistracies had been handed about by the arrogant members of these Illuminated Clubs, and good men of the opposition had been denounced by them at the polls.[949] By the same forces the public press had been deprived of its freedom and the channels of public communication diverted to serve unworthy ends.[950] Missionaries had been sent to frontier communities in the various states, not to propagate religion, but to extend the influence and to increase the power of the societies whose agents they were.[951] The destruction of dissenting bodies had been aimed at and the cause of universal liberty of conscience spurned as an odious thing.[952]

In their efforts to control the instruments of education, the representatives of these Illuminated Clubs had manifested the same illiberal and contracted policy. Public attention had artfully been withdrawn from the schools of the yeomanry and centered upon the colleges which the Illuminati controlled.[953] Some of these institutions had shown themselves subservient in the extreme. The clergy and corporation of Yale had been so narrow as to cause philanthropists to turn the gifts they intended for that institution into other channels, to Harvard particularly.[954] At Dartmouth a spirit quite as contemptible had prevailed.[955] Fortunately the school at Cambridge had escaped from the clutches of these bigoted men. Columbia, too, had recently been placed upon a more liberal foundation, but not without having incurred the hostility of the Illuminati.[956] Everywhere, indeed, that the Edwardean theology was not permitted to flourish unmolested, there the hostility of the New England Illuminati was felt.[957] Venerable, learned, and experienced Catholic, Episcopal, and Baptist clergymen were roughly thrust aside at the seats of learning where these men had control, and dapper young parsons "with neat gowns and bands, and degrees of Doctor of Divinity, bought and obtained by the influence of rich merchants"[958] were permitted to supersede them.

There was no place into which the influence of these men had gone where contentions and persecutions had not followed.[959] But few interruptions of the public tranquility had occurred that could not be traced directly to their door. No hand of sympathy or conciliation had ever been held out by them to the opposition.[960]Should some political despot enlist these men under his banner, disaster would overtake our religion, government, liberty, and property; anarchy and destruction would overspread a land saved by the valor of freemen, by the blood of the fathers.[961]

What, therefore, was to be done with such contumacious and intolerable men? Ogden's answer sounds surprisingly moderate, in view of the extent to which the iron of bitterness had entered his soul:

If the New-England Illuminati proceed unheeded and uncontrolled, this nation will constantly experience the pernicious effects of discord and popular discontent. Wars at home, tumults abroad, the degradation of legislatures, judges and jurors, will be our daily portion.... To dissolve or abolish those societies or clubs would not be to infringe upon the rights of conscience: to counteract them is to establish law and peace.[962]

Such was Ogden's effort to brand the Standing Order of New England with the hateful mark of the Illuminati.[963] His endeavor was supplemented by the oratorical and literary effusions of Connecticut's most shrewd and impudent Democrat, Abraham Bishop, of New Haven. In the course of a year, beginning with September, 1800, Bishop delivered, and later expanded and printed, three orations,[964] in each of which he drew heavily upon his by no means meagre resources of logic, wit, irony, and boldness, to arraign Connecticut Federalism as a hideous conspiracy against the peace of the state and the liberties of the people.

The first of these orations had something of a history, not very extraordinary to be sure, and yet unique enough to throw some light upon the mettle of the man and the nature of the opposition that inflamed his passion. The Phi Beta Kappa Society of Yale College appointed Bishop its orator for the year 1800, in connection with the commencement exercises of the college, then held in the month of September. Exercising the traditional right of selecting his own subject, Bishop elected to prepare an oration on "The Extent and Power of Political Delusion," instead of writing on "broken glass, dried insects, petrifactions, or any such *literary* themes," as he afterwards intimated the Federalists doubtless had expected.[965] The labor of composition completed, Bishop showed his manuscript to the secretary of the society, only to be informed later that on account of the political character of his effort his appointment as orator had been rescinded by the society. Not to be routed by any such expert generalship on the part of the enemy, Bishop rallied his Democratic friends, procured a hall, and on the evening of the Phi Beta Kappa exercises, held forth in the presence of an audience of very gratifying proportions.[966]

And what had Abraham Bishop to say on "The Extent and Power of Political Delusion" which in the view of the Phi Beta Kappas amounted to an abuse of "the confidence of the Society, … involving the members in that political turmoil which disgraces our country"?[967] Much in every way. He devoted several scores of pages to an exposition of the delusive arts of the "friends of order," which, being interpreted, meant the knavery of the Federalists throughout the country in general and in Connecticut in particular. The major portion of his "argument" need not detain us, since Bishop ran the full gamut of political crimination, charging upon the Federalists an amount of deception and chicanery truly appalling. One item only is of interest to us. Among the endless "delusions" that he cited as evidence of the hypocrisy of the Federalists was the clergy's habit of waiving the sacerdotal functions, descending from their high seats made venerable by the respect of the people for religion, and imposing upon their auditories political sermons based upon texts drawn from Robison and Barruel.[968] Happily, he continued, the people were able to penetrate this stratagem, along with the rest.

Robison and Barruel can deceive us no more. The 17 sophistical work-shops of Satan have never been found: not one illuminatus major or minor has been discovered in America, though their names have been published, and though their existence here is as clearly proved as was their existence in Europe.[969]

But Bishop's thought upon the subject of the Illuminati had not yet fully ripened.[970] The circumstances under which this virgin effort of his was executed added considerably to his reputation; so much so that when at the end of the following winter the Democrats of Wallingford adopted the irreverent suggestion of holding a public thanksgiving to celebrate the election of Thomas Jefferson to the presidency, Bishop was asked to be one of the mouthpieces of their joy on that occasion. The ground over which Bishop traveled in the Wallingford oration was much the same as before. Again the "friends of order" were arraigned for their impostures and their oppressions. Such were "blind guides," "a generation of vipers," dispensers of hypocrisy to children in their cradles, "arch impostors and prime movers" of iniquitous works.[971] They were great sticklers for "steady habits"; but what meant their cry of "steady habits" but mortal hostility to republicanism in every form?[972]

These self-styled "friends of order," it should not be forgotten, were not the *people*. They were the commercial aristocrats who insisted that ours was a blessed government because *they* were all becoming rich, plus the clergy, the bench, the bar, and the office-seeking and office-holding" class in general.[973] They united church and state, made religion play a game against civil rights, and strove to make the object of the American Revolution appear impossible of full realization.[974] Affecting to respect and serve the rights of man, they imposed upon the people the funding system, the alien and sedition acts, and the unwarranted enlargement of the navy.[975]They stirred up the animosity of the people against the French, excited the X. Y. Z. mania, and scattered over the country the "*arabian tales* of Robison and Barruel."[976] With respect to religion, they had developed more hypocrisy in New England than existed in any other equal portion of the globe.[977] They had cried aloud that atheism prevailed in New England and infidel books were plentiful; but neither atheists nor infidel publications were actually to be found, unless in the latter case the writings of Robison and Barruel and the sermons preached against infidelity were to be called such.[978] The grave fault of the clerical "friends of order" was that they had not preached the Gospel. Instead, they had insulted the intelligence of the people by revamping the fables of a Scotch monarchist and a Catholic abbé. They imputed infidelity to the Democrats, while they themselves caused infidelity to abound. They directed all their darts of "democratic infidels" and "infidel philosophy" against one man, Thomas Jefferson, and in this way caused their enemies to blaspheme and say, "Where is your God?"[979]

And so on through a hundred pages less one. In a tirade of such interminable length the idea of a Federalist conspiracy against the best interests of the people of New England was worked out in more than ample detail. All that was needed was to apply the term "Illuminati," and the catalogue of incriminations would be complete. This application Bishop proceeded to make in his third oration, which appeared sometime within the year 1802.

Bishop's last effort surpassed all that he had previously achieved in the way of boldfaced and reckless assertion. Constant reiteration and an awkward effort to fashion his composition on the form that Robison and Barruel supplied him, gave to the pamphlet abundant suggestions of insincerity and political rant. The union of church and state in New England was presented as a constant, powerful, and efficient enemy against Christianity and the government of the United States.[980] Thus the true Illuminatists were the political clergy and the Federalist leaders.[981] The charge of infidel conspiracy brought against the Democrats a few years previous constituted nothing more nor less than a specious accusation brought forward "to prostrate the public mind."[982] Robison and Barruel were miserable mixtures of falsehood and folly.[983] The Federalists were well aware of this when they launched their charge of infidel philosophy against Thomas Jefferson and the party that supported him. The Federalists were simply desperate. They were determined to go to any lengths to keep Jefferson out of the presidency. All their works were saturated with sacrilege and impiety. Their public fasts were kept for political purposes.[984] Their cry, "The church is in danger!" was hollow and insincere.[985] Their praise of the Federal administration had no other object than to effect the abasement of the Democrats.[986] Their "Church and State Union" freely sacrificed the highest interests of religion and government to the cause of party.[987]

A more extended report of Bishop's waspish and bitter harangue would neither strengthen his indictment nor elucidate his "proofs." His pamphlet has significance only as an outburst of triumphant but still indignant New England Democracy as it reflected upon the exasperating obstacles which the opposition had thrust in its way as it had pressed forward to power. Nothing could be clearer than that the word "Illuminati" had lost all serious and exact significance and had become a term for politicians to conjure with;[988] or if not that, to give point to the general charge of calloused villainy which Democrats lodged against Federalists at the turn of the eighteenth century.

VITA

The author was born near New London, Ohio, November 23, 1875. His early education was obtained in the public schools of New London and North Fairfield (O.), and in the preparatory department of Hiram College. Upon completing an undergraduate course in the latter institution in 1901, he received the degree of A.B. Ten years were thereupon devoted to the work of the Christian ministry, in pastorates at Cincinnati, Ohio, and Angola, Indiana. He was in residence at Columbia University and Union Theological Seminary for the first half of the academic year 1907–8. In 1911 he returned to these institutions, and in 1912 received from the former the degree of A.M. He completed his residence requirements for the doctorate in 1913. He worked in the seminars of Professors Shotwell, Rockwell, and McGiffert, and in addition took courses under Professors Giddings, Dewey, Robinson, and Monroe. He was called to the position of Dean and Professor of New Testament and Church History in Hiram College in 1913, where his professional service continues.

FOOTNOTES

[1] Reverend Jedediah Morse, born at Woodstock, Connecticut, August 23, 1761, died at New Haven, June 9, 1826, was a man of note. He was the author of the first American geography and gazetteer. His connection with the leading public men of his times, particularly with those of the Federalist party, was both extensive and intimate. His travels and correspondence in the interests of his numerous geographical compositions in part promoted this acquaintance; but his outspoken and unflinching support of the measures of government during the Federalist regime did even more to enhance his influence. Morse was graduated from Yale College in 1783 and settled at Charlestown as minister of the Congregational church in that place in 1789. His wife was Elizabeth Ann Breese, granddaughter of Samuel Finley, president of the College of New Jersey. Quite apart from all other claims to public recognition, the following inscription, to be found to this day on a tablet attached to the front of the house in Charlestown wherein his distinguished son was born, would have rendered the name of Jedediah Morse worthy of regard:

> "Here was born 27th of April, 1791,
> Samuel Finley Breese Morse.
> Inventor of the Electric Telegraph."

W. B. Sprague's *Annals of the American Pulpit*, vol. ii, pp. 247–256, contains interesting data concerning Morse's activities and personality. Sprague also wrote *The Life of Jedidiah Morse, D. D.*, New York, 1874. (Morse's surname appears in the sources both as "Jedediah" and "Jedidiah"). Sawyer's *Old Charlestown, etc.*, p. 299, has an engaging account of Morse's loyalty to the muse of Federalism, and of the painful, though not serious physical consequences, in which in at least one instance this involved him. *Cf.* also *Memorabilia in the Life of Jedediah Morse, D. D.*, by his son, Sidney E. Morse. A bibliography of thirty-two titles by Morse is appended to the sketch in F. B. Dexter, *Biographical Sketches of the Graduates of Yale College*, vol. iv, pp. 295–304.

[2] *A Sermon, Delivered at the New North Church in Boston, in the morning, and in the afternoon at Charlestown, May 9th, 1798, being the day recommended by John Adams, President of the United States of America, for solemn humiliation, fasting and prayer. By Jedidiah Morse, D. D., Minister of the Congregational Church in Charlestown*, Boston, 1798, p. 25.

[3] Robison, *Proofs of a Conspiracy against all the Religions and Governments of Europe, carried on in the Secret Meetings of the Free Masons, Illuminati, and Reading Societies*, Edinburgh, 1797.

[4] An early and yet typical example of this unfavorable view of the moral and religious life of the people after the first generation of the Puritans was gone, may be found in *The Result of 1679*,—a document prepared by the Synod in response to directions from the Massachusetts General Court, calling for answers to the following questions: "What are the euills that haue provoked the Lord to bring his judgments on New England? What is to be donn that so those euills may be reformed?". The following brief excerpt from *The Result* supplies the point of View: "Our Fathers neither sought for, nor thought of great things for themselves, but did seek first the kingdom of God, and his righteousness, and all these things were added to them. They came not into the wilderness to see a man cloathed in soft raiment. But that we have in too many respects, been forgetting the Errand upon which the Lord sent us hither; all the world is witness: And therefore we may not wonder that God hath changed the tenour of his Dispensations towards us, turning to doe us hurt, and consuming us after that he hath done us good. If we had continued to be as once we were, the Lord would have continued to doe for us, as once he did." The entire document, together with much valuable explanatory comment, may be found in Walker, *Creeds and Platforms of Congregationalism*, pp. 421–437. Backus, *History*

of New England, vol i, pp. 457–461, contains a group of similar laments.

[5] Snow, *A History of Boston*, p. 333.

[6] Weeden, *Economic and Social History of New England*, vol. ii, p. 696.

[7] *Acts and Resolves, Public and Private, of the Province of Massachusetts Bay*, vol. iii, pp. 500 *et seq.* The Preamble of this Act is highly interesting: "For preventing and avoiding the many and great mischiefs which arise from publick stage-plays, interludes and other theatrical entertainments, which not only occasion great and unnecessary expenses, and discourage industry and frugality, but likewise tend generally to increase immorality, impiety and a contempt for religion,—Be it enacted", *etc.*

[8] Seilhamer, *History of the American Theatre*, vol. ii, pp. 51 *et seq.*; Winsor, *The Memorial History of Boston*, vol. iv, ch. v: "The Drama in Boston," by William W. Clapp, pp. 358 *et seq.*

[9] Seilhamer, *op. cit.*, vol. iii, p. 13; Dunlap, *History of the American Theatre*, vol. i, p. 244; Snow, *History of Boston*, pp. 333 *et seq.*

[10] *Acts and Laws of the Commonwealth of Massachusetts*, 1792–3, pp. 686 *et seq.*

[11] The public discussion and legislative phase of the situation, together with the disorders occasioned by the determination of the supporters of the theatre to serve their enterprise at any cost, are well covered by Clapp in the chapter already cited in Winsor's *Memorial History of Boston. Cf.* also Seilhamer, vol. iii, pp. 14 *et seq.*; Dunlap, vol. i, pp. 242 *et seq.*; Willard, *Memories of Youth and Manhood*, vol. i, pp. 324, 325; Bentley, *Diary*, vol. i. pp 340, 379, 380, 414, 415, 418, *etc.*

[12] *The Speech of John Gardiner, Esquire, Delivered in the House of Representatives. On Thursday, the 26th of January, 1792*, Boston, 1792, p. 18. Another publication of the same

year, *The Rights of the Drama: or, An Inquiry into the Origin, Principles, and Consequences of Theatrical Entertainments. By Philo Dramatis* (pseud.), discussed the subject in different vein, but with the same object in view. In the final chapter on "The Outlines of a Theatre, it's Necessary Appendages, a Plan of Regulation, Calculation of Expenses, Profits, &c.", doubtless by way of turning the balance of public judgment in favor of the establishment of a local theatre, the author suggests that the following ends may be served: the development of native genius, and thus the elevation of America to a high rank in the republic of letters; the reservation of a certain portion of the revenues of the theatre by the Commonwealth, for the care of the poor of Boston, or of the state, and for the support of the University at Cambridge (Harvard), thus easing the burden of taxation. The closing words of this pamphlet, stripped of their bombast, are not unworthy to stand with Gardiner's: "Whenever I consider this subject, and contemplate the formation of a Theatre, I cannot help feeling a kind of enthusiasm ... I anticipate the time when the Garricks and Siddons of America shall adorn the Stage, and melt the soul to pity. But here let me pause.—Let the most rigid Stoic, or the greatest fanatic in religion, or the most notorious dupe to prejudice, once hearken to the tale of the tragic muse, whose office it is to soften, and to subdue the violent passions of the mind, by painting the real misfortunes and distresses, which accompany our journey through life; or attend to the laughable follies, and vain inconsistencies, which daily mark the character of the human species—the deformity of vice—the excellence of virtue—, and, from the representation of the lively Comedy, 'catch the manners living as they rise,' and then say, if he can, that lessons of instruction are unknown to the Drama. If these have no effect, let him listen, with mute attention, to the occasional symphonies, which burst from a thousand strings, and accompany, and give life and animation to the Comic scene—and then, if sunk below the brute creation, let him be fortified against the impressions of sensibility. The stoicism of man must surpass our comprehension, if the dramatic scene can be contemplated without emotion; more especially when the representation of life and manners is intended to correct and to enlarge the heart...."

[13] *Cf.* (Boston) *Independent Chronicle and Universal Advertiser*, Thursday, March 28, 1793.

[14] *Pseud.: Effects of the Stage on the Manners of a People: and the Propriety of Encouraging and Establishing a Virtuous Theatre. By a Bostonian*, Boston, 1792. The author is insipid enough; none the less the pamphlet is by no means void of a certain practical-mindedness and good sense as the author argues for the frank acceptance of the theatre as an institution in the city's life. The following constitute his chief contentions: The theatre, in some form or other, is bound to come, because of the fact that the people generally are interested in the subject of amusement; the tastes and appetites of the people already give painful evidence of serious debasement and corruption; the acceptance of a "Virtuous Theatre" is the only possible expedient if the people are to be saved from worse debauchment.

The view taken by the Reverend William Bentley, Salem's well-known minister, was less specious, though tinged with a mildly pessimistic view of popular tastes. Under date of July 31, 1792, he wrote: "So much talk has been in the Country about Theatrical entertainments that they have become the pride even of the smallest children in our schools. The fact puts in mind of the effect from the Rope flyers, who visited N. England, after whose feats the children of seven were sliding down the fences & wounding themselves in every quarter." *Diary*, vol. i, p. 384. Later, he wrote: "The Theatre opened for the first time [in Salem] is now the subject. The enlightened who have not determined upon its utter abolition have yet generally agreed that it is too early introduced into our country." *Ibid.*, vol. ii, p. 81. *Cf. ibid.*, pp. 258, *et seq.*, 299, 322. It is clear that Bentley was apprehensive.

[15] Weeden, *Economic and Social History of New England*, vol. i, pp. 188, 195; Bishop, *History of American Manufactures*, vol. i, pp. 245 *et seq.*

[16] *Ibid.*, p. 250; vol. ii, pp. 501, 502. See also Clark, *History of Manufactures in the United States*, p. 480.

[17] *Ibid.* Bishop notes the fact that in 1721 a small village of forty houses, near Boston, made 3000 barrels of cider.

[18] *Ibid.*, p. 269; Weeden, *op. cit.*, vol. i, pp. 144, 148 *et seq.*

[19] The impression that this decline toward a general state of drunkenness set in early will appear from the following excerpt taken from the Synod's report on "The Necessity of Reformation", presented to the General Court of Massachusetts in 1679: "VIII. There is much Intemperance. The heathenish and Idolatrous practice of Health-drinking is become too general a Provocation. Dayes of Training, and other publick Solemnityes, have been abused in this respect: and not only English but Indians have been debauched, by those that call themselves Christians, who have put their bottles to them, and made them drunk also. This is a crying Sin, and the more aggravated in that the first Planters of this Colony did (as in the Patent expressed) come into this Land with a design to Convert the Heathen unto Christ…. There are more Temptations and occasions unto *That Sin*, publickly allowed of, than any necessity doth require; the proper end of Taverns, &c. being to that end only, a far less number would suffice: But it is a common practice for Town dwellers, yea and Church-members, to frequent publick Houses, and there to misspend precious Time, unto the dishonour of the Gospel, and the scandalizing of others, who are by such examples induced to sin against God." *Cf.* Walker, *Creeds and Platforms of Congregationalism*, p. 430.

[20] Hatch, *The Administration of the American Revolutionary Army*, pp. 89 *et seq.* The supplies of beer, cider, and rum furnished the armies were not always held to be adequate. After the battle of Brandywine, Congress ordered thirty hogsheads of

rum distributed among the soldiers as a tribute to their gallant conduct in that battle. *Cf. One Hundred Years of Temperance*, New York, 1886, article by Daniel Dorchester on "The Inception of the Temperance Reformation", p. 113, for comments on the effects of the return of drunken soldiers to the ranks of citizenship.

[21] Weeden, *op. cit.*, vol. ii, p. 883, supplies the following concerning the character of the coasting and river trade, which the exigencies of the war greatly stimulated: "A cargo from Boston to Great Barrington and Williamstown contained 11 hdds. and 6 tierces of rum, 3 bbls. of wine, 2 do. of brandy, 1/2 bale of cotton, and 1 small cask of indigo. The proportion of 'wet goods' to the small quantity of cotton and indigo is significant, and indicates the prevailing appetites".

[22] In 1783 Massachusetts had no fewer than sixty-three distilleries. In 1783 this state distilled 1,475,509 gallons of spirits from foreign, and 11,490 gallons from domestic materials. From 1790 to 1800 in the United States, 23,148,404 gallons of spirits were distilled from molasses; of this 6,322,640 gallons were exported, leaving a quantity for home consumption so large as to supply its own comment. Low grain prices, together with the difficulty of gaining access to the molasses markets, hastened a transition to grain distilling near the end of the eighteenth century, with the result that in 1810 Mr. Gallatin, Secretary of the Treasury, reported not less than 9,000,000 gallons of spirits as having been distilled from grain and fruit in 1801. Bishop, *History of American Manufactures*, vol. ii, pp. 30, 65, 83, 152; Clark, *History of Manufactures in the United States*, p. 230.

[23] *Collections of the Massachusetts Historical Society*, 6th ser., vol. iv, Belknap Papers, pt. iii, p. 440.

[24] *Ibid.*, p. 508.

[25] *Diary of William Bentley*, vol. ii, p. 92: May 31, 1794: "The observation of holydays at Election is an abuse in this part of the Country. Not only at our return yesterday, did we

observe crowds around the new Tavern at the entrance of the Town, but even at this day, we saw at Perkins' on the neck, persons of all descriptions, dancing to a fiddle, drinking, playing with pennies, &c. It is proper such excesses should be checked." *Cf.* also *ibid.*, pp. 58, 363, 410, 444 *et seq. Cf.* also Earle, Alice Morse, *Stage-coach and Tavern Days*, New York, 1900.

[26] *Collections of the Massachusetts Historical Society*, 6th Series, vol. iv, Belknap Papers, pt. iii, p. 456. Jeremiah Libbey writes of the situation at Portsmouth, [N. H.?]: "The common allowance of rum to labourers here is half a pint per day, which has been the rule or custom as long as I can remember. There are several persons in this town that are endeavouring to abolish the custom by giving them more wages in lieu of the *allowance*, as it is call'd; but the custom is so rooted that it is very difficult to break it. The attachment is so great, that in general if you were to offer double the price of the allowance in money it would not be satisfactory to the labourers, and altho' that is the case & it is the ruin of them and familys in many instances … untill a substitute of beer or some other drink is introduced in general, it will be difficult to get over it".

[27] *Diary of William Bentley*, vol. i, pp. 167, 175, 217, 218, 244, 247, 248, 255, 256, 281 *et seq.*

[28] *Autobiography and Correspondence of Lyman Beecher*, vol. i, p. 30.

[29] *Ibid.*, p. 24. The description of the meeting of the Consociation, pp. 214 *et seq.*, is unusually vivid: " … the preparation for our creature comforts in the sitting-room of Mr. Heart's house, besides food, was a broad sideboard, covered with decanters and bottles, and sugar, and pitchers of water. There we found all the various kinds of liquors then in vogue. The drinking was apparently universal. This preparation was made by the society as a matter of course. When the Consociation arrived, they always took something to drink round; also before public services, and always on their return.

As they could not all drink at once, they were obliged to stand and wait, as people do when they go to mill. There was a decanter of spirits also on the dinnertable, to help digestion, and gentlemen partook of it through the afternoon and evening as they felt the need, some more and some less; and the sideboard, with the spillings of water, and sugar, and liquor, looked and smelled like the bar of a very active grog-shop. None of the Consociation were drunk; but that there was not, at times, a considerable amount of exhilaration, I can not affirm." It was Beecher's judgment that "the tide was swelling in the drinking habits of society." *Ibid.*, p. 215.

[30] *Ibid.*, vol. i, pp. 133, 138, 163, 255, 256, 371; vol. ii. pp. 294, 328 *et seq.*

[31] *A Discourse on Some Events of the Last Century, delivered in the Brick Church in New Haven, on Wednesday, January 7, 1801. By Timothy Dwight, President of Yale College*, New Haven, 1801. *Cf.* this author's *Travels in New England and New York*, vol. iv, pp. 353 *et seq.*

[32] Dwight's *Century Sermon*, p. 18.

[33] *Ibid.*, pp. 18 *et seq.*

[34] The testimony of a European traveller should prove as edifying as that of an intimate participant in the country's life. In 1788, Brissot de Warville visited America. He remarked the change which had come over the people of New England, of Boston in particular. The old "Presbyterian austerity, which interdicted all pleasures, even that of walking; which forbade travelling on Sunday, which persecuted men whose opinions were different from their own" was no longer to be encountered. Yet no evidence of the corruption of morals presented itself to the distinguished traveller. On the contrary, he remarked the general wholesomeness and soundness of domestic life, and the general poise and temperance of a people which, "since the ancient puritan austerity has disappeared", was able to play cards without yielding to the gambling instinct and to enjoy its clubs and parties without offending the spirit of

courtesy and good-breeding. The glow upon the soul of Brissot as he contemplates the prosperity and unaffected simplicity of the people of Boston is evident as he writes: "With what pleasure did I contemplate this town, which first shook off the English yoke! which, for a long time, resisted all the seductions, all the menaces, all the horrors of a civil war! How I delighted to wander up and down that long street, whose simple houses of wood border the magnificent channel of Boston, and whose full stores offer me all the productions of the continent which I had quitted! How I enjoyed the activity of the merchants, the artizans, and the sailors! It was not the noisy vortex of Paris; it was not the unquiet, eager mien of my countrymen; it was the simple, dignified air of men, who are conscious of liberty, and who see in all men their brothers and their equals. Everything in this street bears the marks of a town still in its infancy, but which, even in its infancy, enjoys a great prosperity…. Boston is just rising from the devastations of war, and its commerce is flourishing; its manufactures, productions, arts, and sciences, offer a number of curious and interesting observations." (Brissot De Warville, *New Travels in the United States of America*, pp. 70–82.) Equally laudatory comment respecting the state of society in Connecticut is made by Brissot (pp. 108, 109).

John Bernard, the English comedian, who was in this country at the close of the eighteenth century, found the state of society very much like that which he had left in his own country. "They wore the same clothes, spoke the same language, and seemed to glow with the same affable and hospitable feelings. In walking along the mall I could scarcely believe I had not been whisked over to St. James's Park; and in their houses the last modes of London were observable in nearly every article of ornament or utility. Other parts of the state were, however, very different." (Bernard, *Retrospections of America, 1797–1811*, p. 29.) Bernard found in New England abundant evidences of progress such as he had not been accustomed to in England, and splendid stamina of character (p. 30). Nothing, apparently, suggested to him that the people were not virile and sound.

[35] Bentley, *Diary*, vol. i, pp. 253 *et seq.*, discusses at length "the Puerile Sports usual in these parts of New England". Weeden, *Economic and Social History of New England*, vol. ii, p. 696, comments on the dearth of public amusement. *Cf.* also *ibid.*, p. 864. The changed attitude of the public toward dancing, as reported by Weeden, pp. 696 and 864, doubtless finds its explanation in the growing consciousness that the resources in the way of entertainment deserve to be increased. At the close of the century, however, dancing was still frowned upon. Bentley, *Diary*, vol. ii, pp. 17, 232, 233, 296, 322, 363.

[36] Brissot, *New Travels in the United States of America*, p. 72: "Music, which their teachers formerly prescribed as a diabolic art, begins to make part of their education. In some houses you hear the forte-piano. This art, it is true, is still in its infancy; but the young novices who exercise it, are so gentle, so complaisant, and so modest, that the proud perfection of art gives no pleasure equal to what they afford." *Cf.* also Bentley, *Diary*, vol. ii, pp. 247 *et seq.*, 292.

[37] Brissot, *New Travels in the United States of America*, pp. 86 *et seq.* Brissot generously explains this fact upon the ground that in a country so new, whose immediate concerns were so compelling, and where, also, wealth is not centered in a few hands, the cultivation of the arts and sciences is not to be expected. On the side of invention the situation was far from being as bad as a reading of Brissot might seem to imply. Weeden, *Economic and Social History of New England*, vol. ii, pp. 847–858.

[38] Goddard, *Studies in New England Transcendentalism*, p. 18. While the passage cited deals with an earlier situation, the general observation made concerning the well-poised character of the New England type of mind is as valid for the close of the eighteenth century as for the corresponding period of the preceding century; and the failure of New England to take a "plunge … from the moral heights of Puritanism" is all the more impressive in the later period in view of the variety and character of the new incitements and impulses which the people

of New England generally felt in the period following the Revolution.

[39] Conspicuous in this group was the new merchant class. In the wake of the Revolution came an industrial and commercial revival which profoundly affected the life of New England. While the period of the Confederation, on account of its political disorganization and the chaotic state of public finance and the currency, was characterized by extreme economic depression, on the other hand, the adoption of the Constitution communicated to the centers of industry and commerce a feeling of optimism. The sense that a federal government had been formed, equal to the task of guaranteeing to its citizens the rights and privileges of trade, gave early evidence that the economic impulses of the country had been quickened notably. Such evidence is too abundant and too well known either to permit or to require full statement here, but the following is suggestive: The fisheries of New England, which had been nearly destroyed during the Revolution, had so far revived by 1789 that a total of 480 vessels, representing a tonnage of 27,000, were employed in the industry. At least 32,000 tons of shipping were built in the United States, a very large part of this in New England, in 1791. Before the war the largest amount built in any one year was 26,544 tons. But the record of 1791 was modest. From 1789 to 1810, American shipping increased from 202,000 to 1,425,000 tons. Because of the federal government's proclamation of strict neutrality with regard to the wars abroad, the carrying trade of the world came largely into the hands of shipowners and seamen of the United States, with the result that the dockyards and wharves of New England fairly hummed with activity. The exports of 1793 amounted to $33,026,233. By 1799 they had mounted to $78,665,522, of which $33,142,522 was the growth, produce, or manufacture of the Union. Within a very few years after the adoption of the Constitution, American merchants had become the warehousers and distributors of merchandise to all parts of the world. The wharves of New England were covered with goods from Europe, the Orient, the West Indies, and from the

looms, shops, and distilleries of the nation. Directed by resourceful and far-sighted men who had the instinct for commercial expansion, ships sailed from New England ports for Batavia, Canton, Calcutta, St. Petersburg, Port Louis. They carried with them coffee, fish, flour, provisions, tobacco, rum, iron, cattle, horses; they brought back molasses, sugar, wine, indigo, pepper, salt, muslins, calicoes, silks, hemp, duck. The situation is dealt with in detail by Bishop, *History of American Manufactures*, vol. ii, pp. 13–82; Clark, *History of Manufactures in the United States*, pp. 227 *et seq.*; Weeden, *Economic and Social History of New England*, vol. ii, pp. 816–857.

[40] Winsor, *The Memorial History of Boston*, vol. iii, pp. 191, 203; Morse, *The Federalist Party in Massachusetts*, pp. 37, 38; *Harvard Theological Review*, January, 1916, p. 104.

[41] Weeden, *Early Life in Rhode Island*, pp. 357 *et seq.*, calls attention to the spacious and elegant houses which were built at Providence about 1790, and to the new group of merchants which the expansion of trans-oceanic commerce called into existence there. Weeden, *Economic and Social History of New England*, pp. 821 *et seq.*, deals with the situation in a larger way.

[42] Parker, *History of the Second Church of Christ in Hartford*, p. 172. The passage contains a vivid picture of the state of polite society in an important Connecticut center. Love, *The Colonial History of Hartford*, pp. 244 *et seq.*, deals with the transformation of social life with particular reference to the disintegration of Puritanism.

[43] An outcry against the excesses of fashion began to make itself heard. "An Old Farmer," writing to the *Massachusetts Spy*, March 27, 1799, complains on account of the consequent drain upon the purses of husbands and fathers: "I am a plain farmer, and therefore beg leave to trouble you with a little plain language. By the dint of industry, and application to agricultural concerns, I have, till lately, made out to keep

square with the world. But the late scarcity of money, together with the extravagance of fashions have nearly ruined me.... I am by no means tenacious of the *old way*, or of *old fashions*. I know that my family must dress different from what I used to when I was young; yet as I have the interest of husbands and fathers at heart, I wish there might be some reformation in the present mode of female dress.... In better times, six or seven yards of Calico would serve to make a gown; but now fourteen yards are scarcely sufficient. I do not perceive that women grow any larger now than formerly.... A few years since, my daughters were not too proud to wear good calfskin shoes; two pair of which would last them a year: But now none will suit them but morroco, and these must be of the slenderest kind.... Young ladies used to be contented with wearing nothing on their heads but what Nature gave them.... But now they dare not appear in company, unless they have half a bushel of gauze, and other stuff, stuck on their heads". The letter closes with a humorous account of the writer's embarrassing experience with the trains of the ladies' dresses on the occasion of a recent visit to church.

[44] Swift, Lindsay, *The Massachusetts Election Sermons* (Publications of the Colonial Society of Massachusetts, vol. i, Transactions, 1892–1894), pp. 428 *et seq.*

[45] Weeden, *Economic and Social History of New England*, vol. ii, pp. 864 *et seq.*

[46] Scudder, *Recollections of Samuel Breck, with Passages from His Note-Books*, pp. 178 *et seq.* Breck visited New England about 1791. He was impressed with the looseness of life and gross lawlessness which he saw. A fairer judgment appears on page 182: "The severe, gloomy puritanical spirit that had governed New England since the days of the Pilgrim forefathers was gradually giving way in the principal towns", *etc.*

[47] Lauer, *Church and State in New England* (Johns Hopkins University Studies in History and Political Science. Tenth Series), pp. 95 *et seq.*

[48] The term "Standing Order" was generally employed in the speech and literature of the period, and had reference to the alliance between the party of the Establishment and the party of the government.

[49] The scope of inquiry prescribed by the special object of this dissertation renders both unnecessary and unprofitable the tracing of this struggle in detail. Valuable special studies in this field are available. Among these the following are to be commended as of exceptional usefulness: Burrage, *A History of the Baptists in New England*; Greene, *The Development of Religious Liberty in Connecticut*; Reed, *Church and State in Massachusetts, 1691–1740*; Cobb, *The Rise of Religious Liberty in America*; Ford, *New England's Struggle for Religious Liberty*. Lauer's excellent treatise has already been cited. Of contemporaneous treatments, Backus, *A History of New England, with Particular Reference to the Denomination of Christians called Baptists*, though deficient in literary merit, is doubtless the most trustworthy and replete. The citations made from the latter work refer, unless otherwise indicated, to the edition of 1871 (2 vols.).

[50] *The Charter Granted by Their Majesties King William and Queen Mary, to the Inhabitants of the Massachusetts-Bay in New-England*, Boston in New England, 1726, p. 9. The principle of church membership as a qualification for voting was set aside for a property qualification.

[51] Backus, *History of New England*, vol. i, pp. 446 *et seq. Cf.* Reed, *Church and State in Massachusetts, 1691–1740*, pp. 23 *et seq.*

[52] Backus, *History of New England*, vol. i, p. 448.

[53] *Charters and "Acts and Laws" of the Province of Massachusetts-Bay, With Appended Acts and Laws*, Boston,

1726–1735, p. 383. The law provided that "all persons who profess themselves to be of the Church of England", and who were so situated that "there is a Person in Orders according to the Rules of the Church of England setled [*sic*], and abiding among them and performing Divine Service within Five Miles of the Habitation, or usual Residence of any Person professing himself as aforesaid of the Church of England", might have his rate-money reserved for the support of the Episcopal church.

[54] *Charters and "Acts and Laws" of the Province of Mass.*, etc., p. 423. The five-mile limitation formed a part of this legislation, also.

[55] Burrage, *History of the Baptists in New England*, p. 105.

[56] Palfrey, *A Compendious History of New England*, vol. iv, pp. 94, 95.

[57] *Acts and Resolves, Public and Private, etc.*, vol. iii, p. 645.

[58] *Ibid.*

[59] Backus, *History of New England*, vol. ii, p. 140.

[60] *Ibid.*

[61] *Ibid.*

[62] Separatists or Separates were the names by which those were commonly designated who withdrew from the orthodox churches on account of the controversies occasioned by the Great Awakening. See Blake, S. Leroy, *The Separates or Strict Congregationalists of New England*, Boston, 1902, pp. 17 *et seq.*

[63] Hovey, *A Memoir of the Life and Times of the Rev. Isaac Backus*, p. 171.

[64] Backus, *History of New England*, vol. ii, pp. 96 *et seq.* Backus himself suffered imprisonment under this act. See *ibid.*, p. 109.

[65] Greene, *The Development of Religious Liberty in Connecticut*, pp. 235 *et seq.* The process of absorption referred to had much to do with the breaking up of the Separatist movement. Few of these congregations continued to exist until the struggle for religious freedom was fully won. Other contributory causes in the breaking up of the movement were the poverty of the members of these congregations, the difficulties they experienced in securing pastoral care, and the dissensions that arose among them in the exercise of their boasted rights of private judgment, public exhortation, and the interpretation of the Scriptures.

[66] Backus, *History of New England*, vol. ii, pp. 140 *et seq.*

[67] Backus, *op. cit.*, p. 141.

[68] *Ibid.*

[69] *Cf. Minutes of the Warren Association for 1769*, quoted by Burrage, *History of the Baptists in New England*, pp. 108 *et seq. Cf.* the following, taken from a statement and appeal to Baptists, in the *Boston Evening Post*, Aug. 20, 1770: "To the Baptists in the Province of Massachusetts Bay, who are, or have been, oppressed in any way on a religious account. It would be needless to tell you that you have long felt the effects of the laws by which the religion of the government in which you live is established. Your purses have felt the burden of ministerial rates; and when these would not satisfy your enemies, your property hath been taken from you and sold for less than half its value…. You will therefore readily hear and attend when you are desired to collect your cases of suffering, and have them well attested; such as, the taxes you have paid to build meeting-houses, to settle ministers and support them, with all the time, money and labor you have lost in waiting on courts, feeing lawyers, &c.; and bring or send such cases to the Baptist Association to be held at Bellingham; when measures will be resolutely adopted for obtaining redress from another quarter than that to which repeated application hath been made unsuccessfully. Nay, complaints, however just and grievous,

hath been treated with indifference, and scarcely, if at all credited". (Quoted by Backus, *History of New England*, vol. ii, p. 155.)

[70] Backus, *History of New England*, vol. ii, pp. 156 *et seq.*

[71] This standing committee of the Warren Association is itself a token of the strengthened purpose of the Baptists.

[72] The address is given in full in Hovey, *A Memoir of the Life and Times of Isaac Backus*, pp. 218–221. It drew a kindly response from the Provincial Congress, signed by John Hancock as president, pleading the inability of the Congress to give redress and advising the aggrieved parties to submit their case to the General Court of Massachusetts at its next session. This step was taken in September, 1775; but beyond the fact that a bill, drawn to give redress, was once read in the sessions of the Assembly, nothing came at the matter. "Such", remarks Backus, "is the disposition of mankind". (*Cf.* Backus, *History of New England*, vol. ii, pp. 202 *et seq. Cf.* Burrage, *History of the Baptists in New England*, pp. 113 *et seq.*)

[73] *The Laws of the Commonwealth of Massachusetts, Passed from the Year 1780, to the End of the Year 1800*, vol. i, pp. 19, 20.

[74] *Ibid.*

[75] Backus, *History of New England*, vol. ii, pp. 228 *et seq.*, for cases of persecution under the operation of the bill of rights.

[76] The contribution made by the newspapers must not be overlooked in this connection. From about 1770 on there may be traced a growing disposition on the part of dissenters to air their grievances in the public journals. Supporters of the Establishment were not slow to respond.

[77] In addition to the two specifically referred to, Backus published the following: *Policy, as well as Honesty, Forbids the Use of Secular Force in Religious Affairs*, Boston, 1779;

Truth is Great, and Will Prevail, Boston, 1781; *A Door Opened for Equal Christian Liberty, etc.*, Boston, 1783.

[78] Backus, *op. cit.*, p. 13.

[79] Quoted from Backus, *History of New England*, vol. ii, p. 223.

[80] Walker, *History of the Congregational Churches in the United States*, pp. 206–209.

[81] *Cf. A Vindication of the Government of the New-England Churches, etc.*, Boston, 1772. The first edition of 500 copies was quickly subscribed for, and a second was published the same year.

[82] An edition of Wise's tracts was published as late as 1860, by the Congregational Board of Publication. From that edition the citations are drawn. The following from the "Introductory Notice" is of interest: " … some of the most glittering sentences of the immortal Declaration of Independence are almost literal quotations from this essay of John Wise [*i. e., Vindication of the Government of New-England Churches*]. And it is a significant fact, that in 1772, only four years before the declaration was made, a large edition of both those tracts was published by subscription in one duodecimo volume. The presumption which this fact alone suggests, that it was used as a political text-book in the great struggle for freedom then opening, is fully confirmed by the list of subscribers' names printed at the end, with the number of copies annexed." Page xx *et seq.*

[83] *Ibid.*, pp. 48–50, 54, 56.

[84] Wise, *op. cit.*, p. 56.

[85] Backus, *History of New England*, vol. ii, pp. 391–401, furnishes the following table of Baptist strength in New England in the year 1795: Churches, 325; ministers, 232; members, 20,902. Methodism had emerged in New England within the last quarter of the century, and Methodist ministers

were indefatigable in their labors. By the close of the century as generous-minded a Congregational minister as Bentley could not altogether cover over his chagrin on account of the growth and influence of the "sects". *Cf. Diary of William Bentley*, vol. ii, pp. 127, 409, 419.

[86] Backus, *History of New England*, vol. ii, p. 235. *Cf.* Burrage, *History of the Baptist in New England*, pp. 121 *et seq.*

[87] Cobb, *The Rise of Religious Liberty in America*, pp. 509–511.

[88] Backus, *History of New England*, vol. ii, p. 341.

[89] *Ibid.*, pp. 351 *et seq.*, 379.

[90] Backus, *op. cit.*, pp. 353 *et seq.*

[91] *Ibid.*, p. 379.

[92] Actual disestablishment did not come in Massachusetts until 1833.

[93] Since the particular purpose of this chapter is to explain the bitter spirit existing between the orthodox party and dissenters in New England near the close of the eighteenth century, rather than to re-write the history of the struggle for full religious toleration, much that occurred in the long process of severing the bond between church and state may be passed over. Attention will be focused upon the character rather than the chronology of the struggle.

[94] Cobb, *The Rise of Religious Liberty in America*, p. 238; Fiske, *The Beginnings of New England*, pp. 123 *et seq.*

[95] Greene, *The Development of Religious Liberty in Connecticut*, p. 121; Cobb, *The Rise of Religious Liberty in America*, p. 243.

[96] Cobb, *op. cit.*, pp. 244, 246.

[97] *Ibid.*, pp. 240 *et seq.*; Greene, *The Development of Religious Liberty in Connecticut*, pp. 62 *et seq.*, 68.

[98] It was the judgment of Isaac Backus that "oppression was greater in Connecticut, than in other governments in New England". (*History of New England*, vol. ii, p. 404.)

[99] Cobb, *The Rise of Religious Liberty in America*, p. 244. Cobb's statement concerning the lack of harshness and ungentleness which characterized the attitude of the supporters of the state church toward dissent is extreme. The controlling spirit of the Standing Order was doubtless a positive concern for the welfare of the Establishment rather than a desire to weed out dissent; but the clash of interests became so sharp and bitter that motives did not remain unmixed, and in many an instance dissent in Connecticut was compelled to reckon with a spirit of actual persecution.

[100] *The Public Records of the Colony of Connecticut*, vol. i, p. 21.

[101] Cobb, *The Rise of Religious Liberty in America*, pp. 246 *et seq.*

[102] *The Public Records of the Colony of Connecticut*, vol. i, p. 311.

[103] *Ibid.*, pp. 356, 362; vol. ii, pp. 99, 240; vol. iii, pp. 78, 82 *et seq.*

[104] *Ibid.*, vol. iii, pp. 13, 18, 101, 216 *et seq.*

[105] *Ibid.*, vol. iv, pp. 67, 127, 136 *et seq.*

[106] *Ibid.*, vol. vii, p. 554.

[107] *Ibid.*, pp. 334, 335.

[108] *Ibid.*, vol. iii, p. 183.

[109] *Ibid.*, vol. i, pp. 437 *et seq.*

[110] *Ibid.*, vol. iii, p. 104.

[111] Cobb, *The Rise of Religious Liberty in America*, p. 247.

[112] Walker, *The Creeds and Platforms of Congregationalism*, pp. 465 *et seq.*

[113] Walker, *A History of the Congregational Churches in the United States*, pp. 202 *et seq.*; Greene, *The Development of Religious Liberty in Connecticut*, pp. 133 *et seq.*

[114] Walker, *The Creeds and Platforms of Congregationalism*, pp. 491–494.

[115] *The Public Records of the Colony of Connecticut*, vol. v, pp. 51 *et seq.*

[116] *Ibid.*

[117] *Ibid.*

[118] Walker, *The Creeds and Platforms of Congregationalism*, pp. 502–506, where "The Saybrook Meeting and Articles" are printed in full. For expositions, see Backus, *History of New England*, vol. i, pp. 470 *et seq.*; Palfrey, *A History of New England*, vol. iii, p. 342; Dexter, *The Congregationalism of the last Three Hundred Years*, pp. 489, 490.

[119] *The Public Records of the Colony of Connecticut*, vol. v, p. 87.

[120] Greene, *The Development of Religious Liberty in Connecticut*, p 151.

[121] *Cf. supra*, p. 53.

[122] *The Public Records of the Colony of Connecticut*, vol. v, p. 50. It seems clear that either through neglect or evasion a considerable number of congregations failed to qualify under the law. In any event the legislature deemed itself warranted in passing an act, May, 1721, imposing a fine of five shillings on persons convicted of not having attended "the publick worship of God on the Lord's day in some congregation by law

allowed." (See *ibid.*, vol. vi, p. 248.) Churches which for doctrinal or other reasons withdrew from the Establishment suffered serious embarrassments on account of this law respecting the licensing of congregations.

[123] *Ibid.*, vol. v, p. 50. Any infraction of this law was to be punished by a heavy fine. Failure to pay the fine involved heavy bail or imprisonment.

[124] Greene, *The Development of Religious Liberty in Connecticut*, pp. 191 *et seq.*

[125] *The Public Records of the Colony of Connecticut*, vol. vi, p. 106.

[126] *The Pub. Records of the Colony of Conn.*, vol. vi, pp. 237, 257. Unlike the Massachusetts exemption laws passed on behalf of these two bodies, these were perpetual.

[127] *Collections of the Connecticut Historical Society: Talcott Papers*, vol. v, pp. 9–13; Backus, *History of New England*, vol. ii, pp. 98 *et seq.*

[128] Parker, *History of the Second Church of Christ in Hartford*, pp. 117, 119; *Papers of the New Haven Colony Historical Society*, vol. iv: *The Bradford Annals*, pp. 318 *et seq.*; Backus, *History of New England*, vol. ii, pp. 57 *et seq.*, 79 *et seq.* For the account of the difficulties of a particular Separatist congregation, see Dutton, *The History of the North Church in New Haven*, pp. 25–28. *Cf. The Public Records of the Colony of Connecticut*, vol. xi, pp. 323 *et seq.*; also Beardsley, *The History of the Episcopal Church in Connecticut*, vol. i, p. 140.

[129] The bigoted and unfeeling spirit which controlled the authorities is well expressed in the act of May, 1743. Proceeding on the assumption that the Separatists, taking advantage of the act of May, 1708, were responsible for the disruptive tactics and measures of the times, by means of which "some of the parishes established by the laws of this Colony …

have been greatly damnified, and by indirect means divided and parted," the General Court repealed the act in question, and put in its place the following: "And be it further enacted, that, for the future, if any of His Majesty's good subjects, being protestants, inhabitants of this Colony, that shall soberly dissent from the way of worship and ministry established by the laws of this Colony, that such persons may apply themselves to this Assembly for relief, where they shall be heard. *And such persons as have any distinguishing character, by which they may be known from the presbyterians or congregationalists, and from the consociated churches established by the laws of this Colony, may expect the indulgence of this Assembly* [Italics mine.—V. S.], having first before this Assembly taken the oaths and subscribed the declaration provided in the act of Parliament in cases of like nature." (*The Public Records of the Colony of Connecticut*, vol. viii, p. 522. *Cf.* Backus, *History of New England*, vol. ii, p. 58.)

[130] *The Public Records of the Colony of Connecticut*, vol. viii, p. 454.

[131] *Ibid.*, p. 456.

[132] *The Pub. Records of the Colony of Conn.*, vol. viii, p. 456.

[133] *Ibid.*, p. 457.

[134] Backus, *History of New England*, vol. ii, p. 57.

[135] Cobb, *The Rise of Religious Liberty in America*, pp. 274 *et seq.* Greene, *The Development of Religious Liberty in Connecticut*, pp. 244 *et seq.*

[136] *Cf. supra*, Footnote 129.

[137] Backus, *History of New England*, vol. ii, pp. 59 *et seq.*, 62, 65 *et seq.*, 77 *et seq.*, 81 *et seq.*

[138] Greene, *The Development of Religious Liberty in Connecticut*, pp. 248–262. The difficulties experienced by three

congregations in New Haven, Canterbury, and Enfield, are dealt with in detail.

[139] A revision of Connecticut laws took place in 1750. The unjust legislation of 1742–43 and of the following years was quietly left out.

[140] *Papers of the New Haven Colony Historical Society*, vol. iii, pp. 398 *et seq.*

[141] *Acts and Laws of the State of Connecticut, in America*, p. 21.

[142] *Acts and Laws of the State of Connecticut, in America*, p. 21.

[143] Parker, *History of the Second Church of Hartford*, pp. 170, 171. *Cf.* Beecher, *Autobiography, Correspondence, etc.*, vol. i, p. 302. The latter's account of the situation is much softened by his sympathies with the dominant party.

[144] By this time dissenters and Anti-Federalists had largely consolidated their interests. The political program of the latter drew upon the former all the suspicions and antagonisms which the Standing Order entertained toward the foes of Federalism. The acrimonious discussion which arose at this time over the disposition of the Western Reserve and the funds thus derived, admirably illustrates the cross-currents of religious and political agitation in the last decade of the century. *Cf.* Greene, *The Development of Religious Liberty in Connecticut*, pp. 380–392.

[145] This is readily explicable in view of the fact that most of the magistrates were adherents of the Establishment. The comment of Backus touches the pith of the matter, as dissenters saw it: "Thus the civil authority in the uppermost religious party in their State, was to judge the consciences of all men who dissented from their worship." (*History of New England*, vol. ii, p. 345.)

[146] *Acts and Laws of the State of Connecticut*, p. 418.

[147] In September, 1818, by the adoption of the new state constitution, the long wearisome struggle was brought to an end, and State and Church in Connecticut were separated completely.

[148] This point of view was tersely set forth in the election sermon preached by the Rev. Mr. Payson, at Boston, May 27, 1778: "Let the restraints of religion once be broken down, as they infallibly would be by leaving the subject of public worship to the humours of the multitude, and we might well defy all human wisdom and power to support and preserve order and government in the state."—Quoted by Backus, *Church History of New England, from 1620 to 1804* (ed. of 1844, Philadelphia), pp. 204 *et seq.*

[149] The state of feelings shared by the supporters of the Establishment at the time when the blow fell severing the bond between the church and state in Connecticut, is vividly expressed by Beecher: "It was a time of great depression.... It was as dark a day as ever I saw. The injury done to the cause of Christ, as we then supposed, was irreparable. For several days I suffered what no tongue can tell *for the best thing that ever happened to the State of Connecticut.*" (*Autobiography, Correspondence, etc.,* vol. i, p. 304.)

[150] This was the view propounded by President Ezra Stiles, of Yale, in his election sermon of May 3, 1783: "Through the liberty enjoyed here, all religious sects will grow up into large and respectable bodies. But the Congregational and Presbyterian denominations, however hitherto despised, will, by the blessing of Heaven continue to hold the greatest figure in America, and, notwithstanding all the fruitless labors and exertions to proselyte us to other communions, become more numerous than the whole collective body of our fellow protestants in Europe." (Quoted by Backus, *History of New England*, vol. ii, p. 312.)

To this exposition and bold forecast Backus took decided objections, on the grounds (1) that *persecution* and not *tolerance* had promoted the growth of sects in America, and (2) that the numerical increase of the Congregationalists and Presbyterians in this country did not justify any such prediction. *Cf. ibid.*, pp. 403–407.

[151] Perhaps no man more boldly stated this interpretation of the motives that inspired the Standing Order than Abraham Bishop, leader of the forces of Republicanism in Connecticut and arch-enemy of "ecclesiastical aristocrats." "The religion of the country is made a stalking horse for political jockies … Thanksgiving and fasts have been often improved for political purposes and the miserable gleanings from half a year's ignorance of the true interests of our country have been palmed on the people, by the political clergy, as a pious compliance with the governor's very pious proclamations…. The union of Church and State … [is] the grand fortress of the 'friends of order and good government.'" (*Oration delivered at Wallingford, New Haven*, 1801, pp. 46, 83.) That "the church is in danger" has for some time past been one of the most frequent and frantic of all the absurd cries heard in the land, and that New England through her clannishness has produced "patriarchs in opinion" who assume the prerogative of dictating the opinions of the people on all subjects, are further trenchant comments of the same orator. (*Ibid.*, pp. 13, 17.) Bishop's observations respecting the alleged specious and insincere character of those public utterances by which "the friends of order and good government" sought to preserve the *status quo*, are equally pointed. "The sailor nailed the needle of his compass to the cardinal point and swore that it should not be always traversing. So does the New England friend of order: but he cautiously conceals the oppression and imposture, which sustains these habits…. This cry of *steady habits* has a talismanic effect on the minds of our people; but nothing can be more hollow, vain and deceitful. Recollect for a moment that everything valuable in our world has been at one time innovation, illuminatism, modern philosophy, atheism…. Our steady habits have calmly assumed domination over the rights of conscience and suffrage. Certainly the trinitarian doctrine is

established by law and the denial of it is placed in the rank follies. Though we have ceased to transport from town to town, quakers, new lights, and baptists; yet the dissenters from our prevailing denomination are, even at this moment, praying for the repeal of those laws which abridge the rights of conscience." (*Ibid.*, pp. 14, 16.)

[152] Quoted by Walker, in his *History of the Congregational Churches in the United States*, p. 216.

[153] Green, *Life*, pp. 224, 225.

[154] *Cf. supra*, pp. 36 and 37 *et seq.*

[155] See Walker, *Creeds and Platforms of Congregationalism*, p. 287.

[156] The lowest point of religious decline in the history of New England was reached in the first quarter of the eighteenth century. The absence of vital piety was generally remarked. The prevailing type of religious experience was unemotional and formal. The adoption of the Half-Way Covenant in the third quarter of the previous century helped to precipitate a state of things wherein the ordinary distinctions between the converted and the unconverted were largely obscured. Emphasis came to be laid heavily upon the cultivation of morality as a means of promoting spiritual life. Prayer, the reading of the Bible, and church attendance were other "means". In other words, man's part in the acquisition of religious experience came prominently into view. The promoters of the revival attacked these notions, asserting that repentance and faith were still fundamentally necessary and that the experience of conversion, *i. e.*, the conscious sense of a change in one's relation to God, was the prime test of one's hope of salvation. Charles Chauncy, minister of the First Church, Boston, in his *Seasonable Thoughts on the State of Religion in New England* (1743), championed the former position; the great Edwards came to the defence of the latter.

[157] Channing, *Memoirs*, vol. i. pp. 287–290, 387. *Cf.* also Goddard, *Studies in New England Transcendentalism*, pp. 13 *et seq.*

[158] Riley, *American Philosophy*, p. 192. Note: It is not here maintained that radical religious ideas in New England had their earliest roots, or found their sole stimulus, in the controversy which the theological formulations incident to the Great Awakening provoked. Incipient religious liberalism is distinguishable as far back as the publication of Cotton Mather's *Reasonable Religion*, in 1713. In his erudite essay on "The Beginnings of Arminianism in New England," F. A. Christie adopts the position that prior to the Great Awakening there were rumor and alarm over the mere arrival of Arminian doctrines in this country; but that after 1742 the heresy spread rapidly, chiefly due to the growth of the Episcopal church, with its marked leanings to the Arminian theology. *Cf. Papers of the American Society of Church History, Second Series*, vol. iii, pp. 168 *et seq.* But however that may be, the cause of Arminianism during the eighteenth century was promoted by men in New England who drew at least a part of their inspiration from the writings of leaders of thought in the mother country whose theological positions inclined strongly toward rationalism. *Cf.* Cooke, *Unitarianism in America*, pp. 39, 44 *et seq.*, 79. Harvard College, from the close of the seventeenth century on, was increasingly recognized as a center of liberalizing tendencies, although none will dispute that the kernel of intellectual independence was found, all too frequently, well hidden within the tough shell of traditional conceits. *Cf.* Quincy, *The History of Harvard University*, vol. i, pp. 44–57, 199 *et seq.* Independent impulses were largely responsible for the following events which mark the definite emergence of Unitarianism in America: the organization of the first New England Unitarian congregation at Gloucester, Mass., in 1779; the publication in this country, five years later, of the London edition of Dr. Charles Chauncy's *Salvation for All Men*; and the defection from Trinitarian standards of King's Chapel, Boston, in 1785–87. Still it must be maintained that the controversies

which raged around the doctrines of the New Calvinism beyond all other factors stiffened the inclinations and tendencies of the century toward liberal thinking. Such terms as "Arminianism", "Pelagianism", "Socinianism", "Arianism", etc., which occur with ever-increasing frequency from the fourth decade of the century on, are in themselves suggestive of the divergencies in religious opinion which the doctrinal discussion incident to the Great Awakening provoked. Cf. Fiske, *A Century of Science and Other Essays*: "The Origins of Liberal Thought in America", pp. 148 *et seq.*

[159] As a typical illustration the comment of Lyman Beecher may be cited: "The Deistic controversy was an existing thing, and the battle was hot, the crisis exciting." (*Autobiography, Correspondence, etc.* vol. i, p. 52.) The date is about 1798. In the same connection President Dwight of Yale is referred to as "the great stirrer-up of that [*i. e.*, the deistic] controversy on this side the Atlantic." (*Ibid.*) It is certain that Dwight had some acquaintance with the works of the leading English deists, and that he opposed their views. Cf. *Travels in New England and New York*, vol. iv, p. 362; but his main target was infidelity of the French school. Beecher fails to distinguish between the two.

[160] One discovers no convincing evidence that the deistical views of Benjamin Franklin produced any direct effect upon the thought of New England. As respects Thomas Jefferson the case was different. But New England Federalists were so successful in keeping public attention fixed on Jefferson's fondness for French political and religious philosophy, that his alleged "French infidelity" rather than his opinions concerning natural religion became and continued to be the bone of contention. That he was regarded as a deist is, however, not to be questioned. Bentley, *Diary*, vol. iii, p. 20.

[161] Allen's book of some 477 pages bore the following pretentious and rambling title: *Reason the only Oracle of Man, or a Compendius System of Natural Religion. Alternately Adorned with Confutations of a Variety of Doctrines incompatible to it; Deduced from the Most Exalted Ideas which*

we are able to form of the Divine and Human Characters, and from the Universe in General. By Ethan Allen, Esq. Bennington, State of Vermont. The Preface is dated July 2, 1782. Evans records the fact that the entire edition, except about thirty copies, was destroyed by fire, said to have been caused by lightning, an event which the orthodox construed as a judgment from heaven on account of the nature of the book. *Cf. American Bibliography*, vol. vi, p. 266. The author's aim has been interpreted as an effort "to build up a system of natural religion on the basis of a deity expressed in the external universe, as interpreted by the reason of man, in which the author includes the moral consciousness." (Moncure D. Conway in *Open Court* [magazine], January 28, 1892, article: "Ethan Allen's Oracles of Reason," p. 3119.)

[162] *The Literary Diary of Ezra Stiles*, vol. iii, p. 345. The comment of Yale's president is fairly representative: "And the 13th Inst died in Vermont the profane & impious Deist Gen Ethan Allen, Author of the Oracles of Reason, a Book replete with scurrilous Reflexions on Revelation. 'And in Hell he lift up his Eyes being in Torments.'" (*Ibid.*) In 1787, at Litchfield, Connecticut, where Allen's home had once been, there was published an anonymous sermon, from the text: "And he would fain have filled his belly with the husks which the swine did eat." (Luke 15: 16.) The sermon was planned to counteract the effect produced by the "prophane, prayerless, graceless infidel," Allen, through the publication of the book in question. The author, "Common Sense" (apparently Josiah Sherman), adopts for his sermon the caption, "*A Sermon to Swine,*" and explains in the Advertisement the temper of his mood: "By way of apology, I hope Gen. Allen will pardon any reproach that may be supposable, in comparing him to the Prodigal Son, sent by the Citizen into his fields to feed Swine with husks, when he considers, what an infinitely greater reproach he casts upon the holy oracles of God, and upon his Prophets, Apostles and Ministers, and upon the Lord of life and glory himself; at whose tribunal we must all shortly appear; when he represents Him as an impostor and cheat, and all the blessed doctrines of

the gospel as falsehood and lies." (*A Sermon to Swine: From Luke xv: 16 … Containing a concise, but sufficient answer to General Allen's Oracles of Reason. By* Common Sense, A. M., Litchfield, 1787.)

An amusing albeit suggestive episode is recorded by William Bentley in his *Diary*, in connection with certain reflections on the dangers involved in the loaning of books: "Allen's *oracles of reason* … was lent to Col. C. under solemn promise of secrecy, but by him sent to a Mr. Grafton, who was reported to have died a Confirmed Infidel…. The book was found at his death in his chamber, examined with horror by his female relations. By them conveyed to a Mr. Williams … & there examined—reported to be mine from the initials W. B., viewed as an awful curiosity by hundreds, connected with a report that I encouraged infidelity in Grafton by my prayers with him in his dying hour, & upon the whole a terrible opposition to me fixed in the minds of the devout & ignorant multitude." (*Ibid.*, vol. i, p. 82.)

The following extract from Timothy Dwight's poem on *The Triumph of Infidelity* supplies another interesting contemporaneous estimate of Allen's assault upon revelation:

"In vain thro realms of nonsense ran
The great Clodhopping oracle of man.
Yet faithful were his toils: What could he more?
In Satan's cause he bustled, bruised and swore;
And what the due reward, from me shall know,
For gentlemen of equal worth below."

A foot-note explains the point in the last two lines: "In A——n's Journal, the writer observes, he presumes he shall be treated in the future world as well as other gentlemen of equal merit are treated: A sentiment in which all his countrymen will join." (*The Triumph of Infidelity: A Poem.* [Anonymous], 1788, pp. 23 *et seq.* The copy referred to is dedicated by the author "To Mons. de Voltaire.")

[163] *The Age of Reason: Part I,* appeared in America in 1794. *Cf. The Age of Reason by Thomas Paine,* edited by Moncure Daniel Conway, New York, 1901, p. vii; also advertisements of its offer for sale, *Massachusetts Spy* (Worcester), Nov. 19, 1794. The *Connecticut Courant* (Hartford), Jan. 19, and Feb. 9, 1795, contains examples of pained newspaper comment. *Walcott Papers,* vol. viii, 7.

[164] At least fifteen thousand copies of the second part of the book arrived in America in the spring of 1796, despatched from Paris by Paine, consigned to his Philadelphia friend, Mr. Franklin Bache, Republican printer, editor, and ardent servant of radicalism generally. It was clearly Paine's purpose to influence as many minds in America as possible. *Cf.* Conway, *The Writings of Thomas Paine,* vol. iv, p. 15; Paine's letter to Col. Fellows, in New York, explaining the forwarding of the books. This effort to obtain a general circulation of the *Age of Reason* did not escape the attention of men who were disturbed over the prevailing evidences of irreligion. In a fast day sermon, delivered in April, 1799, the Reverend Daniel Dana, of Newburyport, Massachusetts, called attention to the matter in the following fashion: " ... let me mention a fact which ought to excite universal alarm and horror. The well-known and detestable pamphlet of Thomas Paine, written with a professed design to revile the Christian religion, and to diffuse the poison of infidelity, was composed in France, was there printed in English, and an edition containing many thousand of copies, conveyed at a single time into our country, in order to be sold at a cheap rate, or given away, as might best ensure its circulation. What baneful success has attended this vile and insidious effort, you need not be told. That infidelity has had, for several years past, a rapid increase among us, seems a truth generally acknowledged." (*Two Sermons, delivered April 25, 1799: the day recommended by the President of the United States for National Humiliation, Fasting and Prayer.* By Daniel Dana, A. M., pastor of a church in Newburyport, 1799, p. 45). *Cf.* also *ibid.,* p. 20.

[165] *The Age of Reason* was written from the standpoint of a man who believed that the disassociation of religion from political institutions, and the elimination from it of fiction and fable, would bring in the true religion of humanity. The following excerpt sets out the author's approach and aim: "Soon after I had published the pamphlet, 'Common Sense', in America I saw the exceeding probability that a revolution in the system of government would be followed by a revolution in the system of religion. The adulterous connection of church and state, wherever it had taken place, whether Jewish, Christian, or Turkish, had so effectually prohibited by pains and penalties every discussion upon established creeds, and upon first principles of religion, that until the system of government should be changed those subjects could not be brought fairly and openly before the world; but that whenever this should be done a revolution in the system of religion would follow. Human inventions and priestcraft would be detected; and man would return to the pure, unmixed, and unadulterated belief of one God and no more." (*The Writings of Thomas Paine*, vol. ii, pp. 22 *et seq.*) Paine's exposition of the tenets of natural religion was far from scholarly, and as soon as the public became aware of the eccentric and uneven character of the book, the storm of criticism speedily blew itself out. The recoil of Paine's ugly attack upon Washington, in the same year in which the *Age of Reason* was extensively circulated in this country, materially helped to discredit the book.

[166] A partial list of the books and pamphlets, separate discourses not included, which were published in this country immediately following the appearance of the *Age of Reason* will serve to emphasize the depth of the impression which Paine's book made: (1) Priestley, Joseph, *An Answer to Mr. Paine's Age of Reason; being a Continuation of Letters to the Philosophers and Politicians of France, on the Subject of Religion; and of the Letters of a Philosophical Unbeliever.* Second Edition. Northumberlandtown, America, 1794; (2) Williams, Thomas, *The Age of Infidelity: an Answer to Thomas Paine's Age of Reason.* By a Layman (pseud.). Third Edition,

Worcester, Mass., 1794; (3) Stilwell, Samuel, *A Guide to Reason, or an Examination of Thomas Paine's Age of Reason, and Investigation of the True and Fabulous Theology*, New York, 1794; (4) Winchester, Elhanan, *Ten Letters Addressed to Mr. Paine, in Answer to His Pamphlet, entitled The Age of Reason*, Second Edition, New York, 1795; (5) Ogden, Uzal, *Antidote to Deism. The Deist Unmasked; or an Ample Refutation of all the Objections of Thomas Paine, Against the Christian Religion; as Contained in a Pamphlet, intitled (sic), The Age of Reason, etc.*, Two volumes, Newark, 1795; (6) Broaddus, Andrew, *The Age of Reason and Revelation; or Animadversions on Mr. Thomas Paine's late piece, intitled "The Age of Reason", etc.* ... Richmond, 1795; (7) Muir, James, *An Examination of the Principles Contained in the Age of Reason. In Ten Discourses*, Baltimore, 1795; (8) Belknap, Jeremy, *Dissertations on the Character, Death & Resurrection of Jesus Christ ... with remarks on some sentiments advanced in a book intitled "The Age of Reason,"* Boston, 1795; (9) Humphreys, Daniel, *The Bible Needs no Apology; or Watson's System of Religion Refuted; and the Advocate Proved an Unreliable One, by the Bible Itself: of which a short view is given, and which itself gives a short answer to Paine: in Four Letters, on Watson's Apology for the Bible, and Paine's Age of Reason*, Part the Second, Portsmouth, 1796; (10) Tytler, James, *Paine's Second Part of the Age of Reason Answered*, Salem, 1796; (11) Fowler, James, *The Truth of the Bible Fairly Put to the Test, by Confronting the Evidences of Its Own Facts*, Alexandria, 1797; (12) Levy, David, *A Defence of the Old Testament, in a Series of Letters, addressed to Thomas Paine, Author of a Book entitled, The Age of Reason, Part Second, etc.* ... New York, 1797; (13) Williams, Thomas, *Christianity Vindicated in the admirable speech of the Hon. Theo. Erskine, in the Trial of J. Williams, for Publishing Paine's Age of Reason*, Philadelphia, 1797; (14) Snyder, G., *The Age of Reason Unreasonable; or the Folly of Rejecting Revealed Religion*, Philadelphia, 1798; (15) Nelson, D., *An Investigation of that False, Fabulous and Blasphemous Misrepresentation of*

Truth, set forth by Thomas Paine, in his two volumes, entitled The Age of Reason, etc. (This volume appears to have been published pseudonymously. Advertised in Lancaster, Pa., *Intelligencer and Advertiser*, October, 1800); (16) Boudinot, Elias, *The Age of Revelation, Or, The Age of Reason shewn to be an Age of Infidelity*, Philadelphia, 1801.

[167] *Cf.* Morse, *The Federalist Party in Massachusetts*, Appendix I, pp. 217 *et seq.*, for a detailed and fairly satisfactory statement of the character and extent of the discussion which Paine's book precipitated in New England.

[168] Channing, *Memoirs*, vol. i, pp. 60, 61. On the latter page it is asserted that in order to counteract such fatal principles as those expressed in the *Age of Reason*, the patrons and governors of Harvard College had Watson's *Apology for the Bible* published and furnished to the students at the expense of the corporation. This was in 1796. Beecher's *Autobiography, Correspondence, etc.*, vol. i, pp. 30, 35, 52, touches upon the situation at Yale. *Cf.* Dwight, *Theology: Explained and Defended*, vol. i, pp. xxv, xxvi. The extensive prevalence of infidelity among Yale students is commented upon and the statement made that a considerable proportion of the class which President Dwight first taught (1795–96) "had assumed the names of principal English and French Infidels; and were more familiarly known by them than by their own." (*Ibid.*) *Cf.* Dorchester, *Christianity in the United States*, p. 319.

[169] The impression lingered on after the stir caused by the appearance of the *Age of Reason*. In 1803 Paine was in southern New England. His presence was disturbing, as the following comment of William Bentley will show: "Reports are circulated that Thomas Paine intends to visit New England. The name is enough. Every person has ideas of him. Some respect his genius and dread the man. Some reverence his political, while they hate his religious, opinions. Some love the man, but not his private manners. Indeed he has done nothing which has not extremes in it. He never appears but we love and hate him.

He is as great a paradox as ever appeared in human nature."
(*Diary*, vol. iii. p. 37. *Cf. ibid.*, vol. ii. pp. 102, 107, 145.)

[170] Hazen, *Contemporary American Opinion of the French Revolution*, pp. 141 *et seq.*

[171] *Ibid.*, p. 143.

[172] Dwight, *Travels*, vol. iv, p. 361.

[173] *Writings of Thomas Jefferson*, vol. v, pp. 154, 274; *Massachusetts Historical Collections, Sixth Series*, vol. iv, *Belknap Papers*, p. 503.

[174] The entire episode is treated with great fullness and equal vividness by Hazen, *Contemporary American Opinion of the French Revolution*, pp. 164–188.

[175] *Writings of Thomas Jefferson*, vol. vi, pp. 153 *et seq.*

[176] From the first, devotion to the French cause had not been quite unanimous. Here and there, scattered through the country, a man might be found who from the beginning of the Revolution had cherished misgivings as to the essential soundness of the principles of the French in the conflict they were waging with despotism. Occasionally a man had ventured to speak out, voicing apprehension and doubt, although usually preferring to adopt the device of pseudonymity. Conspicuous in this by no means large group were the elder and the younger Adams, the former declaring himself in his "Discourses on Davila" (*Cf. The Life and Works of John Adams*, vol. vi, pp. 223–403), and the latter in the "Publicola" letters, written in 1791, in response to Paine's treatise on "The Rights of Man". Morse, *John Quincy Adams*, p. 18. But *events*, much more than political treatises, were to break the spell which the Revolution in its earlier stages cast over the people of America.

[177] No better testimony concerning the unfavorable impression created by the execution of the French king could be had than that supplied by the comment of Salem's republican minister, the Reverend William Bentley. Under date

of March 25, 1793, he wrote: "The melancholy news of the beheading of the Roi de France is confirmed in the public opinion, & the event is regretted most sincerely by all thinking people. The french lose much of their influence upon the hearts of the Americans by this event." (*Diary*, vol. ii, p. 13. *Cf.* Hazen, *Contemporary American Opinion of the French Revolution*, pp. 254 *et seq.*) This thrill of public horror also found expression in the following lines taken from a broadside of the day:

"When *Mobs* triumphant seize the rheins,
    And guide the *Car* of *State*,
Monarchs will feel the galling chains,
    And meet the worst of fate:
For instance, view the *Gallic* shore,
    A nation, *once* polite
See what confusion hovers o'er,
    A *Star*, that shone so bright.
Then from the scene recoil with dread,
    For LOUIS is no more,
The barb'rous *Mob* cut off his head,
    And drank the spouting gore.
Shall we, the *Sons* of FREEDOM dare
    Against so *vile* a *Race*?
Unless we mean ourselves to *bare* (*sic*)
    The *palm* of their disgrace.
No! God forbid, the man who feels
    The force of *pity's* call,
To join those *Brutes*, whose *sentence* seals,
    Whose hearts are made of gall."

(*The Tragedy of Louis Capet, and Printed next the venerable Stump of Liberty Tree, for J. Plumer, Jun., Trader, of Newburyport.*) (In vol. 21 of Broadsides, Library of Congress.)

[178] Webster, *The Revolution in France considered in Respect to its Progress and Effects*, New York, 1794. Webster's discriminating pamphlet is one of the most suggestive of all American contemporaneous documents. *Cf.* Hazen,

Contemporary American Opinion of the French Revolution, p. 259.

[179] For characteristic outbursts of this nature, *cf.* Adams, *Life and Works*, vol. ii, p. 160; Gibbs, *Memoirs of the Administrations of Washington and John Adams*, vol. i, p. 90. Typical newspaper comment similar in vein may be found in the *Western Star* (Stockbridge, Mass.), March 11, 1794, and the *Gazette of the United States* (Philadelphia), April 13, 1793.

[180] As early as 1790 John Adams had spoken of the French nation as a "republic of atheists." (*Works*, vol. ix, p. 563.) Other leaders responded to similar sentiments. (Hazen, *Contemporary American Opinion of the French Revolution*, p. 266.) Familiarity with French philosophical and religious opinions before the French Revolution had supplied a basis for this concern.

[181] Aulard, *Le culte de la Raison et de l'Être suprême*, pp. 17 *et seq. Cf.* Sloane, *The French Revolution and Religious Reform*, pp. 53, 79, 97. The effort to dechristianize the institutions of religion in France is admitted by both writers, but the superficial occasion of this hostile effort is made clear.

[182] *Cf. infra*, pp. 103 *et seq.*

[183] The practice of looking to the religious situation in France for ammunition to serve the artillery of political parties in America, is well illustrated in the following instances: *The Western Star* of March 25, 1794, dwelt at length upon the depravity of French irreligion, and asserted that the lack of public alarm in this country must be accepted as convincing evidence that the American public has already yielded itself to the seductive influence and power of atheistical opinions. On the other hand, the *Independent Chronicle*, issues of March 6 and July 24, 1794, pounces upon Robespierre's scheme for the rehabilitation of religion under the guise of the cult of the Supreme Being, and with great gusto asserts that here is the positive and sufficient proof that the charge of atheism which has been lodged against the Revolutionists is as baseless as it is

wicked. An examination of the newspaper comment of the day supplies abundant warrant that this crying up and crying down of the charge of French infidelity went far in the direction of investing the political situation in New England with those characteristics of bitter and extravagant crimination and recrimination with which all political discussion in that section, as in fact throughout the entire country, near the close of the eighteenth century, was so deeply marked.

[184] By the adoption of this measure the Catholic clergy in France were turned into state officials. The relation of the Pope to the French clergy became that of a spiritual guide and counsellor only. The principle of territorial limitation on the part of ecclesiastics was also abolished. *Cf.* Sloane, *The French Revolution and Religious Reform*, pp. 121 *et seq.*

[185] Aulard, *The French Revolution*, vol. iii, pp. 152–191, gives an excellent résumé of the dechristianizing movement.

[186] The conservative press of America saw to it that this information did not escape the attention of its readers. *Cf.* Hazen, *Contemporary American Opinion of the French Revolution*, pp. 267 *et seq. Cf.* Morse, *The Federalist Party in Massachusetts*, pp. 80–87, 98 *et seq.*

[187] Hazen, *Contemporary American Opinion of the French Revolution*, pp. 269 *et seq.*

[188] Dwight, *Travels*, vol. iv, p. 362.

[189] Beecher, *Autobiography, Correspondence, etc.*, vol. i, p. 30.

[190] Baldwin, *Annals of Yale College ... From its Foundation to the Year 1831*, New Haven, 1831, p. 146.

[191] Field, *Brief Memoirs of the Members of the Class Graduated at Yale College in September, 1802. (Printed for private distribution)*, p. 9.

[192] Beecher, *Autobiography, Correspondence, etc.*, vol. i, p. 30.

[193] Sprague, *Annals of the American Pulpit*, vol. ii, pp. 164, 165. *Cf. Sketches of Yale College, with Numerous Anecdotes* … New York, 1843, p. 136.

[194] *Memoir of William Ellery Channing*, vol. i, p. 60.

[195] *Ibid.* Sidney Willard, in his *Memories of Youth and Manhood*, vol. ii, p. 101, tones down the picture appreciably.

[196] Morse, *The Federalist Party in Massachusetts*, pp. 88 *et seq.*

[197] *A Sermon Delivered to the First Congregation in Cambridge, and the Religious Society in Charlestown, April 11, 1793.* By David Tappan, A. M., Professor of Divinity in Harvard College, Boston, 1793.

[198] *Ibid.*, p. 16.

[199] David Osgood (1747–1822) was one of the best known New England clergymen of his day. Possessing a fondness for unusual public occasions, such as state and church festivals, he acquired the habit of turning them to account by way of airing his political and religious ideas, a custom which drew to him the cordial support of the Federal school to which he belonged, and the no less cordial contempt of the Republicans. *Cf.* Sprague, *Annals of the American Pulpit*, vol. ii, pp. 75, 76.

[200] The predilection of the New England clergy for political preaching requires a word. The clergy emerged from the period of the American Revolution with their reputation considerably enhanced. The cause of the struggling colonists they had supported with resolution and ability and their moral force had shown itself remarkably effective. It is also to be noted that from the settlement of the country, the clergy had been extraordinarily influential in the direction of public affairs. They were the intimates and advisers of public officials as well as the trusted counsellors of the people. After the setting up of

the government most of the questions which agitated the public mind had definite moral and religious aspects. The New England clergy would have regarded themselves as seriously remiss and therefore culpable had they not spoken out upon the burning questions of the day. With the intrusion of foreign affairs into the sphere of American politics the impulse in the direction of political preaching was decidedly strengthened. Definite issues regarding morality and religion were thus raised, and the passions of patriotism and religious devotion became inextricably woven together. Love, *The Fast and Thanksgiving Days of New England*, p. 363; Swift, *The Massachusetts Election Sermons: Publications of the Colonial Society of Massachusetts*, vol. i: *Transactions*, 1892–1894, pp. 422 *et seq.*

[201] The Democratic Societies (or Clubs), to which fuller attention is given on pp. 104 *et seq.*, instantly assumed a position of first importance in the minds of many clergyman of New England. Coupled as their emergence was with the amazing performances of Genet, they had the effect of suggesting to the clerical mind the fatal thrust at religion which might, and probably would result, on account of their subterranean operations. This idea of a secret combination against the institutions of religion in America, which proved to have a powerful attraction for many clerical minds, was definitely related to the spasm of anxiety and fear which swept the country when the presence of these secret clubs became generally known.

[202] *Cf.* [Osgood, David], *The Wonderful Works of God are to be Remembered. A Sermon delivered on the day of the Annual Thanksgiving, November 20, 1794*, Boston, 1794, pp. 21 *et seq.*

[203] On account of the virulence of party feeling, it was not to be expected that Osgood would succeed in stating the case in a manner acceptable to all. Popular opinion respecting the wisdom and fairness of Osgood's performance was far from unanimous. An opposition, inspired by political interests, quickly developed, to which Republican newspapers willingly

enough gave voice. *The Independent Chronicle* of Dec. 11, 1794, contains typical expressions of adverse comment. An exceptionally forceful counter-attack was made in the guise of an anonymous "sermon", entitled: *"The Altar of Baal Thrown Down: or, The French Nation Defended, Against the Pulpit Slander of David Osgood, A. M., Pastor of the Church in Medford. Par Citoyen de Novion."* The author of this pamphlet, who, as time demonstrated, was none other than James Sullivan, later governor of Massachusetts, right valiantly took up the cudgel in defence of the French. The French, he argues, are to be regarded as a mighty nation by whom our own nation has been preserved from destruction. Their excesses are most charitably and fairly explained in the light of the frightful oppressions which they had long suffered. Their attitude toward religion should not be regarded as hostile. The French strike only at a clergy who have linked their power with that of the nobility, and who together have made the people's lot intolerable. *Cf. ibid.*, pp. 12 *et seq.* The entire sermon abounds in caustic criticism of Osgood for having stepped "out of … line to gratify a party."

[204] *Christian Thankfulness Explained and Enforced. A Sermon, delivered at Charlestown, in the afternoon of February 19, 1795. The day of general thanksgiving through the United States.* By David Tappan, D. D., Hollisian Professor of Divinity in Harvard College, Boston, 1795.

[205] *The Nature and Manner of Giving Thanks to God, Illustrated. A sermon, delivered on the day of the national thanksgiving, February 19, 1795.* By Ebenezer Bradford, A. M., pastor of the First Church in Rowley, Boston, 1795.

[206] The so-called "Whiskey Rebellion" came in for a considerable amount of hostile comment on the part of the Federalist clergy at this time. Generally speaking, the New England clergy felt sure of their ground respecting the alleged causal relation between the Democratic Clubs and the Pennsylvania uprising. Hence it happened that the tone of clerical condemnation with respect to everything which had the

semblance of a secret propaganda was appreciably heightened. The moralizing tendencies of the clergy with respect to the secret combinations which were believed to be back of the "Whiskey Rebellion" is well illustrated in the following: *A Sermon, delivered February 19, 1795, being a day of general thanksgiving throughout the United States of America.* By Joseph Dana, A. M., pastor of the South Church in Ipswich. Newburyport, 1795. *Cf.* also, *Wolcott Papers*, vol. viii, 7.

[207] Tappan's *Sermon*, p. 36.

[208] *A Discourse, delivered February 19, 1795. The day set apart by the President for a general thanksgiving throughout the United States.* By David Osgood, A. M., pastor of the church in Medford, Boston, 1795, p. 18.

[209] *Ibid.*, pp. 18, 19.

[210] *A Sermon, delivered before the Convention of the Clergy of Massachusetts, in Boston, May 26, 1796.* By Jeremy Belknap, minister of the church in Federal-Street, Boston. Boston, 1796, pp. 15 *et seq.* A similar note was struck by Tappan in the convention of the following year. *Cf. Sermon, delivered before the Annual Convention of the Congregational Ministers of Massachusetts, in Boston, June 1, 1797*, Boston, 1797, p. 26.

[211] *A Sermon, delivered on the 9th of May, 1798. Being the day of a National Fast, Recommended by the President of the United States.* By John Thornton Kirkland, minister of the New South Church, Boston. Boston, 1798, pp. 18 *et seq.*

[212] Complaints of the nature indicated, and justifications of ministerial conduct in continuing the practice of "political preaching" increase in number from about 1796 on. The following examples are picked almost at random: *The sermon preached by John Eliot at the ordination of Joseph M'Kean, Milton, Mass., November 1, 1797*, Boston, 1797, p. 33; James Abercrombie's *Fast Day Sermon, May 9, 1798, Philadelphia,* Philadelphia, (n. d.); Eliphalet Porter's *Fast Day Sermon* of the

same date, at Roxbury, Boston, 1798, p. 22; Samuel Miller's *Fast Day Sermon*, also of the same date, at New York, New York, 1798.

[213] *God's Challenge to Infidels to Defend Their Cause, Illustrated and Applied in a Sermon, delivered in West Springfield, May 4, 1797, being the day of the General Fast.* By Joseph Lathrop, minister ... Second Ed., Cambridge, 1803.

[214] *Ibid.*, p. 4.

[215] *A Sermon, preached on the State Fast, April 6th, 1798.* ... By Nathan Strong, pastor of the North Presbyterian Church in Hartford. Hartford, 1798, pp. 14 *et seq.*

[216] *Some Facts evincive of the Atheistical, Anarchical, and in other respects, Immoral Principles of the French Republicans, Stated in a sermon delivered on the 9th of May, 1798.* ... By David Osgood ... Boston, 1798.

[217] One of the curious results of the reflection of the American clergy on the significance of the French Revolution was a marked disposition to treat the Roman Catholic Church with unwonted sympathy and respect. Osgood's implied apology not infrequently received an unblushingly frank statement. *Cf.* for example, Nathan Strong's *Connecticut Fast Day Sermon*, cited above.

[218] This estimate of the case appealed to Osgood's mind and satisfied his fancy. A year later he was heard on the following subject: *The Devil Let Loose; or The Wo occasioned to the Inhabitants of the Earth by His Wrathful Appearance among Them.* For lurid rhetoric Osgood outdid himself on this occasion. "Not in France only, but in various other countries, is the devil let loose; iniquity abounds; unclean spirits, like frogs in the houses and kneading-troughs of the Egyptians, have gone forth to the kings and rulers of the earth, ... the armies of Gog and Magog are gathered together in open hostility against all unrighteousness, truth and goodness." (*The Devil Let Loose,*

etc. Illustrated in a Discourse, delivered on the Day of the National Fast, April 25, 1799, Boston, 1799, pp. 13 *et seq.*)

[219] *Some Facts Evincive, etc.*, pp. 13, 16 *et seq.*

[220] *Acts and Proceedings of the General Assembly of the Presbyterian Church in the United States of America, May 17, 1798*, pp. 11 *et seq.*

[221] *Ibid.*

[222] The *Massachusetts Mercury* (Boston), June 19, 1798, contains the address in full.

[223] This address may be found in the *Independent Chronicle* of July 4, 1799, and the *Newburyport Herald* of June 28, 1799. A further comment, of more than average significance, on the unparalleled degeneracy of the times may be found in the sermon preached by the Reverend William Harris, of Marblehead, Massachusetts, before the annual convention of the Protestant Episcopal Church, held in Boston, May 28, 1799. *Cf. A Sermon delivered at Trinity Church, in Boston. ... By William Harris, rector of St. Michael's Church, Marblehead,* Boston, 1799. A decade and a half later Lyman Beecher preached his famous sermon on "Building Waste Places." The impression which lingered in his mind concerning the period under survey is worthy of consideration. After having discussed the unhappy condition of religious life in the churches of New England during the first half of the eighteenth century, he said: "A later cause of decline and desolation has been the insidious influence of infidel philosophy. The mystery of iniquity had in Europe been operating for a long time. The unclean spirits had commenced their mission to the kings of the earth to gather them together to the battle of the great day of God Almighty. But when that mighty convulsion [Foot-note: The French Revolution] took place, that a second-time burst open the bottomless pit, and spread darkness and dismay over Europe, every gale brought to our shores contagion and death. Thousands at once breathed the tainted air and felt the fever kindle in the brain. A paroxysm of moral madness and terrific

innovation ensued. In the frenzy of perverted vision every foe appeared a friend, and every friend a foe. No maxims were deemed too wise to be abandoned, none too horrid to be adopted; no foundations too deep laid to be torn up, and no superstructure too venerable to be torn down, that another, such as in Europe they were building with bones and blood, might be built.... The polluted page of infidelity everywhere met the eye while its sneers and blasphemies assailed the ear.... The result was a brood of infidels, heretics, and profligates—a generation prepared to be carried about, as they have been, by every wind of doctrine, and to assail, as they have done, our most sacred institutions." *Cf.* Beecher, *Autobiography, Correspondence, etc.*, vol. i, pp. 239, 240.

[224] Robinson, *Jeffersonian Democracy in New England*, p. i; Channing, *History of the United States*, vol. iv, p. 150.

[225] The term "Anti-Federalist" was born out of the struggle which developed over the adoption of the national constitution. The term "Republican" was one of the by-products of the discussion which arose in this country, from 1792 on, over French revolutionary ideals. *Cf.* Johnston, *American Political History*, pt. i, p. 207.

[226] *American State Papers: Foreign Relations*, vol. i, p. 140.

[227] The issues of the *Columbian Centinel* for 1793 abound in addresses of this character.

[228] *Cf.* for example, the issues of the *Connecticut Courant* for July 29, Aug. 5 and 26, 1793, and of the *Independent Chronicle* for May 7, 16 and 23, 1793. *Cf.* Channing, *History of the United States*, vol. iv, p. 128.

[229] The *Connecticut Courant* of May 13, 1793, contains the first announcements of Genet's arrival which that paper made. Subsequent issues are fairly well occupied with accounts of Genet's arrival in Philadelphia, the unconfirmed expressions of cordiality and heated enthusiasm which he encountered there, the congratulatory address which the citizens of that place

presented him, Genet's response, *etc.* In the issue of August 12 mention is made of the Frenchman's arrival in New York. Thus far not the slightest trace of a suspecting attitude of mind is discoverable.

[230] The issues of the *Connecticut Courant* for August 19 and 26, and November 11, 1793, contain articles that admirably illustrate the rising temper of the New England Federalists as they contemplated Genet's absurdities and improprieties.

[231] Luetscher, in his *Early Political Machinery in the United States*, p. 33, asserts that not more than twenty-four separate organizations of this character were formed within the two years which followed their first appearance. These were fairly well distributed throughout the Union. One was in Maine, one in Massachusetts (Boston), three in Vermont, two in New York, one in New Jersey, five in Pennsylvania, one in Delaware, one in Maryland, two in Virginia, one in North Carolina, four in South Carolina, and two in Kentucky.

[232] McMaster, *A History of the People of the United States*, vol. ii, pp. 175 *et seq.*

[233] Hazen, *Contemporary American Opinion of the French Revolution*, pp. 189 *et seq.*

[234] Robinson, *Jeffersonian Democracy in New England*, p. 10, for significant comments upon the effect of the establishment of the Democratic Societies on general political interest. The vote was appreciably increased and elections were more hotly contested on account of the emergence of the Clubs. *Cf.* also *New England Magazine*, January, 1890, p. 488.

[235] Morse, *The Federalist Party in Massachusetts*, p. 75; *Wolcott Papers*, vol. vii, 5, letter of Jedediah Morse to Oliver Wolcott. The *Independent Chronicle* of Jan. 16, 1794, contains the Rules and Regulations and the Declaration of this Society.

[236] *Massachusetts Mercury*, Nov. 29, 1793. *Cf. Works of Fisher Ames*, vol. ii, pp. 146 *et seq.*

[237] Jedediah Morse did not fail to observe the appearance of the Boston organization nor to divine its character and general scope of action. In a letter to Oliver Wolcott, Secretary of the Treasury, and Morse's intimate friend, a letter written close to the date of the organization of the Constitutional Club, Morse wrote optimistically but seriously of the situation:

"Charlestown, Dec. 16th, 1793 … The body of the people repose great confidence in the Wisdom of the President—of Congress, & of the heads of Departments. May they have Wisdom to direct them! The President's speech meets with much approbation—It is worthy of himself—We have some *grumbletonians* among us—who, when the French are victorious, speak loud & saucy—but when they meet with a check—sing small.—They form a sort of political Thermometer, by whh we can pretty accurately determine, what is, *in their opinion*, the state of French politics.—The French *cause* has no enemies here,—their conduct has many.—There are some who undistinguishly [*sic*] & unboundedly approve both—& most bitterly denounce, as *Aristocrats*, all who do not think as they do.—This party, whh is not numerous—nor as respectable as it is numerous—are about forming a Democratic Club—whh I think they call "the Massts. Constitutional Society"—I don't know their design, but suppose they consider themselves as *guardians* of the *Rights of Man*—& overseers of the President, Congress, & you gentlemen in the several principal departments of State—to see that you don't infringe upon the Constitution.—They don't like, nor see through your borrowing so much money of Holland— They are very suspicious about all money matters….

Your friend,
Jed^h Morse."

Wolcott Papers, vol. viii, 5.

[238] *Annals of Congress*, vol. iv, p. 787.

[239] The President's address was printed in full in leading New England journals. *Cf.* for example, *Columbian Centinel,*

Nov. 29, 1794; *Independent Chronicle*, Dec. 1, 1794; *Connecticut Courant*, Dec. 1, 1794.

[240] *Columbian Centinel*, Dec. 6, 10, 1794; *Connecticut Courant*, Dec. 8, 24, 1794.

[241] *Columbian Centinel*, Dec. 13, 1794.

[242] *Ibid.*, Dec. 20, 1794.

[243] *Independent Chronicle*, Sept. 18, 1794. *Cf.* also issues of this paper for Sept. 1, 4, 8, and 15, Dec. 4, 8, and 15, 1794.

[244] *Ibid.*, Aug. 25, 1794.

[245] *Ibid.*, Dec. 8, 1794.

[246] *Independent Chronicle*, Dec. 11, 1794.

[247] *Ibid.*, Nov. 27, 1794.

[248] *Cf. supra*, pp. 89 *et seq.*

[249] *Cf. Independent Chronicle*, Dec. 22, 25, and 29, 1794; Jan. 8 and 15, 1795.

[250] *Ibid.*, Jan. 12, 1795.

[251] *Ibid.*, Jan. 15, 1795.

[252] A more detached and better balanced judgment of the importance of the part played by the clergy in the suppression of the Democratic Societies is that recorded by William Bentley: "When I consider the rash zeal with which the clergy have embarked in the controversy respecting Constitution & Clubs, I could not help thinking of a place in this Town, called Curtis' folly. The good man attempting to descend a steep place, thought it best to take off one pair of his oxen & tackle them behind. But while the other cattle drove down hill, they drew the others down hill backwards & broke their necks. Had the French clergy continued with the people & meliorated their tempers they would have served them & the nobility." (*Diary*, vol. ii, p. 130.)

[253] That a certain depth of impression was made upon the mind of Jedediah Morse by the agitation that developed over these secret organizations will appear from the following letter which he wrote to Oliver Wolcott, late in 1794. It is quite true that the letter shows no trace of apprehension as respects the future; but the man's interest had been keenly solicited and the future was to have suggestions and appeals of its own.

"Charlestown, Dec. 17th, 1794

My dear Sir:

I take the liberty to enclose you Mr. Osgood's Thanksgiving sermon, with whh I think you will be pleased. It will evince that the sentiments of the clergy this way (for so far as I am acquainted he (Mr. Osgood) speaks the sentiments of nine out of ten of the clergy) agree with those of the President, Senate, & house of Representatives, in respect to the Self-created Societies. The Thanksgiving sermons in Boston & its vicinity, with only two or three exceptions, all breathed the same spirit—though their manner was not so particular & pointed as Mr. Osgood's. His sermon is now the general topic of conversation—it has grievously offended the Jacobins.—Poor fellows! they seem to be attacked on all sides. They must I think feel it to be a truth—that "there is no peace for the wicked."—They still make a noise—but it is like the groans of despair.

I could wish, if you think it proper, that the sermon might, in a suitable way, be put into the hands of our *most worthy President*, with this remark accompanying it, that the clergy in this Commonwealth generally approve of the same sentiments. I wish it because it may possibly add to his satisfaction—& will certainly to our honor in his view....

Your friend,

Jed[h] Morse."

To Oliver Wolcott, Comptroller of the U. S. Treas[y].
Philadelphia, Pa."

Wolcott Papers, vol. viii, 9. The explicit proof that the mind of this man, whose personality is of large importance for the purpose in hand, received permanent impressions from the activities of the Democratic Societies, on account of which he found it not difficult to conceive of like secret combinations a few years later, is found in his references to the political clubs in his Fast Day sermon of May 9, 1798, p. 24. *Cf.* also "Note F," p. 67, of his *Thanksgiving Sermon* of Nov. 29, 1798.

[254] An interesting coincidence appears in this connection. The treaty was actually concluded on the very day that President Washington made his address dealing with the uprising in western Pennsylvania (November 19, 1794). It was not submitted to the Senate, however, until June 8 of the following year. On June 24, 1795, it was recommended by that body for ratification, with a special reservation as to the twelfth article. *Cf.* Macdonald, *Documentary Source Book of American History*, p. 244. The promulgation of the treaty came later, as will appear. For comment on the popular resentment which the public announcement of the provisions of the treaty stirred up, *cf.* McMaster, *A History of the People of the United States*, vol. ii, pp. 212 *et seq.* For contemporary newspaper reports of the situation, *cf.* the *Independent Chronicle*, July 9, 13, 16, 23 and 27, 1795. For pertinent observations by Jedediah Morse regarding the apprehensions which the vehement popular disapproval of the treaty awakened in his mind, *cf. Wolcott Papers*, vol. viii, 11.

[255] William Bentley, whose Democratic leanings must not be overlooked, delivered himself in characteristic fashion: "The public indignation is roused, & the papers begin to talk of lost liberties.... The Secrecy under which this business has been covered has served to exasperate the public mind, upon the discovery.... The bells tolled on the 4 of July instead of ringing, & a mournful silence prevailed through the City. In this Town the men who hold securities under the government are sufficiently influential against the disquiets & angry expressions of more dependent people." (*Diary*, vol. ii, p. 146.)

[256] *Independent Chronicle*, July 16, 1795.

[257] *Cf.* reprint of the handbill circulated at Portsmouth, New Hampshire, in the *Independent Chronicle* of July 20, 1795.

[258] *Cf.* extracts from the speech of Fisher Ames in the House of Representatives, April 28, 1796. Quoted by Channing, *History of the United States*, vol. iv, pp. 145 *et seq.*

[259] As a matter of fact, as far as Congress was concerned, the discussion over the treaty was continued for some time to come, because of the measures that were necessary to be taken to put the treaty into effect. *Cf.* Bassett, *The Federalist System*, p. 134. The country, however, showed a disposition to accept the treaty as inevitable when the President's signature was finally affixed.

[260] McMaster, *A History of the People of the United States*, vol. ii, pp. 248 *et seq. Cf. Works of Fisher Ames*, vol. i, p. 161.

[261] Morse, *The Federalist Party in Massachusetts*, pp. 153 *et seq.*

[262] Travelers from abroad who were in the country at this time remarked the extreme virulence of public and private discussion. De La Rochefoucault-Liancourt, *Travels through the United States of North America*, vol. ii, pp. 231 *et seq. Cf. ibid.*, pp. 75 *et seq.*, 256, 359, 381; vol. iii, pp. 23, 33 *et seq.*, 74 *et seq.*, 156, 163 *et seq.*, 250, 274, 366 *et seq. Cf.* Weld, *Travels through the States of North America ... during the years 1795, 1796, and 1797*, p. 62. Writing specifically of the excited state of the public mind in February, 1796, the latter observer of our national life said: "It is scarcely possible for a dozen Americans to sit together without quarrelling about politics, and the British treaty, which had just been ratified, now gave rise to a long and acrimonious debate. The farmers were of one opinion, and gabbled away for a long time; the lawyers and the judge were of another, and in turns they rose to answer their opponents with all the power of rhetoric they possessed. Neither party could say anything to change the sentiments of the other one;

the noisy contest lasted till late at night, when getting heartily tired they withdrew, not to their respective chambers, but to the general one that held five or six beds, and in which they laid down in pairs. Here the conversation was again revived, and pursued with as much noise as below, till at last sleep closed their eyes, and happily their mouths at the same time...." (*Ibid.*, pp. 58 *et seq.*) Such unfavorable reflections are not to be dismissed as representing prejudiced views of the case. A habit of intolerance toward political opponents and of all men who shared contrary opinions, had become one of the characteristics of the times. The agitation over the treaty went far toward fixing this habit. The Alien and Sedition Acts, which came a little later, were the result of an unrestrained freedom of discussion scarcely more perceptible when they were passed in 1798 than at the time of the heat produced by the treaty.

[263] Gibbs, *Memoirs of the Administrations of Washington and John Adams*, vol. i, p. 226, Oliver Ellsworth's letter to Oliver Wolcott. Ellsworth reports that the "argument and explanation [of the treaty], that ''tis a damned thing made to plague the French,' has by repetition, lost its power." This could have been true only in a local sense.

[264] *Cf.* McMaster, *A History of the People of the United States*, vol. ii, pp. 227 *et seq.*, for an ample discussion of this view of the situation.

[265] That this fierce indictment of "British faction" and appeal to republican sentiment was by no means without practical effect, is shown in the result of the general election of 1796. The outcome of that election gave ground for great encouragement to the Democrats; for while their hero and idol, Thomas Jefferson, was not summoned to the presidency, none the less, to the deep chagrin of the Federalists, his opponent, John Adams, received his commission to succeed Washington on the basis of a majority in the electoral college of only three votes. There could be no question that a spirit of confident and undaunted republicanism was abroad in the land, and the good ship Federalism was destined to encounter foul weather. The

state contest held in Massachusetts that same year was even more ominous. After a campaign marked by great vigor on the part of the Federalists, in an effort to rally popular support to their candidate, Increase Sumner, it developed that Samuel Adams, whose enemies had stressed the charge that he desired to enjoy a life tenure of the gubernatorial office, was reelected by a handsome Democratic majority of 5,000 votes. *Cf.* Morse, *The Federalist Party in Massachusetts*, p. 161. Jedediah Morse showed himself to be a fairly astute prognosticator in connection with this election. He is found writing Wolcott, in October, 1795, to the effect that he is conscious of the fact that a severe storm is brewing. It is his conviction that the storm has been gathering for some time and is now about to burst forth. "Disorganizers" have been behind the opposition to the treaty. They have worked subterraneanly, trying to keep opposition alive. *Cf.Wolcott Papers*, vol. viii, 14.

[266] *Cf. supra*, p. 93.

[267] As early as the winter of 1795 William Bentley made the disgusted comment: "The Clergy are now the Tools of the Federalists." *Diary*, vol. ii, p. 129. Commencing with the participation of the clergy in the discussion over the treaty, Democrat newspapers like the *Independent Chronicle* began to administer mild rebukes to the clergy for the unwisdom of their conduct in favoring the British. *Cf.* the issue of the *Chronicle* for July 20, 1795, for one of the earliest utterances of this sort. The spirit of resentment grew apace. Three years later this spirit of moderation had been fully discarded, and the clergy were being lashed unmercifully for their folly. For typical outbursts of this character, *cf.* the *Independent Chronicle* of Dec. 3, 1798. Jedediah Morse paid tribute to the political concern and service of the clergy in a letter to Wolcott, written Dec. 23, 1796: "Very few of ye Clergy of my acquaintance seem disposed to pray for the success of the French, since they have so insidiously and wickedly interferred in the management of our political affairs, & I apprehend the complexion of the thanksgiving sermons throughout N Engd. this year, are

different from those of the last, in respect to this particular. I can speak of more than one with authority." (*Wolcott Papers*, vol. viii, 20.)

[268] Morse, *The Federalist Party in Massachusetts*, p. 121.

[269] Pamphleteers and newspaper writers were much more explicit. *The Pretensions of Thomas Jefferson to the Presidency Examined: and the Charges against John Adams Refuted*, was one of the well known political pamphlets of the day. According to Gibbs, in his *Memoirs of the Administrations of Washington and John Adams*, vol. i, p. 379, it was prepared by Oliver Wolcott and William Smith, the latter of South Carolina. It marshalled the reasons why Jefferson should not be elected to the presidency. Among these "reasons" the charge of a close alliance between Jefferson and the men of the country who were notoriously interested in the cause of irreligion was boldly affirmed. *Cf.* page 36 *et seq.* This pamphlet was published in 1796. Later the charge of impiety was lodged against Jefferson with great frequency. Typical utterances of this nature may be found in the *Library of American Literature*, vol. iv, pp. 249–251: "The Imported French Philosophy" (from "The Lay Preacher" of Joseph Dennie). This disquisition was much quoted in the newspapers of the day. From the position that the leaders of the Democrats were irreligious, it was easy for the Federalists to glide over to the position that the spirit of infidelity, believed to be spreading far and wide through the country, was consciously and deliberately backed by the restless and unscrupulous elements which, in the view of the Federalists, formed the opposition. *The Connecticut Courant* of January 19, 1795, reflects this attitude. "The French", it is asserted, "are mad in their pursuit of every phantom which disordered intellects can image. Having set themselves free from all human control, they would gladly scale the ramparts of heaven, and dethrone ALMIGHTY JEHOVAH. Our own Democrats would do just so, *if they dare.*" *Cf.* also the issue of the *Courant* for January 5, the same year, for a characterization of the program of the Democrats as "a crazy system of Anti-

Christian politics." The offence given to the Democrats by such accusations was great. No man, perhaps, stated the stinging resentment which they felt better than Benjamin Franklin Bache in his *Aurora* of August 15, 1798: "No part of the perfidy of the faction, the insidious monarchical faction, which dishonors our country, and endangers our future peace, is so bare faced as their perpetual railing about a party acting in concert with France—a party of *democrats* and *Jacobins*—a party of *disorganizers* and *atheists*—a party inimical to our independence! What is the plain intent of these impudent and ignorant railings? It is to impose upon the ignorant, to collect and concentre in our focus all the *vice, pride, superstition, avarice,* and *ambition* in the United States, in order to weigh down by the union of such a phalanx of iniquity, all that is virtuous and free in the nation." Abraham Bishop, whose repudiation of the Federalist charge that Jefferson was to be the High Priest of Infidelity was particularly vehement, saw in this cry that an alliance had been made between the forces of democracy and the forces of infidelity, the evidences of a shameless hypocrisy that stripped its makers of all right to be styled Christians. The cry that infidelity abounded meant nothing more nor less than that new electioneering methods were being employed. *Oration Delivered in Wallingford on the 11th of March, 1801* ... by Abraham Bishop, pp. 36, 37.

[270] *The Writings of Thomas Jefferson*, vol. vii, pp. 93 *et seq.* In similar strain, Jefferson wrote Adams a day later, offering his best wishes for his administration, but with the thought of the impending "storm" still well fixed in his mind. *Cf. ibid.*, pp. 95 *et seq. Cf.* Jefferson's letter to Dr. Benjamin Rush, *ibid.*, pp. 113 *et seq.*

[271] The following clause in the treaty seemed to afford ample protection to the rights of France: "Nothing in this treaty contained shall, however, be construed or operate contrary to former and existing public treaties with other sovereigns or states." (*United States Statutes at Large*, vol. viii, p. 128: Article XXV of the treaty.) But France was unable to blind her

eyes to the practical consideration that her European enemy, Great Britain, and an American government, suspicious of if not positively antagonistic to French influence, were to be the interpreters of the treaty.

[272] *Annals of Congress*, vol. vii, p. 103.

[273] Gibbs, *Memoirs of the Administrations of Washington and John Adams*, vol. i, p. 416, letter of Uriah Tracy to Oliver Wolcott.

[274] *Works of Fisher Ames*, vol. i. pp. 232 *et seq.*, Ames' letter to Timothy Pickering.

[275] *Cf. The Writings of Thomas Jefferson*, vol. vii, pp. 127 *et seq.*, letter of Jefferson to Thomas Pinckney. Even Jefferson's steadfast faith and loyalty to France was momentarily put to rout.

[276] *Cf.* Morison, *The Life and Letters of Harrison Gray Otis*, vol. i, p. 69, letter of Otis to Gen. William Heath. This letter was published in full in the *Massachusetts Mercury* of April 17, 1798.

[277] Morison, *The Life and Letters of Harrison Gray Otis*, vol. i, p. 69.

[278] *The Works of John Adams*, vol. viii, pp. 615, 620. President Adams was fully persuaded that French notions of domination "comprehended all America, both *north* and *south*". (*Ibid.*) *Cf.* also *Annals of Congress*, vol. vii, p. 1147, speech of Otis on Foreign Intercourse; *American Historical Association Report for 1896*, p. 807, Higginson's letter to Pickering.

[279] One of the pamphlets of the day, frequently referred to, much quoted in the newspapers, and evidently much read, bore the horrific title: *The Cannibals' Progress; or the Dreadful Horrors of French Invasion, as displayed by the Republican Officers and Soldiers, in their Perfidy, rapacity, ferociousness & brutality, exercised towards the Innocent inhabitants of Germany. Translated from the German, by Anthony Aufrer(e),*

Esq. ... The Connecticut Courant, in announcing a new edition of this work as just off the press, offered the following description of its character: "This work contains a circumstantial account of the excesses committed by the French Army in Suabia. At the present moment, when our country is in danger of being overrun by the same nation, our people ought to be prepared for those things, which they must expect, in case such an event should happen. The pamphlet should be owned by every man, and read in every family. They will there find, from an authentic source, that the consequences of being conquered by France, or even subjected to their government, are more dreadful than the heart of man can conceive. Murder, robbery, burning of towns, and the violation of female chastity, in forms too dreadful to relate, in instances too numerous to be counted, are among them. Five thousand copies of this work were sold in Philadelphia in a few days, and another edition of ten thousand is now in the press in that city." *Cf.* the issue of the *Courant* for July 2, 1798. Another book of horrors which deserves mention in this connection, although it came to public attention in America a little later, was the following: *The History of the Destruction of the Helvetic Union and Liberty.* By J. Mallet Du Pan. This work was first printed in England in 1798, and the following March was reprinted in Boston. A sentence or two taken from the author's preface will convey a fair notion of its nature: "In the Helvetic History, every Government may read its own destiny, and learn its duty. If there be yet one that flatters itself that its existence is reconcilable with that of the French Republic, let it study this dreadful monument of their friendship. Here every man may see how much weight treaties, alliances, benefactions, rights of neutrality, and even submission itself, retain in the scales of that Directory, who hunt justice from the earth, and whose sanguinary rapacity seeks plunder and spreads ruin alike on the Nile as on the Rhine, in Republican Congresses as well as in the heart of Monarchies." Like *The Cannibals' Progress*, this work was much quoted in the newspapers and caught the sympathetic eye of many clergyman, Jedediah Morse among the number. July 29, 1799, Chauncey Goodrich, of Hartford, Connecticut, wrote Oliver Wolcott to the effect that "the facts … in Du Pan, Robinson, Barruel, have got into every farm house; they wont go out, till the stories of the indian tomahawk & war dances around their prisoners do." (*Wolcott Papers*, vol. v, 77.) Nathaniel Ames did not think highly of the veracity of *The Cannibals' Progress*, yet he paid tribute to its influence in the following fashion: "July 31, 1798. Judge Metcalf with his cockade on came down to see Gen. Washington expecting to get a Commission to fight the French & infatuated at the slanders of the Progress of the Cannibals that the French skin Americans, to make boots for their Army, &c." (*Dedham Historical Register*, vol. ix: Diary of Ames, p. 24.)

[280] Channing, *History of the United States*, vol. iv, pp. 176 *et seq.*, gives a brief but entertaining account of the political jockeying on the part of our government which lay back of Monroe's recall and the despatch of Pinckney to France.

[281] Gibbs, *Memoirs of the Administrations of Washington and John Adams*, vol. ii, pp. 15 *et seq. Cf.* McMaster, *History of the People of the United States*, vol. ii, pp. 368 *et seq.*

[282] *Cf. Works of Fisher Ames*, vol. i, p. 225, letter of Ames to H. G. Otis. Ames' comment on the discomfiture of the Democrats was characteristically vigorous: "The late communications [*i. e.*, the X. Y. Z. despatches] have only smothered their rage; it is now a coal-pit, lately it was an open fire. Thacher would say, the effect of the despatches is only like a sermon in hell to awaken conscience in those whose day of probation is over, to sharpen pangs which cannot be soothed by hope."

[283] *The Writings of Thomas Jefferson*, vol. vii, p. 228, Jefferson's letter to Edmund Pendleton.

[284] The elation of Jedediah Morse over the turn affairs seemed to be taking was great. Under date of May 21, 1798, he wrote Wolcott, dilating on "the wonderful and happy change in the public mind. Opposition is shrinking into its proper

insignificance, stripped of the support of its deluded *honest* friends. I now feel it is an honour to be an American." (*Wolcott Papers*, vol. viii, 23.)

[285] Jedediah Morse was far from comfortable over the unwillingness of the President to proceed with vigor in handling affairs with France. An ill-concealed vein of impatience is discoverable in the following letter which he wrote to Wolcott, under date of July 13, 1798: "He [Washington] will unite all *honest* men among us. It gladdens the hearts of some at least, to my knowledge, of our deluded, warm democrats. They say, 'Washington is a good man—an American, & we will rally round his standard!' ... The rising & unexpected spread of the American spirit has dispelled all gloom from my mind, respecting our country. I rejoyce at the crisis, because I believe, the issue will be, the *extinction of French influence among us*, & if this can be effected, treasure & even blood, will not be spilt in vain.—The government is strengthening every day, by the confidence and assertions of the people.—We are waiting with almost impatience to *have war declared agt. France*, that we may distinguish more decidedly between friends & foes among ourselves. I believe there is energy enough in government to silence, & if necessary *exterminate its obstinate & dangerous enemies*." (*Wolcott Papers*, vol. viii, 27.) Eleven months later Morse expressed to Wolcott his grave fears on account of the disposition of the national government to reciprocate the "pacific overtures of the French govt." (*Wolcott Papers*, vol. viii, 24.) It is not French *arms*, but their "principles" which he holds in dread. (*Cf. ibid.*) Back of the fire-eating spirit of this New England clergyman was a genuine moral and religious concern.

[286] The texts of these various acts may be found in *United States Statutes at Large*, vol. i, pp. 566–569, 570–572, 577–578, 596–597. The Naturalization Act extended from five to nineteen years the period of residence necessary for aliens who wished to become naturalized; that is to say, fourteen years of residence, to be followed by an additional five years of

residence after the declaration of intention to become a citizen had been filed. It is obvious that this measure was intended to defeat the process by which the Democrats had been absorbing the foreign vote. The Act Concerning Aliens empowered the President "to order all such aliens as he should judge dangerous to the peace and safety of the United States, or should have reasonable grounds to suspect were concerned in any treasonable or secret machinations against the government thereof, to depart out of the territory of the United States within such a time as should be expressed in such order." Penalties in the form of heavy imprisonment and the withdrawal of the opportunity to become citizens were attached. The Act Respecting Alien Enemies gave the president power when the country was in a state of war to cause the subjects of the nation at war with the United States "to be apprehended, restrained, secured, and removed as alien enemies." The Sedition Act, not only in point of time but in sinister significance as well, stood at the apex of this body of legislation. It provided that fines and imprisonments were to be imposed upon men who were found guilty of unlawfully combining or conspiring for opposition to measures of government, or for impeding the operation of any law in the United States, or for intimidating an officer in the performance of his duty. The penalty was to be a fine not exceeding five thousand dollars, and imprisonment not exceeding five years. Penalties were also provided for publishing false, scandalous, and malicious writings against the government.

[287] At the time the country numbered among its population a very large number of aliens. French refugees from the West Indies, to the number of perhaps 25,000, were here. *Cf. Report of the American Historical Association for 1912*: "The Enforcement of the Alien and Sedition Laws," by F. M. Anderson, p. 116. England, also, had her quota of citizens here, not a few of whom were fugitives from justice, and some of whom, like William Cobbett and J. Thomson Callender (*cf.* McMaster, *History of the People of the United States*, vol. ii, p. 338), either drew the fire of the advocates of French principles

or busied themselves in the affairs of government on this side of the ocean. The amount of scurrilous abuse, aimed at the heads of government, which issued from the public press had become appalling. No innuendoes were too indelicate, no personalities too coarse, no slanders too malicious, no epithets too vile to be of service in the general campaign of villification. The prostitution of the public press in America has never been more abject than it was at the close of the eighteenth and the beginning of the nineteenth centuries. (Duniway, *The Development of Freedom of the Press in Massachusetts*, pp. 143, 144.) Unfortunately, Federalists compromised their position and scandalized their cause by writing as scurrilous and libelous articles as their enemies; but the agencies of administration were in their hands, and, as the Democrats charged, their offences were not noticed.

[288] Morison, *The Life and Letters of Harrison Cray Otis*, vol. i, pp. 106 *et seq.* Morison's treatment of this tempestuous period is characterized by keen discrimination and fine balance. It is one of the most satisfying as well as one of the most vivid accounts of the situation to be found.

[289] *Connecticut Courant*, July 8, 1799.

[290] *Independent Chronicle*, Dec. 3, 1798.

[291] *Report of the American Historical Association for 1912*: "The Enforcement of the Alien and Sedition Laws," by F. M. Anderson, pp. 115 *et seq. Cf. The Writings of Thomas Jefferson*, vol. vii, pp. 256 *et seq.*, 262, letters of Monroe to Jefferson.

[292] Anderson, who appears to have made a painstaking examination of the available records, states his conclusions thus: "I have made a special effort to discover every possible instance and to avoid confusing Federal and State cases. There appears to have been about 24 or 25 persons arrested. At least 15, and probably several more, were indicted. Only 10, or possibly 11, cases came to trial. In 10 the accused were pronounced guilty. The eleventh case may have been an acquittal, but the report of it is entirely unconfirmed." (*Report*

of the *American Historical Association for 1912*, p. 120. *Cf.* Bassett, *The Federalist System*, p. 264.) An important phase of the judicial aspects of the situation, as respects the forming of public opinion, was the widespread publication in the newspapers of the charges made to grand juries by Federal judges who exerted themselves to defend the alien and sedition laws, and whose utterances received caustic criticism at the hands of Democrat writers.

[293] Duniway, *The Development of Freedom of the Press in Massachusetts*, pp. 145, 146.

[294] *The Writings of Thomas Jefferson*, vol. vii, pp. 331 *et seq.*, Jefferson's letter to Elbridge Gerry.

[295] The report of this episode may be found in the *Connecticut Courant* of May 14, 1798. *Cf. The Writings of Thomas Jefferson*, vol. vii, pp. 252 *et seq.*, Jefferson's letter to Madison.

[296] *Ibid.*

[297] *An Answer to Alexander Hamilton's Letter, Concerning the Public Conduct and Character of John Adams, Esq., President of the United States*, New York, 1800, p. 3. In this connection it may be noted that as ardent and hopeful a Democrat as Nathaniel Ames seriously contemplated the outbreak of civil war in the United States as the result of the tense party situation near the end of 1798. *Cf. Dedham Historical Register*, Diary of Ames, vol. ix, p. 63.

[298] *The Works of Alexander Hamilton*, vol. vii, pp. 374–377: Fragment on the French Revolution. The Fragment is undated. It could not have been written later than 1804, of course. There are some slight traces that it was compiled at the time the excitement over the Illuminati was prevalent in America.

[299] Forestier, *Les Illuminés de Bavière et la Franc-Maçonnerie allemande*, p. 103. This author, upon whose recent painstaking researches much reliance is placed in this chapter,

relates that one traveler who was in Bavaria at this time, found 28,000 churches and chapels, with pious foundations representing a total value of 60,000,000 florins. Munich, a city of 40,000 inhabitants, had no less than 17 convents. When a papal bull, issued in 1798, authorized the elector to dispose of the seventh part of the goods of the clergy, the Bavarian government, in executing the pope's directions, deducted 25,000,000 florins, and it was remarked that this amount did not equal the sum which had been agreed upon. *Cf. ibid.*, pp. 103 *et seq.*

[300] Forestier, *op. cit.*, p. 108: "Dans aucun pays du monde, si l'on excepte le Paraguay, les fils de Loyola n'avaient obtenu une victoire plus complète, ni conquis une autorité plus grande." *Cf.* Mounier, *De l'influence attribuée aux Philosophes aux franc-maçons et aux illuminés sur la révolution de France*, p. 189.

[301] *Ibid.*, pp. 109, 100. Duhr, B., *Geschichte der Jesuiten in den Ländern deutscher Zunge im 16. Jahrhundert*, Freiburg, 1907, discusses the earlier development. The work of F. J. Lipowsky, *Geschichte der Jesuiten in Baiern*, München, 1816, 2 vols., is antiquated and is little more than a chronicle.

[302] Engel, *Geschichte des Illuminaten-Ordens*, p. 29.

[303] The suppression of the Jesuits by Pope Clement XIV, in 1773, did not greatly diminish the influence and power of the order in Bavaria. Refusing to accept defeat, the new intrigues to which they gave themselves inspired in their enemies a new sense of their cohesion, with the result that they appeared even more formidable than before their suppression.

[304] Forestier, *op. cit.*, pp. 105 *et seq.*

[305] Forestier, *op. cit.*, p. 19.

[306] *Ibid.*, p. 18. *Cf.* Engel, *op. cit.*, pp. 19, 28, 29.

[307] In the person of Maximilian Joseph, Bavaria found an elector whose earlier devotion to liberal policies gave promise

of fundamental reforms. Agriculture and manufactures were encouraged; judicial reforms were undertaken; the despotism of the clergy was resisted. The founding of the Academy of Science at Munich, in 1759, represented a definite response to the spirit of the *Aufklärung*. However, the elector was not at all minded to break with the Catholic faith. All efforts to introduce Protestant ideas into the country were vigorously opposed by the government. In the end the elector's program of reform miscarried. At the time of his death, in 1777 (the date given by Forestier, p. 106, is incorrect; *cf. Allgemeine Deutsche Biographie*, vol. xxi. p. 30; also Brockhaus, *Konversations-Lexikon*, vol. xi. p. 683.), the absolute power of the clergy remained unshattered.

[308] Forestier, *op. cit.*, p. 107.

[309] As a result of this effort, George Weishaupt, father of Adam, came to the University of Ingolstadt as professor of imperial institutions and criminal law.

[310] Engel, *op. cit.*, pp. 19 *et seq.*

[311] Forestier, *op. cit.*, pp. 19 *et seq. Cf.* Engel, *op. cit.*, pp. 20 *et seq.*

[312] *Ibid.*, pp. 22 *et seq.*

[313] Forestier, *op. cit.*, pp. 16 *et seq.*

[314] Forestier, *op. cit.*, p. 18.

[315] *Ibid.*

[316] Ickstatt withdrew from direct participation in the affairs of the University of Ingolstadt in 1765, but he continued to exercise a controlling influence over the policies of the institution for some time to come. The son of one of his former pupils, Lori, a man of liberal notions, was later chosen co-director of the institution, and with him Weishaupt made common cause in his campaign against the Jesuits.

[317] Forestier, *op. cit.*, p. 21. *Cf.* Engel, *op. cit.*, p. 33.

[318] No clearer illustration of Weishaupt's lack of nobility is needed than his treatment of his protector and patron, Ickstatt. Owing to a marriage which he had contracted in 1773, against the wishes of Ickstatt, a decided chill came over the relations between the two men. All considerations of gratitude were carelessly tossed aside by Weishaupt. Later, in utter disregard of the anticlericalism of his benefactor, Weishaupt entered into an intrigue with the Jesuit professor Stadler, to obtain a coveted ecclesiastical position for the latter. Ickstatt, hearing of this, renounced Weishaupt as an ingrate. Forestier, *op. cit.*, pp. 22 *et seq.*

[319] Engel, *op. cit.*, p. 31.

[320] Forestier, *op. cit.*, p. 21.

[321] *Ibid. Cf.* Engel, *op. cit.*, p. 32.

[322] *Ibid.*, p. 22.

[323] *Ibid.*, p. 25.

[324] *Ibid.*

[325] The motives which led Weishaupt to consider the formation of a secret organization of the general character indicated were not all of a kind. In part they were creditable, in part discreditable. That he had a genuine interest in the cause of liberalism and progress, born largely of the personal discomfort and injury he had experienced at the hands of intolerance and bigotry, there can be no honest doubt. But a thirst for power was also a fundamental element in his nature. The despotic character of the order which he attempted to build up is in itself a sufficient proof of this. Besides, the cast of his personal affairs at the time the organization was launched smacks loudly of the mans over-weening vanity and yearning for personal conquest. His break with Ickstatt had been followed by a breach between him and Lori on account of the constant recriminations in which Weishaupt engaged against his enemies in the university. The secret alliance he had formed

with the Jesuit Stadler likewise soon dissolved. His complaints because of alleged infringements of his freedom of speech as a teacher were vehement. His interference in university affairs outside the proper sphere of his authority was frequent and involved him in numerous acrimonious verbal battles. (Engel seeks to relieve Weishaupt of part of the odium of these charges by shifting somewhat of the burden to other shoulders. (*Cf. Geschichte des Illuminaten-Ordens*, pp. 29–54.) His partiality is, however, sufficiently accounted for by the fact that at the time his work was published, he was the head of the revived Order of the Illuminati. *Cf. op. cit.*, p. 467; *cf. Religion in Geschichte und Gegenwart*, vol. iii: article, "Illuminaten"). Yet none of these experiences brought home to the mind of Weishaupt that he was to blame. As to the matter of motive, Forestier's comment is much to the point: "Ainsi le hardi confesseur de la vérité se trouvait seul à lutter visière levée contre la tourbe des bigots. Une volonté moins bien trempée aurait laissé sombrer dans une résignation inerte ou dans la manie de la persécution ce modeste professeur d'une Université sans prestige, perdu dans un coin de la Bavière, mal payé, mal vu de la majorité de ses collègues, mal noté par le Curateur, surveillé, soupçonné par tous ceux que scandalisait le radicalisme de ses opinions. Mais l'âme de Weishaupt disposait de deux puissants ressorts: la soif du prosélytisme et la volonté de puissance." (*Op. cit.*, pp. 25 *et seq.*) The view adopted by Kluckhohn is not essentially different: "Rachsucht, Ehrgeiz, Herrschbegier mischten sich in ihm mit dem Drange, grosses zu wirken und ein Woltäter der Menschheit zu werden." (Herzog-Plitt, *Real-Encyklopädie für protestantische Theologie und Kirche*, 2. Aufl., vol. vi, Leipzig, 1880: article, "Illuminaten," p. 699.)

[326] Forestier, *op. cit.*, p. 28. Weishaupt readily detected the disparate character of current Freemasonry, and for a brief time he was enthusiastic over the project of developing a rarified type of Masonry to which only men of superior talents should be admitted. For the reasons given, the idea was abandoned.

[327] *Ibid.*, p. 29.

[328] Forestier, *op. cit.*, p. 75. The teaching function of the order is well set out by Forestier in the following: "Faire de l'homme actuel, resté sauvage et férocement égoïste sous le vernis d'une civilisation apparante, un être véritablement sociable, c'est-à-dire respectueux des droits de ses semblables et amène dans ses rapports avec eux, enseigner à ses membres 'l'art de réaliser le bien sans trouver d'opposition, de corriger leurs défauts, d'ecarter les obstacles, d'attaquer le mal à la racine, de faire en un mot ce que jusqu'à présent l'éducation, l'enseignement de la morale, les lois civiles et la religion même ont été incapables d'accomplir,' leur apprendre 'à soumettre leurs désirs au contrôle de la raison,' tel est donc en dernière analyse ce que L'Ordre considère comme sa fin suprême. Société d'enseignement par les occupations qu'il impose à ses adeptes, il est essentiellement, par le but qu'il se propose, un institut d'éducation sociale." (*Op. cit.*, p. 78.)

[329] It was Weishaupt's original purpose to style the new order the "Perfectibilists", but this he later renounced as too bizarre and lacking in the element of mystery.

[330] Forestier, *op. cit.*, p. 46: "Au moment où Weishaupt avait fondé son Ordre, l'organisation de tout le Système était à peine ébauchée dans son esprit. Quand il s'était subitement décidé à jeter les bases de son édifice, il avait hâtivement rédigé des Statuts provisoires, se promettant de les remanier et d'arrêter définitivement dans le silence du cabinet le plan général." *Cf.* Engel, *op. cit.*, p. 90: "Die ersten Ordensstatuten, welche einen Einblick geben über das, was Weishaupt wollte, bestanden nur kurze Zeit; sie waren recht dürftig und unklar." It was not until Baron Knigge came to his assistance, four years later, that Weishaupt was able to rescue the organization of the society from the mire of puerility into which his impractical nature had plunged it.

[331] Engel, *op. cit.*, pp. 56 *et seq.* The recruiting of women, Jews, pagans, monks, and members of other secret

organizations was forbidden. Weishaupt preferred the enrollment of men who were between the ages of 18 and 30.

[332] *Cf. Einige Originalschriften des Illuminaten Ordens*, pp. 49, 50, 56.

[333] *Ibid.*, p. 26.

[334] *Einige Originalschriften des Illuminaten Ordens*, pp. 61–65.

[335] *Ibid.*, p. 63. From time to time the Novice was required to submit to his superiors notations he had made upon interesting portions of books which he had read, in order that his instruction might be properly directed. *Cf. ibid.*, pp. 62, 65. In the pursuit of the art or science that he had chosen as his principal occupation, he was expected to keep in close touch with his enroller.

[336] *Ibid.*, p. 31.

[337] Forestier, *op. cit.*, p. 61.

[338] *Ibid.*, pp. 61–64.

[339] Forestier, *op. cit.*, p. 64.

[340] *Ibid.*, p. 65.

[341] *Ibid.*

[342] *Ibid.*, p. 66. It was in the mind of Weishaupt to make a sort of free university out of this grade. He himself declared: "In der nächsten Klasse [*i. e.*, Minervals], dächte ich also eine Art von gelehrter Academie zu errichten: in solcher wird gearbeitet, an Karakteren, historischen, und lebenden, Studium der Alten, Beobachtungsgeist, Abhandlungen, Preisfragen, und in specie mache ich darinnen jeden zum Spion des andern und aller. Darauf werden die Fähigen zu den Mysterien herausgenommen, die in dieser Klasse etliche Grundsätze und Grunderfordernisse zum menschlichen glückseligen Leben sind." (Quoted by Engel from Weishaupt's correspondence

with Zwack, p. 76.) The grade Minerval is therefore to be regarded as designed to supply the opportunity *par excellence* for imparting the revolutionary ideas of which the founder of the order boasted. Under the direction of their superiors the Minervals were to continue the study of the humanities which they began as Novices; they were to study the works of the ancients, to prepare dissertations upon subjects in those fields to which their special talents were suited, *etc.,*—in a word, to show themselves worthy of membership in an academy of savants. *Cf. Einige Originalschriften des Illuminaten Ordens*, p. 216. *Cf.* Forestier, *op. cit.*, p. 74. Weishaupt entertained extremely ambitious notions of a system of special libraries under the control of the order, and in which the literary and scientific productions of the order should be assembled and preserved. *Cf. Der ächte Illuminat*, p. 46.

[343] Forestier, *op. cit.*, p. 66.

[344] The fantastic element in Weishaupt's mind is well illustrated at this point. In view of the fact that he particularly sought the recruitment of youths between the ages of 15 and 20 years (*cf. Einige Originalschriften des Illuminaten Ordens*, p. 261), it is difficult to see the possibility of sustained satisfaction in such associations. We shall see later that Baron Knigge substantially modified the character of the organization in this particular. Weishaupt did not scruple to employ outright deception with reference to the reputed age and power of the order to enhance in the minds of the members the sense of the value of these secret associations. Forestier, *op. cit.*, p. 82.

[345] *Ibid.*, p. 66.

[346] *Der ächte Illuminat*, p. 94. The notion that the supreme heads of the order, whose identity of course was concealed from the members, were individuals of exceptional purity, was kept before the minds of the "illuminated" Minervals as an added incentive.

[347] From two to four Minervals were given to each Illuminated Minerval, to receive his instructions in the

principles and objects of the order. The selection of these pupils in a given instance was supposed to be based upon their openness to the influence of their particular instructor. *Cf.* Forestier, *op. cit.*, p. 70 *et seq.*

[348] *Ibid.*, p. 71. The principle of espionage was an important element in the administration of the order. Weishaupt acknowledged his indebtedness to the ideal of organization which the Society of Jesus had set before him (*Cf. Endliche Erklärungen*, pp. 60 *et seq. Cf.* Forestier, pp. 97–99), and the principle of one member spying upon another was apparently borrowed from that source. It was Weishaupt's theory that dissimulation and hypocrisy could best be eradicated by proving to the members of the organization the inutility of such courses of life in view of the incessant surveillance under which all the members lived. (*Cf. Der ächte Illuminat*, p. 102.) Accordingly the Novice was left to surmise just how many eyes of unknown superiors might be upon him. The duty imposed upon the Illuminated Minerval of informing upon his disciples has been noted above. Weishaupt seems never to have surmised that this policy of espionage would tend to kill mutual confidence and fraternal regard at the roots.

[349] Forestier, *op. cit.*, p. 71.

[350] Weishaupt's conception of the content of these terms left room for a recognition of the benefits to be derived from society, but denied the value of the state. Man had moved forward, not backward, from his primitive condition. The satisfaction of his needs had supplied the motive force to his progress. In the state of nature, it is quite true, man enjoyed the two sovereign goods, equality and liberty. However, his disposition and desires were such that a continuance in the state of nature was impossible. The condition of misery into which he came resulted from his failure to acquire the art of controlling his faculties and curbing his passions, and from the injustice which he suffered the state to impose upon him. With the erection of the state had come the notions of the subjection of some men to the power and authority of others, the

consequent loss of the unity of the race, and the replacement of the love of humanity with nationalism, or patriotism. But political revolutions were not needed to accomplish the emancipation of the race; such revolutions had always proved sterile because they touched nothing deeper than the constitutions of states. Man's nature needed to be reconstituted. To bring life under the control of reason would enable men again to possess themselves of equality and liberty. A return to man's primitive state is both impossible and undesirable. Social life is a blessing. Only let men learn to govern themselves by the light of reason, and civil authority, having been found utterly useless, will quickly disappear. Forestier, *op. cit.*, pp. 311–316.

[351] *Der ächte Illuminat*, pp. 110, 123.

[352] Forestier, *op. cit.*, p. 78.

[353] Forestier, *op. cit.*, p. 80.

[354] In view of the connections which the enemies of the order later made between the Illuminati and the French Revolution, it is worthy of particular emphasis that Weishaupt eschewed the principle of effecting reform by political revolution, and definitely committed himself to the ideal of moral and intellectual reformation. The slow process of ameliorating the unhappy condition of humanity through the leavening influence of the ideas propagated in the order, *i. e.,* by reshaping private and public opinion, was the pathway which Weishaupt chose. *Der ächte Illuminat*, pp. 10, 205. Such, at least, was the theory in the case. In practise the order abandoned the policy of non-intervention and sought to influence government by putting its members in important civil positions. Forestier, *op. cit.*, pp. 329 *et seq.*

[355] *Einige Originalschriften des Illuminaten Ordens*, p. 339.

[356] *Ibid.*, p. 279.

[357] Forestier, *op. cit.*, p. 88. The anticlerical spirit of the order did not receive an official emphasis commensurate with its importance and weight, doubtless because of Weishaupt's desire to work under cover against his enemies as completely as possible. Forestier's comment seems thoroughly just: "Il ne faut pas oublier que Weishaupt en fondant sa Societé n'avait pas songé seulement à faire le bonheur de l'humanité, mais qu'il avait cherché aussi à trouver des alliés dans la lutte qu'il soutenait à Ingolstadt contre le parti des ex-Jésuites. A côté du but officiellement proclamé, l'Ordre avait un autre but, auquel on pensait d'autant plus qu'on en parlait moins." (*Op. cit.*, 87. *Cf. ibid.*, pp. 92, 110.)

[358] *Ibid.*, p. 90.

[359] *Einige Originalschriften des Illuminaten Ordens*, p. 216. The order was to be used in the circulation of anticlerical and antireligious books and pamphlets, and the work of the priests and the monks was to be held in mind as constituting the chief obstacle to intellectual and moral progress. Forestier, *op. cit.*, pp. 91, 92.

[360] *Ibid.*, p. 317.

[361] *Ibid.*, p. 318.

[362] Forestier, *op. cit.*, p. 318. This was treated as the esoteric doctrine of Christ, coming to the surface here and there in His teachings and acts, and revealed in the *disciplina arcani* of the early church. It is only when this secret teaching is grasped that the coherence of Jesus' utterances and the significance of the true doctrines of man's fall and his resurrection can be understood. It was because man abandoned the state of nature that he lost his dignity and his liberty. In other words, he fell because he ceased to fight against his sensual desires, surrendering himself to the rule of his passions. His work of redemption will be accomplished when he learns to moderate his passions and to limit his desires. The kingdom of grace is therefore a kingdom wherein men live in reason's light.

[363] "Par ses divers caractères avoués ou secrets, l'Ordre des Illuminés était l'expression d'une époque et d'un milieu. Le Système né dans le cerveau de Weishaupt avait trouvé des adeptes en Bavière parce qu'il répondait aux aspirations et satisfaisait les haines de la classe cultivée dans ce pays." (*Ibid.*, p. 99.)

[364] These new centers were Munich, Regensburg, Freising, and Eichstätt. For data concerning the early enrollment of recruits, *cf. ibid.*, pp. 30 *et seq.*

[365] *Ibid.*, p. 45.

[366] The term *Areopagite* was applied to the men who shared with Weishaupt the supreme direction of the order. Each was assigned a pseudonym. With one exception, Xavier Zwack (Danaus), they seem to have been men of very ordinary ability. Forestier, *op. cit.*, p. 232.

[367] *Ibid.*, pp. 231 *et seq.*, 112 *et seq.*

[368] Weishaupt's original plan had been to leave the matter of financial support to the discretion of the members. *Einige Originalschriften des Illuminaten Ordens*, p. 16. Time, however, proved the imprudence of this arrangement, and hence fixed dues, very modest in their character, were imposed. Forestier, pp. 130 *et seq.*

[369] *Ibid.*, pp. 132 *et seq.*

[370] Engel gives the date of the admission of Knigge as July, 1780. *Cf. Geschichte des Illuminaten-Ordens*, p. 114. Forestier is less specific. *Les Illuminés de Bavière, &c.*, p. 217.

[371] Baron Knigge (born near Hannover, October 16, 1752; died at Bremen, May 6, 1796) was a man of considerable distinction in his day. He had studied law at Göttingen, and later had been attached to the courts of Hesse-Cassel and Weimar. Retiring subsequently to private life, he made his home successively at Frankfort-on-the-Main, Heidelberg, Hannover, and Bremen. He was an author of note, a writer of

romance, popular philosophy, and dramatic poetry. His best known work, *Ueber den Umgang mit Menschen* (Hannover, 1788), a volume filled with a discussion of practical principles and maxims of life and characterized by a narrow and egoistical outlook, enjoyed a considerable notoriety in its time. (Knigge's complete works were assembled and published in twelve volumes at Hannover, 1804–1806). He had a decided bias for secret societies, and at the earliest moment that his age permitted had joined a lodge of the Strict Observance, one of the Masonic branches of the period. The Strict Observance was particularly devoted to the reform of Masonry, with special reference to the elimination of the occult sciences which at the time were widely practised in the lodges, and the establishment of cohesion and homogeneity in Masonry through the enforcement of strict discipline, the regulation of functions, *etc.* (Later, the leaders of the Strict Observance found themselves compelled to yield to the popular clamor for the occult sciences which were all but universal in European Freemasonry, and adopted them. Their presence and practice had been influential in attracting Knigge to the Masonic system. *Cf.* Forestier, *op. cit.*, p. 207.) Knigge's Masonic career proved to be of such a nature as to leave him restless and unsatisfied. Because he was not permitted to enjoy the advancement in the order of the Strict Observance that he coveted, he temporarily lost his interest in Masonry only to have it revived a little later by being chosen to assist in the establishment of a new Masonic lodge at Hanau. Meantime his interest in the subjects of theosophy, magic, and particularly alchemy, grew apace. On this account he was led to make an effort to affiliate himself with the Rosicrucians, a branch of Freemasonry notorious for the absurdity of its pretensions and its shameless pandering to the popular desire for occultism. Knigge's advance did not happen to be received with favor; and the result was that, finding himself compelled for the moment to be content with his membership in the Strict Observance, he renounced his interest in alchemy and devoted his reflections to the development of a form of Masonry which should teach men rules of life by the observance of which they might gradually regain that perfection from which their original parents fell. It was at the moment when Knigge's mind was occupied with this project that his membership in the Order of the Illuminati was solicited. *Cf.* Forestier, pp. 214 *et seq.* As to the personality of the man, the following estimate by Forestier is excellent: " … gentilhomme democrate, dilettante par temperament, homme de lettres par necessité, ecrivain abondant et mediocre, publiciste, moraliste, romancier sentimental et satirique, … un personnage interessant moins encore en lui-meme que comme representant d'une caste en dissolution." (*Op. cit.*, p. 202.)

[372] Weishaupt himself, overcoming his earlier antipathy to Freemasonry, had joined the Masons at Munich, in 1777, influenced particularly by his desire to find suggestions for the working out of the higher grades of his order. Out of this connection, and under the persuasion of Zwack, the plan of forming an alliance between the Illuminati and Freemasonry had occurred to Weishaupt's mind before Knigge joined the order. One Masonic lodge, that of Theodore of Good Counsel, located at Munich, had, by the middle of 1779, come so completely under the influence of members of the Illuminati that it had come to be regarded as a part of the order. *Cf.* Forestier, p. 200. But here again the situation waited upon the energetic leadership of Knigge.

[373] *Ibid.*, pp. 133 *et seq. Cf.* Engel, *op. cit.*, pp. 114 *et seq.* Soon after Knigge was admitted to the order, Weishaupt found himself driven to make to the former a most humiliating confession. Knigge hesitated for some time before becoming a member, and to bring him to a decision Weishaupt painted the objects and character of the order before him in flaming colors. The Illuminati represented the greatest advancements in science, the most marvelous speculative philosophy, and a truly wonderful system to carry its purposes into effect. Having joined the order, Knigge's suspicions were aroused on account of the feeble and trifling character of its organization; and Weishaupt, upon being repeatedly pressed for an explanation

concerning the nature of the so-called higher grades, had finally to confess to Knigge that they did not exist. *Cf.* Forestier, pp. 218–226. Knigge's resolution was staggered, but his courage was finally rallied because of the confidence which Weishaupt and the other leaders reposed in him. *Cf. ibid.*, pp. 228 *et seq.*

[374] *Nachtrag von weiteren Originalschriften*, vol. i, p. 108. *Cf.* Forestier, *op. cit.*, p. 250; Engel, *op. cit.*, p. 117.

[375] The ligament to bind the Illuminati and Freemasonry together was supplied by Knigge in the grades of the second class. *Cf.* Engel, *op. cit.*, p. 115.

[376] Apparently these grades were never worked out. See Forestier, p. 250.

[377] Forestier devotes more than forty well-packed pages to a discussion of this phase of the subject. *Ibid.*, pp. 251–294.

[378] *Der ächte Illuminat*, p. 14. Pages 17–37, *ibid.*, contains the description of this grade as revised by Knigge.

[379] *Ibid.*, pp. 39–78.

[380] *Ibid.*, pp. 82–138.

[381] Knigge had, of course, to provide a new ritual and code for these grades. These have not been preserved. They were doubtless similar to those of other Masonic systems, in their Blue Lodge features. "La Franc-Maçonnerie bleue étant le sol commun où poussaient les végétations luxuriantes et diverses des hauts grades et le terrain où tous les Franc-Maçons pouvaient se rencontrer, les différents Systèmes, préoccupés d'établir leur authenticité et aussi pour ne pas dérouter les transfuges des autres sectes, avaient soin de respecter les formes et les usages traditionnels. La Franc-Maçonnerie Illuminée obéit vraisemblablement aux mêmes considérations." (Forestier, *op. cit.*, p. 262.)

[382] Forestier, *op. cit.*, p. 272. *Der ächte Illuminat*, pp. 139–212, contains the ritual and statutes of this grade.

[383] The initiatory rites of this grade were followed by a banquet, which in turn was concluded by a ceremony fashioned after the pattern of the Christian Eucharist. Bread and wine were given to the members, and an effort was made to throw an atmosphere of great solemnity about the observance. *Cf.* Forestier, pp. 278 *et seq.* Christian enemies of the order took special umbrage at this ceremony.

[384] The Chapter was placed under obligation to see that Blue Lodges, not to exceed thirty all told, were established in all the important centers of its district. They had also to see that the Order of the Illuminati secretly obtained a preponderating influence in the lodges of other systems, to reform them if possible, or, failing in this, to ruin them. A Prefect, or Local Superior, who furnished regular reports to his superiors, presided over the Chapter. *Cf.* Forestier, pp. 279–281.

[385] The members of this class were usually referred to as Epopts, and their immediate superiors as Hierophants. These superiors were technically known as Deans. *Ibid.*, pp. 287, 281.

[386] Their admission to the rank was further conditioned upon their advancement in Masonry and the effectiveness of their service in the lower grades of the Illuminati. *Cf. ibid.*, p. 281.

[387] The rites of initiation into this grade expressed a growing tendency in the direction of sacerdotal pomp. *Cf. ibid.*, pp. 283–286.

[388] "Comme toutes les demandes de renseignements leur étaient transmises, ils devaient s'efforcer de satisfaire leurs gens et d'établir des théories solidement construites en faisant étudier et élucider par leurs subordonnés les points restés obscurs." (*Ibid.*, p. 288.) Free *entrée* to all the assemblies of the inferior grades of the order was accorded the Priests, but only in the ceremony of reception into the grade of Scottish Knight did they appear in costume. On other occasions they were not obliged to make their official character known.

[389] The prefectures were grouped together into provinces, of which there seem to have been twelve, to each of which, as to the prefectures and their capitals, pseudonymous names were given. For the geographical divisions of the Illuminati system, *cf.* Forestier, pp. 295 *et seq.*

[390] The title of Regent was also used in this connection.

[391] Provincials, as the term suggests, had control over the various provinces.

[392] An important modification in the government of the order was made by Knigge with respect to its general form. Knigge found the order a despotism, and this he regarded as a fundamental weakness and error. The Areopagites, who chafed excessively under Weishaupt's immoderate zeal to command, and between whom and their leader constant and perilous divisions arose, eagerly sided with Knigge in his efforts to distribute authority. At the latter's suggestion a congress was called at Munich, in October, 1780, at which the position and authority of the Areopagites were definitively settled. The territory, present and prospective, of the order was divided into twelve provinces, each of which was to be governed by a Provincial. The posts of Provincials were thereupon distributed among the Areopagites. Each Provincial was to be left free to administer his province without direct interference on the part of Weishaupt, who remained the supreme head. *Cf.* Forestier, pp. 231–234; *cf. ibid.*, p. 244. Knigge was thus permitted to take pride in the fact that whereas he found the order a monarchy, he left it under "une espèce de gouvernement républicain." (*Cf. ibid.*, p. 305.)

[393] To illustrate: The teaching function of the order was fully worked out and made effective by centering its direction in the grade of Priests. Forestier also notes Knigge's retention of the founder's insistence upon the knowledge of man as "la science par excellence." The principle of espionage was likewise retained. *Cf.* Forestier, pp. 298–304.

[394] The remodeling of the order in order to graft it on to the stem of Freemasonry has already been indicated. No practical result of Knigge's work exceeded this.

[395] Certainly at this point Knigge's feet were planted more solidly upon the earth than those of his fanciful predecessor. *Cf.* Forestier, pp. 240 *et seq.*

[396] The practical considerations which impelled Knigge to adopt this position were dictated by diplomatic rather than by conscientious reasons, although the latter were not wholly wanting. Knigge was well aware of the conditions in Catholic countries like Bavaria which gave rise to the violent anticlerical sentiments that the leaders of the Illuminati echoed. Nor was he out of sympathy with the men of his time who protested against religious intolerance and bigotry. But a spirit of anticlericalism readily enough becomes transmuted into a spirit essentially anti-religious, and Knigge saw that any manifestation of this sort would seriously embarrass the propaganda of the order in Protestant as well as in Catholic lands. Knigge's personal religious views appear to have been liberal rather than ultra radical. For a full and lucid discussion of the whole topic, *cf.* Forestier, pp. 238 *et seq.*

[397] Knigge's proposed modifications of the organization and principles of the order were adopted by the Areopagites, July 9, 1781. *Cf.* Forestier, p. 240. This action amounted to a virtual defeat for Weishaupt and a corresponding triumph for Knigge. In other words, a new epoch had begun. Engel's observations on the significance of the new policies and the respective services rendered by the two men is characteristically biased: "Weishaupt war tatsächlich der einzige im Orden, der streng darauf achtete, sein System der Notwendigkeit unterzuordnen, wohl wissend, dass dadurch allein der Bestand des Ordens gesichert würde. Phantastische Grade entwerfen, ohne eine Spur der Notwendigkeit, dass durch diese der Zweck der Vereinigung sicherer erreicht werde, dann die Mitglieder in die Aeusserlichkeit dieser Form einpressen und einschnüren, ist leider ein vielfach noch jetzt angewandtes, unbrauchbares

Rezept, dem auch Knigge huldigte. Letzterem war es ebenso wie vielen Areopagiten nur darum zu tun, viele Mitglieder zu haben, um dadurch Eindruck zu erzielen, die geistige Qualität stand in zweiter Linie." (*Geschichte des Illuminaten-Ordens*, pp. 123 *et seq.*) Knigge brought more than organizing skill to the languishing order. His accomplishments as a winner of recruits materially helped to fan the smouldering fires of enthusiasm among the earlier leaders. As early as November, 1780, he had begun to enroll adepts (the term commonly applied to members of the order, new and old), and some of these turned out to be most effective propagandists. *Cf.* Forestier, pp. 343 *et seq.*

[398] Forestier is disposed to explain the power of appeal which the new system had for the members of rival Masonic systems on the following grounds: (1) it at least pretended to take more seriously the doctrines of equality and liberty; (2) it emphasized the period of adolescence as the best of all ages for the winning of recruits; (3) it made appreciably less of financial considerations; and (4) it tended to turn attention away from such chimeras as the philosopher's stone, magic, and knight-templar chivalry, which filled with weak heads and visionary spirits the high grades of most of the other systems. *Cf. ibid.*, p. 340. German Freemasonry was far from being in a wholesome and promising condition when the order of the Illuminati emerged. From its introduction into that country sometime within the second quarter of the eighteenth century, it had developed two general types; *viz.*, English Freemasonry and the French high grades. The former was generally disposed to be content with simple organizations. Its lodges were little more than secret clubs whose members had their signs of recognition and their simple rituals, and whose ideals were represented by the terms fraternity and cooperation. The latter developed an excess of ceremonies and "mysteries", and thus opened the door for the introduction of impostures of every sort. Visionaries and charlatans flocked to the French lodges, and alchemy and thaumaturgy found in their secret quarters a veritable hot-house for their culture. It is Forestier's opinion

that this activity and influence of dreamers and mountebanks within the Masonic lodges is to be regarded as a reaction from the dreariness and sterility of current rationalism. *Cf. ibid.*, p. 146. However that may be, in the third quarter of the eighteenth century German Freemasonry generally was catering to a popular thirst for mystery, and the Order of the Illuminati was able to draw advantage from that fact. Certainly the very novelty of the new system had much to do with its attractiveness.

[399] Forestier, *op. cit.*, p. 344.

[400] Engel's treatment of the situation would seem to be inadequate and lacking in accuracy. *Cf.* Engel, *op. cit.*, p. 352. Forestier submits ample proofs of the expansion of the order to include Austria and Switzerland, notably the former. *Cf.* Forestier, *op. cit.*, pp. 346 *et seq.*, 398 *et seq.*

[401] *Ibid.*, pp. 349 *et seq.*

[402] Engel identifies Dalberg as the last elector of Mainz, and, in the time of Napoleon I, grand duke of Frankfort. See *ibid.*, p. 354. Forestier extends the list of civil notables to include Count Metternich, imperial ambassador at Coblenz; Count Brigido, governor of Galicia; Count Leopold Kolowrat, chancellor of Bohemia; Baron Kressel, vice-chancellor of Bohemia; Count Poelffy, chancellor of Hungary; Count Banffy, governor of Transylvania; Count Stadion, ambassador at London; and Baron Van Swieten, minister of public instruction. (The last seven were members of the lodge established at Vienna.) *Cf. ibid.*, pp. 400 *et seq.*

[403] Goethe's connection with the order is fully established by both Engel (*cf. ibid.*, pp. 355 *et seq.*) and Forestier (*cf. ibid.*, pp. 396 *et seq.*). The question whether Schiller belonged to the Illuminati is answered in the negative by Engel. *Cf. ibid.*, p. 356.

[404] "Un pédagogue célèbre, Pestalozzi, figurait parmi les membres de l'Église Minervale de Lautern." (Forestier, p. 349.)

[405] *Ibid.*, p. 399.

[406] In its efforts to obtain a decisive triumph over rival systems of Freemasonry, substantial progress had been made. At Munich, the Secret Chapter of the dominant Masonic fraternity in that city capitulated to the new system. At Vienna, Masons eagerly enrolled as Illuminati with a view to blocking the attempt of the Rosicrucians to extend the hegemony of that branch. The important general congress of Freemasons, held at Wilhelmsbad, in July, 1782, for the purpose of arriving at some conclusion concerning the claims of rival systems, yielded to the Illuminati a double advantage: the pretensions of the Order of the Strict Observance, its most dangerous rival, were disallowed and the opportunity which the congress offered in the form of a field for winning new recruits was adroitly seized by representatives of the Illuminati, with the result that its emissaries retired from the congress completely satisfied. Further, the Order of the Illuminati had apparently put itself on the high road to a complete victory in the Masonic world by securing the enlistment of the two most important personages in German Freemasonry, Duke Ferdinand of Brunswick and Prince Carl of Hesse. The full extent of the order's conquests among the various branches of Masonry is impossible of full and accurate statement, for the principal reason which Engel gives: "Nur wenige Dokumente existieren als Nachweis, denn es ist natürlich, dass solche in der Verfolgungszeit in Bayern vernichtet wurden, um nicht verdächtigt zu werden und äussere Verbindungen ziemlich schroff abgebrochen wurden, als sich die Skandalsucht erhob und dem Orden und deren Leiter all erdenlichen Schlechtigkeiten andichtete. Im Laufe der Zeit sind dann die betreffenden Schriften von den Logen als minderwertig missachtet und beseitigt worden, so dass eine Aufklärung heute ungemein erschwert ist." (*Op. cit.*, pp. 349 *et seq.*) Still, Forestier, in his chapter on "L'Action sur les Loges Allemandes" (pp. 343–388), from which the foregoing isolated facts are drawn, gathers together a very considerable body of evidence, all tending to show that Illuminated Freemasonry was

permitted to enjoy a very gratifying, though brief, period of prosperity.

[407] Writing of the condition of the order at the hour of its apogee, in 1784, Forestier says: "La situation de l'Ordre à cette époque paraît donc des plus prospères. Solidement établi en Bavière, il s'étend sur toute l'Europe Centrale, du Rhin à la Vistule et des Alpes à la mer du Nord et à la Baltique. Il compte au nombre de ses membres des jeunes gens qui appliqueront plus tard les principes qu'il leur a inculqués, des fonctionnaires de tout ordre qui mettent leur influence à son service, des membres du clergé auxquels il enseigne la tolérance, des princes dont il peut invoquer la protection et qu'il espère diriger. Il semble que le Grand Architecte de l'Univers ait spécialement veillé sur lui…." (*Op. cit.*, p. 401.)

[408] The term was no longer in official use, but the men remained. In other words, Weishaupt's Areopagites were Knigge's Provincials.

[409] Forestier, *op. cit.*, pp. 411–413.

[410] Engel asserts that the chief apple of discord was the grade of Priest. Weishaupt believed that Knigge had injected into the ritual of the order at that point expressions of radical religious sentiment which, if once discovered to the public, would be found extremely injurious to the order. *Cf. ibid.*, pp. 133 *et seq. Cf.* Forestier *op. cit.*, p. 415. But this was only one of many bones of contention. At bottom the two men were inordinately jealous, both as to their positions in the order and the systems which they had worked out.

[411] Knigge withdrew from the order April 20, 1784. In July of the same year he put his name to an agreement, pledging himself to restore such papers of the order as he possessed and to maintain silence concerning what he knew of the order's affairs. *Cf.* Forestier, p. 428. Freed from his responsibilities to the order, Knigge resumed his work as a writer, by which he managed to maintain himself very indifferently in funds. He

was finally accorded a government post, as inspector of schools, at Bremen, where he died. *Cf. ibid.*, pp. 549–551.

[412] Carl Theodore, successor to Maximilian Joseph, as Elector Palatinate had been ruler of the provinces of the Rhine since 1742. When he became duke of Upper and Lower Bavaria in 1777, he had established a reputation as a liberal-minded sovereign. The first two years of his rule in Bavaria gave promise of a tolerant reign; but reactionaries, in the persons of his confessor, the ex-Jesuit Frank, a certain Baron Lippert, who was devoted to the cause of ultramontanism, and the duchess dowager of Bavaria and sister of the duke, Maria Anna, worked upon his spirit and easily persuaded the well-meaning but weak-willed monarch to reverse his former policy and come to the defence of the cause of clericalism. See the comments of Professor August Kluckhohn, quoted by Engel, p. 4.

[413] *Cf.* Engel, *op. cit.*, p. 161, where the edict in full may be found. *Cf.* Forestier, p. 453. The Bavarian monarch's bold and, at first blush, precipitate action is explained by the following facts: Flushed with a sense of their growing influence and power, the Bavarian Illuminati for some time past had been guilty of extremely imprudent utterances which had excited the public mind. To certain of their critics, notably the priest Frank and the canon Dantzer, director of the schools of Bavaria, they had not deigned to make a specific reply. (Dantzer, not wholly unfairly, charged the members of the order with interference in the affairs of the public school system of the country). A lofty tone of assumed indifference characterized the leaders; but a spirit of boasting which led the members to profess the exercise of a controlling influence in civil affairs, together with less guarded expressions respecting the extreme religious and political ideals of the order, served to arouse public suspicion. To this extent the Bavarian Illuminati had themselves to blame for the ruin of the order. *Cf.* Forestier, pp. 430–438. On the part of the government, the situation in its main outlines developed somewhat as follows: Early in October, 1783, the duchess dowager, Maria Anna, was made the recipient of a document

that contained detailed accusations against the Illuminati of Bavaria, charging them with holding such vicious moral and religious sentiments as that life should be controlled by passion rather than reason, that suicide is justifiable, that one may poison one's enemies, and that religion should be regarded as nonsense and patriotism as puerility. Finally, and much more seriously from the particular point of view of the duchess, the Bavarian Illuminati were accused of being in the service of the government of Austria, whose efforts at the time to extend its hegemony over Bavaria had created considerable tension in the latter country. For a copy in full of the famous letter, *cf.* Engel, pp. 183–187. *Cf.* Forestier, pp. 440 *et seq.* The author, or at least the inspirer of the document seems to have been one Joseph Utzschneider (Engel disallows this; see *op. cit.*, pp. 187 *et seq.*) who, discontented on account of his slow advancement and enraged by exactions imposed upon him to prove his loyalty, had withdrawn from the Order of the Illuminati, in August, 1783. Later, Utzschneider persuaded several other members, among them Grünberger and Cosandey, fellow professors with him in the Academy of Santa Maria, to follow him in the course he had taken. Obtaining from his associates the ritual of the higher grades of the order, he prepared and despatched his presentment to the duchess. *Cf.* Forestier, pp. 444 *et seq.* The latter, greatly alarmed by the document, carried the accusations, particularly the charge of intrigues in the interests of Austria, to the duke, who thus far had manifested an attitude of indifference to the suspicions that had been engendered concerning the order. His fear being awakened by the considerations of danger to his person and throne that were urged, the duke resolved to bring matters to an immediate crisis. *Cf. ibid.*, p. 452.

[414] Engel, *op. cit.*, p. 161. The leaders of the order in Bavaria exerted themselves to disarm the suspicions of the government with reference to any lack of loyal submission to the interdict. Circular letters containing copies of the edict and commanding the lodges to suspend their labors were addressed to the brethren. A lack of sincerity showed itself, however, in the

efforts of the leaders to convey the impression to their subordinates that the sudden tempest would soon pass and that care therefore must be observed to preserve the cohesion of the order. In one important particular this effort to allay suspicion over-reached itself. In July, 1784, certain members of the order inserted an article in a Bavarian journal, the *Realzeitung* of Erlangen, of the nature of a counter-attack upon the Jesuits, and claiming that the latter, in defiance of the government, were continuing their secret associations. To this a recriminating answer was promptly made, and a war of newspaper articles and pamphlets was soon on. All of this tended, of course, to lend color to the suspicion that the operations of the order continued unabated. *Cf.* Forestier, pp. 454 *et seq. Cf.* Engel, pp. 240 *et seq.* The duchess, Maria Anna, moreover, continued her efforts to strengthen the purpose of the duke. *Cf.* Forestier, p. 467.

[415] The precise occasion, if any existed, for the launching of the second edict remains wholly in doubt. In a final effort to clear the order from the suspicions and calumniations raised against it, an appeal was made to Carl Theodore, in February, 1785, to permit representatives of the order to appear before him and furnish proofs of its innocence. This last desperate device failed. *Cf.* Engel, pp. 283–290, for a copy of this letter. *Cf.* Forestier, pp. 465 *et seq.*

[416] Engel, as in the former instance, copies the second edict in full. *Cf. op. cit.,* pp. 161–164. *Cf.* Forestier, pp. 468, 469. The terms of the second interdict provided that, in view of the alleged degenerate character of the Order of the Illuminati, as well as of the disorders it had occasioned, all its financial resources should be confiscated, half to be given to the poor and half to the informer against the order, "wenn er gleich selbst ein Mitglied wäre … und solcher keineswegs geoffenbart, sondern in Geheim gehalten werden solle." (Engel, p. 164.)

[417] Forestier's comment is trenchant: "Par une ironie du sort, le gouvernement, si indifferent ou si tolerant jusqu'alors, ne

commença à servir que lorsque le danger était passé et, après avoir respecté si longtemps l'organisme vivant, il s'acharna sur le cadavre." (*Op. cit.*, p. 469.)

[418] Cosandey and Renner (the latter also a professor associated with Cosandey on the faculty of the Academy of Santa Maria) were two of the men who supplied important information in this manner. Engel, pp. 291–304, prints their declarations. In this way, also, lists of names of members of the order came into possession of the government. *Cf.* Engel, pp. 303 *et seq.*

[419] A considerable amount of the most valuable papers of the order were either carefully concealed or devoted to the flames immediately after the launching of the second edict. *Cf.* Forestier, p. 469. Later, the government obtained important assistance in its campaign by coming into possession of a considerable portion of those that were spared. *Cf.* Engel, pp. 259 *et seq.*, 276 *et seq.*

[420] *Cf.* Forestier, p. 475. Weishaupt was well out of harm's way when the inquiry began in his home city. He brought lasting discredit upon himself by resorting to precipitate flight two weeks before the proclamation of the second ban. It is evident that he saw the storm gathering, and was resolved to put himself beyond personal danger, whatever might happen to his associates. The excuse he seems to have trumped up to justify his early flight had reference to a difficulty that arose between him and the librarian of the University of Ingolstadt over the latter's failure to purchase two books which Weishaupt held he needed for his classes. He fled across the border to Regensburg, and finally settled at Gotha.

[421] *Cf.* Engel, *op. cit.*, p. 305, for a copy of the order. This measure seemed to be rendered necessary by the fact that the lists of Illuminati which Cosandey and Renner furnished the government contained the names of several officers and other military personages. A later decree called upon ex-members of the order in the army to furnish information concerning the

teachings and membership of the order, and to present such papers and insignia as might be at hand. *Cf.* Forestier, p. 481.

[422] Those who made a frank acknowledgment of their membership in the order were to be pardoned, while those who hesitated or showed themselves contumacious were not only to lose their positions but to suffer other penalties. *Cf.* Forestier, p. 478.

[423] *Ibid.*

[424] *Ibid.*

[425] *Ibid.*, p. 475.

[426] Forestier gives the title of nine such productions that came from Weishaupt's pen within the space of a few months. *Cf. op. cit.*, p. 484. The most notable of these were: *Apologie der Illuminaten*, Frankfort and Leipzig, 1786, and *Vollständige Geschichte der Verfolgung der Illuminaten in Bayern*, Frankfort and Leipzig, 1786. The latter was planned to consist of two volumes, but only one appeared.

[427] Zwack's name had been on the list of members which Renner had put into the hands of the government. He was at the time a councillor of state. A short time before his house was invaded by the police and his papers seized, he had been deposed from his position on account of his relations with the Illuminati. At the time of the seizure he was living at Landshut in circumstances of disgrace and suspicion. *Cf.* Engel, p. 303; Forestier, pp. 480, 498.

[428] These documents were published by the Bavarian government, under the title: *Einige Originalschriften des Illuminaten Ordens*, Munich, 1787. Engel, pp. 259–262, publishes the list compiled by the government.

[429] Among these papers were found two smaller packets which gave a foundation for the most inveterate hostility to the order. These contained intimations of the order's right to exercise the law of life and death over its members, a brief

dissertation entitled, *Gedanken über den Selbstmord*, wherein Zwack, its author, had recorded his defence of suicide (*cf.* Engel, p. 262), a eulogy of atheism, a proposal to establish a branch of the order for women, the description of an infernal machine for safeguarding secret papers, and receipts for procuring abortion, counterfeiting seals, making poisonous perfumes, secret ink, *etc.* (*Cf.* Forestier, pp. 499 *et seq.*) The receipts for procuring abortion were destined to have a very ugly personal association in the public mind. Weishaupt, while still a resident of Ingolstadt, had stained his private life because of a liaison with his sister-in-law. On the 8 of February, 1780, his first wife had died. Her sister, who was his house-keeper at the time, continued in the household, and during the time that Weishaupt was waiting for a papal dispensation, permitting his marriage with her, she was found to be with child. Thrown into a panic on account of the failure of the dispensation to arrive (as a matter of fact it did not reach Ingolstadt until three years after it was first applied for), Weishaupt contemplated recourse to the method of procuring an abortion, in order to extricate himself from his painfully embarrassed position. In August, 1783, he wrote Hertel, one of the prominent members of the order, admitting the facts just stated. This letter fell into the hands of the authorities and was published by them in the volume entitled, *Nachtrag von weiteren Originalschriften*, Munich, 1787, vol. i, p. 14. The stigma of a new disgrace was thus attached to the order. Weishaupt made a pitifully weak effort to suggest extenuating circumstances for his conduct, in his volume, *Kurze Rechtfertigung meiner Absichten*, 1787, pp. 13 *et seq.* Taken in connection with the objectionable papers referred to above, this private scandal of the head of the order made the accusation of gross immorality on the part of the Illuminati difficult to evade. A spirit of intense revulsion penetrated the public mind.

[430] Other secret documents of the order were seized by the police in a search of the quarters of Baron Bassus, whose membership in the order on account of his close friendship with Zwack, brought him under the government's suspicion. The

police visitation referred to yielded no very important result, apart from establishing more solidly the government's claim that the order had not obeyed the first edict. The papers seized in this instance were published by the government under the title, *Nachtrag von weiteren Originalschriften ... Zwei Abtheilungen*, Munich, 1787.

[431] Forestier, pp. 504 *et seq.*

[432] Mändl, in the most cowardly fashion, charged the order with unmentionable practices. He seems to have been the Judas in the order's inner circle. *Cf.* Forestier, pp. 505 *et seq. Cf.* Engel, pp. 331 *et seq.*

[433] Massenhausen was Ajax in the order. The papers seized by the police identified him as one of Weishaupt's intimates.

[434] The "revelations" of Mändl appear to have been immediately responsible for the edict. *Cf.* Forestier, p. 507.

[435] Engel, *op. cit.*, p. 280.

[436] "Unter der nemlichen confiscations—und relegations Straf werden die illuminaten Logen, sie mögen gleich auf diesen oder anderen Namen umgetauft seyn, ebenfalls verbothen, worauf man auch allenthalben gute Spehr' [Späher] bestellen, und die Gesellschaften, welche entweder in Wirth— oder Privathäusern mit versperrten Thüren oder sonst auf verdächtige Weise gehalten werden, als wahre Logen behandeln lassen, und die so leer als gewöhnliche Ausrede, das es nur ehrliche Compagnien von guten Freunden sind, zumal von jenen, welche sich des Illuminatismi und der Freygeisterei vorhin schon suspect gemacht haben, nicht annehmen wird...." Quoted by Engel, p. 280.

[437] Forestier, *op. cit.*, p. 509.

[438] Forestier, *op. cit.*, pp. 511 *et seq. Cf.* Engel, *op. cit.*, pp. 378 *et seq.*

[439] *Ibid.*, p. 369. *Cf.* Forestier, pp. 511 *et seq.*

[440] *Ibid.*, p. 512.

[441] *Ibid.*, pp. 512 *et seq.* An effort to secure the extradition of Weishaupt was defeated by an appeal to Duke Ernst. *Cf.* Engel, pp. 231 *et seq.*

[442] The most significant of these were the following: *Einleitung zu meiner Apologie*, 1787; *Bemerkungen über einige Originalschriften*, published soon after the former; *Das verbesserte System der Illuminaten mit allen seinen Graden Einrichtungen*, also soon after the first mentioned work; *Kurze Rechtfertigung meiner Absichten*, 1787; *Nachtrag zur Rechtfertigung meiner Absichten*, 1787.

[443] A sympathetic and moving account of the last years of Weishaupt's life appears in Engel, *op. cit.*, pp. 380–402.

[444] Forestier, *op. cit.*, pp. 543 *et seq.*

[445] "Es muss die Furcht vor dem verschrieenen Illuminatismus geradezu wie ein Druck in der Luft gehangen haben, denn der Orden selbst existierte in seiner festeren Organisation schon lange nicht mehr, als sich die Gespensterfurcht vor ihm in so allgemeiner Weise breit machte." (Engel, *op. cit.*, p. 425.)

[446] Forestier, *op. cit.*, p. 613.

[447] *Ibid.*, pp. 613 *et seq.*

[448] As late as November 15, 1790, incited thereto by the priest Frank, the duke of Bavaria proclaimed a new interdict against the order. The threat of death as a punishment for membership in the order or activity on its behalf was again imposed. *Cf.* Engel, p. 371; Forestier, pp. 614 *et seq.* The following year the police of the city of Munich compiled a list of ninety-one names (Forestier gives the number as ninety-two, *cf. ibid.*, p. 615), of members of the order who were supposed to be still active, and proceeded to apply the policy of banishing those who were held to be most dangerous. A number suffered in this way. *Cf.* Engel, pp. 371 *et seq. Cf.* Forestier, pp. 615 *et*

seq. A spirit of reckless denunciation ruled in Munich, because of which no suspected man's person was safe. Not until the death of Carl Theodore, in 1799, did this period of hostility to the order on the part of the Bavarian government finally come to an end.

[449] A reorganization of the Rosicrucian system had taken place in 1767, which stressed the antiquity, sanctity, and superior character of the order in its relations to the rest of the Masonic fraternity. According to their claims, the Rosicrucians alone were able to explain the hieroglyphics, symbols, and allegories of Freemasonry. The structure of the order was greatly elaborated at the time indicated, and thus supplementing its traditional appeal to the thirst for alchemy and magic, the order grew rapidly. *Cf.* Forestier, pp. 187–191. *Cf.* Engel, p. 240.

[450] Vehse, in his *Geschichte des Preussischen Hofes*, vol. ii, p. 35, puts the matter thus: "In den Ländern nun, wo sie aufgehoben waren, brauchten die Exjesuiten das Mittel in den geheimen Gesellschaften Aufnahme zu suchen. Sie bildeten hier eine schleichende und deshalb um so sichere Opposition gegen alle Aufklärungstendenzen. In dem Freimaurerorden stifteten sie die sogenannten 'inneren Systeme.' Hier waren sie als Proselytenmacher ganz in der Stille tätig und arbeiteten mit Macht darauf hin, das obscurante Pfaffentum und die despotische Hierarchie in beiden Konfessionen, im Protestantismus sowohl als Katholizismus wieder herzustellen." (Quoted by Engel, pp. 241 *et seq.*)

[451] Forestier, *op. cit.*, p. 191. Engel, *op. cit.*, p. 242.

[452] *Ibid.*, p. 242.

[453] *Ibid.*, pp. 247 *et seq.* Forestier brings into connection with this effort of the king of Prussia to check the supposed operations of the Illuminati, a further reproach which came upon the order on account of the course pursued by the Rosicrucians in spreading the report in the Masonic world that the Eclectic Alliance, an ill-fated effort to unite and dominate

German Freemasonry, launched in 1783, was a survival of the Order of the Illuminati. The unpopularity and suspicion which the Eclectic Alliance incurred were due in part to its attempts to eliminate the high grades of Masonry, but more especially to the charges made against it by representatives of rival Masonic systems that it had at heart the undermining of the Christian religion. *Cf. ibid.*, pp. 617 *et seq.*, 383–388. The Illuminati had had affiliations with the Eclectic Alliance, and hence a certain justification had been given for the accusations which were transferred from the former to the latter.

[454] The loose use of the term "Illuminati" involved in these statements is only partially illustrated in the following comment of Mounier: "On a donné par dérision la qualité d'*Illuminés* à tous les charlatans mystiques de ce siècle, à tous ceux qui s'occupent d'alchimie, de magie et de cabale, de revenans, de relations avec des esprits intermédiaires, tels que les Saint-Germain, les Cagliostro, les Swedenborg, les Rose-croix et les Martinistes: mais il a existé une autre espèce d'illuminés en Allemagne" (*i. e.*, Weishaupt's system). (*De l'influence attribuée aux philosophes, aux franc-maçons et aux illuminés, sur la révolution de France*, p. 169.) Not these systems alone, but the representatives of the diffused forces of the Enlightenment were appointed to share the mantle of the ambiguous term.

[455] Baron Knigge. In responding to Bahrdt's appeal to assist him in working out the system of the German Union, Knigge violated the pledge he had made to the Bavarian government not to concern himself again with secret organizations. For his indiscretion he paid the penalty of an unpleasant notoriety. *Cf.* Forestier, p. 629.

[456] Bahrdt's career was objectionable from almost every point of view. He had been first a pastor, and later a professor of sacred philology at the University of Leipzig. Here, as at Erfurt, the place of his next professional labors, his dissolute conduct involved him in public scandals which lost him his post. In 1771 he went to Giessen as preacher and professor of

theology. Later, after numerous changes of location and in the character of his educational activity, he took refuge at Halle, where he conducted courses in rhetoric, eloquence, declamation, and ethics. A man of low tastes, his life was without dignity and solid convictions. *Cf.* Forestier, pp. 624 *et seq.*; Mounier, pp. 201 *et seq.*; P. Tschackert, in Herzog-Hauck, *Realencyklopädie*, 3. Aufl., ii, (1897), pp. 357–359.

[457] These associations were to be divided into six grades: Adolescent, Man, Elder, Mesopolite, Diocesan, and Superior. A ritual was provided and the low initiation fee of one *thaler* imposed. The system, never fully developed, conveys the impression of crudeness and absurdity.

[458] Mounier, pp. 201 *et seq.* Forestier makes the added suggestion that Bahrdt saw in the formation of the Union a chance to further his own literary ambitions and pecuniary interests. *Cf.* Forestier, p. 627.

[459] *Ibid.*, pp. 629, 630.

[460] *Ibid.*

[461] Mounier, p. 186.

[462] "Die merkwürdigste, aber auch gleichzeitig groteskeste Beschuldigung, die jemals dem Illuminatenorden nachgesagt worden ist, war die, dass er die französische Revolution zur Explosion gebracht habe. Es gehörte recht viel Kombinationsvermögen und Taschenspielerei in der Logik dazu, um den Beweis für diese wundersame Behauptung zusammenzuleimen, aber in jener Zeit wurde tatsächlich alles geglaubt, sobald es sich darum handelte, dem Illuminatismus eine neue Schurkerei aufzuhalsen." (Engel, pp. 402, 404. *Cf.* Mounier, pp. 124, 215 *et seq.*)

[463] Published anonymously at Munich, in 1794.

[464] Title in full: *Illuminatus Dirigens oder Schottischer Ritter. Ein Pendant zu der nicht unwichtigen Schrift: Die neuesten Arbeiten, etc.*, Munich, 1794.

[465] The grades of Priest and Regent were reproduced in the first of these two works. The most objectionable principles of the order were reserved to these two grades.

[466] Forestier brings into connection with the publication of these pamphlets the appearance of certain brochures of Knigge's, wherein he espoused with great ardor the cause of the French Revolutionists. The special import of this requires no comment. *Cf. ibid.*, pp. 636 *et seq.*

[467] Hoffman had himself been a member of the Illuminati, at Vienna. *Cf.* Forestier, *op. cit.*, p. 646.

[468] The date was early in 1792 (!). *Cf. ibid.*, p. 646.

[469] Forestier, whose treatment at this point is characteristically thorough, gives the titles, or otherwise refers to not less than fourteen pamphlets or brochures, in addition to numerous magazine articles. *Cf. ibid.*, pp. 649–658.

[470] Forestier, *op. cit.*, pp. 649–658.

[471] Johann Joachim Christoph Bode (1730–1793), by no means a distinguished representative of the German literati of his period, occupied a fairly important rôle in the history of the Order of the Illuminati. After Weishaupt's flight to Ingolstadt he was the most active leader in the ranks of the persecuted order. *Cf.* Forestier, pp. 543 *et seq.* He was profoundly interested in Masonry. In 1790 he projected a plan for the union of all the German lodges of Masonry. The effort proved futile.

[472] The *Philalèthes* were conspicuous among French Freemasons for their unequalled devotion to alchemy and theurgy. The order was founded about 1773.

[473] Staack, in his *Der Triumph der Philosophie im 18. Jahrhundert* (1803), vol. ii, p. 276, represents von dem Busche as a military official in the service of the Dutch government, and as a member of Weishaupt's order. Mounier (p. 212) refers to him as a major in the service of the landgrave of Hesse-

Darmstadt. His figure is of no historical importance apart from its chance connection with the Illuminati legend.

[474] This bizarre and preposterous explanation of the genesis of the French Revolution was a favorite with contemporary German and French writers of the special-pleader type. It was used, as we shall see later, by both Robison and Barruel in their discussions of the rôle played by the Illuminati in the great French political and social debacle. Its classic statement was made a few years later by Staack, in his *Der Triumph der Philosophie im 18. Jahrhundert*, vol. ii, pp. 348 *et seq.*

A more silly exposition of the relation of the Illuminati to the French Revolution is that found in the fabulous tale related by the notorious Sicilian impostor, Giuseppe Balsamo ("Count" Alessandro Cagliostro), who, in 1790, having been arrested at Rome and interrogated by officials respecting his revolutionary principles, attempted to divert suspicion by recounting experiences he claimed to have had with two chiefs of the Illuminati, at Mitau, near Frankfort, Germany. Revelations had been made to him at that time (1780), he alleged, to the effect that the Order of the Illuminati was able to number 20,000 lodges, scattered through Europe and America; that its agents were industriously operating in all European courts, particularly, being lavishly financed with funds drawn from the immense treasures of the order; and that the next great blow of the order was to be delivered against the government of France. *Cf.* Sierke, *Schwärmer und Schwindler zu Ende des 18. Jahrhunderts*, pp. 407 *et seq.* Both Engel (pp. 420 *et seq.*) and Forestier (pp. 658 *et seq.*) devote an unnecessary amount of space to Cagliostro's foolish "revelations". It is sufficient for our purpose to remark in passing that, in any case, Cagliostro was not discussing the affairs of Weishaupt's order, but the affairs of the Strict Observance whose growing credulity and occultism caused the term "Illuminati" sometimes to be applied to them.

[475] "Ses principes étaient directement contraires à ceux des illuminés; il n'était pas homme à placer ses espérances dans un

intervalle de mille ans. Il n'a jamais pensé qu'un peuple pût devenir assez vertueux pour se passer de lois et de magistrats. Il a soutenu la vraie théorie de la balance des pouvoirs, et combattu le despotisme populaire, toutes les fois que l'amour de la célébrité et l'intérêt de son ambition ne le faisaient pas agir contre sa propre doctrine, et les illuminés n'auraient été capables, ni d'ajouter à ses lumières, ni de changer sa théorie, ni de corriger ses vices." (Mounier, pp. 216 *et seq.*) This judgment of a sensible and impartial critic of the French Revolution, first submitted to the public in 1801, is as valid now as then.

[476] Without citing his authority, Forestier makes the statement that von dem Busche's interest in the reform of the debased order of the *Philalèthes* led him not only to accompany Bode but to offer to pay his expenses. *Cf.* Forestier, p. 666.

[477] The theories and *séances* of the empiric, Mesmer, were greatly agitating Paris at the time and attracting attention throughout Europe.

[478] Mounier, pp. 212 *et seq. Cf.* Forestier, pp. 664 *et seq.* While Bode was in Paris he kept in close correspondence with his German friend, Frau Hess, of Hirschberg. Engel, who made an examination of this correspondence in the Royal Library at Dresden, was unable to discover the slightest intimation that Bode's mind, while he was in Paris, was occupied with anything more revolutionary than the turning of the *Philalèthes* away from their craze for alchemy, cabala, theosophy, and theurgy, or in Mesmer's theories. *Cf.* Engel, pp. 409–415. When Bode returned to Germany it is undeniable that he carried with him an unfavorable opinion of French Masonry. *Cf.* Forestier, p. 668.

[479] In addition to the two elaborated upon in the remainder of this chapter, the following are most worthy of note: Staack, *Der Triumph der Philosophie im 18. Jahrhundert*, vols. i, ii, 1803 (already noted); Proyard, *Louis XVI et ses vertus aux prises avec la perversité du siècle*, Paris, 1808 (4 vols.); De Malet,

Recherches politiques et historiques qui prouvent l'existence d'une secte révolutionnaire, son antique origine, ses moyens, ainsi que son but, et dévoilent entièrement l'unique cause de la Révolution Française, Paris, 1817; De Langres, *Des Sociétés Secrètes en Allemagne et dans d'autres contrées, de la Secte des Illuminés, du Tribunal Secret, de l'assassinat de Kotzebue*, 1819; Le Couteulx, *Les Sectes et Sociétés politiques et religieuses*, Paris, 1863; Deschamps, *Les Sociétés Secrètes et la Société*, vols. i, ii, iii, Avignon, 1874–1876. As late as 1906, in an article in the *Edinburgh Review* of July of that year, Una Birch traversed much of the ground covered thus far in this and the preceding chapter and, on the theory that an event as spontaneous (?) as the French Revolution *must* have originated in a definite coördination of ideas and doctrines, reaffirmed the general notion that the Masonic lodges of France, having been inoculated with the doctrines of the Illuminati, became the principal points of associative agitation for, and thus the direct cause of, the French Revolution. This essay may also be found in the volume of essays entitled, *Secret Societies and the French Revolution* (London and New York, 1911), by the same author.

[480] Later editions of this work, which in their number and geographical extent strongly suggest the degree of interest the subject had for the reading public, appeared as follows: second edition, London, 1797; third edition, London, 1798; fourth edition, London and New York, 1798; a French translation, London, 1798–99 (2 vols.); a German translation, Königslutter and Hamburg, 1800; a Dutch translation, Dordrecht (n. d.). See Wolfstieg, *Bibliographie der Freimaurerischen Literatur*, vol. i, pp. 192, 193.

[481] Robison was a mathematician, scientific writer, and lecturer in the field of natural philosophy, of considerable ability and distinction. The son of a Glasgow merchant, he was born in Scotland in 1739. He received the benefits of a thorough education, graduating from Glasgow University in 1756. The connections he enjoyed throughout his life were of

the best. Subsequent to his graduation he became tutor to the son of Sir Charles Knowles, the English admiral, and later was appointed by the government to service in the testing out at sea of the newly completed chronometer of John Harrison, the horologist. Still later he went to Russia as private secretary to Sir Charles. While in Russia he was called to the chair of mathematics established in connection with the imperial sea-cadet corps of nobles. Abandoning this post, he returned to Scotland, and in 1773 became professor of natural philosophy in Edinburgh University, lecturing on such subjects as hydro-dynamics, astronomy, optics, electricity, and magnetism. His distinction in this general field seems clearly demonstrated by the fact that he was called upon to contribute to the third edition of the *Encyclopaedia Britannica* articles on seamanship, the telescope, optics, waterworks, resistance to fluids, electricity, magnetism, music, *etc.*, as well as by the fact that when the Royal Society of Edinburgh was organized under royal charter in 1783, Robison was elected general secretary of that distinguished organization, an office he continued to hold until within a few years of his death. The versatility of the man is further evidenced by the fact that he was deeply interested in music, attaining the mastery of several instruments, and in the writing of verse. His reputation was not confined to Great Britain. In 1790 the College of New Jersey (Princeton University) conferred upon him the degree of LL.D. (*Cf. General Catalogue of the College of New Jersey*, 1746–1896, p. 177. *The Dictionary of National Biography*, vol. xlix, p. 58, incorrectly gives the date for the bestowal of this degree as 1798.) Later, his alma mater, Glasgow University, bestowed upon him a like honor.

In addition to his encyclopaedia articles and his book on the Illuminati, Robison edited and published the lectures of Dr. Black, the chemist, and the following scientific works, the product of his own intellectual activity: *Outlines of a Course of Lectures on Mechanical Philosophy*, Edinburgh, 1797, and *Elements of Mechanical Philosophy*, Edinburgh, 1804. The latter was intended to be the initial volume of a series, but its successors were not forthcoming. A posthumous work of four volumes entitled, *A System of Mechanical Philosophy, with Notes by David Brewster, LL.D.*, was published at Edinburgh in 1822. The death of Robison occurred in 1805. (For the material incorporated in the foregoing the writer is chiefly indebted to the *Dictionary of National Biography*, vol. xlix, pp. 57, 58, and to casual references in the *Transactions of the Royal Society of Edinburgh*, vols. i–v.)

[482] "Die Neuesten Religionsbegebenheiten mit unpartheyischen Anmerkungen mit Beihülfe mehrerer von H. M. G. Köster, Professor in Giessen, herausgegeben Jg. 1–20 Giessen, 1778–97 verfolgten gleichfalls den Zweck, von den wichtigsten Vorfällen aus der Religionsgeschichte der Gegenwart eine deutliche, gründliche und nützliche Beschreibung zu liefern, doch beschränkten sie sich dabei vornehmlich auf Deutschland und richteten sich in erster Linie an Laien und Nichttheologen" (Herzog-Hauck, *Realencyklopädie*, 3rd ed., vol. xxiv, Leipzig, 1913, p. 673).

[483] Though a Mason, Robison was by no means an ardent supporter of Freemasonry. The English Masonic lodges with which he was acquainted impressed him as having no higher function than that of supplying "a pretext for passing an hour or two in a sort of decent conviviality, not altogether void of some rational occupation." He found the lodges on the continent, however, "matters of serious concern and debate." *Cf. Proofs of a Conspiracy, etc.*, pp. 1 *et seq.* (The edition of Robison's book here as elsewhere referred to is the third [London] edition of 1798.) Robison professed to have visited lodges at Liège, Valenciennes, Brussels, Aix-la-Chapelle, Berlin, Königsberg, and St. Petersburg. Everywhere he found an elaboration of ritual, joined with a spirit of grave interest in the affairs of Freemasonry, which filled him with astonishment and seemed to call for explanation. *Cf. ibid.*, pp. 2 *et seq.*

[484] Robison, *op. cit.*, p. 7. Robison also made use of several of the works which the disturbances occasioned by the Bavarian Illuminati called forth on the continent. Conspicuous

among these were the documents of the order published by the Bavarian government. *Cf. ibid.*, pp. 133, 185, 186, 205, *etc.* He also made use of Hoffman's violently hostile sheet, the *Wiener Zeitschrift. Cf. ibid.*, pp. 358, 393. Robison's knowledge of the German language was, however, far from perfect, as he himself freely admitted (*Cf. ibid.*, pp. 14, 499), so that his handling of his sources must be viewed as neither capable nor complete. The meagerness of his resources is perhaps best illustrated in his treatment of the conspiracy which he assumed underlay the French Revolution. Such "proofs" as he made use of in this connection amounted to little more than the political manifestoes of certain secret lodges and clubs, fugitive revolutionary documents which chanced to blow across his path, current historical conjecture and gossip, *etc.* The whole was pieced together in the spirit of one who ventured to hope that his "scattered facts" might be of some service to his generation. (*Cf. ibid.*, pp. 493–496.)

[485] Robison, *op. cit.*, pp. 10, 11, 15.

[486] An illustration of the carelessness with which Robison handled his dates is found on pages 15 and 133 (*cf.* p. 103) of the *Proofs of a Conspiracy, etc.*, in the matter of the date of the founding of the Order of the Illuminati. Far more serious in its reflection on the author's lack of accuracy and insight is such looseness and general unsoundness of treatment as permitted him to represent the Jesuits as frequenters of English and French Masonic lodges, while at the same time indicting the latter as fully committed to a free-thinking propaganda which sought nothing less than the eradication of *religion*, not to speak of its institutions. *Cf. ibid.*, pp. 22 *et seq.* Robison's superficial explanation of the anticlericalism of Weishaupt might be cited as another illustration of the blundering method pursued in the book. *Cf. ibid.*, pp. 101, 103 *et seq.* His weak and practically pointless digression in order to find opportunity to comment on the educational projects of Basedow will serve to illustrate the discursive quality in his work. *Cf. ibid.*, 85 *et seq.*

[487] Robison's exposition of the elements of uncontrolled curiosity and conjecture as elements in his purpose in writing the book is not without significance: "I must entreat that it be remembered that these sheets are not the work of an author determined to write a book. They were for the most part notes, which I took from books I had borrowed, that I might occasionally have recourse to them when occupied with Free Masonry, the first object of my curiosity. My curiosity was diverted to many other things as I went along, and when the Illuminati came in my way, I regretted the time I had thrown away on Free Masonry. (But, observing their connection, I thought that I perceived the progress of one and the same design. This made me eager to find out any remains of Weishaupt's Association. I was not surprised when I saw marks of its interference in the French Revolution.) In hunting for clearer proofs I found out the German Union—and, in fine, the whole appeared to be one great and wicked project, fermenting and working over all Europe." (*Ibid.*, pp. 493 *et seq.*) Encouraged by his friends, Robison "set about collecting my [his] scattered facts." (*Ibid.*, p. 494.)

[488] *Ibid.*, pp. 28 *et seq.*

[489] Robison does not wholly miss the true point in his survey of the backgrounds of the French Revolution. He points out numerous "cooperating causes" which served to make the Revolution inevitable. "Perhaps there never was a nation where all these cooperating causes had acquired greater strength than in France. Oppressions of all kinds were at a height. The luxuries of life were enjoyed exclusively by the upper classes, and this in the highest degree of refinement; so that the desires of the rest were whetted to the utmost. Even religion appeared in an unwelcome form, and seemed chiefly calculated for procuring establishments for the younger sons of insolent and useless nobility. For numbers of men of letters were excluded, by their birth, from all hopes of advancement to the higher stations in the church. These men frequently vented their discontents by secretly joining the laics in their bitter satires on

such in the higher orders of the clergy, as had scandalously departed from the purity and simplicity of manners which Christianity enjoins. Such examples were not unfrequent, and none was spared in those bitter invectives.... The faith of the nation was shaken; and when, in a few instances, a worthy Curé uttered the small still voice of true religion, it was not heard amidst the general noise of satire and reproach. The misconduct of administration, and the abuse of the public treasures, were every day growing more impudent and glaring, and exposed the government to continual criticism." (Robison, pp. 60 *et seq. Cf. ibid.*, pp. 362 *et seq.*) These "cooperating causes" receive little emphasis, however, in Robison's zealous effort to trace the revolutionary spirit to its lair in the Masonic lodges of France.

[490] *Ibid.*, pp. 40 *et seq.*

[491] Robison, *op. cit.*, pp. 43 *et seq.*

[492] *Ibid.*, p. 51. Robison's account of this phase of the situation has little to commend it. Upon his own unsupported assertions many of the Revolutionary leaders, as, for example, Mirabeau, Sieyès, Despremenil, Bailly, Fauchet, Maury, Mounier, and Talleyrand, are brought into direct connection with one or another of the French Masonic systems. *Cf.* Robison, pp. 49 *et seq.* Similarly, it is maintained, it was among Masonic lodges that the ideas contained in such books as Robinet's *La Nature, ou l'Homme moral et physique*, Condorcet's *Le Progrès de l'Esprit humain*, Lequinio's *Les préjugés vaincus par la raison*, and the book *Des Erreurs et de la Vérité*, were first disseminated. Indeed, some of these books are said to have sprung out of the very bosom of the lodges. *Cf. ibid.*, pp. 43 *et seq.*

[493] *Ibid.*, pp. 67 *et seq.* Comparison with Forestier, pp. 141 *et seq.*, will make clear the paucity of the data upon which Robison drew in attempting to write the earlier chapters of the history of German Freemasonry.

[494] Robison, *op. cit.*, p. 64.

[495] Robison's language is absurdly strong. "In half a year Free Masonry underwent a complete revolution all over Germany." (*Ibid.*, p. 70.)

[496] The sheer puerility of the treatment is indicated by the following: "A Mr. Rosa, a French commissary, brought from Paris a complete wagon-load of Masonic ornaments, which were all distributed before it had reached Berlin, and he was obliged to order another, to furnish the Lodges of that city. It became for a while the most profitable business to many French officers and commissaries dispersed over Germany, having little else to do." (Robison, *op. cit.*, pp. 69 *et seq.*)

[497] *Ibid.*, p. 73.

[498] *Ibid.*, pp. 65 *et seq.*

[499] *Ibid.*, pp. 78, 79. Robison read into this situation a deliberate effort on the part of the leaders of French Freemasonry to extend the hegemony of the latter. He surmised that political uses and benefits were thus aimed at. *Cf. ibid.*

[500] Robison's term for the representatives of the *Aufklärung*. *Cf.* Robison, p. 81.

[501] *Ibid.*, p. 80. This declension of faith and morals Robison, more wisely than he was aware, traced in part to the clash between the Roman Catholic and Protestant systems in Germany and the spirit of free inquiry which was thus promoted. See Robison, pp. 80 *et seqq.*

[502] It is in this connection that Basedow is brought into relations with Robison's devious exposition. *Cf. ibid.*, pp. 85 *et seq.*

[503] *Ibid.*, pp. 82 *et seq.*

[504] Robison, *op. cit.*, pp. 92 *et seq.* " … Germany has experienced the same gradual progress, from Religion to Atheism, from decency to dissoluteness, and from loyalty to rebellion, which has had its course in France. And I must now

add, that this progress has been effected in the same manner, and by the same means; and that one of the chief means of seduction has been the Lodges of the Free Masons. The French, along with their numerous chevaleries [*sic*], and stars, and ribands, had brought in the custom of haranguing in the Lodges, and as human nature has a considerable uniformity everywhere, the same topics became favorite subjects of declamation that had tickled the ear in France; there were the same corruptions of sentiments and manners among the luxurious or profligate, and the same incitements to the utterance of these sentiments, wherever it could be done with safety; and I may say, that the zealots in all these tracts of free-thinking were more serious, more grave, and fanatical. These are assertions *a priori*. I can produce proofs." (*Ibid.*, pp. 91 *et seq.*) The "proofs" here referred to concern the Masonic career of Baron Knigge, whose antagonism to orthodox Christianity Robison distorts both as to its temper and its effect.

[505] *Ibid.*, pp. 126 *et seq.*

[506] *Ibid.*, pp. 100 *et seq.*

[507] *Ibid.*, pp. 101 *et seq.* These connections Robison almost wholly misconceived. *Cf. supra*, pp. 150, 163 *et seq.*

[508] Robison, *op. cit.*, p. 103.

[509] *Ibid.*, p. 105. The ulterior object of the order is later stated by Robison in the following manner: "Their first and immediate aim is to get possession of riches, power, and influence, without industry; and, to accomplish this, they want to abolish Christianity; and then dissolute manners and universal profligacy will procure them the adherence of all the wicked, and enable them to overturn all the civil governments of Europe; after which they will think of further conquests, and extend their operations to the other quarters of the globe, till they have reduced mankind to a state of one indistinguishable chaotic mass." Robison, pp. 209 *et seq.*

[510] *Ibid.*, p. 126.

[511] *Ibid.*, p. 212.

[512] Robison omitted nothing in his effort to fasten the stigma of moral obliquity upon the order. The published papers of the order were appealed to show that crimes of bribery, theft, and libertinism were not uncommon on the part of the leaders. See Robison, pp. 144 *et seq.* The unsavory documents of the order referred to on page 181 of this dissertation likewise received Robison's zealous attention. *Cf. ibid.*, pp. 138 *et seq.* Weishaupt's personal immorality in his relations with his sister-in-law is made to do full duty as "a brilliant specimen of the ethics which illuminated" the leaders. *Cf. ibid.*, pp. 164 *et seq.* (If a particular illustration of Robison's bungling way of handling his German sources were needed, that might be found in the fact that our author identified the victim of Weishaupt's lust as the sister-in-law of Zwack. *Cf. ibid.*, p. 167.)

[513] To Robison's mind this constituted the crowning infamy of the order. "There is nothing in the whole constitution of the Illuminati that strikes me with more horror than the proposals of Hercules and Minos to enlist women in this shocking warfare with all that 'is good, and pure, and lovely, and of good report'…. Are not the accursed fruits of Illumination to be seen in the present humiliating condition of women in France? … In their present state of national moderation (as they call it) and security, see Madame Tallien come into the public theatre, accompanied by other *beautiful* women, (I was about to have misnamed them Ladies), laying aside all modesty, and presenting themselves to the public view, with bared limbs, *à la Sauvage*, as the alluring objects of desire…. Was not their abominable farce in the church of Notre Dame a bait of the same kind, in the true spirit of Weishaupt's *Eroterion?*" (Robison, pp. 243, 251, 252.)

[514] Robison, *op. cit.*, pp. 110–200.

[515] *Ibid.*, pp. 201 *et seq.*

[516] *Ibid.* Although offered to the public with every show of confidence, Robison's list was largely chimerical. He had

depended upon isolated references in the papers of the order, many of which he must have misread. Doubtless in numerous cases he took the *hopes* of the ambitious leaders of the order as sober statements of fact. The importance of the reference to America will, of course, appear later.

[517] *Ibid.*, p. 272.

[518] *Ibid.*, p. 286.

[519] *Ibid.*, p. 290.

[520] Robison, *op. cit.*, pp. 315 *et seq.*

[521] *Ibid.*, p. 322.

[522] *Ibid.*, p. 321.

[523] *Ibid.*, p. 317. "All the Archives that were found were the plans and lists of the members, and a parcel of letters of correspondence. The correspondence and other business was managed by an old man in some inferior office or judicatory, who lived at bed and board in Bahrdt's house for about six shillings a week, having a chest of papers and a writing-desk in the corner of the common room of the house." (*Ibid.*)

[524] *Ibid.*, pp. 291, 296, 297.

[525] *Ibid.*, p. 299. Bahrdt's fantastical program called for the division of these societies into Provinces or Dioceses, each directed by its Diocesan, and subordinate to a central organization. *Cf. ibid.*, p. 292

[526] *Ibid.*, p. 294.

[527] Robison, *op, cit.*, p. 297.

[528] *Ibid.*, pp. 322 *et seq.* " … although I cannot consider the German Union as a formal revival of the Order under another name, I must hold those *United*, and the members of those Reading Societies, as *Illuminati* and *Minervals*. I must even consider the Union as a part of Spartacus's work." (*Ibid.*)

[529] *Ibid.*, pp. 355 *et seq.* "Thus I think it clearly appears, that the suppression of the Illuminati in Bavaria and of the Union in Brandenburgh were insufficient.... The habit of plotting had formed itself into a regular system. Societies now acted everywhere in secret, in correspondence with similar societies in distant places. And thus a mode of cooperation was furnished to the discontented, the restless, and the unprincipled in all places, without even the trouble of formal initiations, and without any external appearances by which the existence and occupations of the members could be distinguished." (*Ibid.*)

[530] *Ibid.*, p. 355. *Cf. ibid.*, p. 286.

[531] *Ibid.*, p. 358.

[532] Robison, *op. cit.*, p. 371.

[533] *Ibid.*, pp. 393 *et seq.*

[534] *Ibid.*, pp. 397 *et seq.*

[535] *Ibid.*, p. 374.

[536] *Ibid.*, p. 398.

[537] The Grand Orient, according to Robison, represented the association of all the *improved* Masonic lodges of France. Its Grand Master was the Duke of Orléans. *Cf. ibid.*, p. 381.

[538] *Ibid.*, pp. 400 *et seq.*

[539] *Ibid.*, p. 376.

[540] *Ibid.*, pp. 376 *et seq.*

[541] Robison, *op. cit.*, p. 405.

[542] *Ibid.*, p. 402. Robison regarded the famous Jacobin Club in Paris as "just one of those Lodges." (Robison, p. 406. *Cf. ibid.*, p. 402.) He allowed his statement to stand, however, without making any effort to substantiate it. Further, he held that the political committees in these "illuminated" lodges of France were in correspondence with similar committees in

Germany, Holland, Austria, and Switzerland. *Cf. ibid.*, pp. 406 *et seq.*, 414 *et seq.*, 420. The contradictory character of his "evidence" is perhaps best illustrated by the fact that he treats the Masonic lodges of Paris as trying to seduce the lodges of German Freemasons. *Cf. Ibid.*, p. 418.

[543] *Ibid.*, p. 402.

[544] *Ibid.*, p. 405.

[545] The London edition of 1797–8 (4 vols.) was reprinted in five volumes at Hamburg, Augsburg and Braunschweig; and a new edition, revised and corrected by the author, was issued at Lyons in 1818. Barruel himself put forth an English translation at London in 1798; and this was reprinted at Hartford, Conn., New York, and Elizabeth-town, N. J., the following year. Continental allies of the ex-Jesuit must have been responsible for translations into Polish, Dutch and Portuguese, which enjoyed but one printing apiece, as well as for the three editions of the Spanish translation, and for two of the three Italian editions. During the anti-Masonic campaign of the swindler Leo Taxil (1887), the Italian translation was reprinted at Rome by the *Tipografia de Propaganda Fide*.

Abridgements and excerpts were also circulated in several languages, including English. In this connection the following titles may also be noted: *Application of Barruel's Memoirs of Jacobinism to the Secret Societies of Ireland and Great Britain*, London, 1798; *The Anti-Christian and Antisocial Conspiracy. An extract from the French of Barruel, to which is prefixed "Jachin and Boaz,"* Lancaster, (U. S.), 1812.

Cf. Sommervogel, C., *Bibliothèque de la Compagnie de Jésus*, i, Bruxelles, 1890, coll. 938–941; also Wolfstieg, *Bibliographie der Freimaurerischen Literatur*, vol. i, pp. 324, 325.

[546] Augustin Barruel (1741–1820) was a French controversialist and publicist, whose zeal was aroused in the defence of traditional ecclesiastical institutions and doctrines, in opposition to rationalistic tendencies manifest in the

eighteenth century. Barruel entered the Society of Jesus in 1756 and was later driven from France when that order was suppressed by the French government in 1773. Permitted the next year to terminate his exile, he gave himself to literary pursuits. As might be expected, the turbulent condition of public affairs in France drew him into the currents of political discussion. His loyalty to the interests of the church would brook no silence. The civil oath demanded of ecclesiastics and the promulgation of the civil constitution in the earlier period of the Revolution specially roused his spirit, and led to the publication of a number of pamphlets from his pen. His ecclesiastical loyalties and political antagonisms were such that when the full fury of the revolutionary storm broke, Barruel became an *emigré* and sought asylum in England. There he continued his literary employments, and published in 1794 his well-known *Histoire du clergé de France, pendant la révolution française*. In that same year he brought out an English translation at London. This work Barruel dedicated to the English people in grateful recognition of the hospitable treatment which they accorded the persecuted ecclesiastics of his own land. Later, and while still in England, he wrote his *Memoirs of Jacobinism*. The number of editions through which this work passed is in itself a gauge of its claim upon popular interest. After the fall of the Directory, and after he had given his pledge of fidelity to the new government, Barruel again was permitted to return to France. With a view to healing the schism in the French church which the Revolution had produced, he championed the cause of the government in a work entitled, *Du Pape et ses droits religieux*, 1803. As the Napoleonic regime drew towards its close, Barruel came to be regarded as an *emigré* priest, and suffered arrest at the hands of the government. In August, 1816, Barruel was allowed to make his profession in the Society of Jesus. Shortly before this he wrote to its General: "Je m'étais toujours regardé comme lié par mes voeux, sans cesser d'être vraiment Jésuite, ce qui heureusement a fait pour moi une douce illusion dans laquelle je remercie Dieu de m'avoir laissé vivre jusqu' au moment où vous vous prêtez avec tant de bonté à la demande que j'ai faite pour ma profession." (*La Compagnie de Jésus en France, Histoire d'un siècle, 1814–1914*, Par Joseph Burnichon, S.J., Tome 1er, Paris, 1914, pp. 74 *et seq.*) The last years of Barruel's life were spent in retirement. A list of his writings may be found in Quérard's *La France Littéraire*, Tome Premier, pp. 196, 197, and a more elaborate one, in Sommervogel, *op. cit.* i, coll. 930–945.

[547] Barruel, *op. cit.*, pp. i, vi.

[548] *Ibid.*, pp. xiii *et seq.*

[549] Barruel's term was *Sophistes*.

[550] Barruel, *op. cit.*, pp. xiv, xv.

[551] *Ibid.*, p. 2.

[552] *Ibid.*, p. 1.

[553] Barruel's main reliance is the correspondence of Voltaire, as published in the edition of Kehl.

[554] Barruel, *op. cit.*, vol. i, pp. 25 *et seq.*

[555] *Ibid.*, pp. 26, 27, 33.

[556] *Ibid.*, pp. 54 *et seq.* Barruel represents the Encyclopedists as arguing that force could not be employed until there had first been a revolution in all religious ideas; hence *L'Encyclopédie*, with all its insinuating doubts, its artful cross-references, its veiled impiety, was planned to give the first great impulse in that direction. Thus the old forms of thought would perish "as it were, by inanition;" later, the laying of the axe to the altar would not be hazardous.

[557] *Ibid.*, pp. 75 *et seq.*

[558] *Ibid.*, pp. 127 *et seq.*

[559] *Ibid.*, pp. 163 *et seq.* According to Barruel, the conspirators numbered among their adepts the following: Joseph II of Germany, Catherine II of Russia, Christian VII of

Denmark, Gustave III of Sweden, Poniatowski, king of Poland, and the landgrave Frederick of Hesse-Cassel.

[560] *Ibid.*, p. 154.

[561] Barruel, *op. cit.*, p. 157.

[562] *Ibid.*, pp. 321 *et seq.*

[563] *Ibid.*, vol. ii, pp. 9, 10, 13 *et seq.*, 21.

[564] *Ibid.*, pp. 52 *et seq.*, 66, 76. Barruel labors hard to save himself from the cruel necessity of including Montesquieu in the list of conspirators. He finds it "painful to apply such a reproach to this celebrated writer." (*Ibid.*, p. 76.) With some cleverness he remarks: "He [Montesquieu] did not conspire by setting up his systems, but his systems formed conspirators." (*Ibid.*, p. 98.)

[565] *Ibid.*, p. 101.

[566] Barruel, *op. cit.*, pp. 130, 131, 157 *et seq.*

[567] *Ibid.*, pp. 159 *et seq.*

[568] Barruel contended that the popular uprisings of the period in Geneva, Bohemia, Transylvania, and even among the negroes of St. Domingo, were all directly due to the conspiracy. *Cf.* Barruel, pp. 205 *et seq.*, 255 *et seq.*, 260 *et seq.*, 271.

[569] Barruel's estimate of Freemasonry was appreciably lower than that of Robison. Its mysteries were to be traced to Manes, and to the introduction of Manichaeism into Europe in the period of Frederich II (1221–1250). Condorcet was appealed to for proof in this connection. *Cf.* Barruel, pp. 399 *et seq.* The general idea that the Freemasons were responsible for the campaign against monarchy and the Catholic religion which, many believed, characterized the greater part of the eighteenth century, had already been made familiar to the French by the ecclesiastics Larudan and Lefranc. *Cf.* Forestier, pp. 684 *et seq.*

[570] By the occult lodges Barruel meant those whose members had received the higher mysteries and degrees. *Cf.* Barruel, vol. ii, p. 293.

[571] *Ibid.*, pp. 276, 277, 278, 279.

[572] *Ibid.*, pp. 436 *et seq.*

[573] *Ibid.*, p. 436.

[574] *Ibid.*, p. 438.

[575] *Ibid.*, pp. 444 *et seq.*

[576] *Ibid.*, pp. 455 *et seq.*

[577] *Ibid.*, pp. 471 *et seq. Cf. ibid.*, p. 437.

[578] "Under the name of ILLUMINES a band of Conspirators had coalesced with the Encyclopedists and Masons, far more dangerous in their tenets, more artful in their plots, and more extensive in their plans of devastation. They more silently prepared the explosions of the Revolutionary volcano, not merely swearing hatred to the Altar of Christ and the Throne of Kings, but swearing at once hatred to every God, to every Law, to every Government, to all society and social compact; and in order to destroy every plea and every foundation of social contract, they proscribed the terms MINE *and* THINE, acknowledging neither Equality nor Liberty but in the *entire, absolute and universal overthrow of all* PROPERTY *whatever.*" (Barruel, *op. cit.*, p. 478. *Cf.* vol. iii, pp. 17, 22 *et seq.*)

[579] Barruel attributed little or no success to the efforts which Weishaupt's associates made to strip him of much of his despotic power. *Cf.* Barruel, ch. xviii.

[580] The discussion of the character of the order fills the entire third volume of the *Memoirs*. It is not too much to say that Barruel's analysis of the organization is characterized by no little soundness of judgment as well as by literary skill. The documents upon which he draws are not only those published

by the Bavarian government, but also the apologetic writings of Weishaupt and Knigge, as well as a considerable part of the polemical literature which developed after the suppression of the order. Yet it need scarcely be said, the author's bias is nowhere obscured. On page after page he conveys the impression that he is dealing with the sum of all villainies. His judgment of Weishaupt was, of course, severe: "An odious phenomenon in nature, an Atheist void of remorse, a profound hypocrite, destitute of those superior talents which lead to the vindication of truth, he is possessed of all that energy and ardor in vice which generates conspirators for impiety and anarchy. Shunning, like the ill-boding owl, the genial rays of the sun, he wraps around him the mantle of darkness; and history shall record of him, as of the evil spirit, only the black deeds which he planned or executed.... Scarcely have the magistrates cast their eyes upon him when they find him at the head of a conspiracy which, when compared with those of the clubs of Voltaire and D'Alembert, or with the secret committees of D'Orléans [sic], make these latter appear like the faint imitations of puerility, and show the Sophister and the Brigand as mere novices in the arts of revolution." (Barruel, op. cit., pp. 2, 3, 7.)

[581] Ibid., p. 293. Cf. ibid., p. 413: "Will not hell vomit forth its legions to applaud this last Spartacus, to contemplate in amazement this work of the Illuminizing Code? Will not Satan exclaim, 'Here then are men as I wished them'".

[582] Ibid., vol. iv, p. 379. Cf. ibid., p. 387: " ... in this den of conspirators ... we find every thing in perfect union with the Occult Lodges, to which it only succeeds. Adepts, object, principles, all are the same; whether we turn our eyes towards the adepts of impiety, of rebellion, or of anarchy, they are now but one conspiring Sect, under the disastrous name of Jacobin. We have hitherto denominated some by the name of Sophisters, others by that of Occult Masons, and, lastly, we have described those men styled Illuminées. Their very names will now

disappear; they will in future all be duly described by the name of Jacobin."

[583] Barruel, *op. cit.*, ch. ix.

[584] *Ibid.*, ch. x.

[585] *Ibid.*, p. 326.

[586] *Ibid.*, ch. xi.

[587] *Ibid.*, p. 370.

[588] *Ibid.*, pp. 370 *et seq.*

[589] *Ibid.*, pp. 375 *et seq.*

[590] *Ibid.*, p. 376.

[591] *Ibid.*, p. 377.

[592] *Ibid.*, p. 379.

[593] Barruel, *op. cit., passim.*

[594] *Ibid.*, pp. 468 *et seq.*

[595] *Ibid.*, pp. 472 *et seq.*

[596] *Ibid.*, pp. 476 *et seq.*

[597] *Ibid.*, pp. 482 *et seq.*

[598] *Ibid.*, pp. 493–551. Barruel found no difficulty in making the conspiracy broad enough in Prussia to take in Immanuel Kant. *Cf. ibid.*, pp. 523 *et seq.* The *Professor of Königsberg* and the *Professor of Ingolstadt* developed systems which ultimately lead to the same end (!). *Cf. ibid.*, p. 526.

[599] *Ibid.*, pp. 493 *et seq.*

[600] The reference is to the United Irishmen, an organization whose affairs got somewhat mixed with the discussion of the Illuminati in America. *Cf. infra*, pp. 271 *et seq.*

[601] A foot-note connects the French minister, Adet, with the Illuminati campaign in North America. *Cf. ibid.*, p. 494.

[602] Robison, *op. cit.*, p. 535.

[603] *Ibid.*, p. 537.

[604] *Ibid.*, p. 538.

[605] Barruel, *op. cit.*, vol. iii, p. xiv.

[606] Barruel, *op. cit.*, vol. iii, p. xiv.

[607] *Ibid.*, p. xv.

[608] *Ibid.*, pp. xv, xvi.

[609] *Ibid.*, p. xviii.

[610] *The Works of John Adams*, vol. ix, pp. 169 *et seq.*

[611] *Cf. supra*, p. 10.

[612] *A Sermon, Delivered at the New North Church in Boston, in the morning, and in the afternoon at Charlestown, May 9th, 1798, being the day recommended by John Adams, President of the United States of America, for solemn humiliation, fasting and prayer.* By Jedidiah Morse, D. D., minister of the congregation in Charlestown, Boston, 1798, pp. 5–12.

[613] *Ibid.*, p. 13.

[614] Morse was one of those New England clergymen whose earlier enthusiasm for the French Revolution had been pronounced. In a sermon preached on the occasion of the national thanksgiving of 1795, he confessed his profound interest in the French cause, on account of what that people had accomplished in breaking the chains of civil and ecclesiastical tyranny. At the same time he voiced his concern because a spirit of *vandalism* had lately arisen in France, by which all the salutary results of the Revolution were gravely imperiled. Still, his hopes for the recovery of the nation's self-control were strong. *Cf. The Present Situation of Other Nations of the World,*

Contrasted with our Own. A Sermon, delivered at Charlestown, in the Commonwealth of Massachusetts, February 19, 1795; being the day recommended by George Washington, President of the United States of America, for Publick Thanksgiving and Prayer. By Jedidiah Morse, D. D., minister of the congregation in Charlestown, Boston, 1795, pp. 10–16. *Cf.* also the Preface to Morse's *Fast Day Sermon* of April 25, 1799.

[615] Morse, *Sermon on the National Fast*, May 9, 1798, p. 13.

[616] The X. Y. Z. despatches.

[617] Morse, *Sermon on the National Fast*, May 9, 1798, pp. 14 *et seq.*

[618] Morse, *op. cit.*, p. 17.

[619] *Ibid.*, p. 19.

[620] *Ibid.*, p. 20.

[621] Morse, *op. cit.*, p. 20.

[622] Morse's first acquaintance with Robison's volume is thus explained by him: "The first copies which were sent to America, arrived at Philadelphia and New York, at both which places the re-printing of it was immediately undertaken, and the Philadelphia edition was completed ready for sale in the short space of 3 *weeks*. This was about the middle of April. Happening at this time to be in Philadelphia, and hearing the work spoken of in terms of the highest respect by men of judgment, one of them went so far as to pronounce it the most interesting work that the present century had produced; I was induced to procure a copy, which I brought home with me...." (*Independent Chronicle*, June 14, 1798.) In Sprague's *Life of Jedediah Morse*, pp. 233 *et seq.*, it is affirmed that Dr. Erskine, one of Morse's Scottish correspondents, wrote Morse in January, 1797, informing him of the alarm which had sprung up in Europe with respect to the "conspiracy", and calling attention to Robison's volume which was then being prepared for the press.

[623] Morse, *Sermon on the National Fast*, May 9, 1798, p. 21.

[624] *Ibid.*

[625] *Ibid.*, pp. 22 *et seq.*

[626] *Ibid.*, p. 23.

[627] *Ibid.*

[628] *Ibid.*, p. 24.

[629] Robison's reference to the "several" societies established in America previous to 1786 (*cf. supra*, p. 210) is specifically referred to. *Cf. Sermon on the National Fast*, May 9, 1798, p. 23.

[630] *Ibid.*, p. 24.

[631] Morse, *op. cit.*, p. 24.

[632] Morse had been at pains in his sermon to recommend Robison's volume as throwing a flood of light upon "the causes which have brought the world into its present disorganized state." (*Ibid.*, pp. 24 *et seq.*) Later it must have occurred to him that the silence he had maintained in the pulpit respecting Masonry's part in the conspiracy was bound to be noticed by all who upon his recommendation read Robison's volume.

[633] *Ibid.*, p. 21.

[634] Morse, *op. cit.*, p. 21.

[635] *Ibid.*, p. 22.

[636] *Ibid.*, pp. 21, 22. For the time being Morse was content to follow the example of Robison. The latter, in his discussion of English Freemasonry, made a fairly sharp distinction between the English system and the Masonic systems of the continent. That distinction, on the whole, was decidedly favorable to English Freemasonry. By every consideration of precedent and prudence Morse must have felt strongly impelled to pursue the same course.

[637] *Ibid.*, p. 22.

[638] Morse, *op. cit.*, p. 25.

[639] *Ibid.*, pp. 25 *et seq.*

[640] *Cf. supra*, ch. i, 2.

[641] *Cf. supra*, pp. 125 *et seq.*

[642] The editor of as loyal and resourceful a Federalist sheet as the *Columbian Centinel*, for example, insisted upon treating as a whole the performances of the clergy on the occasion of the national fast, and refused to make discriminations with respect to the special import or merit of any particular minister's performance: "Wednesday last was observed throughout the United States as a day of Fasting and Prayer. (Within the sphere of our information we can say, that on no occasion were there ever exhibited more moral patriotism, and more ardent devotion.) The Clergy on this occasion came forward with a zeal which added greatly to the high character they have long enjoyed, as Patriots. We could instance numerous traits of Federalism, which would do them honour; but when all of them are entitled to praise, it would be invidious to make distinctions." (*Columbian Centinel*, May 12, 1798.)

[643] *Wolcott Papers*, viii, 23.

[644] *A Discourse, Delivered at the Roman Catholic Church in Boston on the 9th of May, 1798.* ... By the Reverend John Thayer, Catholic Missioner, Boston, 1798.

[645] *Ibid.*, p. 23.

[646] *Op. cit.*

[647] *Independent Chronicle*, May 31, 1798.

[648] *Ibid.* The "observations" referred to really threw no new light upon the situation. They amounted to nothing more than proof of the fact that the editor of the *New York Spectator* had

accepted the idea of the Illuminati conspiracy. This being the case he was anxious to warn his readers that if they would escape from the designs of the French government they must make their choice, and that speedily, between "INDEPENDENCE and SUBMISSION."

[649] *Independent Chronicle*, June 14, 1798.

[650] The extracts in question boldly championed Robison's cause, and while admitting that all the tenets and secret manoeuvers of the Illuminati could not be said to have been fully brought to light, Morse did not hesitate to draw the following summary conclusion: "There is however sufficient known to call forth the indignation of every person who professes to be a friend to religion or virtue, and to put every one on their guard who knows and respects the rights of private property, and of good government." (*Ibid.*)

[651] *Ibid.*

[652] *A Discourse delivered in the Chapel of Harvard College, June 19, 1798, Occasioned by the Approaching Departure of the Senior Class from the University.* By David Tappan, D. D., Hollis Professor of Divinity in said College, Boston, 1798.

[653] *Ibid.*, pp. 4–13.

[654] As far as the present writer has been able to discover, President Dwight did not deal publicly with the Illuminati charge until a little later. Tappan's reference must therefore be to general discussions of infidelity, a favorite topic with Yale's president, as we have seen.

[655] The reference is to Robison. Whether or not Tappan had personally read Robison's volume at this time is not altogether clear. The general impression created by his sermon is that he had.

[656] *Cf.* Tappan's *Sermon*, p. 19.

[657] *Ibid.*, pp. 15 *et seq.* (foot note).

[658] *Cf.* Tappan's *Sermon*, pp. 15 *et seq.* (foot note).

[659] *THE DUTY OF AMERICANS IN THE PRESENT CRISIS. Illustrated in a Discourse, Preached on the Fourth of July, 1798*; by the Reverend Timothy Dwight, D. D., President of Yale-College; at the request of the citizens of New-Haven. New-Haven, 1798.

[660] *Ibid.*, p. 8.

[661] The elaboration of this point necessarily led to some emphasis upon the spirit of irreligion and savage persecution that had thus manifested itself, and this in turn necessitated an effort to find a way out of the embarrassment of seeming to approve this persecution. The following ingenious foot note appended to the text of the published sermon admirably illustrates the inventive resourcefulness of many a New England clergyman of the day who found it necessary to rescue himself from such an *impasse* as Dwight's method of exegesis produced: "In the mention of all these evils brought on the Romish Hierarchy, I beg it may be remembered, that I am far from justifying the iniquitous conduct of their persecutors. I know not that any person holds it, and all other persecutions, more in abhorrence. Neither have I a doubt of the integrity and piety of multitudes of the unhappy sufferers. In my view they claim, and I trust will receive, the commiseration, and, as occasion offers, the kind offices of all men possessed even of common humanity." (*Ibid.*, p. 9.) The truth is that in some cases Protestant clergymen in New England, out of their concern for Christianity in general, went so far as to deprecate the persecutions which Roman Catholicism suffered.

[662] Dwight offered as his sources of authority Robison's *Proofs* and an article on Barruel's *Memoirs of Jacobinism* which he had discovered in the *British Critic*.

[663] *Cf.* Dwight's *Sermon*, p. 11.

[664] *Ibid.*

[665] *Ibid.*

[666] *Cf.* Dwight's *Sermon*, pp. 11, 12.

[667] *Ibid.*, p. 12.

[668] *Ibid.*, p. 13.

[669] *Cf.* Dwight's *Sermon*, p. 15.

[670] *Cf.* Dwight's *Sermon*, pp. 20, 21.

[671] *Ibid.*, p. 22.

[672] The commanding position that Dwight occupied in the Standing Order, as well as the unenviable distinction which in the eyes of the opposition belonged to him, is certified to by the fact that he was commonly referred to as "Pope Dwight." *Cf.* Beecher, *Autobiography, Correspondence, etc.*, vol. i, p. 289. *Cf.* Stiles, *Diary*, vol. ii, p. 531.

[673] The *Connecticut Journal* of July 11, 1798, comments as follows upon New Haven's celebration of the previous Fourth: "The exercises of the day at the Meeting-house were a Sermon by President Dwight, from the 16th chapter of Revelations, 15th verse, accompanied with prayers. An Oration by Noah Webster, jun., Esq., and sundry pieces of excellent music. We forbare [*sic*] to remark particularly on the Sermon and Oration, as the public eye will be speedily gratified in perusing them…. We shall only say that an enlightened audience, composed of the citizens of New-Haven, the members of our university, and many clergymen, civilians, and other respectable inhabitants from the adjacent towns, listened with profound attention while Doct. Dwight and Mr. Webster exposed to their view, in a feeling manner, those principles of modern philosophy which desolate Europe, and threaten the universe with mighty evils."

[674] *An Oration, pronounced at Sharon, on the Anniversary of American Independence, 4th of July, 1798.* By John C. Smith, Litchfield, (n. d.), pp. 6 *et seq. Cf. ibid.*, pp. 7 *et seq.*

[675] *Theodore Dwight: An Oration spoken at Hartford, in the State of Connecticut, on the Anniversary of American Independence, July 4th, 1798.* Hartford, 1798, p. 23.

[676] *Ibid.* On a later page, in commenting upon Robison's reference in his *Proofs of a Conspiracy* to the lodges of the Illuminati which had been established in America, Dwight said: "I know not who belonged to that society in this country; but if I were about to make proselytes to illuminatism in the United States, I should in the first place apply to Thomas Jefferson, Albert Gallatin, and their political associates." (*Ibid.*, p. 30.) This early use of the outcry against the Illuminati for political purposes was prophetic.

[677] *An Oration on Party Spirit, Pronounced before the Connecticut Society of Cincinnati, convened at Hartford, for the celebration of American Independence, on the 4th of July, 1798.* By Thomas Day, (n. d.), p. 15.

[678] *Ibid.*

[679] That "Censor's" tone of moderation was assumed and not genuine is further evinced by his assertion of contempt for Robison's *absurd* supposition that the Illuminati had kindled the French Revolution and for his "unjustifiable attacks upon certain worthy characters." If the Illuminati had never existed the Revolution would have occurred on account of the arbitrary and excessive despotism of the old French government, the insupportable weight of taxation, the luxury and dissipation of the nobility and clergy, the prohibition of free religious and political discussion, and the dissemination of liberal sentiments during the previous fifty years. That Robison, without sufficient warrant, should have attacked such characters as "the worthy La Fayette," "the venerable Duke de Rochefoucault," Dr. Priestley, *et al.*, caused his book to appear as one born of "incorrigible prejudices, acting upon an inflamed imagination." As for the author of the fast day sermon, he may judge for himself whether he was too hasty in recommending such a book to the public. The times may be full of peril, but surely

this does not justify those who terrify their fellow citizens by means of groundless alarms. One's fellow citizens also need to be put on their guard against the danger of becoming "the dupes of every foolish tale which the prejudices or ignorance of Europeans may fabricate." Such were further comments by "Censor." *Cf.* Day, *op. cit.*

[680] These articles began in the issue of the *Mercury* for August 3, and were continued through the issues of August 10, 14, 17, 21, 28, and 31. Because of an effort which the Reverend Josiah Bartlett made to absolve the Masons of this country of the suspicion that had been cast upon them, they found a certain continuation in the issues of the *Mercury* for September 7, 14, 18, 21; but these are reserved for the special treatment of the Masonic aspects of the case. *Cf. infra*, pp. 330 *et seq.*

[681] *Massachusetts Mercury*, Aug. 3, 1798.

[682] *Ibid.*

[683] *Massachusetts Mercury*, Aug. 3, 1798.

[684] *Ibid.*, Aug. 10.

[685] *Ibid.* In this connection Morse seeks to extract comfort from the fact that the editors of the *British Critic*, having compared Robison's *Proofs* and Barruel's *Memoirs of Jacobinism*, have recorded their verdict that the two works are highly confirmatory of each other, "barring certain unimportant particulars." He likewise observes that the marks of precipitation and certain faults of style and expression which some of the impartial English reviewers have been able to point out, have yet not been allowed to alter their judgment that the book as a whole is a credit to its author, and contains much valuable information. The clamor that has arisen against the book, Morse insists, is to be traced to the hostility of men who have been incensed because their secrets have been exposed. At this point it may be said in passing that Morse allowed himself to be drawn into the expression of a sentiment, gratuitous in its nature, which served to precipitate the very thing he had been

anxious to avoid, *viz.*, a break with the Masons. Irritated by his critics, he wrote: "The Free Masons can not be angry with him [Robison].... If therefore any are really angry here, it must be because he has touched and exposed their secret friends."

[686] The reference is to Professor Tappan's sermon before the senior class of Harvard. *Cf. supra*, pp. 244 *et seq.*

[687] In this instance the reference is not to President Dwight's Fourth of July sermon: that sermon had not yet been seen by Morse; but to an allusion made by Dwight to Robison's book in a note appended to the following pamphlet: *The Nature and Danger of Infidel Philosophy. Two Discourses, to the Candidates for the Baccalaureate, in Yale College, September 9, 1797....* New-Haven, 1798. *Cf. Massachusetts Mercury*, Aug. 17, 1798.

[688] Theodore Dwight's Fourth of July oration is referred to. *Cf. supra*, pp. 246 *et seq.*

[689] *Massachusetts Mercury*, Aug. 17, 1798.

[690] *Ibid.*, Aug. 21, 1798.

[691] *Massachusetts Mercury*, Aug. 21, 1798. Morse's article in this issue of the *Mercury*, perhaps more discursive and less convincing than anything he had previously written on the general subject, at various points descends to the level of abuse, in which Robison's hostile English reviewers, the Reverend William Bentley (for reasons that will appear later), and "Censor" are made to share.

[692] *Massachusetts Mercury*, Aug. 28, 1798. In explanation of the delicacy and difficulty of such a task as Robison's, Morse offered to his readers the following: "The schemes and views of Conspirators are often veiled in language and signs intelligible only to themselves; they correspond under fictitious names; their papers are sparingly multiplied, artfully detached, and most cautiously concealed." (*Ibid.*) The apologetic motive is evident.

[693] *Ibid.* With a "summary account" of the documents upon which Robison had relied in the composition of his book and of which Morse had no first-hand knowledge, and with an examination of the alleged differences between the accounts of the "conspiracy" by Robison and Barruel (*cf. ibid.*, Aug. 31, 1798), Morse's prolix discussion of the subject came to a close. During the time that his articles were in process of publication, "Censor" contributed a fresh article to the *Mercury*, admitting that his faith in the existence of the European Illuminati was growing, but still protesting that Robison was to be regarded as extremely blameworthy on account of the false and calumnious attacks that he had made on worthy private characters in his *Proofs. Cf.* the *Massachusetts Mercury* of August 28 for this article by "Censor." What degree of unmixed comfort this may have afforded Morse, we may guess.

[694] As yet Barruel's *Memoirs of Jacobinism* was known to Americans only in the literature of English reviews.

[695] *Massachusetts Mercury*, Nov. 3, 1798: article by "A Customer."

[696] *Massachusetts Mercury*, Nov. 13, 1798.

[697] *Ibid.*

[698] *Ibid.*, Nov. 16, 1798. Extracts from Barruel's *Memoirs*, garnered from English reviews, were offered in evidence by this writer. The charge of *contradiction* was hotly commanded by him to give place to the darker charge of *designed perversion* on the part of Robison's enemies.

[699] *Ibid.*, Nov. 30, 1798.

[700] *Massachusetts Mercury*, Nov. 30, 1798.

[701] *Massachusetts Mercury*, Oct. 26, 1798.

[702] *Ibid.*

[703] *A Sermon, Preached at Charlestown, November 29, 1798, on the Anniversary Thanksgiving in Massachusetts. With*

an Appendix, designed to illustrate some parts of the Discourse; exhibiting proofs of the early existence, progress, and deleterious effects of French intrigue and influence in the United States. By Jedediah Morse, D. D., pastor of the church in Charlestown…. Boston, December, 1798. Two reprints of the sermon were issued early in the next year.

[704] Morse, *op. cit.*, p. 9.

[705] *Ibid.*, pp. 10–14.

[706] Morse, *op. cit.*, p. 15.

[707] *Ibid.*

[708] *Ibid.*

[709] *Ibid.*, p. 16.

[710] *Ibid.*, p. 18.

[711] The sermon was preached in two parts, morning and afternoon, and concerning Morse's discussion of the Christian religion this explanatory mote appears in the printed report: "The last article, respecting the *Christian Religion*, which constituted the whole of the forenoon sermon, being a *common*, though always *interesting* subject, has been considerably abridged." (*Ibid.*, p. 4.) This is only one of many marks of the great care Morse took to get the printed report of the sermon before the public in the most impressive form possible. He was fully conscious of the fact that he had an allegation to defend as well as a demurrer to oppose.

[712] Morse, *op. cit.*, pp. 20–22.

[713] Morse's *Anniversary Thanksgiving Sermon*, pp. 22 *et seq.* The sermon of Lathrop referred to bears the following title: *A Sermon, on the Dangers of the Times, from Infidelity and Immorality; and especially from a lately discovered Conspiracy against Religion and Government, delivered at West-Springfield and afterward at Springfield.* By Joseph Lathrop, D. D., Springfield, September, 1798. The statement that Morse

quotes appears on page 14 of Lathrop's sermon. *Cf.* Cunningham, Abner, *Practical Infidelity Portrayed and the Judgments of God Made Manifest*, (3rd. edition), New York, 1836, pp. 42–46, where a somewhat similar situation in Orange County, New York, is referred to, and with suggestions of secret revolutionary designs not unlike those made by Lathrop. The situation referred to by Cunningham is also dealt with by F. M. Ruttenber, in his *History of the County of Orange, with a History of the Town and City of Newburgh* .... Newburgh, N. Y., 1875, pp. 164 *et seq.* Woodbridge Riley's article on *Early Free-Thinking Societies in America* (Harvard Theological Review, July, 1918, pp. 247–284) came to the attention of the author of this study when the entire dissertation was in page proof.

[714] Some of these dated as far back as 1782, and none of them need have been disturbing to a calm mind.

[715] The following letter, written by Morse to Timothy Pickering, throws considerable light upon the sources from which the most of these documents were derived and the manner and spirit in which they were compiled.

"Charlestown, Jan. 22d, 1799.

Dear Sir

I take the liberty to enclose for your acceptance a copy of my Thanksgiving Discourse. The Appendix contains some documents not before published. I hope the publication of them, in the manner I have done, will not be deemed premature. I did it by the advice of some of the wisest & best informed men in this vicinity.

I think it my duty, confidentially to make known to you the sources from which I obtained my information, that you may better know how to appreciate its authenticity. It will rest with you, Sir, to make what use of it you may think expedient. I wish it may be communicated to the President.

Mr. J. Jackson, Supervisor, favored me with Mr. Marbois' Letter, & the Letter p. 41 whh is from Mr. Adams.—I should not have published the latter, had it not before appeared in print in a political pamphlet printed in Phila lately. The member of Congress from whom I derived the documents contained between pages 43 & 52, is Mr. S. Higginson, who also wrote the Letters whh follow to page 56. Note E, p. 66 & G, p. 69 & H, p. 70 were furnished (at least the information they contain) by Mr. G. Cabot. The Letters under Note H, from a diplomatic character in Europe, are from Mr. K—g—. [Rufus King?] The Emigrant mentioned p. 69—was the Duke de Liancourt, whose name I see in Porcupine's Gazette of January 11, as about to revisit this Country. The American was Mr. G. C. above mentioned. The note concerning Volney, p. 21 was furnished by Genl. K—x [General Henry Knox?] & Mr. G. C. The fact mentioned p. 68 relative to Paine's Age of Reason, 15,000 copies of which are asserted to have been poured into this Country at one time from France, rests chiefly on the authority of a well written piece published last summer in Porcupine's Gazette. I wish, Sir, if you are knowing to the fact, or can ascertain the truth, you would do me the favor to furnish me with the evidence. I know not that it will be controverted, but should it be it is well to have it in my power to substantiate it. I feel prepared to substantiate all other of my assertions.

I am persuaded, Sir, you will properly appreciate my motives in making the above communication, as also in publishing the Sermon & Appendix. I live among a people many of whom err in Sentiment & Conduct through their want of information. It was especially for their benefit that the Appendix was compiled. With great and very sincere respect,

I am, Sir, your most Obd. Servt,

JED^H MORSE."

Pickering Papers, vol. xxiv, 29.

[716] Morse's *Thanksgiving Sermon*, "Note F," pp. 67 *et seq.*

[717] Morse's *Thanksgiving Sermon*, p. 67. The reference is, of course, to the Democratic Clubs.

[718] Morse's *Thanksgiving Sermon*, pp. 68 *et seq.*

[719] *Ibid.*, p. 67.

[720] *Ibid.* This secret organization referred to by Morse was founded in Ireland about 1791. It was in part the outgrowth of republican sentiments which the French Revolution inspired in the Irish people, in part of similar sentiments earlier received. *Cf.* Madden, *The United Irishmen*, vol. i, pp. 3–44. The object of the organization was to obtain complete emancipation for both Catholics and Dissenters, and to reform the Irish parliament. The group manifested a bold revolutionary spirit. When the English government resorted to strong repressive measures, many of its members came to America. The Irish Rebellion of 1798 sent other Irish political exiles here; with the result that by many in this country the situation was adjudged to be alarming. William Cobbett ("Peter Porcupine") was one of the most aggressive opponents of the movement in America. *The Proceedings of the Society of the United Irishmen of Dublin* was published at Philadelphia in 1795. The same year Cobbett published *A Bone to Gnaw, for the Democrats; or Observations on a Pamphlet entitled "The Political Progress of Britain."* Part ii of Cobbett's pamphlet was devoted to the *Proceedings* just mentioned. Cobbett's paper, *Porcupine's Gazette*, to a considerable extent was devoted to the raising of an alarm against the United Irishmen. Cobbett urged that the United Irishmen represented a conspiracy on the part of France to ruin the United States. See *Porcupine's Gazette*, May 8, 10, 1798. Since Cobbett was one of the men in America deeply interested in Robison's *Proofs of a Conspiracy* (*cf.* particularly *Porcupine's Gazette* for May 18, July 14, and Aug. 13, 1798), and since Cobbett printed in his paper much that Morse published on the subject of the Illuminati (see, for example, *Porcupine's Gazette* for Aug. 9 and 13, 1798; Feb. 25, 26, and June 3, 1799), it is at least believable that Morse took from Cobbett the suggestion about the identification of the Illuminati with the United Irishmen. *The Commercial Advertiser* of New York was another newspaper that gave attention to the subject of the United Irishmen. The issue of that paper for Nov. 1, 1798, carried an extended article copied from the *Gazette of the*

United States, calling upon the citizens of this country to be on their guard against the United Irishmen. The author of this article identified the United Irishmen and the French party in the United States as one. *Cf.* also the *Commercial Advertiser* for Nov. 5, 1798. Thus Morse had abundant warrant in precedent if not in fact for the suggestion he made at this point in the Appendix to his thanksgiving sermon.

[721] One may be sure that the following caustic comment of the editor of the *Independent Chronicle* is to be set down to instinctive repugnance and hostility, and is thus representative only of rabid partisanship: "Actions speak louder than words. If the parish observe the Minister busy about many things; if they find him more anxious about the *geographical* description of the City of Washington or the Georgia Lands, than the *New-Jerusalem* or the *Land of Canaan*; if they find him neglect his parish on a Sunday and employ himself during the week, to collect ridiculous fables to swell an appendix to a political publication. If he will do these things, he must expect that his Flock will not increase, and that at the year's end, while he is exploring the territory of the United States, and hunting up Robinson's [*sic*] straggling Illuminati, he must not be surprised if some of his *own sheep* have strayed across the river, and become the care of a more attentive shepherd." (*Ibid.*, Jan. 7, 1799.)

[722] *A Memorial of Divine Benefits. In a Sermon, delivered at Exeter, on the 15th, and at Haverhill, on the 29th of November, 1798, days of Public Thanksgiving, in New-Hampshire and Massachusetts.* By Abiel Abbot, pastor of the First Church in Haverhill. Haverhill, Massachusetts, 1798, pp. 18 *et seq.*

[723] *A Sermon, delivered on the day of Public Thanksgiving, at Deerfield; Nov. 29, '98.* By John Taylor. A. M., pastor of the church at Deerfield. Greenfield (n. d.), p. 13.

[724] Taylor's *Thanksgiving Sermon*, p. 13.

[725] *A Sermon, delivered on the Anniversary Thanksgiving, November 29, 1798, with some additions in the historical part.*

By Jonathan French, A. M., pastor of the South Church in Andover. Andover, 1799. p. 23.

[726] *Ibid.*, pp. 23 *et seq.*

[727] *Ibid.*

[728] *A Discourse, delivered on the Public Thanksgiving Day, November 29, 1798.* By Joseph Eckley, D. D., minister of the Old South Church, Boston. Boston, 1798, pp. 9, 15, 18.

[729] Connecticut kept a state thanksgiving at the same time as Massachusetts.

[730] *Political Instruction from the Prophecies of God's Word,—a Sermon, preached on the State Thanksgiving, Nov. 29, 1798.* By Nathan Strong, pastor of the North Presbyterian Church in Hartford, Connecticut. Hartford, 1798. This sermon is characterized by an ingenious effort to remove the stigma "mother of harlots" from the Catholic hierarchy and attach it to the Revolutionary leaders in France. "It is the Talleyrands and their associates," said Strong, "whom I conceive to be the most properly designated by the mother of harlots, in the present period of the great apostacy." (*Ibid.*, p. 17.)

[731] *A Sermon preached at Billerica, November 29, 1798, being the day of the Anniversary Thanksgiving throughout the Commonwealth of Massachusetts.* By Henry Cumings, A. M., pastor of the church in said town. Boston. 1798, p. 22.

[732] *Ibid.*

[733] The following excerpt from a letter of Jedediah Morse to Timothy Pickering, under date of Feb. 11, 1799, is significant in this connection: "An editn. of 450 of my Sermon and Appendix is nearly gone—& a second of 800 is in the press. A number of gentlemen in Boston have thought it might be useful to send a copy to every clergyman in the commonwealth, & have agreed with the printer to furnish them, & they will be distributed when the members of the Legislature return home." (*Pickering Papers*, vol. xxiv, 71.)

[734] The full title of this journal was *The Columbian Centinel and Massachusetts Federalist*. Here was an instance in which Masonic affiliations quite overrode ardent Federalist loyalty. To this the following letter of editor Benjamin Russell to William Bentley testifies:

"Boston, Aug. 9, 1798. … As to Morse, I think him meddling in an affair which but little concerns him, and of which he has less knowledge. It would be better to let him flounder on, and he will speedily blow himself out. He cannot hurt the craft,—and his wit is as pointless, as his holy zeal is unchangeable. Although I wish not to engage in a controversy, which has no politick in its ingredients, I should nevertheless have published your communication had I received it.—As it is it may be best that the controversy should be carried on in one paper. You will see by this day's Mercury, that M. is still floundering.—I intend to barb him a little at the Installation at Reading, if he is present. If not he shall *hear* of a toast or two." (*William Bentley Correspondence*, vol. iv, 117).

[735] *Columbian Centinel*, Sept. 8, 1798.

[736] *Ibid.*, Sept. 12, 1798.

[737] *Ibid.*, Jan. 5, 1799.

[738] *Ibid.*

[739] *Columbian Centinel*, Jan. 5, 1799. This communication including the Böttiger letter, was promptly copied by the *Massachusetts Mercury*, and thus given a wider publicity. *Cf.* the *Mercury* of Jan. 11, 1799.

[740] *Op. Cit.*

[741] Somewhat later the *Mercury* offered to its readers relevant passages from Lathrop's sermon of the preceding September and from French's thanksgiving sermon. *Cf.* the *Mercury* for Jan. 11 and Feb. 26, 1799.

[742] The attention of Thomas and Abijah Adams, editors of the *Independent Chronicle*, during the fall and winter of 1798–99 was mostly occupied with very pressing personal considerations. In October, 1798, Thomas Adams was arrested under the Sedition Act. While his trial was in progress objectionable comments on the state and federal governments continued to appear in the *Chronicle*, with the result that his clerk and acting editor, Abijah Adams, was likewise arrested and put on trial. Thomas Adams died before his case was concluded; but Abijah Adams was later convicted and had the sentence of the court imposed upon him. Duniway, *The Development of Freedom of the Press in Massachusetts*, pp. 144 *et seq.* These facts supply a new angle from which to view the relative silence of the *Independent Chronicle* with regard to the Illuminati controversy.

[743] *Independent Chronicle*, April 15, 1799. *Cf. ibid.*, Jan. 7, 1799.

[744] Outside of Boston the newspapers of Massachusetts appear to have been generally content to furnish their readers an occasional article bearing on the controversy, copied in most cases from the columns of Boston or Hartford journals, or from papers which entered New England from without, particularly from New York and Philadelphia. Some of these Massachusetts newspapers are to be noticed later in connection with the effort that the Masons made to clear themselves of guilt.

[745] *American Mercury*, Aug. 16, 1798.

[746] The following quotation bears upon the topic, and does full justice to the abilities of the rhymster, although offering only slight suggestion respecting the variety of subjects which the poem, after the manner of its kind, touched upon:

"Of late the pulpits roar'd like thunder
To bring the Whore of Bab'lon under;
But now she's down, the tone is turn'd,
And the old Whore is sadly mourn'd.
    This brings us on to Politicks,—

For fruitful argument,—(sweet chicks!)

....

The Jacobin's head-end we've had,
To see his *tail*, most would be glad.
Of late, Old England was a moon,
To bay and snarl at, night and noon:
That's over:—now her Queenship seems
A splendid Sun with *golden* beams.
But pauvre Sanscolotte [*sic*] is given
A diff'rent lot, by will of heaven.

....

From *Anno Lucis* till our time,
Masonic Treason's been a crime:
Now *Robison's* in every pocket,
And up he's flown to fame, like rocket."

Cf. American Mercury, Jan. 3, 1799: "Ode on Ends; or, The Boy's Address, who carries the *American Mercury*."

[747] Babcock's adverse attitude is dealt with on pp. 313 *et seq.* of this dissertation.

[748] *Cf.* issues of the *Courant* for July 2, 30, Aug. 6, 13, Sept. 17, 1798; and for May 27, June 10, 17, 24, July 1, 8, 15, 22, 29, Aug. 5, 12, 19, 26, Sept. 2, 9, 16, 23, Oct. 7, Dec. 16, 1799.

[749] *Ibid.*, Aug. 6, 1798.

[750] *Ibid.*, Aug. 13, 1798.

[751] *Ibid.*, Sept. 3, 1798. This view that the *Courant* sought to turn the agitation over the Illuminati to political account is confirmed by the following extract from "Guillotina," the new year's poem that the editors of the *Courant* presented to their patrons early in 1799.

"O thou who spurn'd monarchial sway,
    E'er nature sprang to birth;
Lord of each Jacobinic fray,
    In ev'ry clime on earth.

"Tho' plung'd from thy once high estate,
   For turning *Order's* foe;
We joy that thou a Prince so great,
   Dost rule the world below.

"We joy that when like falling star,
   Thy footsteps downward drove;
The *Democratic Cause*, from far,
   Came cow'ring from above.

"That *France* has caught the livid flame,
   Affords supreme delight;
And that Genet has spread the same,
   To our admiring sight.

....

"May thy Iluminati then
   In ev'ry clime be found;
All busy as a clucking hen,
   That peeping chicks surround."

Connecticut Courant, Jan. 7, 1799: "Guillotina, for the year 1799, addressed to the Reader's of the Connecticut Courant."

[752] *Porcupine's Gazette*, April 12, 13, 1798.

[753] *Ibid.*, July 14, 1798.

[754] *Porcupine's Gazette*, July 14, 1798. An illustration of the dearth of vital data bearing on the existence of the Illuminati, as well as of the absurd way in which those who sought to prove their existence grasped at straws, is to be found in this issue of *Porcupine's Gazette*. Cobbett published a letter which he had recently received from a certain William Smith, of Norwalk, Connecticut, who claimed that the chaplain of the ship of a French Admiral had made statements in his presence that corroborated Robison's contentions. This letter speedily found its way into several New England newspapers, and passed for evidence in the case. *Cf.* for example, the *Salem Gazette*, Aug. 7, 1798.

[755] *Ibid.*, Aug. 13, 23, 24, 30, 1798.

[756] *Porcupine's Gazette*, Feb. 25, 1799.

[757] *Porcupine's Gazette*, Feb. 25, 1799.

[758] *Ibid.*, Feb. 26, 1799.

[759] By this abbreviated title Bache's paper was generally referred to.

[760] *Aurora*, Aug. 3, 1798.

[761] *Aurora*, Aug. 3, 1798.

[762] *Ibid.*, Aug. 10, 1798. Bache's death occurred in September.

[763] *The Life and Works of John Adams*, vol. ix, p. 172.

[764] *Ibid.*, pp. 172 *et seq.*

[765] Reverend Ashbel Green, who was chaplain of Congress at the time, accounts for the presence of this quality in the proclamation in the following manner. The President requested Green to assist him by preparing a draft of such a proclamation as the latter deemed suitable for the purpose. Aware of the complaints that had been made respecting previous proclamations, on the ground that while they called the people to the religious duties of thanksgiving and fasting, they were yet somewhat lacking in the manifestation of "a decidedly Christian spirit," Green resolved to prepare for the President's benefit a proclamation of such a thoroughgoing evangelical character that no such objection could possibly be lodged against it. This he endeavored to do. The President adopted Greens draft and published it, "with only the alteration of two or three words out of all affecting the religious character of my [his] production." (*The Life of Ashbel Green*, pp. 260 *et seq.*) The "decidedly Christian spirit" of the proclamation did not make the instrument immune from criticism. "An Old Ecclesiastic" contributed a highly censorious article to the *Aurora*, sharply rebuking the President for proclaiming the fast, objecting also to his "very improper and impolitic … language

… when speaking of the French nation," and questioning his right to direct the people as to what they should pray for. *Cf. Aurora*, April 4, 1799. This article was copied by the *Independent Chronicle* for the benefit of New England readers, and drew from "A Real Ecclesiastic" a valiant defence of the President's action and language. In the eyes of this writer, "the observations … by an Old Ecclesiastic … are so artfully fitted to excite groundless suspicions and prejudices against that GREAT AND GOOD MAN [President Adams], and especially to prepossess unwary readers against the approaching Fast recommended by him, that it seems important to defeat the writer's manifest intention by a few seasonable remarks." The nation was a *Christian* nation, and therefore the President had a right to *recommend* the observance of a day of *Christian* humiliation and prayer. *Cf. Massachusetts Mercury*, April 16, 1799.

[766] *A Sermon, Exhibiting the Present Dangers, and Consequent Duties of the Citizens of the United States of America. Delivered at Charlestown, April 25, 1799, the day of the National Fast.* By Jedediah Morse, D. D., pastor of the church in Charlestown. Charlestown, 1799.

[767] Morse, *op. cit.*, p. 5.

[768] Morse, *op. cit.*

[769] *Ibid.*, p. 9.

[770] *Ibid.*, p. 7.

[771] *Ibid.*, p. 9.

[772] *Ibid.*, p. 12.

[773] Morse, *op. cit.*, pp. 13 *et seq.* Morse gave as his authority in this instance Robert Goodloe Harper's "Sketch of the Principal Acts of Congress during the session which closed the 3d. of March". See Note A, p. 33, of Morse's *Sermon*. Reference to Benton's *Abridgement of the Debates of Congress*, vol. ii, pp. 339, 343, discloses the fact that

sentiments embodying this apprehension were expressed in the Third Congress. The struggle which France and England waged for the control of the island of St. Domingo, a struggle that had as its principal development the insurrection of the blacks of the island under the leadership of Toussaint l'Ouverture, properly enough was full of deep interest for Americans. *Cf.* Hildreth, *The History of the United States of America*, vol. v, pp. 269 *et seq.* For a recent discussion of American policy with respect to St. Domingo and the state of affairs within the island, see Treudley, Mary, *The United States and Santo Domingo, 1789–1866* (doctoral dissertation, Clark University), pp. 125–138.

[774] *Cf.* Morse's *Sermon*, pp. 12–14.

[775] *Cf.* Morse's *Sermon*, p. 15.

[776] *Cf.* Morse's *Sermon*, pp. 15–17. The allusion to a hostile attitude towards the clergy, with which the extract closes, led Morse to dwell at length upon the anticlerical spirit of the whole French system. *Cf. ibid.*, pp. 17 *et seq.* Wherever that system operates, there, Morse asserts, the clergy are the first to feel its power and to become the victims of its sanguinary revolutionizing spirit. Here in the United States this same malignant spirit is visibly at work. And all that the clergy have done to provoke this deadly hostility may be summed up in the phrase, "they have preached politics." (*Ibid.*, p. 18). They are now "censured and abused, and represented as an expense, useless, nay even, noxious body of men" for doing what "only twenty years ago they were called upon to perform as a *duty*." (*Ibid.*, p. 19). No clergyman of the Standing Order could possibly have felt keener resentment on account of the growing antagonism to that group of men than Jedediah Morse. His state of mind is a bit more clearly revealed by the contents of the following note by which the printed sermon was accompanied. This note, it should first be explained, was called out by the fact that a bill had been presented in a recent session of the Massachusetts legislature, providing for the suspension of the obligation to support the clergy of the Standing Order in all

cases where it was possible for individuals to produce certificates, showing that they were otherwise contributing to the support of public worship. "Had this Bill passed into a law, it is easy to see that it would have justified and protected (as was no doubt the intention of the Bill, though by no means of all who may have voted for it) the disaffected, the irreligious, and the despisers of public worship and of the Christian Sabbath, in every town and parish, in withdrawing that support of the Christian ministry which the laws now oblige them to give." (Note D, p. 49 of the *Fast Sermon*).

[777] The concluding sections of the sermon were devoted to (a) a depiction of the awful calamities which would come upon America if ever French armies were permitted to work their remorseless ravages here, and (b) an analysis of the duties which arose out of the dangers that had been presented. The duties named required one (1) to stand by one's post of duty, despite the gloomy but not utterly hopeless aspect of affairs; (2) to avoid all political connections with those nations which seem devoted by Providence to destruction, and to make a zealous effort "to watch their movements, and detect and expose the machinations of their numerous emissaries among us; to reject, as we would the most deadly poison, their atheistical and destructive principles in whatever way or shape they may be insinuated among us;" and, *especially*, (3) to promote the election to offices of trust of only such men as have "good principles and morals, who respect religion and love their country, who will be a terror to evil doers, and will encourage such as do well."

[778] *Ibid.*, p. 34. For the benefit of his readers, Morse supplied the following translation:

"At the East of the Lodge of Portsmouth in Virginia, the 17th of the 5th month, in the year of (V∴ L∴) True Light 5798./:
The (R∴ L∴ Pte∴ Fse∴) respectable French Provincial Lodge, regularly appointed under the distinctive title of WISDOM, No. 2660 by the GRAND ORIENT OF FRANCE.

To

The (T∴ R∴ L∴) very respectable French Lodge, *The* Union, No. 14, constituted by the *Grand Orient* of New-York.

S∴ F∴ V∴
TT∴ CC∴ and RR∴ FF∴

The plate or opening (*la planche*) with which you have favoured us in date of the 16th of the 2nd month of the current year (Mque∴) Masonic, came to us but a few days since. It was laid before our (R∴ L∴) respectable Lodge, at its extraordinary session on the 14th inst.

We congratulate you TT∴ CC∴ FF∴ upon the new Constitutions or Regulations which you have obtained from the Grand Orient of New York. We will therefore make it our pleasure and duty to maintain the most fraternal or intimate Correspondence with your (R∴ L∴) respectable Lodge; as also with all the regular Lodges who are willing to favour us with theirs.

It is on this ground (*a ce titre*) that we think it our duty to inform you of the establishment of two new Masonic workshops (*attellieres*) regularly constituted and installed according to the French ritual, by our Provincial (R∴ L∴) respectable Lodge; one, more than a year since, under the title of Friendship in the East side of Petersburg in Virginia; the other more recent, under the title of PERFECT EQUALITY, in the East of Port de Paix in the Island of St. Domingo.

We herewith transmit to you some copies of our List (*Tableau*) for this year, which our Lodge prays you to accept in return for those which it hath received from your Lodge with thankfulness.

May the Grand Architect of the Universe bless your labours, and crown them with all manner of success. With these sentiments we have the favour to be,

P∴ L∴ N∴ M∴ Q∴ V∴ S∴ C∴
TT∴ CC∴ and TT∴ RR∴ FF∴
Your very affectionate FF∴

> By order of the very respectable
> Provincial Lodge of Wisdom,
>
> Guieu,
> Secretary."

Morse's *Sermon*, p. 35.

[779] These documents may be found on pp. 36–45 of Morse's *Sermon*. For the motto Morse supplied the following translation: "*Men believe their eyes farther than their ears. The way by precept is long, but short and efficaceous by example.*" (*Ibid.*, pp. 46 *et seq.*)

[780] *Ibid.*, pp. 46 *et seq.*

[781] *Ibid.*, p. 46.

[782] Morse's *Sermon*, p. 46.

[783] *Ibid.*

[784] *Ibid.*

[785] *Ibid.*

[786] Morse's *Sermon*, p. 46.

[787] *Ibid.*, pp. 46 *et seq.*

[788] *Ibid.*, p. 47.

[789] *Ibid.*

[790] *Ibid.*

[791] Naturally, Morse had not failed to make use of his European authorities in preparing his sermon for the eyes of the general public. There was, of course, no new evidence to be derived from this source.

[792] Morse's *Sermon*, p. 48. The immediate source from which Morse obtained the documents of which he made such large and confident use in this sermon, constitutes an interesting subject of inquiry. Happily that source is fully

disclosed in the following extract from a letter which Morse addressed to Wolcott, Dec. 6, 1799:

… I wish all the evidence whh can be procured to substantiate the truth of what I have published. As the documents came through your hands, I have thought it proper to apply to you on the subject, as well as for evidence as for your advice as to the manner of exhibiting it.—I wish only to be assisted in defending myself to the satisfaction of candid & good men." (*Wolcott Papers*, vol. viii, 30.)

The canniness of Oliver Wolcott's Federalism is quite as much illuminated by this letter as is Jedediah Morse's caution and generosity in assuming responsibility for the publication of the documents referred to. That Wolcott had been instrumental in furnishing Morse's quiver with the arrows which Morse discharged from his bow on the occasion of the 1799 fast, was soon suspected in Democratic circles. *Cf. Aurora*, Feb. 14, 1800. (In this connection it may be remarked that Wolcott was not the only New England Federalist who came into possession of portions of the correspondence of Wisdom Lodge. The *Pickering MSS.*, vol. xlii, 37, presents a copy of another letter which in this instance was sent by the Portsmouth lodge to the lodge Verity and Union, in Philadelphia. The letter bears date of April 12, 1798. Its value for the purposes of this investigation is *nil*. How it came to be in Pickering's possession is not known. The implication is strong that the Federalists were eager to exploit the documents to the utmost.)

[793] As far as the records show, no other minister in New England may be said to have spoken emphatically upon the subject on the occasion of the fast. It was Morse alone who galvanized the issue into new life. The general tenor of the utterances of the clergy on the day of the fast may be judged from the following typical examples. At Concord, the Reverend Hezekiah Packard, who made it known that he had read Dr. Morse's thanksgiving sermon and its appendix, descanted on the dangers to be apprehended from the existence of foreign intrigue among the citizens of this country. His language was

general, though certainly expressive of profound concern. *Cf. Federal Republicanism, Displayed in Two Discourses, preached on the day of the State Fast at Chelmsford, and on the day of the National Fast at Concord, in April, 1799.* By Hezekiah Packard, pastor of the church in Chelmsford. Boston, 1799. At Franklin, Mass., the Reverend Nathaniel Emmons discoursed in similar vein. The French were pointed out as a nation which had corrupted every people whom they had subjugated. Further, Emmons asserted that things were happening in the United States which made it certain "some men [were] behind the curtain … pushing on the populace to open sedition and rebellion." No direct reference to the Illuminati was made, however. *Cf. A Discourse, delivered on the National Fast, April 25, 1799.* By Nathaniel Emmons, D. D., pastor of the church in Franklin. Wrentham, Mass., 1799, p. 23. The pastor of the church in Braintree had also been reading Morse's thanksgiving sermon. However, he had no definite word to speak on the subject of the Illuminati. France, he said, had her secret friends here, and the real truth of her designs were hidden from the American people. *Cf. A Discourse, delivered April 25, 1799; being the day of Fasting and Prayer throughout the United States of America.* By Ezra Weld, A. M., pastor of the church in Braintree. Boston, 1799. At Newburyport, the Reverend Daniel Dana saw an exceedingly dark and ominous situation confronting him and his hearers. He spoke of a "deep-laid infernal scheme to hunt Christianity from the globe." It was his firm belief that all the foundations of religion and morality were frightfully imperiled. But he gave no clear intimation that he was thinking of the Illuminati. *Two Sermons, delivered April 25, 1799; the day recommended by the President of the United States for National Humiliation, Fasting and Prayer.* By Daniel Dana, A. M., pastor of a church in Newburyport. Newburyport, 1799, p. 45. In addition to Morse there was at least one other exception to the general reticence. A congregation at Sullivan, N. H.(?), heard a sermon full of wild and hysterical utterances, containing frequent references to the Illuminati, to Robison and Barruel, with much stress laid upon the lugubrious idea that the church in America was about to drink a cup of persecution exceedingly bitter. This sermon, however, was much too irrational to be of special significance. *The Present Times Perilous. A Sermon, preached at Sullivan, on the National Fast, April 25, 1799.* By Abraham Cummings, A. M., (n. d.). It would not be altogether incorrect to observe that the New England clergy, on the occasion of the national fast of 1799, took their cue direct from the President's proclamation rather than from the literature which had previously been published on the subject of Illuminism.

[794] This is certainly a reasonable inference from the fact that the interest of the public in Morse's sermon made necessary four different issues of it during the year in which it appeared. One of these was printed at Charlestown, another at Boston, a third at Hartford, and a fourth at New York.

[795] Here it may be noted that when Morse's sermon appeared in print, it was accompanied by a note setting forth the author's account of the progress of his thought regarding the Illuminati. In part the note ran as follows: "In my Discourse on the National Fast, May 9th., 1798, after giving some account of Robison's *Proofs of a Conspiracy, etc.*, a work which had just arrived in America, I said, 'There are too many evidences that this order [the Illuminati] has had its branches established, in some form or other, and its emissaries secretly at work in this country, for several years past.'

"Being often publicly called upon for evidence to support this insinuation, I engaged, when my health and leisure would permit, to lay it before the public. This engagement was in part fulfilled, in the Appendix to my Thanksgiving *Sermon* of Nov. 29, 1798, Note (F), p. 73, to which I refer the reader.

"Since this I have received a letter from President Dwight, confirming the fact which he had asserted in a note to his Discourse of the 4th of July, 1798, viz, that 'Illuminatism exists in this country; and the impious mockery of the Sacramental Supper described by Mr. Robison has been enacted here.' ...

"But if all this evidence, added to that which arises *prima facie* from the existing state of things; from the wonderful and alarming change which has been suddenly and imperceptibly produced too generally in the principles and morals of the American people, be insufficient to convince and satisfy candid minds of the actual existence, and secret and extensive operation, of Illuminatism in this country, the following documents which were received through a most respectable channel, and for the authenticity of which I pledge myself, must, I conceive, remove every doubt remaining in the minds of reasonable men. If any branches of this Society are established in this part of the United States, the members no doubt will feel irritated at this disclosure, and will use all their secret arts, and open endeavours, to diminish the importance of these documents and the reputation of him who makes them public." (Note B, pp. 33 *et seq.*) The note concludes with a solemn statement by its author to the effect that he stands prepared to sacrifice all, even his life if necessary, for the cause of religion and his country. See also the preface of the sermon.

[796] *Wolcott Papers*, vol. viii, 26.

[797] *Wolcott Papers*, vol. viii, 26.

[798] On the very day of the national fast the editor of the *Chronicle* busied himself at his familiar task of rebuking the clergy on account of their practice of indulging in "political preaching". The latter were again admonished to confine their attention to the divine book of Revelation and to abandon their interest in the reveries of Robison. This, however, was only such a jibe as had intermittently issued from this source.

[799] *Independent Chronicle*, May 9, 1799.

[800] *Ibid.*

[801] *Independent Chronicle*, May 30, 1799.

[802] *Ibid.*

[803] *Ibid.*

[804] *Ibid.*, June 10, 1799.

[805] *Cf.* especially the *Independent Chronicle* of May 9, 13, 16, 20, 27, 30, and June 3, 6, 10, 13, 1799.

[806] *Ibid.*, May 13, 1799.

[807] *Independent Chronicle*, May 20, 1799.

[808] *Cf. supra*, pp. 281 *et seq.*

[809] The ship Ocean was a vessel of the United States concerning which, in the spring of 1799, the statement got into circulation that it had been captured by the French and every soul on board foully murdered. No such massacre actually took place. Morse, however, heard the story, believed it, and made reference to it in his fast sermon of April 25, 1799. Later, and not unnaturally, he became disturbed over the part he had played in giving publicity to the story. His integrity, he believed, was involved; likewise the faith of the public in other pronouncements he had made, *e. g.* with regard to the Illuminati. See *Wolcott Papers*, vol. viii, 27. And this was the view of the case that his enemies took. *Cf.* for instance, the *Aurora*, June 6, 1799.

[810] *American Mercury*, June 6, 1799.

[811] Printed at Walpole, N. H.

[812] *American Mercury*, Aug. 29, 1799. *Cf.* also *The Bee* (New Haven), Aug. 21, 1799.

[813] *Cf.* issue of May 7, 1799.

[814] *Cf.* issue of May 10, 1799.

[815] *Connecticut Courant*, May 27, 1799.

[816] *An Oration delivered at Ridgefield on the Fourth of July, 1799, before a large concourse of people, assembled to commemorate their National Independence.* By David Edmond. Danbury…MDCCXCIX, p. 10.

[817] *An Oration, on the Apparent and the Real Political Situation of the United States, pronounced before the Connecticut Society of the Cincinnati, assembled at New-Haven ... July 4th, 1799.* By Zechariah Lewis, ... New-Haven, 1799, p. 16.

[818] *An Oration spoken at Hartford ... on the Anniversary of American Independence, July 4th, A. D., 1799.* By William Brown. Hartford ... 1799, pp. 6 *et seqq.*

[819] *An Oration, pronounced July 4th, 1799, at the request of the Inhabitants of the Town of Boston, in Commemoration of the Anniversary of American Independence.* By John Lowell, Junior. Boston, 1799, p. 21.

[820] *An Oration, delivered before the citizens of Portland ... on the Fourth of July, 1799 ...* By A. Stoddard. Portland, 1799, pp. 10, 11, 13, 29 *et seq.*

[821] *An Oration delivered at Byfield, July 4, 1799.* By Rev. Elijah Parish, A. M. Newburyport (n. d.).

[822] *An Oration, delivered at Roxbury, July 4, 1799. In Commemoration of American Independence.* By Thomas Beedé. Boston, 1799.

[823] The *Connecticut Courant* of June 10, 1799, carried to its readers the announcement that "the IIIrd volume of the History of Jacobinism" had just been received by Messrs. Hudson & Goodwin, the editors, and, along with volumes i and ii, was on sale.

[824] Jedediah Morse was certainly one of those who hoped for much from the appearance of Barruel's work in America. On October 3, 1799, he wrote to the American publishers of the *Memoirs of Jacobinism*, expressing his gratification over the receipt of six copies of volumes i and ii (bound in one) of the same, and arranging to have the remaining volumes forwarded to him at the earliest possible date. *Cf.* Morse's letter to Messrs. Hudson & Goodwin, in the *Ford Collection*, New York Public

Library. Morse's urgency in the case is partly explained by the fact that at this time he was being drawn deeply into the Ebeling-Huntington-Babcock-Bentley-Morse controversy, to be noticed below.

[825] *Wolcott Papers*, vol. v, 77. *Cf. Salem Gazette*, Aug. 13, 1799.

[826] *Cf.* the issues of the *Courant* for June 24, July 1, 8, 15, 29, Aug. 5, 12, 19, 26, Sept. 2, 9, 16, 23, 30, Oct. 7, 1799. The partisan object in view in making and publishing this abridgment of Barruel is thinly veiled in the following statement of the editors: "We have not, indeed, much to apprehend from external invasion, but our greatest dangers arise from a disorganizing party among ourselves, who will recognize no government, except in bacchanalian curses, and the sanguinary notions of a blind, seditious, and corrupted crowd—who will be guided by no laws except what are conceived in the womb of crime, the weakness and absurdity of which will be calculated to establish the reign of licentiousness, and consolidate the empire of sedition and conspiracy." (*Connecticut Courant*, July 8, 1798.)

[827] *Cf.* the issues of the *Mercury* for July 30, Aug. 9, 13, 16, 20, 27, Sept. 3, 6, 17, 24, Oct. 1, 8, 22, 29, 1799. Other papers, the *Columbian Centinel*, for example, began the publication of the Abridgement, but discontinued the series before the end was reached.

[828] The entire indifference to the Abridgement which many New England editors manifested was the occasion of no little disappointment and chagrin on the part of those who had hoped for material assistance and comfort from this source. *Cf. Connecticut Courant*, July 22, 1799. With regard to the general impression which the *Memoirs of Jacobinism* made in this country, the comments of Thomas Jefferson are of interest. Though based upon an imperfect acquaintance with Barruel's work, considerable sound criticism is expressed. "I have lately by accident got sight of a single volume (the 3d.) of the Abbé

Barruel's 'Antisocial Conspiracy', which gives me the first idea I have ever had of what is meant by the Illuminatism against which 'Illuminate Morse', as he is now called, and his ecclesiastical and monarchical associates have been making such a hue and cry. Barruel's own parts of the book are perfectly the ravings of a Bedlamite. But he quotes largely from Wishaupt [*sic*] whom he considers the founder of what he calls the order ... Wishaupt seems to be an enthusiastic philanthropist. He is among those (as you know the excellent Price and Priestley also are) who believe in the infinite perfectibility of man. He thinks he may in time be rendered so perfect that he will be able to govern himself in every circumstance, so as to injure none, to do all the good he can, to leave government no occasion to exercise their powers over him, and, of course, to render political government useless. This, you know, is Godwin's doctrine, and this is what Robison, Barruel, and Morse have called a conspiracy against all government. ... The means he proposes to effect this improvement of human nature are 'to enlighten men, to correct their morals and inspire them with benevolence'. As Wishaupt lived under the tyranny of a despot and priests, he knew that caution was necessary even in spreading information, and the principles of pure morality. He proposed, therefore, to lead the Free Masons to adopt this object. ... This has given an air of mystery to his views, was the foundation of his banishment, the subversion of the Masonic Order, and is the color for the ravings against him of Robison, Barruel, and Morse, whose *real fears are that the craft* would be endangered by the spreading of information, reason, and natural morality among men. ... I believe you will think with me that if Wishaupt had written here, where no secrecy is necessary in our endeavours to render men wise and virtuous, he would not have thought of any secret machinery for that purpose ... ". (*The Writings of Thomas Jefferson*, vol. vii, p. 419: Letter to Bishop James Madison.)

[829] Christopher D. Ebeling (1741–1817) was a German geographer and historian who was greatly interested in

everything relating to America. In 1794 he was elected a corresponding member of the Massachusetts Historical Society. He was in correspondence with such public characters in America as Morse, Dr. Jeremy Belknap, President Stiles, and Thomas Jefferson. After his death, Ebeling's large and valuable library became the property of Harvard University.

[830] *Cf. op. cit.*

[831] *Ibid.*

[832] *American Mercury*, Sept. 26, 1799. The entire article was well calculated to nettle the feelings of Morse. He was referred to therein as "a celebrated calumniator of Masonry" and "an eagle-eyed detector of Illuminatism." The concluding statement was peculiarly humiliating and irritating: "Many people wonder why the Rev. Granny, who has officiated at the birth of so many *mice* (when Mountains have travailed), had not published the letter he has lately received from Professor Ebeling: many others suppose he will publish it as an Appendix to his next Fast-Day Sermon." In addition to the *American Mercury*, the *Bee* and the *Aurora* both published this account of the Ebeling-Morse letter. *Cf.* the edition of the former for Oct. 9, 1799, and of the latter for Nov. 25, Dec. 6, 9, 1799. Thus wide publicity was given to the matter, on account of which Morse was justly aroused.

[833] *American Mercury*, Nov. 7, 1799 *Cf. Columbian Centinel*, Nov. 23, 1799.

[834] Morse's letter to Babcock, editor of the *American Mercury*, bore date of October 4, 1799. It drew no further response from Babcock than a private epistle, calling upon Morse to refute the statements which had appeared in the Mercury, and promising that then the editor's "man" would be produced. *Cf. American Mercury*, Nov. 7, 1799.

[835] *American Mercury*, Nov. 14, 1799. *Cf. Columbian Centinel*, Nov. 23, 1799.

[836] *American Mercury*, Nov. 14, 1799. The affidavits of Tappan and Pearson were actually offered in evidence later. *Cf. Connecticut Courant*, May 19, 1800; *Massachusetts Mercury*, May 23, 1800.

[837] *Cf.* the issue of this paper for Sept. 30, 1799.

[838] *Ibid.*, Nov. 4, 1799.

[839] *Cf.* article by "Candidus" in the issue of this paper for Nov. 23, 1799.

[840] *Cf.* the issue of this paper for Dec. 27, 1799.

[841] *Cf. Bee*, Nov. 20, 1799.

[842] *Ibid.*

[843] *Ibid.*, Nov. 20, 27, 1799.

[844] *Ibid.*, Nov. 20, 1799.

[845] *Cf. Aurora*, Nov. 16, 25, Dec. 6, 9, 1799.

[846] *Ibid.*, Nov. 16, 1799.

[847] *Ibid.*

[848] *Ibid.*

[849] This fact was acknowledged by Ebeling. *Cf. Ebeling MSS.*: Ebeling's letters to Bentley, July 28, 1800; July 1, 1801.

[850] From 1798 on, Bentley's *Diary* is replete with ill-tempered and abusive references to Morse. *Cf.* for example, vol. ii, pp. 278, 291, 296, 302, 329, 334, 384, 391; vol. iii. pp. 9, 32, 141, 149, 217, 218, 342, 357 *et seq.*, 431; vol. iv, pp. 209, 241. Bentley's enthusiastic devotion to Freemasonry and his rancorous republicanism were largely responsible for his personal feeling towards Morse; but there also appears to have been a disagreeable and petty personal element in the situation. Bentley was peevish and spiteful towards Morse because he believed that the latter had stirred up one of the creditors of the

elder Bentley to attempt to collect a debt from the son. *Cf.* Bentley, *Diary*, vol. iv, pp. 241 *et seq.* Even before the Illuminati agitation broke out in New England, Bentley found it impossible to repress his low opinion of Morse as a geographer and as a man. *Cf. ibid.*, vol. ii, pp. 64, 70.

[851] *Cf. Ebeling MSS.*: Ebeling's letter to Bentley, March 13, 1799.

[852] *Ibid.*: Ebeling's letter to Bentley, March 23, 1799.

[853] *Ibid.*

[854] In view of the fact that Ebeling had instructed Bentley that his letter was not to be given to the public, and that if by any chance it should find its way into print, it was to be expurgated and presented to the public only in part, he felt aggrieved at Bentley for paying attention to none of his instructions. Ebeling's great fear seems to have been that his mention of living personages in European politics would be likely to create serious embarrassments. Nevertheless, he assured Bentley that he was not disposed to be deeply hurt over the appearance of the letter in the American press. *Cf. ibid.*: Ebeling's letters to Bentley, July 28, 1800, July 1, 1801.

[855] Morse had ample justification for thinking himself thoroughly ill-used in this situation. The embarrassment that he experienced over the appearance of the letter in the *Aurora* and the *Bee* was enhanced by the fact that the account of the Ebeling-Morse letter published in the *American Mercury*, which tallied with the *Aurora-Bee* letter, was due to a confidence that Morse had given to a man whom he supposed to be friendly to his cause. A certain Samuel Huntington had visited him, to whom Morse read the letter he had received from Ebeling. Trusting to his memory, Huntington afterwards sent a communication to the *American Mercury*, purporting to contain a true account of the epistle that Morse had read to him. *Cf. Bentley Correspondence*, vol. i, 40: J. Eliot's letter to Bentley, July 26, 1802. *Cf. The Mercury and New-England*

Palladium [successor to the *Massachusetts Mercury*], April 28, 1801.

[856] The agitation against Morse became highly abusive and threatening. He was made the recipient of scurrilous and intimidating epistles, which did not stop short of promising physical chastisement. *Cf. Wolcott Papers*, vol. viii, 32, for a specimen of such documents. *Cf. ibid.*, 30: Morse's letter to Wolcott, Dec. 6, 1799.

[857] *Wolcott Papers*, 31. *Cf. National Magazine, or a Political, Historical, Biographical, and Literary Repository*, vol. ii, pp. 26 *et seq.*: article by *Philalethes*. Parker's observations are fully corroborated by this pseudonymous writer. That Wisdom Lodge was a regular Masonic lodge, organized under the *Grand Orient* of France, is further testified to by Mackey, *The History of Free Masonry*, vol, v, p. 1420. Treudley, *The United States and Santa Domingo, 1789–1866*, pp. 111–125, adequately presents the essential facts bearing on the presence of the French refugees in the United States.

[858] *Wolcott Papers*, vol. viii, 31.

[859] Payson (1753–1820) was a Harvard graduate, who located at Rindge in 1782, and continued in the pastorate at that place until death removed him, forty-eight years later.

[860] *Proofs of the Real Existence, and Dangerous Tendency, of Illuminism. Containing an abstract of the most interesting parts of what Dr. Robison and the Abbe Barruel have published on this subject; with collateral proofs and general observations.* By Seth Payson, A. M., Charlestown, 1802.

[861] *Ibid.*, pp. iii, 217 *et seq.*, 245 *et seq.*

[862] Mackey, *Lexicon and History of Freemasonry*, pp. 183 *et seq.* One of the most active and influential New England Masons of the period was the Reverend William Bentley. The following references in his *Diary* throw light upon this phase of

the situation: vol. ii, pp. 6–8, 11, 12. *Cf.* also Myer's *History of Free Masonry and Its Progress in the United States*, p. 15.

[863] *Cf.* for example, a small volume entitled, *Eulogium and Vindication of Masonry. Selected (and Improved) from Various Writers*, Philadelphia, 1792. The following excerpt is fairly typical: "There are brethren who, careless of their own reputation, disregard the instinctive lessons of our noble science, and by yielding to vice and intemperance, not only disgrace themselves, but reflect dishonor upon Masonry in general. It is this unfortunate circumstance which has given rise to those severe and unjust reflections, which the prejudiced part of mankind have so illiberally bestowed upon us." (*Ibid.*, p. 11. *Cf. ibid.*, p. 19.) This representation of the case is fully confirmed by *The Freemason's Monitor; or Illustrations of Masonry: in Two Parts*. By a Royal Arch Mason … Albany, 1797, pp. 18 *et seq.*. The following sermon, delivered by a non-Mason, is also suggestive in this connection: *A Discourse delivered in the New Presbyterian Church, New York: Before the Grand Lodge of the State of New York … June 24th, 1795*. By Samuel Miller, one of the Ministers of the United Presbyterian Churches in the City of New York, 1795. Miller dwelt at length upon the suspicion and prejudice that existed against the Masons, due, as he argued, to (1) the order's veil of secrecy, (2) the number of men who have been admitted to membership who were known to be the open enemies of religion and morality and a disgrace to human nature itself, and (3) the "scenes of vanity and folly" and "the froth of nonsense" by which too many Masonic gatherings were characterized. *Cf. ibid.*, pp. 25 *et seq.* Despite the fact that the sermon was full of frankest criticism, Miller's composition was ordered printed by the Grand Lodge, doubtless for the principal reason that he had been at pains to distinguish between *genuine* and *spurious* Masons. Thaddeus Harris, a prominent Massachusetts Mason, in a sermon preached at the consecration at a lodge at Groton, Mass., Aug. 9, 1797, took account of the same criticism of the order. *Cf.* also, Bentley's *Diary*, vol. i, p. 379. Reference to such Masonic compilations as *The Vocal Companion and*

Masonic Register, Boston, 1802, and *The Maryland Ahiman Rezon of Free and Accepted Masons* ... Baltimore, 1797, will not leave the reader in doubt that a good deal of the poetry and music employed in the lodges was excessively hilarious and coarse.

[864] In addition to the sermons of Miller and Harris cited in the foregoing note, *cf. A Discourse on the Origin, Progress and Design of Free Masonry. Delivered at the Meeting-House in Charlestown, in the Commonwealth of Massachusetts, on the Anniversary of St. John the Baptist, June 24, A. D. 1793.* By Josiah Bartlett, M. B., Boston, 1793. p. 17. The Rev. Ashbel Baldwin, chaplain of the grand lodge of Connecticut, in 1797, came to the defence of Masonry against the same charge. *Cf. The Records of Free Masonry in the State of Connecticut, etc.* By E. G. Storer, Grand Secretary, New Haven, 1859, vol. i, pp. 97 *et seq.*

[865] Jedediah Morse's efforts, in his fast sermon at May 9, 1798, to avoid giving mortal offence to the Masons of New England, have already been noted. See *supra*, pp. 235 *et seq.* As Robison had sought to exculpate the Masons of England, so Morse sought to exculpate the Masons of "the Eastern States." We shall see plenty of evidence, however, that New England Masons were not deceived. From the first they recognized with more or less clearness that *Masonry* itself was involved. The good name and integrity of their entire institution were at stake.

[866] General Joseph Warren, the Revolutionary patriot and hero, who fell at Bunker Hill, one of the most honored leaders of American Freemasonry.

[867] *Cf. Columbian Centinel*, June 30, 1798; also *Massachusetts Mercury*, Aug. 21, 1798, for the address of the Grand Lodge in full, together with the President's cordial response.

[868] Harris was Past Grand Chaplain of the Grand Lodge and Chaplain of the Grand Royal Arch Chapter of Massachusetts.

[869] *A Charge delivered before the Morning Star Lodge, in Worcester, Massachusetts, upon the festival of Saint John the Baptist, June 25, A. L. 5798.* By the Rev. Brother William Bentley, of Salem, Massachusetts. Worcester, June, A. L. 5798. (The initials A. L. in the foregoing title stand for *Anno Lucis*, and represent a common Masonic usage). This charge not only found independent publication, but got into the New England newspapers generally, and did much to distinguish its author as a bold defender of the craft.

[870] *Ibid.*, p. 9.

[871] Bentley, *op. cit.*, p. 16.

[872] *Ibid.*, pp. 22 *et seq.*

[873] *Ibid.*, p. 31. Bentley rarely, if ever, made as generous a reference to Morse from this time on. His resentment toward the chief calumniator of Masonry, as Morse came to be regarded, grew apace.

[874] *Discourses, delivered on Public Occasions, Illustrating the Principles, Displaying the Tendency, and Vindicating the Design of Freemasonry.* By Thaddeus Mason Harris…. Charlestown, Anno Lucis, 1801.

[875] Harris, *op. cit.*, pp. 51 *et seq.*

[876] *Ibid., Discourses ii, vii, viii,* and *x,* particularly.

[877] This became one of the terms by which Bentley was alluded to.

[878] *A Sermon delivered before the Grand Lodge of Free and Accepted Masons of the Commonwealth of Massachusetts, at a Public Installation of Officers of Corinthian Lodge, at Concord, … June 25, 1798.* By Jedediah Morse, D. D., minister of the congregation in Charlestown (n. d.).

[879] *An Oration, delivered before the Right Worshipful Master and Brethren of St. Peter's Lodge, at the Episcopal Church in Newburyport, Massachusetts, on the festival of St.*

John the Baptist; celebrated June 25, 5798. By Worshipful Brother Charles Jackson, p. M., Newburyport, March, A. L. 5799.

[880] *Ibid.*, p. 18.

[881] *Ibid.*, p. 17.

[882] *Ibid.*, pp. 19 *et seq.*

[883] *Ibid.*, p. 23.

[884] *Cf. supra*, pp. 254 *et seq.*

[885] *Massachusetts Mercury*, Aug. 7, 1798. Bartlett was Grand Master of the Grand Lodge of Massachusetts.

[886] *Ibid.*

[887] In his address before the Worcester Lodge, June 25, Bentley had gone so far as to designate Morse "a madman" for accepting Robison's book at its face value. This led to a retort in kind on the part of Morse. Bentley, according to Morse, was incapable of making himself understood; one must always have a commentator in reading him. *Massachusetts Mercury*, Aug. 3, 1798.

[888] *Ibid.*, Aug. 10, 1798.

[889] *Ibid.*, Sept. 7, 1798.

[890] *Massachusetts Mercury*, Sept. 18, 1798.

[891] *Ibid.*

[892] The Masons appear to have paid little if any attention to the thanksgiving sermon of November 29, 1798. There was little reason why they should.

[893] See *Salem Gazette*, Dec. 25, 1798.

[894] *Salem Gazette*, Dec. 25, 1798.

[895] *Ibid.*

[896] *Salem Gazette*, Dec. 25, 1798.

[897] Hayden, *Washington and His Masonic Compeers*, p. 176.

[898] *Ibid.*, pp. 176 *et seq.*

[899] The address of the Maryland Grand Lodge was presented early in June, 1798. The President's response followed in due course. Both documents were freely copied in the newspapers of the day, the New England papers not excepted. *Cf.* for example, the *Salem Gazette*, Aug. 10, 1798.

[900] *An Address, delivered in Essex Lodge, Massachusetts, Dec. 27, 5798 (1798), on the festival of St. John the Evangelist, at the induction of officers.* By William Bentley. Essex Lodge was located at Salem, Bentley's home. The address may be found in the Freemason's Magazine, February, 1812, pp. 333 *et seq.* Bentley's further reflections upon President Adams's unsatisfactory response to the Vermont Grand Lodge led him to make even more pointed observations. Under date of Feb. 4, 1799, he wrote in his diary: "My address to Essex Lodge out of press. Pres. A. talks like a boy about the danger of the institution. Men of sense who ridicule or oppose the Institution are surprised at his simplicity. If he affects to be afraid, he loosens by the pretence because indifferent persons consider it as a weakness & his judgment suffers, so that he gets neither aid nor confidence." (*Diary*, vol. ii, p. 296.)

[901] *An Oration, delivered in the Meeting house of the First Parish in Portland, Monday, June 24th, 5799 ... in celebration of the anniversary festival of St. John the Baptist.* By Brother Amos Stoddard ... Portland, 1799.

[902] *Ibid.*, p. 9.

[903] *Ibid.*, p. 10.

[904] *Ibid.*

[905] *Ibid.*

[906] *A Sermon delivered before Mount Moriah Lodge: at Reading in the County of Middlesex; at the celebration of St. John: June 24th, A. D. 1799.* By Caleb Prentiss, A. M., pastor of the First Parish in said town ... Leominster (Mass.) ... Anno Lucis, 5799.

[907] Prentiss, *op. cit.*, pp. 12, 13.

[908] *A Sermon, at the Consecration of the Social Lodge in Ashby, and the Installation of its Officers, June 24, A. D. 1799.* By Seth Payson, A. M., pastor of the church in Rindge, Amherst, N. H. 1800.

[909] *Cf. supra*, p. 321.

[910] Payson's *Sermon*, p. 8.

[911] Payson's *Sermon*, p. 9.

[912] *Ibid.*

[913] Bentley, *op. cit.*, vol. ii, p. 316.

[914] *Ibid.*

[915] *The Secrets of Masonry Illustrated and Explained; in a Discourse, preached at South-Kingston, before the Grand Lodge of the State of Rhode-Island, etc., September 3d, A. L. 5799.* By Abraham L. Clark, A. M., rector of St. John's Church, Providence. Providence, 1799. p. 13.

[916] *An Address, delivered December 18, 1799. Before the Brethren of Montgomery Lodge; at their Masonic Hall in Franklin....* By Brother James Mann, P. M. Wrentham, 1800, p. 16.

[917] *Masonry in Its Glory: or Solomon's Temple Illuminated.* By David Austin, Jun.: Citizen of the World. East-Windsor, Connecticut, 1800, p. 32. *Cf.An Oration, pronounced at Walpole, Newhampshire [sic] before the Jerusalem, Golden Rule and Olive Branch Lodges of Free and Accepted Masons, at their celebration of the festival of St. John the Baptist, June*

24th, A. L. 5800. By Brother Martin Field, A. B. Putney, October, 1800.

[918] *An Oration pronounced before the Right Worshipful Master & Brethren of St. Peter's Lodge, at the Episcopal Church in Newburyport, on the festival of St. John the Baptist, June 24th, 5802*. By Brother Michael Hodge, Jun. p. M. Newburyport, ... 5802, p. 12.

[919] *An Address, delivered before the Grand Lodge of Massachusetts, on the festival of St. John the Evangelist, Dec. 27th, A. L. 5805....* By Henry Maurice Lisle, P. M. R. A. C. and Master of Union Lodge, Dorchester. Boston, 1805, pp. 14 *et seq.*

[920] Bentley, *Diary*, vol. iii, p. 228.

[921] *An Address, delivered at the Grand Convention of the Free Masons of the State of Maryland; held on the 10th May, 1802,—in which the observance of secrecy is vindicated, and the principal objections of Professor Robison against the institution, are candidly considered.* By John Crawford, M. D., Grand Master. Baltimore, 1802, pp. 5, 8, 9, 30.—In this connection, the following table showing the numerical increase of certain Massachusetts lodges during the period 1794–1802, compiled from the records of these lodges as contained in their published histories, will be of interest. In three instances, *viz.*, St. John's, Corinthian and Columbian, both those who received membership and those who took degrees are included.

	1794	1795	1796	1797	1798	1799	1800	1801	1802
St John's, Boston	11	11	6	23	3	0	31	14	14
Tyrian, Gloucester	5	11	2	3	3	3	5	3	2
Essex, Salem	2	2	1	8	7	1	9	8	8
Washington, Roxbury (constituted in				13	10	13	10	6	5

1796)

King Solomon's Charlestown	7	14	7	7	4	5	7	4	1
Corinthian, Concord (constituted in 1797)			28	27*	5	17	16	16	
Columbian, Boston (constituted in 1795)		10	51	25	23	19	25	52	21
St. Andrews, Royal Arch, Boston	1	7	7	6	10†	3	14	3	5
Totals	26‡	55‡	74‡	113	87	49	118	106	72

* Only one new member admitted after May.
† Only one new member admitted after Sept. 3.
‡ Incomplete.

[922] *A Masonic Oration, pronounced on the festival of St. John the Evangelist, December 26, 1799.... In Middletown.* By Alexander Collins, Esq. Middletown, 1800.

[923] *Ibid.*, p. 5.

[924] *Ibid.*, p. 15. An interesting episode in Washington's Masonic career may here be alluded to. In the summer of 1798, the Reverend G. W. Snyder, a Lutheran clergyman of Frederickstown, Md., wrote Washington, expressing his fear that Illuminism might possibly gain an entrance into the American lodges and appealing to Washington to exert himself to prevent such an unhappy consummation. Snyder accompanied his letter with a copy of Robison's *Proofs of a Conspiracy*. Washington replied to Snyder's letter to the effect that he had heard much about "the nefarious and dangerous plan and doctrines of the Illuminati," but that he did not believe

the lodges of this country had become contaminated thereby. Later Snyder again addressed Washington on the subject, expressing surprise that the latter was doubtful concerning the spread of the doctrines of Illuminism in this country. To this Washington made answer that he had not intended to impart the impression by his former letter "that the doctrines of the Illuminati and the principles of Jacobinism had not spread in the United States." On the contrary, he professed himself fully satisfied on that point. But what he had meant to say formerly was this: he "did not believe that the lodges of freemasons in this country had, as societies, endeavoured to propagate the diabolical tenets of the former, or pernicious principles of the latter." (*Cf.* Sparks, *The Writings of Washington*, vol. xi, pp. 314 *et seq.*, 377. *Cf.* Hayden, *Washington and His Masonic Compeers*, pp. 177–189.) A recent study of this correspondence has appeared. *Cf.* Sachse, *Washington's Masonic Correspondence*, Philadelphia, 1915, pp. 117–139. The author manifests undue eagerness to acquit Washington of serious interest in the controversy over the Illuminati. His unnecessary emphasis upon Snyder's private character, his remark that "Brother Washington evidently surmised that this letter from Snyder was nothing more or less than a scheme to entrap him" (*Ibid.*, p. 124), and his characterization of Washington's second letter to Snyder as "sharp," all strongly imply that Sachse failed to view the episode in its true setting. That Washington had a genuine interest in the controversy over the Illuminati the following letter gives added proof:

"Mount Vernon, 28th Feb^y, 1799.
Rev. Sir,

The letter with which you were pleased to favor me, dated the first instant, accompanying your thanksgiving sermon, came duly to hand.

For the latter I pray you to accept my thanks.—I have read it, and the Appendix with pleasure, and wish the latter, at least, could meet a more general circulation than it probably will have, for it contains important information, as little known, out of a small circle as the dissemination of it would be useful, if spread through the community.

With   great

respect,

I am,—Revd. Sir,
Your most Obdt. Servant,
G°. Washington."

The Rev^d. M^r. Morse

Washington Collection, New York Public Library.

Washington's copy of Morse's sermon may be found in the Athenaeum, Boston.

[925] *The Fraternal Tribute of Respect Paid to the Masonic Character of Washington, in the Union League, in Dorchester, January 7th., A. L. 5800.* Charlestown, 1800, p. 11. (The address appeared anonymously.)

[926] Charlestown Masons went so far as to hold out the olive branch of peace and good-will to Morse, in connection with the Masonic mourning which followed Washington's death. It is recorded that the lodge in Charlestown presented to Morse the cloth which for a time hung under the portrait of its "beloved Brother, George Washington." The gift was gratefully accepted by Morse and was made into a coat which he afterwards wore. *Cf. By-Laws of King Solomon's Lodge, Charlestown, etc.* Boston, 1885, p. 83.

[927] Robison, *Jeffersonian Democracy in New England*, pp. 26 *et seq. Cf.* Bentley, *Diary*, vol. ii, pp. 289, 346, 421, 429, 458.

[928] The situation is well covered by McMaster, *History of the People of the United States*, vol. ii, pp. 441 *et seq.*

[929] On account of the supposed place of concealment of the imaginary papers, this was commonly referred to as the "tub plot."

[930] The public report of this story by Morse has already been noted. *Cf. supra*, p. 306.

[931] *Independent Chronicle*, April 18, 1798. *Cf. Constitutional Telegraph* (Boston), Oct. 2, 1799.

[932] *To the Freemen of Rhode-Island, etc.*, p. 4. This pamphlet was issued anonymously and without date. Its author was Jonathan Russell, and the date of its publication fell within the period of the Adams-Jefferson contest for the presidency, *i. e.*, 1800–1801. The passage from which the quotation is taken is marked by not a little dignity and comprehension. "The people have been continually agitated by false alarms, and without even the apparition of a foe. They have been made to believe that their government and their religion were upon the eve of annihilation. The ridiculous fabrications of plots, which have been crushed out of being by the weight of their own absurdity; and the perpetration of massacres which never existed, but in the distempered malevolence which preached them, have been artfully employed to excite an indignation which might be played off for the purposes of party. Tubs have arrived at Charlestown. The crews of the Ocean and Pickering have been murdered…. No falsehood which depravity could invent, has passed unpropagated by credulity; and no innocence which virtue could render respectable and amiable has escaped unassailed by federal malignity. Bigotry has cried down toleration, and royalism everything Republican." (*Ibid.*)

[933] *Aurora*, June 5, 1799.

[934] The pamphlet's full title follows: *A View of the New England Illuminati: who are indefatigably engaged in Destroying the Religion and Government of the United States; under a feigned regard for their safety—and under an impious abuse of true religion.* The pamphlet passed through at least two editions. The citations of this study are from the second.

[935] Ogden (1740–1800) was rector of St. John's Church (formerly Queen's Chapel), Portsmouth, N. H., from 1786 to 1793. He was a well-meaning but an exceedingly erratic man.

Perry, *The History of the American Episcopal Church, 1587–1883*, vol. ii, p. 79. He is said to have been the first Episcopal clergyman to be ordained in the city of Boston. *Cf. ibid.*, p. 488. His death occurred at Chestertown, Md.

[936] *A View of the New England Illuminati*, pp. 2, 3.

[937] *Ibid.*, p. 3.

[938] *Ibid.*

[939] *Ibid.*, p. 5. Ogden's observations in this connection are caustic enough. "The people generally attended the public exercises in the meeting-houses, but had no share in the deliberations of the ministers. Dinners were prepared, by private donations, of the most delicious food of the season, which could be procured by the parishioners; and *a day of conviviality* was thus observed once a month by the clergy, to their gratification and the increase of their association." (*Ibid.*)

[940] *Ibid.*, pp. 4 *et seq.*

[941] Ogden, *op. cit.*, p. 5. Ogden made a delicate thrust at this point. He professed to see an explanation of the prevalence of sceptical and deistical notions in New England in the discussions of the dark and obscure questions that consumed the attention of the clergy in their monthly meetings, before they became interested in the affairs of the French Revolution. *Cf. ibid.*

[942] *Ibid.*, pp. 5 *et seq.*

[943] *Ibid.*, p. 6.

[944] *Ibid.*, p. 7.

[945] Ogden, *op. cit.*, p. 7.

[946] *Ibid.*, p. 8.

[947] *Ibid.*, pp. 8, 18.

[948] *Ibid.*, p. 18.

[949] *Ibid.*, p. 9.

[950] *Ibid.*

[951] Ogden, *op. cit.*, pp. 9 *et seq.*

[952] *Ibid.*

[953] *Ibid.*, pp. 11, 16.

[954] *Ibid.*, p. 11. President Dwight is dubbed by Ogden "the head of the Illuminati." (*Ibid.*) "In his sermon preached on the fourth of July, 1798, in New-Haven, he has given us a perfect picture of the Illuminati of Connecticut, under his control, in the representation he has made of the Illuminati of Europe.... Birth, education, elevation, and connections have placed Doctor Dwight at the head of the Edwardean sect and Illuminati.... Science he forsakes, and her institutions he prostrates, to promote party, bigotry, and error." (*Ibid.*)

[955] *Ibid.*, pp. 11 *et seq.*

[956] *Ibid.*, p. 14.

[957] Ogden, *op. cit.*, p. 19.

[958] *Ibid.*, p. 12.

[959] *Ibid.*, p. 19.

[960] *Ibid.*, p. 15.

[961] *Ibid.*, p. 20.

[962] Ogden, *op. cit.*, pp. 10, 11.

[963] Ogden's pamphlet was in high favor with the Democrats from the first. The *Aurora* of Feb. 14, 1800, has the following reference to it: "This book, within a few months, has attained a very rapid and extensive circulation, in all parts of the union. It is the 'clue' to the tyrannies at the northward, which have assumed the control of our affairs, under the sanction of federalism, or an union of church and state, & which has

associated in one focus, federalism, religion, war, aristocracy, monarchy, and prelacy." Ogden was responsible for two other pamphlets, somewhat similar in tone, but less striking. One of these bore the title: *Friendly Remarks to the People of Connecticut, upon their College and Schools*. It was published anonymously, and without indication of date or place of publication. The other bore the following title and imprint: *A Short History of Late Ecclesiastical Oppressions in New-England and Vermont. By a Citizen. In which is exhibited a Statement of the Violation of Religious Liberties which are ratified by the Constitution of the United States*. Richmond, … 1799. Neither of these is worthy of special notice.

[964] In the order of their composition and appearance these were: (1) *Connecticut Republicanism. An Oration on the Extent and Power of Political Delusion, delivered in New-Haven, on the evening preceding the public commencement, September, 1800*. By Abraham Bishop. Philadelphia, 1800; (2) *Oration delivered at Wallingford, on the 11th of March, 1801, before the Republicans of the State of Connecticut, and their general thanksgiving for the election of Thomas Jefferson to the Presidency and of Aaron Burr to the Vice Presidency of the United States of America*. By Abraham Bishop. New-Haven, 1801; (3) *Proofs of a Conspiracy, against Christianity, and the Government of the United States; exhibited in several views of the union of church and state in New-England*. By Abraham Bishop. Hartford, 1802.

[965] *Oration delivered at Wallingford, on the 11th of March, 1801*, p. 101.

[966] Plenty of bad political blood was back of the whole episode. Bishop's father, who was charged with holding no less than five political offices *simultaneously* under Jefferson, had recently had his responsibilities extended by being appointed Collector of Customs for the Port of New Haven. The indignation of the Federalists was unutterable. A wrathy protest was sent to Jefferson, among whose specifications was the claim that on account of Bishop Senior's advanced age (he was

in his seventy-eighth year), the work would fall to his son who was a foe to commerce and an enemy to order. *Cf.* McMaster, *History of the United States*, vol. ii, pp. 585 *et seq.* In these circumstances Abraham Bishop seems to have found an adequate *casus belli*.

[967] *Connecticut Courant*, Sept. 15, 1800.

[968] *Connecticut Republicanism. An Oration, etc.*, p. 39.

[969] *Ibid.*, p. 43.

[970] The reception of Bishop's oration by the Federalists gave strong impulse in that direction. The pamphleteers and newspaper scribblers of that political persuasion promptly attacked him. Noah Webster replied to Bishop in *A Rod for the Fool's Back.* "Connecticutensis" wrote and published *Three Letters to Abraham Bishop. Cf. Oration delivered at Wallingford, on the 11th of March, 1801*, pp. 103 *et seq.*

[971] *Ibid., passim.*

[972] *Ibid.*, p. 18.

[973] *Ibid.*, pp. 22, 44.

[974] *Ibid.*, pp. 26 *et seq.*

[975] Bishop, *op. cit.*, pp. 47 *et seq.*

[976] *Ibid.*, pp. 50, 51.

[977] *Ibid.*, p. 68.

[978] *Ibid.*, p. 87.

[979] *Ibid.*, p. 92.

[980] *Proofs of a Conspiracy against Christianity and the Government of the United States*, preface.

[981] *Ibid.*, pp. 15, 16.

[982] *Ibid.*, p. 54.

[983] *Ibid.*, pp. 60 *et seq.*

[984] *Ibid.*, p. 64.

[985] *Ibid.*, p. 59.

[986] *Ibid.*, p. 64.

[987] Bishop, *op. cit.*, preface.

[988] The practice was not confined to New England. In New York, for example, the political enemies of the Clinton family employed the term "Illuminati" to embarrass the adherents of that faction. *A Full Exposition of the Clintonian Faction, and the Society of the Columbian Illuminati; with an account of the writer of the narrative, and the characters of his certificate men, as also Remarks on Warren's Pamphlet.* By J[ohn] W[ood]. Newark, 1802.

Made in the USA
Monee, IL
05 March 2022